MICHAEL POWER

MCGILL-QUEEN'S STUDIES IN THE HISTORY OF RELIGION
Volumes in this series have been supported by the Jackman Foundation of Toronto.

Series Two *In memory of George Rawlyk*
Donald Harman Akenson, Editor

❧ Michael Power ❧

THE STRUGGLE TO BUILD THE CATHOLIC CHURCH ON THE CANADIAN FRONTIER

Mark G. McGowan

McGILL-QUEEN'S UNIVERSITY PRESS
MONTREAL & KINGSTON · LONDON · ITHACA

© McGill-Queen's University Press 2005
ISBN 0-7735-2914-4

Legal deposit second quarter 2005
Bibliothèque nationale du Québec

Printed in Canada on acid-free paper that is 100% ancient-forest
free (100% post-consumer recycled), processed chlorine free

This book has been published with the help of a grant from the
Episcopal Corporation of the Roman Catholic Archdiocese of
Toronto.

McGill-Queen's University Press acknowledges the support of
the Canada Council for the Arts for our publishing program.
We also acknowledge the financial support of the Government
of Canada through the Book Publishing Industry Development
Program (BPIDP) for our publishing activities.

LIBRARY AND ARCHIVES CANADA CATALOGUING
IN PUBLICATION

McGowan, Mark George, 1959–
Michael Power: the struggle to build the Catholic Church on the
Canadian frontier / Mark McGowan.
(McGill-Queen's studies in the history of religion; 40)
Includes index.
ISBN 0-7735-2914-4
1. Power, Michael, 1804–1847. 2. Catholic Church – Ontario –
Toronto – Bishops – Biography. 3. Catholic Church – Canada –
History – 19th century. I. Title. II. Series.
BX4705.P711M34 2005 282'.092 C2004-907250-1

Typeset in 10/12.8 Sabon with Poetica Supplemental Ornaments
Book design and typesetting by zijn digital

FOR

> JOHN SARGENT MOIR <

PROFESSOR EMERITUS

DEPARTMENT OF HISTORY

UNIVERSITY OF TORONTO

TEACHER, MENTOR, FRIEND

✑ Contents ✑

∿ Acknowledgments ∿

I did not intend to write this book. On a chilly morning in January 1998, Richard Alway, president of the University of St Michael's College, and Monsignor Sam Bianco, rector of St Michael's Cathedral, invited me to lunch to discuss how one "might" write a biography of Michael Power. Evidently, His Eminence Aloysius Cardinal Ambrozic of Toronto had become fascinated by the founding bishop of his diocese and was disappointed that Power had never been the subject of a full-length scholarly enquiry. With the absent-mindedness of an academic or, perhaps, in a spirit of pure naïveté, I accepted their invitation and prepared my opinion. Just after dessert, and en route to a comfortable sitting room in the episcopal palace, I began to have the uncomfortable feeling that I was not simply going to be asked for my impressions of how this project might be undertaken, but I was also going to be offered the assignment. The sting was in place, and in the first month of a needed research leave, with only little projects on my docket, I could hardly cite overwork as an excuse. In the next hour, I managed to capitulate completely to this dynamic duo while convincing myself that writing Power's biography might be an interesting project after all.

My initial hesitation about researching and writing a biography of Michael Power was well-founded. I was a social historian of religion and ethnicity who, when in graduate school, had regarded biography as old-fashioned and, in the spirit of Collingwood, scarcely history at all. Beyond my prejudice lay even more pressing challenges: Power was just shy of forty-three years of age when he died, had been bishop of Toronto for less than six years, and had left behind only two thin file cases of personal papers and two small volumes of his own outgoing correspondence. Few of the letters he received remained – they were either destroyed after his death (or during his life) or, heaven forbid, lost in the

century and a half between his death and the beginning of my assignment. Finally, there was almost no known narrative of his life during
the thirty-seven years prior to his becoming bishop of Toronto. My first
problem – that of "doing biography" – melted away as I devoured dozens
of excellent biographies in order to prepare for my task. They were generally well researched, usually well written, and represented a more imagi-
native medium than is sometimes afforded to scholars who write focused
microhistories. To solve the second problem – the paucity of sources – I
had to play the role of detective, pursuing bits of Power material and
fragments of evidence across eastern Canada, the United Kingdom, and
Italy. I also corresponded with dozens of archivists worldwide. In the
end, the book I did not want to write has become an adventure I have
enjoyed immensely.

The journey from the January "ambush" to the book launch, seven
years later, was not a solitary one. Many fellow pilgrims assisted me as I
hunted down the mysterious Michael Power. First, I would like to thank
Rick and Sam for setting the trap. Cardinal Ambrozic arranged a generous expense account, which allowed me to travel, hire assistants, and
acquire a mountain of photocopies. I am also thankful to His Eminence
for his encouragement and patience, despite the fact that as I worked
on this project, I continued to teach and fulfill my duties at St Michael's
College, University of Toronto and then accepted an appointment as the
college's fourth principal. I would like to thank William Broadhurst and
his successor, John McGrath, who offered moral support for the project
and expedited the financial arrangements in their role as vice-chancellor
of the Archdiocese of Toronto. Similarly, archdiocesan chancellor John
Murphy made arrangements for my accommodation in Rome, where I
was treated to the warm hospitality of Emilius Goulet, PSS, then rector
of the Canadian College, now archbishop of St Boniface. At St Michael's,
my predecessor as principal, Dr Joseph Boyle, was highly supportive of
the project and made it possible for me to be released from some teaching duties when I was preparing the first draft of the manuscript. Carl
Amhrein, former dean of arts and science at the University of Toronto,
provided a generous research fund upon which I could draw while principal. I am indebted to the spirit of support and kindness exuded by both
the university and the archdiocese.

Many archivists assisted me in my quest to discover written and illustrated evidence of Power's life. I owe an enormous debt of gratitude to
Marc Lerman, archivist of the Archdiocese of Toronto, and his staff,
particularly Sue Lout, who helped me exhaust every possible avenue as

I gathered evidence in their superb archives. Without their co-operation, friendship, and good humour, this project would never have taken
flight. I would also like to thank Archbishop Terrence Pendergast of the
Archdiocese of Halifax and the archdiocesan archivist, Karen White,
for opening their archives to me; Karen postponed her holidays to do so.
As well, I would like to thank the archivists and ordinaries of the following Quebec archives, without whose assistance chapters 2 to 5 could
never have been written: Father Armand Gagné (Archdiocese of Quebec),
Monique Boisvert (Diocese of Valleyfield); the staff of the archives of
the Archdiocese of Montreal, Lucy Gorman McCoy (Archdiocese of
Gatineau-Hull), Father Jacques Leduc, PSS (Grand Seminary, Montreal),
Bishop Raymond Saint-Gelais (Nicolet), and Bishop Jacques Berthelet,
CSV (St Jean-Longeuil). In Ontario, I would like to recognize the assistance of Father M.J. Lynch (Kingston), Diane Baltaz (Hamilton), Glenn
Wright (National Archives, Ottawa), Sister M. Teresita Kennedy, CSJ
(London), Dr Jacques Monet, SJ (Jesuit Archives, Toronto), Sister Juliana
Dusel, IBVM (Loretto Archives, Toronto), and the staff of the Archives
of Ontario. In Europe, my friends Professor Luca Codignola and Professor Matteo Sanfilippo helped me navigate the Roman archives, providing me with excellent inventories and a familiarity with Rome and its
history. Finally, chapter 1 (on Power's early life in Halifax) would never
have been completed had it not been for the intrepid work of researcher
Dorothy Pollock, who managed to lay out numerous leads for me and
made my research excursions in Nova Scotia rewarding and pleasant.
I am ever grateful to my colleague Dr Elizabeth Smyth for connecting
me with Dorothy.

Through each phase of the journey, there were persons who made it
possible for me to pursue a line of thought, posed tough questions of
me, helped me when my work hit a dead end, or threw me a lifeline
when certain nineteenth-century French idioms bested me. My colleague
Dr Yannick Portebois of the Sablé Centre at St Michael's helped me verify my translations of some of Power's French-language correspondence
and recommended to me two talented graduate students: Dr Jeanne
Humphries, who provided crisp translations for French passages appearing in this book, and Ms Diana Shepherd, who transcribed the French
minuscule from photocopied double-sided onion-skin pages so that my
middle-aged eyes could read the text in typed form. My thanks are also
extended to my colleague Dr Jennifer Harris, who verified my Latin
translations (when I discovered shades of the apocalyptic in Power), and
to my student Jesse Pagliaroli, who verified and corrected my transla-

tions of Italian documents. Another of my doctoral students, Ms Indre Cuplinskas, assisted me in the initial phases of transcribing some nearly indecipherable documents from the Jesuit Archives in Rome. Dr Richard Toporoski of St Michael's College provided the first modern English translation of the constitutions passed by the first Synod of Toronto (1842). Richard's valuable contribution is appendix 1 to this book. Jo Godfrey, my assistant in the principal's office, helped in ways too numerous to mention, despite our vocal disagreements about our respective baseball loyalties. I am thankful that Martina Nemoianu used her expert computer skills to scan and improve the images used in the book. My eldest son, Patrick McGowan, who has greater facility with the new technologies than his father, assisted me in entering corrections and preparing the final version of the manuscript for publication. I would also be remiss if I did not thank Alan Keefer, a friend in Whitby, who, on a monthly basis, asked for updates on my progress. While he may think his role minor, the anticipation of his questions forced me to be disciplined and productive during the writing stages of the project.

I have also had the pleasure of sharing Power with my fellow travellers in the historical profession. David Wilson – who is currently writing a biography of Thomas D'Arcy McGee – and I have had an ongoing conversation on the problems and pleasures of writing biography, and Allan Greer helped me immeasurably by providing me with microfilms and advice pertaining to the rebellions of 1837 and 1838 in Lower Canada. Sam Bianco and John Moir read the second draft of the manuscript and offered encouragement and good advice. Jacques Monet, SJ, graciously and painstakingly scoured the manuscript, bringing to the fore his immense knowledge of Catholicism and British North America. His suggestions have spared me serious embarrassment and enhanced the narrative appreciably. I am responsible for any errors of commission or omission that may be obvious in the pages that follow. McGill-Queen's University Press has once again been supportive, and my sincerest thanks go to Donald Akenson (who has been unfailing in his interest in my projects), Kyla Madden, Joan McGilvray, and Roger Martin. Copy editor Mary Williams has put excellent finishing touches on this book. Confirming that truth is stranger than fiction, fellow historian Michael Power (no relation to the deceased bishop) has prepared an excellent index.

As always, this book or any of my little ventures would never have been possible without the love and support of my wife, Eileen, and our five children, Erin, Patrick, Brendan, Kathleen, and John-Francis. In some ways, they lived the Power story from inception to completion, and they probably wish to forget Dad's "Power grand tour of 2003," including pilgrimages to Quebec churches, a stroll on Hollis Street in Halifax, frustration in Montreal's traffic gridlock, burgers in the St François Valley, and a visit to Papineau's berry bushes at Montebello. I cherish their patience, treasure their love, and forgive them should they pursue things other than Canadian history. Finally, this book is dedicated to John Sargent Moir, professor emeritus, Department of History, University of Toronto. John directed my doctoral dissertation with rigour and gentle encouragement; over the years, he has been a wise mentor and scholar, whose love of early Canadian history has been infectious. He once told me that he would have liked to have written a biography of Power, one of several Roman Catholic bishops (including Plessis and Briand) for whom he had great admiration. His labour has become mine. His love of history has transformed my vocation. His friendship has been a pearl of great price.

MICHAEL POWER

↜ Eulogy for a Bishop ↝

THEY HAD BARELY KNOWN HIM. Yet hundreds of Torontonians stood ankle-deep in the muck of Queen Street enjoying a brief appearance of the noonday sun and a respite from the torrents of rain that had been falling since the previous evening. Those in the crowd who had read the papers leading up to 5 October 1847 or engaged in gossip amid the stalls at the St Lawrence Market would have known only the basics about the man for whom they waited.[1] He was born in Nova Scotia, educated in Montreal, ordained a priest of Quebec, appointed first Roman Catholic bishop of Toronto in 1841, and now, just shy of his forty-third birthday, he was dead of the dreaded typhus fever, which he had caught while offering succour and solace to Irish potato famine refugees. Power had resided in Toronto a scant five years, much of which he had spent travelling throughout his gargantuan diocese, but his funeral mass had filled St Paul's Church to capacity, and hundreds kept vigil outside on Queen Street. His funeral train stretched at least half a mile as it bore his body through the streets to the cathedral's crypt.[2]

Michael Power's final journey had begun at 6:30 on the morning of 1 October, when his physician pulled a white sheet over the bishop's face and announced to his horrified colleagues and friends that he had succumbed to the typhus he had been battling for nearly two weeks. Prayers were said at his bedside and his body was washed, dressed in episcopal attire, and gently carried down the stairs to the parlour of the bishop's palace, where it lay in state for three days. On Monday, 4 October, Power's remains were conveyed to St Paul's Church, the acting cathedral, where they were laid in a triple casket. At 5:30 a.m. on 5 October, local priests celebrated a High Mass in the presence of their deceased bishop, which was followed four and a half hours later by the public Mass of Christian Burial. Dignitaries, Catholic and non-Catholic, filled the tiny nave of St Paul's, while at the front of the church, average citizens stood on Power Street, named in the bishop's honour, awaiting the beginning of the final procession.[3]

It may have been, to that point in the city's history, Toronto's largest display of public mourning. Michael Power's casket was placed on a wagon, the priests and dignitaries lined up at its head and rear in two-by-two formation, and the entire ensemble walked in a slow, sombre, and dignified manner to the shell of his unfinished cathedral, at the corner of Church Street and what is now Shuter Street. There, Power would be laid in a bricked vault directly below the sanctuary, joining his old friend William Peter MacDonald and Sir Charles Chichester, who had already been buried close by in the crypt. En route, across Queen and up Church, Power was accompanied by his doctors, priestly colleagues, leading members of the city's Catholic laity, church trustees, police officers, the mayor and city aldermen, members of the Board of Education, the president of King's College and the heads of all its departments, and what the *British Colonist* described as "an immense number of CITIZENS."[4]

As diverse as was the crowd that slogged its way through the muddy streets behind his bier were the reasons individuals in this throng were paying their final respects to Michael Power. In the lead was Father John Carroll, the celebrant of the Mass and, perhaps, Power's only close link to his Nova Scotia roots. Power's senior by several years, Carroll had buried Power's father and one of his brothers before leaving the fractured and rambunctious Catholic parish in Halifax to assume duties under Toronto's first Catholic bishop. Carroll was among Power's most trusted colleagues, so much so that Power had named him co-administrator of the diocese just days before he died. Trudging along the wheel ruts behind Carroll, holding his cassock above the ooze, was Jean-Baptiste Proulx, a colleague of Power's when both men served in Lower Canada. For several years, Power had depended on this expatriate French Canadian priest to administer the Catholic missions in Georgian Bay and Lake Huron. Proulx was not only a living link to Power's French Canadian formation, he was also indispensable to Power in his willingness to assume difficult assignments in the diocese. Partnered with Proulx in the cortège was Patrick McDonagh, pastor of St Catharine's and the Welland Canal area. His memories of Power were less happy, as he'd often felt the sting of Power's pen when he failed to live up to his bishop's high standards of church discipline and the strict application of canon law. Today, however, was a day to bite his tongue and walk in sober respect for his deceased leader.

The honourable John Elmsley, one of the chief mourners, would place himself directly behind Power's casket. One of the wealthiest and most influential Catholics in the western section of the province, Elmsley counted Power among his dearest friends. Together they had planned the building of the cathedral, a considerable portion of the funding for which came out of Elmsley's pocket. He mourned not only a friend, but also a man he identified as a zealous defender of the Catholic faith with a deep commitment to the delivery of Catholic education to Upper Canadian Catholic children. Power's educational views drew others to the procession, as well. Ironically, close to the rear of the train walked J. George Hodgins, chief clerk of the Board of Education, and the surviving members of that board, which Power had chaired. Hodgins – standing in for the chief superintendent, Reverend Egerton Ryerson, who was on school business in Brantford[5] – was there to honour a Catholic prelate whom he and his fellow Protestants considered to be a great supporter of common public education for all children, regardless of creed. The board, in fact, issued a public statement paying tribute to Power by describing him as a voice of moderation, "liberality and good sense."[6]

Much the same sentiment could account for the presence of Mayor W.H. Boulton, who was keeping pace with his councillors just a few metres ahead of Hodgins and company. Like many non-Catholic politicians of his day, Boulton held Power in high esteem as a moderate, wise, and loyal Catholic leader who sought to live in harmony with his Protestant fellow citizens. The presence of the mayor, civic officials, and those "professing other creeds"[7] was a testament to the belief that Power's British Empire citizenship was integral to his person and that Power did not consider his citizenship to be in conflict with his deep devotion to the teaching and practices of the Roman Catholic Church. Instead, non-Catholics would identify him as one who "promoted brotherly love among those of all creeds."[8] For this reason, they withstood rain and mud to pay him a final tribute.

As the funeral train rounded the corner of Queen and Church and proceeded north, it became clear that the two-by-two military precision of the marching dignitaries was only a herald to the chaotic mob of Catholics and Protestants who wanted to complete the journey with Power. In this mob were men wearing cloth caps, homespun trousers, and the remnants of cheap leather shoes, accompanied by women wrapped in woollen shawls, children in tow. These were the recently arrived Irish. They followed the train because they believed that Power had died for them. He had been a presence in the immigrant sheds and the fever hospital, and he had stood and prayed at gravesides as their kith and kin, having lost their battle with typhus, were lowered into Canadian soil. They would remember Michael Power as one who had walked with them, become infected with them, and died with them. Of all the images of Power summoned by those who mourned him in those few short hours, that of the Irish would persist the strongest and the longest: "As is well known he died a martyr to his zeal and charity in [sic] behalf of the fever-stricken immigrants of '47."[9]

After the lid on his vault was sealed, Michael Power became a bishop for whom the most memorable action of his life was his death. At the time of his passing, newspapers across the Province of Canada and elsewhere in North America imparted little about his background or his work as Bishop of Toronto, from 1841 to 1847. Instead, they focused on the journalistic hook that was his death, hanging his life story on it. "He shrunk not from the battleground of duty," remarked the Toronto *Mirror*, but, "serene and unmoved, he made his way to the hovels of the poor, and to be at the bedside of the stricken."[10] Writers referred to him as a "martyr of duty,"[11] a "martyr of his charity,"[12] a modern-day Charles Borromeo who died in the service of the poor of his diocese,[13] or as one whose "martyrdom in the hospitals ... [was] the seal of his sanctity."[14] Later newspaper reports, memorial services, eulogies delivered during services of commemoration, and Power's first biographers would deviate little from the theme of the "Irish bishop" and "martyr of charity." In 1856, at an immigrant aid convention in Buffalo, New York, Power was briefly memorialized as having first raised the idea of immigrant aid during the famine.[15] In its inaugural, January 1863, issue, the *Irish Canadian*, an Irish nationalist weekly with a Canada-wide distribution published in Toronto by Patrick Boyle, immortalized Michael Power and his heroic actions and sacrifice on behalf of the Irish: "If there is one man of our race in Canada more than another whose memory should be revered and cherished, it is the subject of this short and imperfect memoir, and we feel confident that none of our country-men who are not Catholics will be displeased ... for they as well as his own flock learned to love him. His mission was one of peace and good will ... a great good man – one who was in reality the father of his flock, the counsellor of the poor, and the comforter of the exiled."[16]

The image of Power that persisted thereafter was not just one of good man who died a martyr of charity, but also of an Irish leader who died for the exiles of Ireland. Such images passed from Boyle's pen into the historical record, appearing as late as 1880 in the much publicized and very popular book *The Irish in America*. Continuing in this vein, the

Portrait of Michael Power at St Michael's Cathedral,
likely adapted from a painting in the collection of
Father E.B. Gauvreau (St Michael's Cathedral)

Irish nationalist author and politician John Francis Maguire recounted
the details of Power's passing, right down to the "feeble" handwriting
that weakened and trailed off as he wrote his will on his deathbed.[17]

Nearly thirty years after the *Irish Canadian* published that front-page
story, Boyle's wish for a Michael Power biography was at last fulfilled.
In 1892, H.F. McIntosh, an amateur historian, wrote a brief essay on
the "life and times" of Michael Power for Father John R. Teefy's *Jubilee
Volume*, which commemorated the fiftieth anniversary of the Diocese
of Toronto.[18] The essay drew on materials from the Archives of the Arch-

Portrait of Michael Power, artist
unknown (ARCAT, PH 992.02/04)

diocese of Toronto, several Catholic and secular newspapers, and the
rather nationalistic spin that had been placed on Power's life by the *Irish
Canadian* so many years before.[19] McIntosh ably filled in the historical and ecclesiastical context of Power's appointment to Toronto but
offered little more than a page of information on Power's life from birth
to becoming bishop.[20] Predictably, his essay is prefaced and concluded
by the scriptural quotation "Greater love than this no man hath, that a
man lay down his life for his friends."[21] While a considerable amount
of biographical and historical detail is covered in this short article, the
theme announced in the Biblical verse at its outset builds to a crescendo in the last quarter of the paper, thus situating McIntosh's work
squarely within the forty-five-year-old "memory tradition" of Michael
Power as "martyr."

For almost one hundred years, McIntosh's short essay was the standard work on Michael Power. In fact, part of it was reprinted in 1923,
when McIntosh wrote a lengthy essay entitled "The Catholic Church in
Toronto" for Edgar Middleton's multivolume history of Toronto.[22] While
Murray W. Nicolson's essay "Michael Power, First Bishop of Toronto,
1842–1847," published in 1987 by the Canadian Catholic Historical
Association, provided some details of Power's life in Toronto, it did not

Portrait of Michael Power, artist unknown; a
chubby version of the bishop (from Reverend
Edward Kelly, *The Story of St Paul's Parish,
1822–1922* [Toronto, 1922])

venture significantly from McIntosh's well-beaten path. Nicolson ended
the essay on a familiar note: "he left to a laity which was to encounter
degradation and hardship the example of true Christian charity – the
gift of his life."[23] Nicolson's short tribute to Power was derived from
his lengthy doctoral dissertation, which chronicled the migration and
settlement of Irish Catholic immigrants in mid-Victorian Toronto. In
the dissertation and essays derived from it, Nicolson placed very little
emphasis on the episcopate of Power.[24] At the end of his biographical essay, for example, Nicolson concluded that Power left his diocese
much as he had found it: "in chronic need of priests, religious orders,
and institutions."[25] This set the stage for Nicolson to argue that it was
the career of Power's successor, Armand de Charbonnel, that essentially
built the infrastructure of the diocese.

Line drawing of Michael Power, likely adapted from previous portraits (from *Jubilee Volume of the Archdiocese of Toronto, 1842–1892*, ed. J.R. Teefy [Toronto: George T. Dixon, 1892])

Robert Choquette's entry on Michael Power in the *Dictionary of Canadian Biography* appeared the same year as Nicolson's essay, but it broke some new ground. Originally submitted to the DCB in 1979, and partially the fruit of Choquette's ongoing research on the Catholic Church in French-speaking Ontario, this new biographical sketch of Power included French-language primary sources that had never been mined by Power's earlier biographers. While working in the Archives of the Chancery of the Archdiocese of Montreal, Choquette had uncovered a treasure trove of letters exchanged by Power and his mentor Bishop Ignace Bourget. It only stood to reason that a visit to Montreal would yield additional information on Power, given that he had spent twenty-six of his nearly forty-three years – from 1816 to 1842 – either studying in Montreal or serving in the parishes and missions of the St Lawrence and Ottawa Valleys. The inclusion of this new material established a paper trail linking Power formally with church leaders in Quebec, although the remainder of the biography did not add much to what McIntosh and Nicolson had already written.[26]

Historians have faced a great many obstacles in trying to chronicle Power's life and assess the significance of his work as a priest and bishop in Canada. The powerful martyr of charity image and the nationalist interpretation of his death as a martyrdom for the Irish are irresistible to many, and they have become a driving force behind discussions of Toronto's first Roman Catholic bishop. Moreover, historians who challenge these almost sacred precepts of the collective memory or attempt to peer around them often do so at the peril of their reputations. These scholars risk stirring the wrath of the religious or cultural stakeholders in the Power memory and those who judge any biography veering from these "truths" as, at best, profane secular history or, at worst, a denigration of the sanctity of Power. Nevertheless, the gaps in Power's story are wide – about thirty-eight years fall into them. Few of us would be amused if we knew that our life's chronicle omitted the first 80 per cent of the story or relegated those years to a footnote or a sweeping summary. Without knowledge of Power's earlier years – the pre-episcopal years – how can we arrive at an understanding of his personality, the evolution of his character, or the ongoing development of his spirituality and his ideas?

Michael Power left very little behind in terms of documentary evidence with which one could answer these questions and build a profile of the man, particularly the man who developed before his consecration to the episcopacy. In the Archives of the Archdiocese of Toronto, one of the finest collections and best-organized depositories in Canada, there remain only two slender cases of documents containing fragments of his incoming correspondence, a few family letters, some purchase receipts, and drafts and copies of some letters. Portions of two letter books contain copies of several hundred outgoing letters, but few letters of reply. For a more robust portrait of Power, one must ferret out the missing letters in memos held in the Catholic chancery offices of Montreal, Quebec, and dozens of other dioceses, and in the archives of the Propaganda Fide, the Colonial Office, the Generalate of the Society of Jesus, and the mother house of the Institute of the Blessed Virgin Mary. Additional sleuthing leads the historical detective to government archives, newspapers, court transcripts, wills, and such routinely generated records as the shipping news, property tax assessments, and the Canadian censuses. Sometimes, these investigations lead nowhere; other times, the detective feels like the Hebrews who, while in bondage in Egypt, were forced to make bricks without straw. What follows are the fruits of my search. This book is not an attempt to debunk the martyr memories; it is an attempt to glimpse the whole life behind them.

Three elements appear to be woven into the fabric of Michael Power's brief life. First, he had developed into a strong-willed man of faith, deeply devoted to the Roman Catholic Church, its doctrine, its mission, and its institutional structures. Though seemingly oriented to the priestly life as a preadolescent, he struggled with his faith as a young man, and as a young pastor he was outspoken when his bishop made what he considered unreasonable demands of him. Power had a legalistic mind, and in time he began to enjoy teasing questions and interpretations from the canon law and pondering their applications in pastoral life. His embrace of the ultramontane revolution of the late 1830s and 1840s, his personal devotion, and his legalistic perspective fuelled a greater ambition to build a hierarchically administered, orderly, and canonically disciplined Roman Catholic Church on the Upper Canadian frontier.

Michael Power was also, by choice, a loyal subject of the British Crown and a proud citizen of the British Empire. He was raised in a garrison town that hummed to the rhythms of the Royal Navy. The sights and sounds of the British military structure were all about him, floating in Halifax harbour, parading in the public squares, or hewn out of stone on the heights above Bedford Basin. He was trained by clergy in Halifax, Montreal, and Quebec City who were noted for their fidelity to the church and their loyalty to the British monarch, and he imbibed these lessons liberally. From pastors and teachers like Joseph-Octave Plessis, Edmund Burke, and the Sulpicians, he gleaned a perspective of church and state that regarded the interests of the Catholic Church and those of the British Empire as complementary, inclusive of one another, and, perhaps, mutually reinforcing. He adopted a demeanour of personal discipline and a respect for order, which he applied to both his spiritual life and the behaviour of those who served him. He also applied it in the public square, were he sought civil peace and a respect for legitimate authority and the rule of law. Though his resolve would sometimes be tested by political radicalism, armed insurrection, religious prejudice, and thick-headed bureaucrats in the corridors of empire, Michael Power did not waver in his belief that Catholics would never take lightly, nor take for granted, their citizenship in the world's largest and strongest colonial empire.

Finally, the Canadian frontier – its vastness, its unknowns, its relaxation of the norms of "civilized life," and its reluctance to be conquered – was a constant force in Power's life. Born on the empire's frontier, he encountered the economic, social, political, and religious idiosyncrasies that often characterize regions far from metropolitan centres. As a novice priest, he spent six years on the settlement frontiers of Lower Canada and in the Ottawa and St François Valleys, where he found his formal seminary training to be of little help in the face of the irregularities and flexibility of religious practice. In such places, church law was difficult to enforce and clerical authority impossible to impose. The frontiers – the settlement frontier and the missionary frontier – would challenge him, provoke him, make him ill, test his patience, and force him to take risks. His unwanted appointment to the Diocese of Western Upper Canada, later Toronto, a great expanse of lake, rock, forest, swamp, and meadow stretching from the small towns and villages of the lower Great Lakes to the little-known lands north of Lake Superior, became Michael Power's ultimate challenge.

Power's fidelity to Catholicism, loyalty to the Crown, and attempts to order religious life on the frontier were the three principal forces that shaped his person and his self-understanding. Once one understands these transforming impulses of his life and work, one can then view the last weeks of Power's life with greater clarity and deeper insight. The human train that departed from the front doors of St Paul's Church on 5 October 1847 was only embarking on the final leg of a much longer pilgrimage undertaken by a man who felt a constant call to put out into the deep.

CHAPTER ONE

∿ Land and Sea ∿

EACH SPRING, THE MEN OF WATERFORD put out into the deep. As had been their ritual for decades, wives, children, and kin would crowd the wharves and quays of Waterford City and wave as their menfolk slipped away for another season in the fishery. One by one, the sails disappeared on the Atlantic horizon, the currents of the great ocean carrying the vessels to their final destination – *Talamh an eisc*, or, "land of fish." Some of the men would drop their nets into the cod-rich waters off the Grand Banks of Newfoundland. Others would spend months on the inhospitable rocks of the Avalon Peninsula slapping fillets of salted cod onto wooden drying frames. Still others would provision the stores of St John's, the major port in a colony built on a fishery. And others would criss-cross the North Atlantic, exchanging their cargoes of Newfoundland salted cod for hemp, tar, ships' provisions, salted meat, bacon, and grain from Irish farms. Once their ships were loaded, they would make another run to the land of fish. Meanwhile, the women of Waterford and district would wait until the autumn, when the men would return. Then the season would be over, and their income would be secure.

This rhythm of life, which married the fortunes and expectations of Waterford with the resources of the New World, continued from the mid-seventeenth century to 1830, with few interruptions.[1] Each year, merchant captains – Coughlans, Doyles, Kellys, McCarthys, and Powers – collected their crews and labourers at Waterford and Bristol and set out to earn a living, making southeast Ireland one of the most prosperous regions in the United Kingdom. Their odysseys would take them to Britain's North American colonies, the coves and ports of the new American Republic, and to the cane fields and distilleries of the British Caribbean. Yet, for the families of Waterford and environs, Newfoundland and the neighbouring colony of Nova Scotia held the keys to prosperity.

For generations, bonds of family and finance linked southeast Ireland to Britain's north Atlantic colonies. Despite the wealth of the fishery, however, British authorities never intended to establish a permanent settlement in Newfoundland, but sailors and their captains had other ideas.[2] The men who spent their summers at the onshore drying racks began to winter in the "land of fish." Their women no longer had to wait in Waterford – families reunited and began to create new lives for themselves in the coves and inlets that form the shore of what is now called the "Irish loop" on the southern stretch of the Avalon Peninsula.[3] In time, Britain's best-laid plans for Newfoundland lay in ruins as families from Waterford, Cork, Wexford, and South Tipperary laid claim to the land, giving each bay, headland, and hamlet an Irish flavour and a colourful name: Ferryland, Bay Bulls, Trepassy, and Witless Bay. To the alarm of the admiralty and others less disposed to the Irish, the women and men of Waterford were re-creating their old world in the new.[4] This Irish diaspora would eventually spread across much of eastern Newfoundland, eventually spilling over into the neighbouring colonies of Cape Breton, Prince Edward Island, the Miramichi Valley of northern New Brunswick, and the port of Halifax, Nova Scotia.

Captain William Power was a Waterford man who annually put out into the deep. The vital statistics collected in the late eighteenth century in southeast Ireland reveal precious little about William Power and his extended family. Our knowledge of Irish Catholics like Power is scant for good reason. The English conquest of Ireland, which began during the reign of Edward I and gathered force under the Tudors during the Reformation in the sixteenth century, had never anticipated the tenacity of Roman Catholics in maintaining their faith tradition. It was as if the Irish were sending a message to their Protestant conquerors that they would hold fast to their Catholicism to spite the English. Even the penal laws implemented by the Stuarts in 1701, which deprived most Catholics of the right to hold public office, own land, or enter the liberal professions, failed to dislodge the majority of the Irish from their allegiance to Catholicism.[5] Priests and laypersons continued to teach the faith in illegal schools, while itinerant clergy continued to administer the sacraments that marked the significant rites of passage in Irish life. Eventually, the penal laws became a dead letter, as small parishes continued to survive and priests went about their work unmolested by civil authorities. The casualty of these years, however, was record keeping. While the Church of Ireland (Anglican), the state church, has left a legacy of meticulous registers and records, the records of the unofficial Catholic majority are scant for the eighteenth century and vary in quality from village to village and county to county.

What can be deduced from the available fragments, generally from obituaries, is that William Power was likely born in Waterford City in the mid-1770s, the son of William Power Sr. and Bridget Phelan. The Powers were among the largest and most prosperous of the region's families. The family name Power, however, was not indigenously Irish. Originally called dePaor or dePeur, meaning "the poor," the Powers were descendants of Norman raiders who captured southern Irish ports in the eleventh century.[6] In the years between the Norman Conquest and the seventeenth century, the Powers betrayed the original meaning of their family name. In 1746, the Powers of Gardenmorris were one of the leading Roman Catholic families in County Waterford.[7] The navigation and trade records of the time reveal that the Powers were active merchants and sailors and numbered among the first settlers of Placentia Bay, Newfoundland.[8] Moreover, Powers were also in the ranks of the clergy; in 1815, a Father John Power was one of the first Irish missionary priests to venture to Newfoundland.[9] Earlier, in 1787, his kinsman Thomas Power served the Acadian Catholics who had returned to Arichat and Cape Breton Island after the 1755 mass expulsion from Nova Scotia. This Power also served the Irish Catholic enclave in Halifax and was recruited specifically for that mission because he was a native Irish speaker, a skill considered necessary for success among the Catholics of the colonial capital.[10] With the expansion of the Waterford trade to eastern North America and the subsequent arrival of increasing numbers of women and children from southeast Ireland, the family name Power became one of the most common in eastern Newfoundland. Moreover, as either direct migrants or sojourners from Ireland or as "two-boaters" from Newfoundland, the Powers made their name as common in Halifax as it was in St John's or Waterford City. In fact, like the Powers, a substantial majority of the Irish migrants to Britain's Atlantic coast colonies could trace their ancestry back exclusively to southeast Ireland, specifically the region of the Suir Estuary.[11]

Like so many Waterford men of his own family, William Power became a sailor in the region's merchant fleet. While it is not clear whether he owned his own ship – several Waterford men bearing the name Power did – William Power earned the title of captain, suggesting that he had earned the honour, in the very least, through faithful and skilled service to other Waterford owners and investors. The meagre family papers reveal that he had extensive knowledge of the waters off North America's northern coast, from the sunker-riddled depths off Newfoundland to the coral reefs and shoals hidden beneath the currents swirling about Jamaica and Cuba.[12] Given the economy of his times, young Captain Power would have loaded his ship with Irish bacon, barrels of salted meat and cereal grains, and boxes of Irish farm butter and then sailed into Bristol, or St John's, or Kingston, Jamaica. On his return voyage to Waterford, the holds of his ship would have been filled with cane sugar destined for refining, casks of rum from Dominica, Jamaica, and Trinidad, or salted cod from Newfoundland.[13] Until the onset of yet another European war, in the 1790s, which continued into the first decade of the new century, the North Atlantic trade in which Power was engaged was lucrative and reasonably secure under the protection of the Royal Navy.[14]

In his late twenties, for reasons known only to his contemporaries, Captain William Power settled in Halifax, Britain's principal naval and military installation in eastern North America. Founded in 1749 by Lord Cornwallis as a counterweight to the French fortress at Louisbourg, on Île Royale (Cape Breton), Halifax was blessed with a deep harbour protected by a narrow opening to the Atlantic. Cornwallis and successive military governors built a massive stone fortress on the heights above the western side of the harbour. This citadel, at the centre of which was Fort George, came to be the dominant landmark around which frame houses, shops, shipyards, and warehouses were constructed. During the American Revolution (1775–83), which would have only been a childhood memory to Captain Power, the Royal Navy strengthened its presence at Halifax, and once Britain had lost the rich colonies to the south, the Nova Scotia port became its most important North American garrison.

As trade increased in the North Atlantic triangle, and as contraband trade with the "Boston States" (New England) flourished, Halifax became a target for migrants from the British Isles. Both the merchant trade and the military infrastructure of Halifax demanded a ready pool of artisans, provisioners, sailors, and labourers, an array of opportunities that attracted large numbers of Irish, some directly from the homeland, others from the recently settled outports and villages of Newfoundland.[15] The latter earned the name "two-boaters" because they took one boat from Ireland to Newfoundland and then travelled on to a second destination in another boat.[16] In 1792–93, city administrators counted only 99 Irish Catholics among Halifax's 1,051 taxpayers. By 1800, however, with the weakening of the Waterford economy, Irish families from the counties of Wexford, Tipperary, Cork, and Waterford continued to stream across the Atlantic to Newfoundland and Halifax.[17] On the eve of the collapse of the fishing trade, in 1830, these Catholic migrants from southeast Ireland created distinctive enclaves in Halifax, encouraged members of their extended families to join them, gave birth to a new generation of Irish, and, eventually, comprised one-quarter of the city's population of 14,439.[18]

In 1802, in this new Irish Catholic community, William Power found a port of call and the love of his life. On 29 November of that year, he married Mary Roach at St Peter's Chapel, the ceremony officiated by the newly arrived missionary priest Edmund Burke.[19] As she often expressed in her letters, Mary Roach Power possessed a deep Catholic faith and a personal piety, which she would attempt to impart to each of her children. Her parents, Robert Roach of Waterford and Margaret Doyle of Youghal, were already residents of Halifax, participants in the well-established Irish trade pattern to eastern North America. Margaret Doyle's family may have converted to Catholicism, since the records of late-eighteenth-century Youghal show that the only resident Doyles were members of the Church of Ireland.[20] Much of the family history remains as shrouded as a ship in a North Atlantic fog. We have little sense of when the Doyles converted to Catholicism, or whether the religious divisions that marked her recent past accounted for Mary Roach Power's Catholic zeal and her determination to implant her spiritual passions in her children, particularly her eldest son.

William and Mary took up residence on Hollis Street, which ran parallel to the harbour, though three blocks to the west.[21] Hollis Street was a busy artery, cutting through the city's business and commercial section. The Power home was assessed variously at between £200 and £400, depending upon the year of assessment, and it would have been considered a dwelling of mid-range value. Many of their neighbours were professionals and businessmen, including a Dr. Petrie, G.M. Haliburton, and Jeremiah Vickers of J. Vickers and Sons.[22] Moreover, when the Powers resided on Hollis, the street provided access to the wood-frame Government House, seat of the Colonial Assembly, which sat at the northern terminus of the street.[23] Given the location of Hollis Street and the lack of Irish Catholic residents in the neighbourhood, it appeared that William and Mary Power were less concerned with being part of the Irish ghetto than with being in close proximity to the areas of highest priority in their lives. Mary would have been satisfied that they were within a short walking distance of the only Catholic

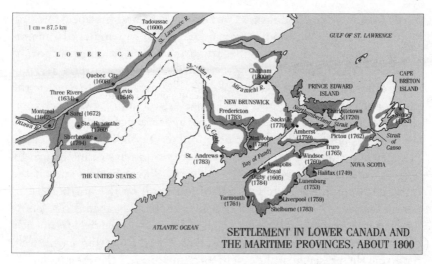

"Settlement in Lower Canada and the Maritime Provinces, about 1800" (courtesy of McGraw-Hill Ryerson)

church in the city, St Peter's Chapel, at the corner of Grafton Street and Spring Garden Road.[24] Captain Power would have been pleased to have the harbour and his fellow navigators close at hand; these navigator-merchants included Captains Walsh, Crowder, Cleary, and Smilie.[25] In terms of raising a family, the Hollis Street home was also satisfactory, because it was at a safe distance from the streets near the citadel, notorious for their "brothels, grog shops and dancing houses."[26] Mary Power would have been somewhat comforted by the knowledge that her children were insulated from the noises and spectacles of inebriation occurring in alleys and lanes immortalized by such names as "Knock Him Down Street."[27] This peace of mind would have been critical to Mary Power, since for most of her childbearing years she had to raise her family almost single-handedly.

With his wife safely ensconced in a good section of town, Captain William Power continued his life at sea. In 1805 and 1806, he commanded the *Thomas and John*, sailing her from Halifax to Sydney, Cape Breton, and to Tobago and Jamaica in the British Caribbean.[28] Three years later, he took charge of both the *Loyalty* and the brig *Regulator*, which made frequent runs between Halifax and Newfoundland. In later years, Power could be found at the helm of several other vessels: the *Hanna*, the *Thomas Jeffery*, the *Lark*, and the *Prudent*.[29] In most cases, his principal task was to do what he and his ancestors had done for several generations – transfer cargos of raw materials, manufactured goods, food, and supplies from one British colonial outport to another – in addition to making several runs to Boston. Upon arriving in port, he would rest for several weeks, contract himself to either the same merchant or a new one, and embark upon another voyage. Typical of this pattern was his eighty-day voyage to Jamaica at the wheel of the *Thomas Jeffery*, which concluded on 10 October 1809. His cargo of sugar and rum was brought to market within days of his return by retailer C. Hians. In the following winter, Power headed off on the *Lark*, en route to the Dutch colony of Surinam, on the north coast of South America.[30] In addition to hauling cargo, Power and his fellow merchants served as intelligence for the admiralty, since they frequently came in contact with French warships. Power performed this service well, reporting the presence of the Rochefort Squadron of the French fleet in the Mona Passage off Jamaica while he was en route to Tobago in 1805 and offering a disputed report of enemy frigates near Guadaloupe when he was homebound from Dominica in 1810.[31]

Upon returning to Halifax from his adventures at sea, the captain would usually discover that he was a father again. William and Mary Power had eight children who survived childbirth. Born on 17 October 1804, Michael was their first.[32] The birth of the future bishop was followed by the arrival of three boys and four girls: William Junior (died 1827), James (1806–22), John (born 1811), Margaret (1813–83), Mary Ann (born 1815), Elizabeth (born 1816), and Frances (born 1818).[33] While such large families were certainly not uncommon among Irish Catholics in the nineteenth century,[34] the Powers were fortunate that most of their children avoided the typical childhood diseases and epidemics that claimed the lives of many Halifax infants before they reached the age of five. In the nineteenth century, severe winters, contaminated water and food, and periodic outbreaks of fever and smallpox took their toll among the children of Nova Scotia.[35] During Michael's childhood, however, his family had little cause to hang the black crepe of mourning on the front door.

From all available evidence, Captain Power's sustained employment in the merchant fleet provided the means to keep his family fed, clothed, and educated. They survived the economic downturn of 1803, the result of a temporary collapse in the market for fish.[36] In fact, the captain's income was sufficient to cover the cost of maintaining a pew at St Peter's

Chapel, send his eldest son to a school that charged modest fees, and, by May 1816, permit him to join the Charitable Irish Society of Halifax (CIS).[37] Power's membership in the CIS required him to pay an initial fee of four dollars (Halifax currency), additional payments of two shillings per quarter, and the secretary's fee of two shillings and sixpence per year.[38] Although the CIS had been founded in 1786 as an ecumenical benevolent association to assist the city's Irish poor, it also served as an important social club for Halifax's business and political elite and those who considered themselves respectable citizens.[39] The importance of this social function was clear to all. For instance, the CIS became notorious for its St Patrick's Day banquets, some of which involved over fifty toasts; on one occasion, the festivities were not terminated until the sun rose on March 18.[40] To join this philanthropic and sometimes tipsy fraternity, one had to be nominated and approved by its members. In the society's earliest days, the approval procedure was conducted using black and white beans – nominees who ended up with a black one were damned to exclusion.[41] William Power, by remaining a CIS member in good standing (although he was not a regular participant due to his long voyages), not only confirmed his respectable position among the leading men of the city but also gave him access to the highest levels of political, social, and financial power in the colony.[42] CIS presidents included such luminaries as John Howe, the Honourable Charles Morris, Lawrence Doyle, and scions of the Uniacke family. A merchant with a growing family, a CIS member with a reputation for numbering among those most loyal to the Crown, Captain Power had status in his community.[43] It is therefore not surprising that when, in 1863, the *Irish Canadian* reviewed the career of Bishop Power it unabashedly characterized his father as "honest, sober, peaceful and industrious."[44]

Although the unwritten rules of domestic politics dictate that parents love their children equally, Mary Power favoured her eldest son. Even as he grew in her womb, she dedicated him to the service of God and resolved to push him – whether he assented to it or not – towards an ecclesiastical vocation.[45] As a child, he was simply her Mick, a curly-haired boy with dark colouring. But by the time he reached adolescence, Mick understood that his mother considered him the hope of the family. When he went away to study, far from home, Mary made it abundantly clear that his service to the church would do great honour to his family and his parish community in Halifax.[46] No records of his early years survive, so it is difficult to pinpoint the extent of Mary's ambitions for her son. When one examines Mick's actions, however, one can detect Mary's hand at work, shaping his sense of commitment to the tiny parish community of St Peter's. Here the evidence is clear – as an altar server and a participant in weekly catechism classes, he slowly absorbed the basics of his mother's faith and a sense of active participation in liturgy.

The church was not his only childhood influence. Young Mick Power needed few reminders that he had been born in a bustling colonial out-post of Britain's vast global empire. From the rooftop of his Hollis Street home, he could view Halifax harbour to the east. Throughout his youth, the wharves and quays bustled with sailors, stevedores, and longshore-men loading and unloading ships or outfitting frigates and men-of-war, preparing them for battle with the warships of Napoleon or, by 1812, the corsairs of the American republic. Young Mick's world was filled with the sights and sounds of war. The Halifax economy boomed as the admiralty poured thousands of pounds into ship repair, provisioning, naval stores, and the recruitment of sailors and longshoremen. News of Britain's wars drifted into Halifax weeks or even months after the fact, and Haligonians celebrated Nelson's victory over the French at Trafalgar and Wellington's destruction of Napoleon's army at Waterloo.[47]

On several occasions, Mick and his friends witnessed the devastating effects of war in Halifax harbour. On 6 June 1813, the locals crammed onto the piers to view the HMS *Shannon* tow the battered hulk of the USS *Chesapeake* into view. Later, the Royal Navy permitted the public to tour the spoils of war, reportedly still ripe with the stench of blood and rotten flesh, the remains of the American sailors who had defended the Chesapeake to the last. For many Haligonians, the conquest appeared complete when a silent cortège of sailors carried the lifeless body of the American Captain Lawrence through the capital en route to the public cemetery for temporary burial. Lawrence did not live long enough to see his last order – "don't give up the ship" – go unrequited. In 1814, Mick Power also shared in his fellow Haligonians' relief and sense of celebration when word came that Napoleon had been exiled to Elba; they rejoiced again in August 1815, when the news arrived that a rejuvenated Napoleon had fallen at Waterloo.[48]

When Mick's wanderings took him away from the harbour, the visual reminders of empire were rarely far from his sight. To the west of his home, the citadel loomed over the city, as did the city's famous clock tower, erected in 1799 by the Duke of Kent, the fourth in line to the throne of King George III.[49] Beyond the citadel, Hollis Street extended

View of Halifax harbour in the early nineteenth century
(NA, Peter Winkworth Collection, R 9266-237)

south, the end of the street affording a clear view of the harbour's
mouth, McNab's Island, and the open ocean beyond. The young Power
spent much of his time exploring his native city. He frequently ventured
south along Hollis, past the frame and stone houses of the merchants and
the ample wooden homes of the Halifax elite. Just beyond Alexander
McLean's house, he would turn west onto Morris Road and then make
his way along a dirt road (now Tower Road). At its end was his favourite
wild haunt – a forested area that now encompasses Point Pleasant Park.
These rambles in the woods and rises of the south end nourished Mick's
love of the outdoors, and particularly his interest in the variety of trees,
shrubs, and flowers that could be found in abundance less than fifteen
minutes from the harbour. He committed to memory the Latin names
of the Acadian flora, grew adept at identifying the shapes, colours, and
varieties of wildflowers, and found peace from school, Hollis Street, and
his growing family. Yet, even in the quiet of the king's forest, the presence of empire intruded – his jaunts always took place within sight of
the Martello tower built by the British on the heights of Point Pleasant.[50]

The sense of imperial citizenship was also evident in Mick's home and
his church. Captain Power's income was tied to the fortunes of the British
merchant trade, which in turn was protected by the Royal Navy, which
endeavoured to keep the shipping lanes of the North Atlantic triangle

safe from privateers and enemy warships. By holding a CIS membership, Captain Power demonstrated his family's loyalty to the British Empire, this at a time when bloody revolution in Ireland was still fresh in people's minds – it had occurred in 1798, just six years before Mick's birth. The captain thus assured his benefactors that he was a safe investment and no romantic follower of the ghost of Irish revolutionary Wolf Tone.[51] On Sundays, he served Mass for Father Edmund Burke, a friend who played a major role in all of the Power family rites of passage, including Mick's baptism. Burke himself was renowned for his public expressions of loyalty, to the annoyance of his superior, Bishop Joseph-Octave Plessis of Quebec, who believed that the Halifax priest was far too preoccupied with Britain's war with Napoleonic France.[52] At home, in church, at school (his teacher was the Anglican chaplain to the garrison at Fort George), and in the streets and green spaces of the city, young Michael Power drank liberally from the wellspring of imperial sentiment. His sense of British citizenship was well established.

Loyalties aside, Mick would have known that he and his family were citizens, but different. They were faithful Catholics in an overtly Protestant town. The Powers belonged to St Peter's Roman Catholic Chapel, the first and only place of Catholic worship in Halifax, serving 1,000 faithful, mostly of Irish extraction, and large numbers of soldiers billeted at the citadel.[53] The small, red wood-framed building was considered a blessing to Catholics in a community that had been under the strictures of Nova Scotia's penal laws until the late eighteenth century.[54] In 1758, for instance, during yet another war with Catholic France, colonial officials had imposed heavy sanctions against Nova Scotia's Catholic population: "every Popish person, exercising any ecclesiastical jurisdiction, and every popish priest or person exercising the function of parish priest shall depart out of this province on or before the twenty-fifth day of March 1759."[55]

The Nova Scotia penal laws imposed a penalty of fifty pounds upon any person harbouring a Catholic priest and added the further indignity of time in the pillory. Catholics were also barred from owning property, building churches, and seeking or holding public office. It is interesting to note that while Nova Scotia's Catholics suffered such penalties until 1783, their Catholic neighbours in the conquered province of Quebec, unlike other British Empire Catholics, enjoyed the Crown's tolerance under the terms of the Quebec Act.[56]

Relief from some penal laws was already evident in Ireland from 1778 to 1782, and in 1783, Nova Scotia repealed its own prohibitions on Catholic worship and the upward political and social mobility of Catholic males.[57] Representatives of Halifax's growing Irish Catholic minority petitioned Governor John Wentworth for permission to build a chapel. Previously, Catholics had worshipped in private homes, where they were served by itinerant Catholics priests, some of whom were of rather dubious character.[58] In 1784, St Peter's Chapel was completed, and the following year the congregation completed its adjoining presbytery.[59] The visiting priest from Quebec, under whose jurisdiction Halifax fell, described the new church as "spacious and beautiful ... perfectly finished on the outside and well advanced inside."[60] With the Diocese of Quebec unable to provide Halifax with sufficient English-speaking clergy, the parish trustees arranged for the transfer of Irish priests to Nova Scotia. In 1785, Bishop John Butler of Cork sent Capuchin friar James Jones to Halifax, whereupon Bishop Louis-Philippe d'Esgly of Quebec, despite having been embarrassed by the unilateral action of the St Peter's trustees, appointed Jones superior of the Nova Scotia mission.[61] Although Michael Power would never meet Jones, who left the city under a cloud four years before Power was born, the young altar server did come to understand Jones's difficulty with the trustees through his friendship with Jones's second successor, Father Edmund Burke.

Jones had fought a drawn-out battle with the parish trustees over jurisdictional and financial matters. By 1800, the laymen who held title to the parish and controlled its finances had won, and Jones departed the city in frustration. His successor, a Dominican named Edmund Burke (the first of two pastors with this name), found himself caught in the same fierce power struggle waged by assertive churchwardens on one side and, on the other, the pastor and his supporters from the far less affluent parish rank and file, who refused to pay the subscriptions demanded by the wardens for the upkeep of St Peter's. In 1801, when the "popular" faction resisted the wardens' threats to deny them parish rights, including burial in the church cemetery, the wardens appealed to Bishop Pierre Denault, who removed Burke. He replaced him with a secular priest of the same name.[62] The new Edmund Burke was also appointed Denault's vicar-general for Nova Scotia, perhaps in the hope that the bishop's authority could be exercised more effectively to keep peace in the region.

Born in Ireland in 1753 and educated in Paris, Burke had been a professor of Latin and Greek at the Quebec Seminary from 1786 to 1791.[63] Having laboured for four years as pastor of two francophone parishes on Île d'Orléans, northeast of Quebec City, Burke was sent as a missionary to Niagara on the Upper Canadian frontier, where he served for seven years.[64] At Fort Niagara, a British officer wrongfully accused Burke of an "indiscretion" with his wife, and to avoid scandal Denault moved Burke to Halifax, where he remained for the rest of his life.[65] In the three years leading up to his death in 1820, Burke served as vicar apostolic of Nova Scotia – he was essentially a missionary bishop who reported directly to the Propaganda Fide in Rome. There is little evidence to suggest that the cloud under which Burke left Niagara followed him to Nova Scotia; in Halifax, he pursued a distinguished career as a cleric, community leader, and public advocate for Catholic rights in the colony.

For young Michael Power, Burke was not just a pastor, he was also a model of the priestly vocation. Burke had officiated at the marriage of William and Mary in 1802; he had baptized Michael on 23 October 1804;[66] he had supervised the young Power's catechism classes; and he had mentored him as he served Mass at St Peter's Chapel. While records of Michael Power's early years are fragmentary, at best, it is clear that Burke was a constant presence in his life, and he was perhaps Michael's most consistent male role model, given that Captain Power's work kept him away from home for long periods. Michael's activities and interests later in life suggest that he had been a careful observer of Burke as a priest and pastor and a witness to Burke's measured but forceful ventures into the public sphere.[67]

The Burke years at St Peter's stood in marked contrast to the mission's troubled early history. Burke was far more successful than his predecessors at keeping the often aggressive lay churchwardens in check. Buoyed by Bishop Denault's intervention into parish affairs in 1801, and sustained by the force of his own personality, Burke was the undisputed master of the parish. The elected churchwardens neither challenged Burke openly nor asserted their former jurisdictional claims. As had been mandated by Bishop Denault, their meetings could take place only in Burke's presence, and the pastor's signature was required on all of their decisions and resolutions.[68] In this way, it was made clear that episcopal authority was paramount in the parish and, as Denault's vicar-general, Burke had the final word on all matters relating to life at St Peter's. Reporting back to Denault, Burke happily concluded, "In obedience to the instructions conveyed in Your Lordship's pastoral letter, of the 8th of Sept. 1801 ... We think it our duty to inform your Lordship, that the whole of this arduous business has been conducted without a contradiction and to the entire satisfaction of all parties. To your Lordship's paternal vigilance and effectual attention to our wants as

"The South End of Argyle Street," by Colonel Alexander C. Mercer. Here we see St Mary's Church, which replaced St Peter's Chapel in the 1820s (NA, 1989–397–10)

soon as made known we stand indebted for that Harmony which now subsists."[69] According to Terrence Murphy, Burke developed a "system of parish administration which protected the authority of both bishop and priest."[70] For young Power, the first and lasting images of parish life would be those of clerical authority and lay submission to the priest.

Mick Power would have also become aware of Burke's intellectual skills and his ability to engage in articulate debate in both the public press and local politics. The most immediate experience for Power was as Burke's student in weekly catechism classes. It is certain that some bond grew between the two. Burke recognized in Michael Power intellectual and theological gifts, which, he believed, could not be fully cultivated in Nova Scotia, where neither Catholic elementary schools nor academies of Catholic higher education existed. Eventually, Burke would become the principal catalyst in Power's decision to leave home to study in Quebec.[71] But it was during the time he spent under Burke's tutelage at the parish manse that Power moved from the forms of worship he had learned from his mother to a more formal intellectual training in Catholicism. In the absence of records, one can assume that Burke's curriculum was similar to other Catholic instruction offered at the time:

the study of Bible history and the unpacking of Catholic doctrine by means of catechisms. While catechetical texts had been commonly used in the Diocese of Quebec since the appearance of Bishop Saint-Vallier's *Catéchisme du Diocèse de Québec*, first printed in 1702, Burke would likely have preferred the approved English-language text developed by Archbishop James Butler of Cashel.[72] Like most catechisms, Butler's edition included a compendium of prayers in addition to sections on basic points of doctrine, an analysis of the Ten Commandments, or "decalogue," and a section on the Seven Sacraments of the church. Having observed Power's intellectual talents, Burke would surely have exceeded the regular curriculum and introduced his young ward to his own Latin and Greek favourites.

Power may also have been aware of Burke's unwavering loyalty to the Crown and his close attention to imperial politics. Burke followed Denault's instruction of 1803 that "God Save the King" ("Domine salvum fac regem") be sung at the conclusion of all church services. Given Burke's public pronouncements of loyalty to the Crown, this was not simple compliance with episcopal authority. In his pamphlet "Letter of Instruction to the Catholic Missionaries of Nova Scotia and its Dependencies," published in February 1804, Burke was unequivocal about Catholic loyalty to a Protestant monarch: "our most gracious sovereign extending his paternal care to all his subjects, having directed his Parliament, the Supreme Legislature of the Empire, to permit his subjects of the Roman Catholic Communion to profess the faith of their ancestors on condition of attesting their Allegiance ... that one indispensable rule of Catholic morality, tho it strictly forbids a compliance with any order contrary to the divine law or known Principles of Religion, does not in any case permit active resistance ... Insurrection is an evil so great in itself that no abuse of power can justify it ... obedience is due to him [the prince] not because he is a just and virtuous man, but because he is the ruling Prince, in whom the Supreme power is invested."[73]

Accordingly, Burke followed the campaign against Napoleon closely, opposed the American Revolution, and expressed concern that Nova Scotian students would be corrupted in American schools, should they be sent there, because they would be inculcated with "principles inimical to our constitution."[74] Even when he was attacked for disloyalty, Burke was effusive about his friendship with John Graves Simcoe, the former lieutenant-governor of Upper Canada, and the Duke of Kent, son of King George III.[75] Young Power would have noted that his teacher and pastor was, unflinchingly, a priest of the Catholic Church and a subject of the British Empire.

The sometimes difficult balancing act of maintaining Catholic faith while professing loyalty to a Protestant monarch would pose daily challenges for Power, especially when he was beyond the range of Burke's watchful eye. Before 1819, there were no formal Catholic schools in Halifax.[76] As early as 1786, Governor John Parr had lifted the penal laws restricting Catholics from operating their own denominational schools.[77] Catholics did not respond immediately to this new freedom, since neither sufficient capital nor a large number of potential school ratepayers could be secured. In 1802, Burke successfully petitioned the Legislative Assembly to establish a state-funded common school for poor Irish children. The combination of fierce opposition from the local Anglican bishop, Charles Inglis, a lack of qualified teachers or Catholic teaching sisters or brothers, and a shortage of private donations to bolster public funds delayed the establishment of a Catholic school for nearly two decades.[78] Thus, apart from Burke's Sunday school classes, Michael Power's formal education would be conducted in a non-Catholic school environment.

As an adolescent, Michael attended Halifax Grammar School, located at Barrington and Sackville Streets, not far from the Power home. The school had been founded in 1780, but the building itself was not completed, nor did classes commence, until 1789. The headmaster was William Cochrane.[79] The school's principal goal was to prepare young men to enter King's College and "to furnish such as pretend to a complete collegiate education with a cheap and convenient means of attaining such useful knowledge as their future destination in life may admit or require."[80] At the time of Michael Power's arrival at the school (which is not precisely known), the Reverend George Wright, Cochrane's brother-in-law, was headmaster.[81] Wright, who assumed control of the school in 1799, was an active member of the Society for the Propagation of the Gospel in Foreign Parts (SPGFP) and chaplain to the Halifax garrison. Members of the Cunard family had attended the school, as had the children of many of Halifax's leading Protestant families. Some maintain that newspaper editor and political reformer Joseph Howe also attended the school.[82] Given their ages – all were born in 1804 – it is possible that Howe, Power, and Catholic barrister Lawrence O'Connor Doyle were classmates under Wright.

With the exception of Doyle, Power found himself surrounded by Protestant British loyalists. The Nova Scotia government mandated a curriculum including writing, arithmetic, a variety of maths, English, Latin, French, writing, geography, and philosophy. As did other Anglican-run institutions in Upper Canada and New Brunswick, the Halifax

Grammar School inculcated in its students principles of "conservatism, social hierarchy, monarchism, and anti-Americanism."[83] In such an environment, Power's experience of clericalism and loyalism in his relationship with Edmund Burke would have been reinforced. Despite Burke's consternation over Catholic children attending Protestant schools, Power's time under George Wright seems to have had little effect on his practice of Catholicism. In fact, with both Burke and Wright as his mentors during his formative years, Power would have been subject to a doubly powerful model of imperial citizenship, duty, and public virtue. From Burke, Power learned that it was possible to be both a faithful Catholic and a loyal subject of the king; Wright underscored the importance of the latter through teaching and example.

In 1815, Power experienced one of the great events of his youth: Bishop Joseph-Octave Plessis's visit to Halifax. Plessis's diocese, one of the largest in the Christian world, stretched south to north from the Great Lakes to Hudson Bay and the *terra incognita*, and from west to east from the great interior plains to the Atlantic Ocean, excluding the colony of Newfoundland. While Plessis's principal pastoral focus was the French Canadian population of Lower Canada, most of which was settled in the valley of the St Lawrence River and along the river's tributaries, the bishop was also responsible for First Nations peoples across the hinterlands of the diocese, English- and Gaelic-speaking peoples in Upper Canada and the Maritime colonies, and the French-speaking Acadians who had resettled in the Atlantic region. Although many of his anglophone Catholics living both east and west of Lower Canada had accused him of centralizing control and asserting his metropolitan dominance over their regions, to his credit, Plessis visited the frontiers of his diocese to assess the state of the faith there and to ascertain more effective ways of shepherding their disparate Catholic populations.[84] As Bishop Denault had done before him, Plessis travelled to the growing Catholic communities beyond the Gulf of St Lawrence. He made visits in 1811 and 1812 to the Magdalen Islands, northern New Brunswick, and Prince Edward Island. He had hoped to reach Halifax in 1812, but the trip was cut short when war erupted between Great Britain and the United States. With the cessation of hostilities in 1815, Plessis determined to undertake the first episcopal visit to Halifax since Denault had gone there in 1803, the year prior to Michael Power's birth.[85] He knew that he must deal with sensitive issues relevant to the future of the church in Nova Scotia.

As Denault's vicar-general in Upper Canada, Burke had been adamant that the huge Diocese of Quebec be divided into more manageable units, and his view remained unchanged. He envisioned the authority centred in four regions: Quebec, Montreal, Upper Canada, and the Maritimes. Between 1796 and 1797, while he was still in Niagara, Burke had actively sought apostolic-mission status for the upper colony.[86] Similarly, in Halifax he wanted greater autonomy for the fledgling churches east of the St Lawrence, and he hoped to create a central administration and a seminary for the Maritimes in Halifax. For Burke, the logic of such a move was clear. He recognized that Plessis had few priests to spare, and no anglophones at that, and if Nova Scotia and New Brunswick were to be properly served, the initiative to recruit clergy would have to come from the region itself.[87] One solution, proposed by Plessis himself, was to send Maritime men to the minor seminaries and ultimately the Seminary of Quebec for training.[88] A second, and more costly, option was for Burke to establish his own seminary in Halifax, staff it, and prepare priests locally. Finally, Burke could also resume the traditional recruitment pattern of having Irish bishops send their surplus clergy to British North America.[89] Whichever means, or combination of means, they adopted, one critical fact remained in Burke's view: Halifax and district required anglophone priests, and Nova Scotia, with its linguistic, social, and cultural distinctions, needed autonomy from Quebec.

Some of these plans were already being implemented. In 1814, Plessis sent Father Pierre-Marie Mignault to serve as Burke's assistant, and one year later he transferred Father Antoine Manseau to assist Mignault while Burke was in Europe.[90] Neither spoke English as a first language, thus confirming Burke's contention that Quebec priests could only act as temporary replacements. As for the local seminary, Burke had neither the money nor a teaching order of priests to run what he envisioned as a regional centre for English-language clerical education and the centrepiece of a diocese independent of Quebec. The third option, Irish recruitment, probably held the best prospects for a short-term solution to the shortage of priests in the Maritime colonies. The vicar-general of the Diocese of Kilkenny, James Mansfield, pledged his support to Burke by permitting some of his seminarians to be sent to Halifax. The venture did not bear fruit until 1817, when the Apostolic Vicariate of Nova Scotia was created and several men, including Burke's nephew John Carroll, were sent to Halifax.[91] Carroll was ordained in Halifax in 1820. He would eventually move to Toronto, where he would become one of Michael Power's most trusted priests and, after Power's death, the administrator of the diocese.

These recruitment schemes produced only a trickle of men suited to the Nova Scotia church, and by 1815 Burke had decided to emulate a program that his colleague Bernard MacEachern of Prince Edward Island had already established. Islanders were participating in Plessis's plan to train local men in the seminaries of Quebec, after which they would return home to minister to their English- and Gaelic-speaking communities.[92] Burke sent five men from Nova Scotia to Quebec, just as some Irish Catholics from the region had sent their daughters to be educated by the Ursuline sisters.[93] Sending young men to Quebec would also be more cost-efficient that sending them to the Jesuits at Stoneyhurst, England, where some of Halifax's wealthier Catholic families were sending their sons.[94]

When Plessis finally arrived in Halifax, on 14 July 1815, Burke was preparing to leave for Europe, citing medical reasons. In fact, Burke, who was indeed ill, was en route to Europe and the Papal States, where he hoped to visit the recently restored Pope Pius VII and request the creation of a new bishopric in Nova Scotia. Burke remained with Plessis only two days before departing on a sabbatical that would keep him away from Halifax for almost a year. Undaunted, Plessis maintained his rigorous schedule of meetings, luncheons with local leaders, pastoral visits, and confirmations. Michael Power, now nearly eleven years old, was one of the confirmandi who received the sacrament from Plessis at either the 15 July or 23 July ceremony.[95] The presence of Plessis and the experience of his confirmation, the first in his family, may have firmed Power's resolve to become a priest. Shortly after returning to Quebec, Plessis received a letter from Father Vincent, a Trappist serving as one of Mignault's assistants in the absence of Burke. While Vincent appeared to be concerned primarily with Father Mignault's failing health and local missionary activity, he closed the letter with a discussion of "little Michael Power," who had expressed a desire to study in Montreal, Mignault's home. "He is a child of much promise," added Vincent, and "he wants to be a priest." Vincent, though concerned that Power might be too young to undertake such a project, conceded that the boy had made up his mind, and he awaited episcopal approval.[96]

To some extent, Power himself may have been the catalytic agent in a process already initiated by Burke and nurtured by Mignault. It is still not entirely clear whether Burke considered Power a good candidate to join the contingent of young men to be sent to Quebec. Edward William Bennett and Henry Lelievre of Halifax were already studying at the Collège de Montréal, but we do not know whether Burke had formally sent them.[97] It is probable, however, that prior to his departure Burke told either Vincent or Mignault about Power's selection; they had already been impressed by the boy's piety and intellectual promise.[98] Since Burke appeared to have some personal differences with his assistants – he may even have actively disliked Mignault[99] – it was unlikely that he would have left the selection of "the candidates" to his French Canadian curates. He may well have made his selections before leaving for Europe, having decided that Power – and perhaps Power's cousin William Cleary and Charles McCullagh – would go to Montreal to begin their studies in the fall of 1816.[100]

Despite Burke's absence, the Plessis visit was a triumph for all concerned. Civil and military officials – Governor Sherbrooke, politicians, and representatives of the admiralty – were anxious to meet and dine with the bishop. Plessis was a seasoned prelate who had garnered a stellar reputation as a skilled negotiator between the Catholic Church and the British Crown.[101] His most recent laurels had been won between 1812 and 1814, when he gave staunch public support to the British war effort against the United States. The bishop's assessments of the local church were glowing. He was particularly pleased that of the 600 parishioners at St Peter's, a mere one in ten had not made their Easter duty.[102] But Plessis may have underestimated the actual size of the parish of St Peter's, since if one takes into account the Africans, Acadians, soldiers, *matelots*, and *caboteurs* living in the vicinity of Halifax, the total number of Catholics may have been as high as 2,000.[103] Nevertheless, he had strong words of praise for what he saw in the outports and the villages surrounding the city, singling out the work of the missionary priests. Plessis impressed upon Governor Sherbrooke that Catholics ought not to be treated as an inferior class. For one thing, they should not be prevented from ringing their church bell before 10:00 a.m. on Sundays in deference to the first toll of the bells at St Paul's Anglican Cathedral. Pleased with the success of his interventions, the prelate commented that the Catholic Church would be emancipated from such forms of servitude in the future.[104] From an Anglican perspective, there was no counter-argument, since, according to Plessis, Bishop Inglis had "retombe en enfance," a gentle way of describing his rival's senile dementia.[105]

With the departure of Plessis on 24 July, Michael Power's Halifax years were nearing an end. His confirmation marked a significant ecclesiastical rite of passage into spiritual adulthood and the near-completion of his grammar school education. Many of his Halifax Grammar School classmates would, by merit of their Anglicanism, be assured of admittance to King's College. Power, a Catholic, would have to seek his higher education elsewhere. Burke and Mignault, no doubt with the assent of

St Mary's Church, Halifax, 1838. Power would not have seen this church
until the 1840s, but his family had worshipped there since the 1820s

William and Mary Power, decided that Michael would leave the colony
to pursue his studies in a minor seminary with the long-term objective
of ordination to the priesthood. Michael Power, William Cleary, and
Charles McCullagh likely left Halifax in late July or early August to
arrive in time to settle in and start classes in the autumn. There is no
record of anyone accompanying the three lads to Quebec; Mignault
would not return to Lower Canada until after 21 August 1817, the date
he preformed his last baptism in Halifax.[106] Burke had most probably
returned in time to give the boys the funds to pay for their first year of
studies and bid them farewell.[107] Mignault may have accompanied the
boys part of the way, since he does not appear in the registers between
30 July and 17 August; he would have had enough time to acclimatize
the boys to the trip but not to sail to Quebec and back unless conditions,
climate, and the river pilot's skills were optimum.[108] We do know that the
boys boarded a ship bound for the Gulf of St Lawrence and, ultimately,
Quebec City and Montreal. If her letters are any indication – and they
remain the only reliable record of Michael's family life – it was a pain-

ful parting for Mary Power. While she had great trust and respect for Mignault and his decisions, she still fretted over the loss of her eldest and most cherished child. Perhaps neither she nor her Mick knew how long he would be gone, although her hopes were buoyed by the fact that when he did return for good, he would be a priest, a credit to his parish, and the pride of his family.[109]

Michael Power could not have imagined how final his goodbyes would be. He would never see his father again. It is fortunate that Captain Power was even there to see his son off on his journey. On 22 May 1816, Captain Power and the crew of the schooner *Trafalgar* arrived in Halifax having subsisted on nothing but fish and tea for the previous fortnight. They had run aground on Sable Island "in a violent gust of wind" twenty days before.[110] The captain's fortunes continued to sour as the mercantile trade took a downward turn in the second decade of the century, and he was cursed by more wrecks and brushes with death on the high seas. In 1823, he was shipwrecked twice – once off the coast of Jamaica, and again off the treacherous gulf coast of Newfoundland, at that time some of the most dangerous waters to be navigated by commercial vessels.[111] The captain became unable to pay his dues to the Charitable Irish Society, from which he retired in 1823, or his municipal property taxes.[112] By 1824, cash-strapped, humiliated, broken, and ill, Captain William Power retired. He died within the year.[113] His death was preceded by that of his sickly son, James, who died of lung inflammation in 1822; another son, John, who had turned his back on the sea and embraced his studies the way his brother Mick had, died soon after the captain.[114] William, who followed his namesake to the sea, died of natural causes off the coast of Jamaica on 24 July 1827. Thus, by the time of his ordination to the priesthood, Michael Power was the sole remaining male in his family.

Mary Power and her daughters continued to live in the three-storey family home on Hollis Street. Pressed for cash (she could barely afford postage for her letters to Michael), Mary rented the ground floor to a bookbinder.[115] The rent money and income from some casual employment permitted her to support local church initiatives and contribute to the mission collections sponsored by the Society for the Propagation of the Faith. The Power family witnessed the appointment of their pastor, Father Burke, as vicar apostolic of Nova Scotia and his foundation of a new cathedral. Burke died in 1820.[116] Of Michael's sisters, only Mary Anne married; in 1842, she wed William Mooney. The couple moved to the United States, and in 1848 Mary Anne gave birth to the only known successor to this branch of the Power family. Michael Power Mooney was born in Boston and named in honour of his deceased uncle.[117]

Michael Power would not return to his native Halifax until 1840, when Bishop Ignace Bourget granted him a brief leave from his pastoral duties at Laprairie.[118] His family, parish, and city had changed much since 1816 when he had first put out into the deep.

CHAPTER TWO

◄ Forming the Heart, ► the Spirit, and the Body

EVERYTHING WAS DIFFERENT. Michael Power was not quite twelve years old in August 1816, when he and his companions set out from Halifax for Quebec. Behind him was the comfort and security of his home, his family, his parish, and the streets and parks of his birthplace. Ahead was the unknown – a foreign colony, a foreign people who spoke a foreign language, and no familiar faces save for his two companions. He was putting out to sea for the first time. In Montreal, he would be educated, and if God's will be done – and Mary Power's dreams fulfilled – he would be ordained a priest and return to serve his fellow Nova Scotians. Not even the most clairvoyant could predict that this voyage to the seminaries of Quebec and Montreal would eventually carry him to the frontiers of the Eastern Townships of Lower Canada and the Upper Ottawa Valley. Confronted with a new wave of Irish immigrants, shanty hamlets in the bush, cholera epidemics, and political unrest among the *habitants*, Power would become part of a new generation of Quebec priests trained to deal with urban and village parish structures, but he would also be expected to tame and order the frontier for the church. In the process, he, like all seminary graduates of the 1820s, would have to struggle to contain political revolution while fostering the devotional revolution that was slowly making its way across the Atlantic from France and the Papal States.

Power experienced many new things on that spring voyage. Although he was familiar with the blue line of the Atlantic as viewed from the water's edge in what is now Point Pleasant Park, that view paled in comparison to the vast maritime panorama he now beheld. He was no sailor. He had been the bookworm of the family, preferring dry land to the open seas that were the playground for his father and brothers. The ship on which he and his companions travelled slipped by the eastern tip of

McNab's Island, it fortifications appearing as grey flecks on a green canvas, and it entered the open ocean. Power was leaving Nova Scotia for the first time in his life and would soon voyage through the gulf and along the St Lawrence River. The stands of pine and hardwood along the shores of the great river dwarfed the familiar scrubby spruce that clung to the rocks surrounding Halifax. And nothing in his previous experience could have prepared him for the sight of the sheer rock that towered above the Saguenay, squeezing that river into the St Lawrence at Tadoussac. As the cliffs receded and the riverbanks closed in, Power glimpsed tiny white specks on the shore. These specks, which had been noted by many travellers before him, became larger, taking on the shape of the houses that anchored the rangs, or strips of land, of tenant farmers to the great river.[1]

We do not know how long it took Power and his mates to reach Quebec. Vessels travelling up the St Lawrence usually had seasoned pilots who knew the currents, shoals, and rocks of what could be a "last and fatal" passage along the St Lawrence.[2] Although schooners and brigs going from Quebec to Halifax usually completed the voyage in eight to ten days, they had the advantage of the current and the westerly winds that filled their sails, carrying them towards the gulf. Power's ship was sailing against the current and, in the absence of easterly breezes, it would likely have had to tack its way along the St Lawrence, thereby prolonging the journey. After what could have been as long as two weeks, Power, Cleary, and McCullagh arrived at Quebec, where the river narrowed substantially. Due to river conditions, changing depths, sandbars, and hazardous rocks, they transferred to a lighter sailing craft to complete the journey to Montreal. The young men may have remained in Quebec for a short visit, perhaps at the seminary, or they may have moved on immediately, but even a glimpse of the town from the vantage point of the river would have given Power some reassurance, as the fortifications on the heights of Quebec would have reminded him of Fort George on Citadel Hill, in whose shadow he had been raised. As a bustling port, Quebec was similar to Halifax, but it was too far inland to be refreshed by the sea air.

The Montreal that greeted Power in 1816 may have both excited and, upon closer inspection, disappointed him. Approached by river, the island city would have seemed almost majestic, nestled between the St Lawrence and the green hills of the Laurentians to the north and the Monteregian drumlins to the south. Offshore, from a distance, the city appeared little different from the town that had capitulated to the English

View of Montreal harbour, 1830, by R.A. Sproule (NA, C-002641)

fifty-six years before. Montreal was comprised of about 2,500 two- and three-storey buildings of stone and wooden planks extending along the south shore of the island,[3] and Mount Royal sloped gently upward from its northern edge. As Power's vessel neared the shore, however, the view and the smell would have been far less appealing. The earthy odour of the river mingled with the stench of sewage, which locals dumped freely into St Peter's creek, which, in turn, spewed it into the harbour.[4] In place of Halifax's fine long wharves were plank-and-duckboard structures projecting out from the riverbank to receive new arrivals. The harbour area, if one dared call it that, was littered with logs, driftwood, and flotsam, giving first-time visitors a poor impression of a town that had been dedicated to the Blessed Virgin Mary.[5]

Montreal, however, was a place of contrasts. Although founded in 1641 by Sieur de Maisonneuve and the proponents of the Catholic Counter-Reformation (some of whom were members of the secret society La compagnie de Saint-Sacrament),[6] the Catholic visionary's Ville Marie had transformed itself into Lower Canada's largest, wealthiest, and busiest commercial centre. The "new Jerusalem" of Maisonneuve, Jeanne Mance, and Madame de la Peltrie had become the sanctuary of Mammon – conveniently located at the confluence of several important trading routes. As it had since the 1640s, Montreal received annual shipments of furs from traders via the Ottawa River. Located at the island's west end, the village of Lachine became the principal departure point for trade goods and immigrants headed for the younger colony of Upper Canada. To the south, American trade was funnelled through the Lake Champlain and Richelieu River system and via road and ferry connections from the American border to Laprairie, a small village on the south shore of the St Lawrence opposite Montreal.

At the time of Power's arrival, Montreal's commercial success had altered its social, political, and religious character. What had once been envisioned as the New World capital of French Catholicism[7] was now an ethnic, linguistic, and religious mosaic. The city boasted some 16,000 inhabitants, of whom roughly 10,000 were French-speaking and overwhelmingly Roman Catholic. There were about 1,500 English residents, most of whom worshipped at the local Church of England, located in the same neighbourhood as the Catholic parish church, Notre Dame. The English Protestants were joined by nearly 2,000 Scots, most of whom were Presbyterian and prominent members of the city's merchant class, and 1,000 Irish, who were evenly divided between Protestantism and Catholicism.[8] This spiritual mosaic, while similar in some ways to the mix of faith groups Power had known in Halifax, would offer the young man his first opportunity to live in a centre where Roman Catholicism was the dominant religion. Signs of the Catholic faith were everywhere: there were chapels, schools, hospitals, convents, and social service agencies sponsored by the church. The public calendar was filled with the events and celebrations of Montreal's Catholic majority; feasts and religious festivals could be celebrated by Catholics with impunity. Yet, while the rhythms of public life and the material culture of Montreal may have been welcoming to Power, it was all expressed in French, a language he could not speak.

There were other things to which Power would have to acclimatize himself. He was certainly not prepared for the bitter cold of the Montreal winters. Sub-zero temperatures, made even more bone-numbing by the winds that swept down the Ottawa Valley, across the island, and up the St Lawrence, transformed Montreal into a river-bound block of ice. Tons of accumulated snow clogged the already narrow streets, making it difficult for carriages to pass.[9] In April, warmer temperatures and frequent rains prompted a spring thaw, transforming the streets into rivers of slush and mud. Creeks to the west of the city, in the suburb of Récollet, were fed generously by the mountain, and they overflowed their banks, carrying water and refuse to the swollen St Lawrence. As the floods subsided and April gave way to May and June, the creeks became breeding grounds for mosquitoes, which feasted upon the population until the summer heat dried their breeding pools.[10] Power would have longed for a cooling ocean breeze as he suffered through the humidity that blanketed the Montreal basin in the summer. During the dog days of August, when school adjourned for a holiday, the fortunate ones, including Power's professors and fellow students, would take refuge on the farms and at the summer homes scattered through the pleasant fields, orchards, and glades on the slopes of Mount Royal and beyond.[11]

For eight cycles of the seasons, from 1816 to 1824, Power would call the Collège de Montréal his home. At Mignault's suggestion, the three young Haligonians would be educated by the Sulpicians. Mignault himself would return home one year later, but he was immediately made pastor of St Joseph's Parish in Chambly, and it is uncertain whether he was able to visit his former parishioners at the college.[12] If he had, he would have seen only Cleary and Power, since McCullagh had left the institution by the end of 1816.[13] The college was housed in a relatively new building. Erected in 1806 at the corner of St-Paul and McGill Streets, it stood outside the walls of the old city, in Récollet. For Power, accustomed to the cramped Halifax Grammar School, the college was palatial. Its enormous central building (210 feet by 35 feet) was flanked by two equally large wings, and, from an aerial view, it would have resembled a giant letter *H*.[14] Power would find within the confines of this *petit séminaire* facilities and opportunities scarcely imaginable in Halifax. His quarters were in one of the two wings. He would be surrounded by, at most, 120 young men, some of whom were following the academic program offered by the Sulpicians in preparation for further study in the professions or the priesthood.[15]

While most of Power's classmates would speak French, the college's working language, the student body would include other young English-speaking Catholics and some Protestants from across the colonies and the United States. He would discover a few Halifax boys in the mix: Edward Bennett would study with Power until 1818, at which point William McAaron would arrive and remain until well after Power had graduated. In fact, of the eight Halifax scholars at the college during this period, only Power and McAaron would complete their courses and enter the seminary and the priesthood. Power would also have been able to converse in English with students from Upper Canada, sent by Father Alexander Macdonell, soon to be the upper province's

ANCIEN COLLÉGE DE MONTRÉAL

Collège de Montréal as it would have looked in Power's time
(Séminaire St-Sulpice)

first bishop, and with others from Ireland and New England.[16] Each day, students would meet in the central building, where they would eat all of their meals, borrow books from the library's extensive collection (it held some 6,000 volumes by 1860),[17] recover from illnesses in the infirmary, meet with professors, hear Mass, and attend lectures.[18] Within the highly disciplined environment of the college, Michael Power would spend his entire adolescence.

    Arriving in late summer, Power would have had some time to explore his new neighbourhood and become acquainted with Montreal; classes began on the first day of October. The college would have been quiet, since most students had returned home to their families and others divided their time between doing chores at the college and visiting the Sulpician-owned estates at the foot of Mount Royal. Although Power left no written account of his early education, spending time on these farms would have greatly appealed to him – it would have reminded him of his rambles through the forests and parks of Halifax.

The farming estates, now the site of the Grand Séminaire complex on Sherbrooke Street, would have offered a welcome contrast to the bustling and noisy environs of the college.[19] Beyond the college's courtyards, which were filled with acacias and poplars, the city was busy gobbling up its suburbs and extending its thoroughfares westward. Venturing out, Power would discover St Peter's Creek, or what college promotional literature referred to as "a small rivulet" that "flows through the gardens and yards and rolls at the foot of the College walls."[20] In fact, the creek was an open sewer in the spring, the source of a stygian stench and a breeding ground for disease – many of the students at the college contracted throat infections.[21] Not far from the college were Montreal's principal military barracks, still active in 1816 due to the recently concluded war with the United States.[22] Young Power would also have noted that the college was just a short stroll away from the city's new market (now Carleton Square), which was underused because Montrealers favoured the old market, located inside the city walls. At the old market, patrons jostled one another as they purchased produce at noisy stalls, drank ale in the many taverns, or sought other pleasures in the thinly disguised brothels.[23] Power would witness the dismantling of the old-city walls within a year and the ensuing expansion of commercial and residential Montreal to the west and north, well past the once peaceful college, gradually encroaching on Mount Royal.[24]

Although Power was aware of all this rapid change affecting his new home, much of his time would be spent focusing on the day-to-day activities at the college. When he started classes, in October 1816, the pattern of his life was set for the next eight years. He and his fellow students began their day at 5:30 a.m. They had about forty-five minutes to rise, wash, dress, and dash off to morning prayer in the chapel. The college had no official uniform policy, but it did impose certain restrictions on garish colours and frilly cuffs and recommended that students wear a hooded blue frock coat, or *capot*, tied with a *ceinture sauvage*.[25] Mary Power kept her son supplied with white linen shirts, which she shipped to Montreal via her son's "uncles" (one of whom was Captain Patrick Cleary) – William Power's fellow navigators.[26] Having dressed and prayed, the students attended Mass, ate breakfast, and undertook a full schedule consisting of catechism, the regular school curriculum, and recreation.[27] Once classes were in session, residential students were not permitted to leave the college grounds without the permission of the prefect, and, in a gesture towards equality, day students were forbidden to leave the parish.[28]

The program of study was organized on an eight-year cycle. The first two years, conducted in either English or French, Latin compulsory, provided a philosophical foundation. There was a daily regimen of seven classes. Over his eight years at the college, Power would study progressive levels of mathematics, geography, Latin syntax, classics, astronomy, botany, natural science, literature, history, rhetoric, and composition.[29] He reported to his mother that in his final year, much to his delight, he was finally studying Greek.[30] This would be Power's fourth language, since his philosophy courses were taught in Latin, and French was the language of instruction in the later years of the program. By the time he graduated, in the summer of 1824 (classes ended on 15 August), Michael Power would boast an education that his Sulpician teachers described as offering "formation of the heart, the spirit and the body."[31]

The influence of the Sulpicians permeated college life. As *seigneurs* of Montreal, they controlled the only parish church, Notre Dame, the adjoining seminary, and the college itself, which served as a diving board to the priesthood and the professions. During the *ancien régime*, the Suplicians had been a force to reckon with. They were an ecclesiastical authority that rivalled the bishop of Quebec. As Gallican in their political thought, they were closely aligned with the French Crown and, by association, with the governors of New France. Their alliance with the civil rulers did not change significantly during the period of the British conquest. After 1760, the Sulpicians supported British policy, and in return the British allowed them to continue controlling the church in the Montreal district.[32] In Power's years at the college, his Sulpician teachers were noted for their moral rigour as derived from the theology of their founder, Jean-Jacques Olier, and French philosopher Pierre Cardinal Bérulle; they were also known for their deference to, and accommodation of, British civil authorities.[33] Such tendencies were reinforced in the 1790s, when eighteen Sulpicians, exiles from the French Revolution, were given sanctuary in Lower Canada. They brought with them a vociferous anti-revolutionary disposition and a wariness of the emergent liberal-democratic political movements in French Canada.[34] As mentors and teachers, the Sulpicians had ample opportunity to shape impressionable young minds. No doubt Power, already familiar with the political conservatism espoused by his earliest mentor, Edmund Burke, was favourably impressed by his new teachers. As bishop of Toronto, he would bequeath his personal property to the Sulpicians and designate Sulpician superior Vincent Quiblier as principal beneficiary.[35]

Although the Sulpicians imposed a strict discipline on their students and tried to instill in them a sense of loyalty to the Crown, not all of Power's classmates were easily convinced. The years of Power's residency, 1816 to 1824, were also the years in which a new generation of French Canadian civil leaders came of age, and many of them trained at the college. The sons of artisans, professionals, and well-established farmers flocked to the college, not only because of its location in the heart of Lower Canada's fastest-growing region, but also because of its excellent curriculum. During Power's time, some 109 young men passed through the college, and not all of them were aspiring priests.[36] After the implementation of the Constitution Act of 1791, which created the provinces of Upper and Lower Canada, French Canadian males were accorded both suffrage and the right to sit in the Legislative Assembly, the Executive Council, and the Legislative Council. Such political rights were not accorded uniformly to Catholics in the rest of the British Empire. Even in the neighbouring Atlantic colonies, Catholics would not gain political emancipation until the 1820s and 1830s.[37]

For young French Canadian men, the new political culture, when combined with the growth in commerce and insecurity in the traditional agricultural economy, offered new prospects in the liberal professions. The political climate had become increasingly charged in the province, and questions of constitutional reform, social change, and economic crisis were frequent topics of conversation among some of Power's colleagues. Power had not simply landed in a theological college – he had entered the nursery of French Canada's next generation of political radicals and reformers. He would share meals with the likes of Louis-Hippolyte LaFontaine, the first prime minister of a responsible government in the Province of Canada; Jean-Baptiste Meilleur, a physician and first head of a school of administration in the province; scions of the famous Papineau family; and George-Étienne Cartier, a future *patriote* turned Father of Confederation.[38] Although later in life Power would lean towards the loyalist-conservative politics of his Sulpician mentors, he would demonstrate a sensitivity and respect for political reform by constitutional means. No doubt his social interaction with budding liberal professionals helped him to understand such sensibilities.

Power's years in the *petit séminaire*, however, appear to have been complicated by three factors: language, his family finances, and personal doubts about his vocation. The first and most obvious barrier to his education was the fact that he had arrived in Montreal speaking only English, although he did possess some Latin and Greek reading skills, passed on to him by Edmund Burke. While there was a small English-language program at the college, the working environment and the "grand program" of studies was in French and Latin. Yet Burke and Mignault proved correct in their observation that young Power was a quick study. By the time he had finished his minor seminary training, he was fluent in French and Latin and had a working knowledge of Greek. His linguistic abilities became known to Bishop Panet of Quebec, who in 1826 would send him to St-François-du-Lac on the south shore of the St Lawrence to learn Abenaki.

Family finances proved to be a greater obstacle than language limitations. Few records exist to explain how Power was able to pay for his education. One possible explanation is that he and his family relied heavily on Burke, who had encouraged Power and the other Nova Scotians to train in Quebec with the object of becoming priests in Nova Scotia. The apostolic vicariate of Nova Scotia may have covered their tuition fees and board, but since Power had been recruited before the creation of the vicariate, he may have been financed by Bishop Plessis. James Lambert has argued that Plessis was resented by some Lower Canadian priests because, they claimed, he lavished attention on the frontiers of the diocese and spent a lot of money "educating missionaries to work there."[39] Yet neither Burke's correspondence, nor seminary records, nor the parish financial ledgers at St Peter's reveal the source of Power's funding. Presumably, for a time Captain William Power, given his success in commercial shipping, could have financed his son. Packages addressed to Michael Power containing Halifax currency and clothing arrived in Montreal at least until the early 1820s. But in 1823, when the captain's fortunes deteriorated and he lost his sailing career, the financial lifeline linking Michael to his home appears to have snapped. Mary Power claimed that she could not afford the postage to Montreal and therefore asked the captain's former associates to take packages to her son. Captain Cleary, likely the godfather to William and Mary's son James and father to Michael's classmate William Cleary, frequently brought Michael mail and news of home. Mary, by now forced to rent out the ground floor of their house, was blunt about their financial situation: William, she wrote to her son, had been "very little help ... this [past four] years."[40]

William Power seems to have fallen into a depression. Having lost his health and unable to honour his financial responsibilities, he dropped out of Halifax social life. Similarly, unable to fulfill his paternal responsibilities and provide for his eldest son, he stopped communicating with him. His embarrassment effectively ended their relationship. Michael's financial woes were compounded at this time by a seemingly endless stream of bad news from home. By 1824, his brothers James and John had died, and so had his father. Although he was in his final year of study, he offered to return to Halifax to piece together the fragments of his family and assist his mother and surviving siblings. Mary rebuffed the offer. She was determined that he complete his studies – it was a matter of family and parochial honour. Mary prevailed, and Michael remained at the college. He was likely able to finish his program with the assistance of the Sulpicians, who recognized his potential, and with whom he had forged a very strong friendship.[41]

But Michael Power's most pressing and potentially most debilitating obstacle was a personal crisis he encountered involving his vocation. At the age of seventeen, after six years at the college, he appears to have been assailed with doubts about his aspirations to the Roman Catholic priesthood. Given the fact that he was very young when he first arrived in Montreal, he was forced to endure a prolonged separation from his family, he had suffered the loss of loved ones in his absence, and he must have been experiencing the typical growing pains of a teenage boy, such doubts were understandable. Mary Power, however, would have none of it. As devout and determined as ever, she lectured her son sternly: "I am told that you are not disposed for the Church[.] [I]f such be the case ... you have deceived your father and mother[.] Write to me the particular of everything[.] Conceal nothing from your parents for the[y] love you tenderly Mick[.] I made an offering of you to the almighty before you were born and indevoured [*sic*] to senctify [*sic*] your [illegible] to the seccers [*sic*] of your God[.] ... [T]here is great expectations of you in the progress of your studeyes [*sic*.] [T]here is more expected from you than from anyone that left this place."[42]

While Michael's return correspondence to his mother has not survived, Mary's subsequent letters continue to refer to his spiritual struggle and his ambivalence about the priesthood. Ten months after her initial warning to her son, Mary was just as frank in expressing her opinions about his future. She offered her advice freely and clearly stated what his family and friends in Halifax expected of him: "At the same time that you prepare yourself for an ecclesiastical state[.] By a virtuous life remember to join with the exercises of piety diligent application to study in order to qualify yourselfe [*sic*] for serving God in that calling you are obliged to[.] [I]t is in conscience and if you apply not to your selfe carefully to it you render yourselfe unworthy of that calling because thou hast rejected knowledge faith in the Almighty[.] I well respect that thou shall not do the office of priesthood to me [illegible] that you render your selfe guilty in the sight of God of all the mischief which happens through your ignorance ... in deed my dear there is a great deal more expected from you than from all that has left our perrish [*sic*.] I hope you will not disappoint your friends [*sic*] expectations."[43]

Now eighteen, with only fifteen months of study remaining, Power was under duress. He had a difficult decision to make, and his mother was applying pressure. A change in the tone of her letters and the fact that he registered for his final year are the only existing indications of Power's decision to complete his formation at the college. His strength of character is revealed through the focus he brought to bear on his studies during this stressful time.

In the summer of 1824, he left the Collège de Montréal and was admitted by Bishop Panet to the Grand Séminaire at Quebec. We know almost nothing about the brief interval between his periods of study in Montreal and Quebec, except that during it Mary Power became frustrated that she had not heard from him for several months.[44] Power had been to Quebec at least once before, when he and the other Halifax boys had changed boats on their journey to Montreal eight years earlier. We do not know whether he ever travelled outside of Montreal and its immediate vicinity during his annual 15 August to 1 October holiday, but considering the state of his personal finances it seems unlikely. What we do know is that his acquired fluency in French meant that he was no longer a stranger when he ventured beyond the college walls and when he finally left Montreal, having matriculated from the college. Moreover, as a man of twenty wearing the soutane as a sign of his intent to enter the clerical estate, Power would have been accorded respect by those whom he met in Montreal, Quebec, and points in between.

In contrast to Montreal, Quebec City retained its Old World feel. Perched on its rock high above the St Lawrence, its fortifications intact, it almost seemed to be daring intruders to take it on. There was much to remind Power of home: Quebec was close to the forest; its network of forts and earthen defences indicated the British military presence; its port was alive with activity; and it had an adjacent expanse of parkland, which extended from the Plains of Abraham. Power's new home was located in the Catholic complex in the southeast section of Upper Town, within the walls of the old city. At the head of Rue de la Fabrique was the seat of Canada's only bishop. From his episcopal palace, Bishop Bernard-Claude Panet held jurisdiction over all Roman Catholics living between the Gulf of St Lawrence and the Red River.[45] Rome had awarded the title of archbishop to his predecessor, Joseph-Octave Plessis, but the title was not used publicly until 1844, when Rome erected the Metropolitan See of Quebec. Until that time, the Colonial Office had been displeased that Rome had moved unilaterally to raise the status of Quebec, particularly because the quasi-established church of Canada, the Church of England, had no archbishop. Therefore, some viewed the use of the title by Catholics when it was designated in 1819 as an insult to the Crown and its church.[46] The church may have proven its loyalty to the British Crown during times of crisis in 1775 and 1812, and the Crown may have accorded it certain freedoms with the Quebec Act, but the bishop of Quebec was still conscious of the fact that not all the problems associated with being a church in a "conquered" territory had been resolved.

Adjoining the palace and the cathedral was Quebec's Grand Séminaire, an institution noted for its particular emphasis on spiritual exercises, piety, and discipline in the context of a theological curriculum typical of its time.[47] Despite its stature as Canada's oldest and largest Catholic institution of higher education, in the 1820s the Grand Séminaire was not operating at full capacity. Clergy throughout the province had a weak hold on their parishioners, and lay initiative and assertiveness prevailed – although this would change a century later – so vocations to the priesthood were not plentiful.[48] Moreover, young men could aspire to other vocations should they wish to pursue their education beyond the confines of the local parish. The rise of the liberal professions in Lower Canada after 1800 offered new and more exciting opportunities to ambitious young men.[49] Many of Power's Collège de Montréal classmates, LaFontaine and Cartier included, elected to become lawyers, notaries, physicians, or accountants, opting not to pursue Holy Orders. Earlier bishops, like Joseph-Octave Plessis, recognizing the implications of this, tried to ward off a crisis by recruiting priests from Europe, and especially from the United Kingdom, whose services would be most valuable to the frontier missions of the Eastern Townships, the Ottawa Valley, and western Upper Canada. Between 1814 and 1836, the bishops of Quebec secured twenty-four English-speaking men of American, Irish, English, and Scottish backgrounds, including Michael Power.[50] From 1766 to 1836, the bishops, drawing upon the graduates of the Grand Séminaire of Quebec and the seminaries at Nicolet, St-Hyacinthe, St-Sulpice, and Bishop Jean-Jacques Lartigue's fledgling seminary in Montreal, ordained 453 men. An upswing in vocations in the early 1820s gave way to a dearth later in the decade that extended well into the 1830s. Of the 109 candidates for the priesthood who studied between 1820 and 1836, fifty-six abandoned their vocation prior to ordination.[51] The dropout rate when Power was a student was as high as 22 per cent, and given his own vocational struggles he might well have contributed to that figure. With the dramatic increase in the Catholic population in Lower Canada by 1830 – it rose to 400,000 – the church faced a serious shortage of individuals qualified to manage and administer the sacraments, which were deemed essential to the life of the faithful.[52]

Power's daily routine at the Grand Séminaire paralleled his Collège de Montréal routine. At 4:30 each morning – except in winter, when the time was switched to 5:00 a.m. – he began a day of prayer, meditation, and study.[53] Under superior Jérome Demers, director of vocations Joseph Fortinat Aubry, and prefect of studies Antoine Parent, Power would have been responsible for digesting a program that included scripture study, ecclesiology, systematic theology, canon law, sacramental theology, moral theology, catechetics, and liturgy.[54] The proposed three-year program was constructed on the six-volume *Compendiosae Institutiones Theologicae* (revised edition, 1778), which had been in common use at the seminary at Poitiers, France.[55] Each volume consisted of 900 pages or more, and its coverage of the sub-fields of theology was thorough. This seminary education replicated models of study already proven effective in Europe. It adequately prepared priests for urban areas and well-established parishes, but it was of limited value when it came to preparing students for what awaited them as seculars serving in frontier parishes and missions. Wedded tightly to French norms, this type of education failed to anticipate what might actually be demanded of a priest where the authority of canon law was weak, parish infrastructure was rudimentary, and the Catholic laity had become accustomed to a high degree of independence in their spiritual and temporal lives. Moreover, the daily regimen of Power's training was highly disciplined and exhausting. In light of all of these factors, it is not surprising that between 1827 and 1836, only forty young men completed the final stages of their priestly formation.[56]

Michael Power spent only two years at the Quebec seminary. The shortage of priests was so acute, and the burnout rate among the existing *curés* so high, that bishops were forced to send younger, partially formed seminarians to serve in parishes as associates, or to assist as teachers in the local colleges, in the hope that a competent pastor in the field would be available to complete their training. Due to these circumstances, it was understood that a young seminarian's last year of study, for the sake of expediency, would be amalgamated with his pastoral year. As they did in the late 1820s and 1830s with the critical shortage in vocations, the bishops of Quebec sought special dispensations from Rome to ordain men who were well short of the minimum age for ordination (twenty-four) under canon law. Despite the initial reluctance of Bishop Joseph-Octave Plessis and his seminary instructors to dip into the pool of underage seminarians, by the 1820s, they were fast-tracking twenty-two and twenty-three year olds into the diaconate and priesthood. Within a year of entering the seminary, as was the custom, Michael Power was tonsured by Bishop Plessis, who had effectively provided for Power's recruitment from Halifax. On Christmas Eve 1825, Plessis and his successor, Bernard-Claude Panet, raised Power to minor orders in the chapel of the seminary. Power still was required to complete a year and a half of his theological studies before he was canonically eligible for ordination to the priesthood.[57]

However, the rumblings of a discontented priest at St-François-du-Lac, near Nicolet, disrupted Power's timetable. Since 1821, Father Laurent Amiot had been serving the Odanak mission and its Abenaki First Nation. He had begun as an associate of Father Paquin, but by 1823, he was in charge of both the First People's mission and a mission station for the local French Canadian population. After five years of service, Amiot was exhausted, and he requested a transfer.[58] But, due to the shortage of clergy and the difficulty of finding a replacement for Amiot who could speak the Abenaki language, Bishop Panet resisted his request. In September 1826, he offered Amiot an alternative: he would send Power to assist the beleaguered priest. Although Power was still a year away from completing his studies, Panet described him to Amiot as being a bright young man who had an "aptitude pour apprendre de vous même & au village la langue."[59] Panet added that Power could also handle most of Amiot's paperwork – he could fill out baptismal certificates, maintain the mission registers, and produce copies of important documents. Receiving no response from Amiot, Panet wrote again to emphasize that young Power was "a boy of good character and talents."[60] While awaiting a reply, Panet refused Power permission to enter the seminary for that academic year – he was confident that Amiot would train him at St-François-du-Lac, just as Paquin had trained Amiot.[61] But Amiot's silence persisted. In early November, an exasperated Panet ordered Amiot to make up his mind, lest Power become "perplexed." Amiot's continuing silence was an act of defiance and an expression of his disappointment, and it provoked Panet to exercise his episcopal rights and send Power to St-François-du-Lac without Amiot's assent. The bishop's final orders to the obdurate missionary were that he was to receive Power, instruct him, and "continue a work that was well commenced."[62]

In 1826, Michael Power journeyed upriver to St-François-du-Lac, where he would complete his theological education under the reluctant Amiot while beginning his formal instruction in the Abenaki language. The hope that he might remain there working among Lower Canada's First Peoples was short-lived. Farther up the St-François River, at the new settlement of Drummondville, another drama was unfolding. The resident missionary for the St-François River Valley, Father John Holmes, was unhappy in Drummondville and wished to be transferred, preferably to the Quebec seminary, where he could take a teaching position. Holmes was a frustrated academic who detested his frontier appointment, and he was most unpopular with the seigneur and the local inhabitants. Panet agreed to transfer Holmes and proposed that the priest's successor be given the added responsibility of the mission of St-Hughes, thus ensuring a sufficient income for the new missionary.[63] At that time, Lower Canadian priests relied upon the generosity of their parishioners, who contributed to the *dîme*, or tithe – an annual gift to the local church of either a portion of their crops, produce, or cash income.[64] While in the larger, well-established parishes the *dîme* could amount to a handsome income for the *curé*, in the small, rural parishes and missions, priests complained constantly of paltry collections with which they were unable to sustain their households. Panet was therefore aware that if he sent Power to the Drummondville mission, he would either have to add territory to the jurisdiction or see the young missionary impoverished by his first placement.

The attempt to ordain Power, however, did not go as Panet planned. In February 1827, the bishop informed Amiot that Jean-Jacques Lartigue, Panet's episcopal vicar in the Montreal district, would ordain Power to the subdiaconate and the diaconate. Amiot was instructed to administer the oath to Power so that he could work in the missions of the diocese; as soon as he had accomplished this, he was to send Power to Montreal, where Lartigue would ordain him. Panet also instructed Amiot to publish banns of Power's ordination on the Sunday preceding Lent, adding that Lartigue would be responsible for formally examining Power to determine his theological preparedness for the priesthood, especially if this had not already been done by Father Rambault, who made frequent visits to the Odanak mission. Perhaps thinking of Amiot's past tardiness, he held out a carrot to the missionary: he promised that when all of these matters had been attended to, Michael Power would return to St-François prepared to preach in both its Native and French Canadian churches.[65] Panet then cemented the plan, ordering Lartigue to proceed with Power's ordination, as arranged, before Lent, at which point the young man would be dispatched to Ste-Marguerite-de-Blair-findie Parish at L'Acadie, southeast of Montreal.[66]

The carefully laid plans went awry. Power did not arrive in Montreal when expected, although we can only hypothesize the reason for the delay. Perhaps he was not properly prepared for his examinations; no mention of his test by either Lartigue or Rambault has been recorded. Perhaps Power himself felt that at twenty-two he was still too young to proceed with such a plan and wanted more time to prepare himself for his mission. Given his high academic standing and Panet's esteem for his intelligence, it seems highly unlikely that Power failed his examinations. However, as his later behaviour would demonstrate, he possessed a humility that could have led him to doubt his own fitness for ordination, and he had a shy and distant personality, which made relations with others awkward.[67] But the most likely scenario is that Amiot saw through Panet's plan and sensed that he was about to lose his much-needed assistant at Odanak permanently. True to his record as a procrastinator, he may have tactically delayed acting upon Panet's orders to expedite Power's ordination. Panet's correspondence is unclear, suggesting that either the letters never arrived or that Power was unready.[68] Yet, whether due to Amiot's inaction, Power's personal struggle with his vocation, humility, and self-doubt, or something entirely different, the fact remains that Michael Power was not ordained in May 1827.[69]

The frustrating attempt to ordain Power continued into the summer. Panet, scheduled to make an official visitation to the seminary at Nicolet in July, requested that Power travel the short distance from St-François-du-Lac to Nicolet, where he would be examined to establish his eligibility for ordination to the subdiaconate.[70] At this point, Amiot appeared to be co-operating in the process, reporting to Panet that Power was an exemplary man who had worked hard in the parish and had worn *l'habit et la tonsure* every day. He was ready for ordination.[71] The only change in plan was that Joseph Signay, the coadjutor bishop of Quebec and Panet's vicar-general, travelled to Nicolet, met with Power and, on 7 July, elevated him to the subdiaconate.[72] Later, on 12 August, Power reported to Montreal, where he was ordained to the diaconate by Jean-Jacques Lartigue. His way had been paved for him by a report from the bishop that described him to Lartigue in the most favourable terms. Panet explained that Power was "a young well instructed man of gentle and good character."[73] The following Sunday, 19 August, again in Montreal, Michael Power was ordained to the priesthood by Bishop Jean DuBois, who had been visiting the Montreal district, which bordered on his Diocese of New York.[74] That year, the Diocese of Quebec produced a bumper crop of priests, particularly when compared to the general rates of ordination for the years 1810 to 1840. In 1827, Power was one of the two men ordained who were destined to become bishop; the other was Colin Francis McKinnon of Arichat (later Antigonish). Also ordained that year were John Larkin, the man originally selected to succeed Power in Toronto, but who declined the daunting task, and George Antoine Belcourt, who had a distinguished career as a missionary in the upper country beyond Lake Superior. At twenty-two, Power was the second youngest to be ordained. The median age was twenty-four, and the average age of the ordinands in 1827 was 24.8 years.[75]

At the time of his ordination, Power knew where he would begin his ministry. On 1 August, Panet had informed him that upon ordination he would proceed immediately to the St-François Valley to take control of the mission of St-Frédéric from Father John Holmes. There he would await further instructions.[76] Panet also told Amiot that Power would not be returning to Odanak, which must have greatly distressed the missionary and confirmed his suspicions.[77] Amiot stuck it out alone at St-François-du-Lac for two more years, enduring fierce competition from a Protestant Abenaki preacher.[78] Panet mandated John Holmes to familiarize Power with the St-Frédéric mission and its territory and offer the new priest "necessary instructions for his good government."[79] The bishop had also been trying to find a way to secure adequate remuneration for Power – Holmes had been required to supplement his income with grants from the Diocesan bank. If Power retained the Abenaki mission as part of his territory, he might get an additional fifty pounds, which he could apply to his travel and lodging expenses as he travelled up and down the St-François Valley.[80] But, in the end, Panet decided that the mission of St-Hughes, not Odanak, ought to be added to Power's territory.[81]

Holmes fulfilled the bishop's requests, left the mission, and moved on to the Quebec seminary. There, he became a distinguished professor and, among other things, penned one of French Canada's first common-school geography textbooks.[82] But Power was not yet ready to assume his ministry. There remained some obstacles to be cleared, because Panet had neglected to attend to some of the relevant canonical details before he ordained Power. This was partly the bishop's fault and partly due to the fact that Power was a native of Halifax. According to canon law, Power remained under the authority of the apostolic vicar of Nova Scotia; Burke was the one who had sent him to Quebec to be trained and ordained, and his object had been to prepare Power for priestly work in Nova Scotia. As early as 1824, however, it had become increasingly clear to all who knew Power, and perhaps to Power himself, that his talents could be put to better use in the growing church of Lower Canada. Even Mary Power confessed that despite the pain it caused her to be separated from her son, there was little future for him in Halifax, where there was already a full complement of priests.[83] Thus, on 26 July 1824, Michael Power applied for dismissal and release from the apostolic vicariate of Nova Scotia. Burke, however, had been dead nearly four years, and the vicariate's administrator, Father John Carroll, was in a quandary, since there was no successor to the deceased bishop and no official seal to authenticate the administrator's permission to grant Power his exeat. Power was aware of the problem that this situation posed. He told Carroll that his friend Patrick Phelan had had to wait to be ordained because Phelan's dismissal letters from the Diocese of Boston did not bear the seal of Bishop Cheverus. The young man was obliged to wait until the proper letters had been submitted. Carroll himself had been willing to approve Power's exeat, but he was uncertain of his authority to do so.[84] The matter would remain unresolved until 1827, when Panet appealed to the new apostolic vicar of Nova Scotia, Bishop William Fraser, to grant Power his exeat. Fraser was a little miffed because he could have used Power in the parishes and missions outside Halifax. Moreover, it bothered him that Panet was seeking Power's release after Power had been ordained and instructed to serve in Lower Canada.[85] However, Fraser did give his consent, and Michael Power officially became a priest of the Diocese of Quebec.

In the end, Power's exeat from Nova Scotia seemed appropriate. He had not returned to his home province after his departure in 1816. In October 1827, he was a twenty-three-year-old man who had spent his most formative years in Lower Canada. He was now fluent in French, and he appeared to have mastered Latin and Abenaki. His Nova Scotian companions had either abandoned their studies or returned home for ordination. His new friends were his classmates and colleagues from Montreal and Quebec, and judging by his correspondence, his working language was French. He had been indoctrinated in French seminary traditions in order to serve in a French-language parish, and he had absorbed a Gallican ecclesiology wherein the *marguilliers*, representing the laity, effectively controlled the temporal affairs of the parish. His life had changed more dramatically than he had ever anticipated. The Irish Nova Scotian boy had been transformed into a priest of Quebec.

CHAPTER THREE

◂ Saddlebag Christianity ▸

EUROPEAN-STYLE SEMINARIES did not prepare young men very well for what would greet them on the North American frontier. Curricula based on tried-and-true models originating in France, Rome, Austria, or Spain offered adequate theological and pastoral foundations for men who would end up in urban parish settings, villages, and towns, or in well-established rural areas. In most western European dioceses, recently ordained men would apprentice as curates in a variety of parish settings under the watchful eye of an elder or more experienced priest. With this type of mentorship, the young man – sometimes one of a number – would gain the pastoral knowledge that he would not have had access to in the cloistered world of the seminary. As assistants, these young men would learn how to administer the sacraments, pour water over the heads of squirming and screaming babies, ensure that betrothed couples had complied with the canons necessary for lawful marriage, and anoint the wrinkled brows of elderly parishioners wheezing their last breaths. They would be shown how to complete registers, hear confessions, celebrate Mass, and police social iniquities. Arriving in most western European dioceses, the newly ordained found themselves in well-established parish cultures with high administrative expectations and clearly defined moral and devotional norms.[1]

To expect such conditions on the North American frontier was folly. In the French and British North American colonies, the Catholic missions were undertaken first by members of religious orders, who, in the seventeenth and eighteenth centuries, had conflicting ideas about how to proclaim the Gospel, primarily to the First Nations peoples of Acadia and New France. The Récollets (the Franciscans), bent on frenchifying and then evangelizing, failed in their principal missions because those to whom they were proselytizing had little interest in abandoning their own cultures and traditions for the gods of the French. At the other end of the mission spectrum, the Society of Jesus (the Jésuits) made special efforts to inculcate the First Peoples they encountered with the Christian faith, couching the major tenets of Christianity in Native-culture terms.[2] Whether they were culturally relativistic, like the Jesuits, or openly assimilationist, like other orders, most clergy working on the frontier were frustrated by what they perceived as the wild and immoral behaviour of the European Catholics, whom they considered to be poor examples to the Natives.[3] While there is much to dispute in Frederick Jackson Turner's frontier thesis of American history, there is little argument that the newness and remoteness of the frontier offered Europeans freedom from the restraints and structures of the Old World.[4] Even those specially trained by religious orders to work within frontier settings – be they spiritual, cultural, or environmental – discovered that it would be difficult to replicate the European church in North America.

In the nineteenth century, the churches maintained a dual focus as they pushed into the frontier. They wanted to convert the Native peoples and to keep the European immigrants in the Christian faith. Both the Catholic and Protestant churches found that ministering to the latter, particularly given the vastness of the agricultural frontier and the dispersal of its population, the enormous distances between villages, and the traveller's dependence upon poor roads and dangerous rivers, was extraordinarily difficult. In Michael Power's time, the practice of covering preaching circuits on horseback was already well established. In Nova Scotia, prior to Power's birth, Henry Alline and his followers had sparked a "new light" evangelism among anglophone Protestant settlers on either side of the Bay of Fundy.[5] Similarly, in Power's day, Methodist preachers toting bibles in their saddlebags penetrated the Upper Canadian frontier, criss-crossing the landscape, fomenting religious revival at large camp meetings. Even Anglican clergy mounted horses in the upper province in order to maintain the presence of the established church, fearing that their absence would leave citizen farmers susceptible to the ministrations of the Methodists and Baptists who were already flogging their own forms of saddlebag Christianity. Settlers on the Canadian frontier lacked formal religious training and a commitment to regular participation in meetings and services, and although the Methodists could whip these people into spiritual ecstasy during revivals, the long-term challenge was finding a way to harness that fervour and secure it within the church's four walls.[6] Yet, on the whole, the frontier was not a vehicle for transforming the eastern churches in some Turnerian fashion; instead, it eventually gave rise to churches that resembled those of the previously settled and ordered east. Moreover, the job of taming and institutionalizing frontier Christians was difficult, and there were many casualties – priests and preachers were weakened and broken by their ministry.

In the early nineteenth century, the Catholic Church in Lower Canada was confronted with the expansion of Catholic settlement beyond the old seigneuries into the upper Ottawa Valley, the Châteauguay Valley, and the Eastern Townships. Without the services of the religious orders, upon whom the Catholic Church had formerly relied for frontier ministry, the bishops of Quebec depended heavily on secular clergy. The selection of priests for frontier ministry was complicated further by issues of language and culture. Since many of the new immigrants to these frontier regions of the colony were of Irish, Scottish, or American origin, the bishops could not simply call upon unilingual francophone clergy to cover the mission districts. Furthermore, in these areas of new settlement, the general population encompassed a mix of religions, with significant numbers of Anglicans and Protestants, a situation foreign to most French Canadians living outside of Montreal and to their *curés*, who had become accustomed to the near universal presence of Roman Catholics within their parish boundaries. Jean-Jacques Lartigue, the episcopal vicar for the bishop of Quebec who oversaw the district of Montreal, would discover that the most valuable priests for service on the frontier were anglophone men who had command of French. But these Irish, Scottish, and American priests would have to be assured of an income. This was a problem of some gravity, because settlers who had grown accustomed to independence from the parish would now be expected to sustain a priest, and the incomes of these recently established farmers were already meagre. For Michael Power and his generation of young priests, the frontier posed challenges to education, physical health, patience, and pocketbook.

Michael Power's time in the St-François Valley did not begin well. The outgoing pastor, John Holmes, an American and a convert to Catholicism from Methodism, politely refuted Panet's grand design for financing the new missionary. Holmes thought that attaching the lucrative Odanak mission to the financially less sound mission at Drummondville was a mistake. It would mean drawing the priest away from Drummondville too frequently, leaving local Catholics at the mercy of the itinerant Protestant ministers who were serving the Protestant majority in the region. Holmes told the bishop that due to the population growth in the townships adjoining Drummondville, there would be sufficient revenue from the enlarged *dîme* to pay Power.[7] Seemingly convinced, Panet abandoned the idea of giving Power the Odanak mission and resolved to keep the Drummondville mission intact, with the expectation that the Catholic population within its jurisdiction would increase considerably. However, Panet was still being questioned by Lartigue, who did not approve of Power's appointment to Drummondville, favouring Father Jean-Baptiste McMahon as Holmes's replacement. While he considered both to be capable young men, Lartigue argued that Power was newly ordained, whereas McMahon had three years of experience to prepare him for a frontier mission. Power, asserted Lartigue, was in need of a parish "apprenticeship."[8] But Panet would have none of this, and in September 1827, Power – a newly ordained priest just one month shy of his twenty-third birthday – found himself in Drummondville.[9]

In retrospect, Lartigue had been correct in his assessment of the needs of Drummondville and Holmes had been wrong. Michael Power's four years in that mission constantly challenged his skill, health, intellect, and – perhaps most of all – his patience. In the upper St-François River Valley, he came face-to-face with the enormous challenge of implanting the institutions and disciplines of the Catholic Church in settlers who seemed little interested. This missionary frontier presented Power with five formidable obstacles: difficult terrain connected to the outside world by poor transportation routes and communications; an immigrant population spread thinly over a wide geographical area; a lack of religious discipline and moral consistency among his flock; an insufficient level of personal income due to the poverty of the new immigrants; and the susceptibility of the Catholic population to the Protestant majority and to enterprising individuals posing as Catholic priests. Furthermore, Power would learn that what a religious institution prescribed was not essentially what its followers practised. He would be forced to make tough decisions when the letter of the canons and the will of the local magisterium collided with the expectations of the Catholics settlers. Trained to respect the church's legal traditions, and lacking experience, Power would take refuge in the laws, applying them as best he could.

The mission of St-Frédéric at Drummondville was new by Lower Canadian standards. Situated in the upper St-François River Valley, it was to become the gateway to the colonization route that extended into the Notre Dame range of the Appalachian highlands. It was part of the region referred to by locals as *les cantons de l'est* ("eastern townships") – British-style townships that had formed after the fall of the seigneurial system. After 1815, the entire region between the St Lawrence and the American border, cut by the Richelieu and St-François river systems, became the target of Irish and British settlers who arrived via the St Lawrence, and American immigrants who entered from the south.[10] In 1815, during the period when the British Crown was awarding the first land grants to veterans of the War of 1812, General Frederick George Heriot brought his famed Voltigeurs regiment to the Drummondville area. A descendant of Huguenots with a lineage tracing back to the island of Jersey, Heriot named the new settlement after the governor general under whom he had served, Sir Gordon Drummond.[11] The vast majority of the settlers in Heriot's new town and environs were Protestant, as were the hundreds of Americans entering the valley from the south. The latter founded the village of Ascott, later renamed Sherbrooke, at the confluence of the Magog and St-François Rivers.[12]

Michael Power would reside in Drummondville, from which he would oversee his extensive mission territory. He had a small church and rectory, blessed as St-Frédéric Church in honour of General Heriot, who had donated the land to local Catholics. Built in 1822 by volunteer work parties, the church was a modest wood-frame structure measuring only fifty-six feet long by thirty-six feet wide and reflecting the style of the day: a rectangle with a tower and belfry at the main entrance.[13] From this chapel, Power was expected to visit the nearly 500 Catholics scattered across the townships of Drummond, Wickham, Shipton, Kingsley, and Sherbrooke, which was the second principal node of Catholic settlement in the region.[14] He could only maintain the mission by travelling constantly up and down the river valley – a round trip of over 200 kilometres – and, since the river was only partially navigable because of rapids, he covered the distance on horseback. The colonization roads, dating from the time of Governor General Sir James Craig, were little more than trails cut through the bush characterized by ruts, fallen logs, and embankments created by the intruding Appalachian highlands. It is little wonder that one reason Holmes wanted out of the mission was that he suffered a hernia due to long hours in the saddle.[15]

The missionaries believed that all of this travel was necessary for several reasons. At a time when English-speaking Protestants were arriving in the region in record numbers, there was concern that the small pockets of Catholics would be targeted by Protestant proselytizers.[16] This situation was made more acute by what both Holmes and Power had identified as the problem of distance between these pockets; the willynilly settlement pattern of Catholic farmers made those settlers even

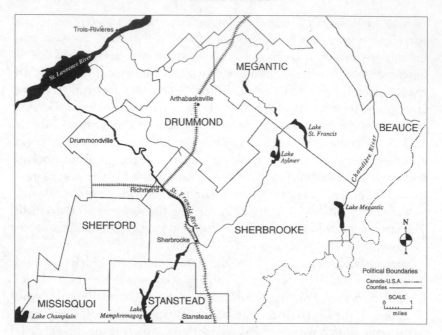

Counties of the Eastern Townships, highlighting the St-François Valley, where Power first served as a missionary priest (from J.I. Little, *State and Society in Transition* [Montreal and Kingston: McGill-Queen's University Press, 1997]).

more vulnerable. Catholics were vastly outnumbered in every section of Power's mission. In the township of Sherbrooke, for example, by 1831, only 9 per cent of the population was Catholic, amounting to 747 souls.[17] Holmes had already warned Panet that if Power spent too much time away from Drummondville, then the local Protestants would take advantage of the leaderless Catholic minority. Power would soon see for himself that the local Protestant ministers were aggressive – he reported to Lartigue that certain Protestant leaders had circulated calumnious rumours to the effect that Lartigue's loyalty to the British Crown was questionable.[18] Power also noted that the danger faced by Catholics appeared subtle and was perhaps even the product of covert Protestant activity. In light of all this, he lamented the apostasy of four Catholic women who had married zealous Protestants. Likewise, Holmes had witnessed at least thirty mixed marriages as he made his rounds through the mission territory.[19] Although the number of Protestants in the region would become proportionally less significant in the coming decades as Catholic migration increased, Power and other missionary priests of his generation became preoccupied with establishing a visible Catholic presence as a focus of community life and as a bulwark against potential dominance of non-Catholics in political and social institutions.

One unmistakable sign of Power's intention to establish a Catholic presence was the erection of church buildings. When he arrived in Drummondville, the village had the only completed Catholic church building in the entire mission territory. Making his rounds through his territory, Power administered the sacraments and gathered the faithful outdoors and in private homes – "cathedrals in the wilderness." At Sherbrooke, however, the tiny Catholic population led by Patrick Read and Anna Maria Valls Felton, wife of local Anglican leader Colonel William Bowman Felton, were attempting to build their own chapel. These Sherbrooke Catholics – primarily Irish immigrants, some loyalists, and the spouses of several leading Protestants – did not have the financial means to erect a large structure, let alone maintain it. Power was aware of their relative poverty but conscious of the importance of this project as a Catholic statement in the "centre of Protestantism."[20] Such an edifice, he thought, would encourage further immigration of Catholics to the region, thus building a Catholic presence not only architecturally but also, more importantly, in terms of actual numbers. Without a strong core of Catholic settlement, he feared, a trend that he had noticed since his arrival would persist: in places where there was no regular service by a Catholic priest, Catholic immigrants tended to move on, leaving the area open to a strong non-Catholic majority. So strong were his beliefs in this regard that he made a donation to the Sherbrooke chapel fund from his own paltry savings,[21] which helped to compensate for the fact that he had failed to convince Panet to provide episcopal funds for the project or approve a call for a general subscription throughout the diocese. Perhaps, taking the advice of experienced missionary Holmes, Panet had concluded that the community was too small to bear the maintenance costs of the endeavour. He was evidently correct, since the chapel project debt was still outstanding as late as 1843.[22] Undeterred, Sherbrooke Catholics, led by the Griffith family, erected the building with volunteer labour, and in 1830, Power blessed the new church, which was named St Columba, after the famous Irish missionary.[23]

Power also discovered that itinerant Protestant preachers were not the only threat to his scattered flock. Settlers who did not receive regular visits from their priest lacked discrimination when faced with a stranger

Woolen mill in the 1830s, Sherbrooke, reflects the ruggedness of the
southernmost settlement in Power's mission territory
(NA, 1970-188-2386)

in a black cassock claiming the authority to hear their confessions,
baptize their infants, and marry their children. Many settlers thought
that if the stranger looked like a priest, talked like a priest, and had
the bearing of a priest, then he must be a priest. In the summer of
1831, Power confronted a certain Father Francis Grady. Grady arrived
in Drummondville wearing a soutane and bearing letters from Joseph
Signay, the coadjutor bishop of Quebec, but Power suspected that not all
was as it appeared to be.[24] Grady seemed preoccupied with the incoming Irish Catholic immigrants, and he made his way to Shipton to take
up a collection among them. This alone raised Power's suspicions, but
when Grady passed through Drummondville and avoided the presbytery,
he knew that something was terribly amiss. While making a sick call
outside of town, Power ran into Grady. Conversing with him in Latin –
an obvious test – Power saw that Grady's clerical dress was incomplete
and demanded to see Signay's letters. During a second confrontation,

this time at Drummondville, Grady demanded his letters back. Instead of complying, Power quizzed him on his theological knowledge, thereby confirming that Grady was "an impostor of great insolence."[25] Whether Power was correct in his assessment or Grady was simply a poorly trained priest who had fled Ireland looking for work made little difference to Lartigue. The bishop sided with Power, fearing that the "impostor" had already harmed the recently arrived Irish.

Power had enough trouble tending his flock without having to deal with suspicious strangers. In his letters to Panet, he confessed that on the frontier, Catholic worship, piety, and discipline did not resemble that which he had experienced among the Catholic citizens of Quebec, Montreal, and Halifax. In part, Power's difficulties were symptomatic of his new circumstances: frontier Catholics had infrequent contact with their pastors; there were few permanent sacred spaces where Catholics could worship; and Catholics lived either in isolation from one another or in an environment where it was easy to ignore or stretch the canon laws and moral norms prescribed by the church. His problems were compounded by the very nature of the communities he served – communities of French Canadians with origins in the seigneurial system and Irish Catholics who had recently arrived in Canada. The troubles within the French Canadian parishes that occurred between the conquest of 1760 and the religious revolution of the early 1840s have been well documented. Priests in the old seigneurial parishes complained to their bishops of the moral laxity of their flocks, exemplified by concubinage among young people, anticlericalism among the male population, rambunctious behaviour among the youth who attended services, and spotty church attendance.[26]

Similarly, many of the recently arrived Irish Catholics demonstrated a relaxed attitude towards attending Mass and maintaining the moral norms of the church. Prior to the devotional revolution in Ireland in the late 1840s and the 1850s, institutions in the Archdiocese of Dublin and urban centres were lightly attended and poorly supported by the laity.[27] In rural areas, men usually shied away from regular Sunday Mass attendance, church facilities were impoverished, and there was little sense of a formal religious vitality among the people, who generally maintained the outward appearance of Catholicism while adhering to a rather syncretic blend of Christian beliefs, older Celtic practices, and a strong veneration of local saints.[28] In occupying Ireland, the British had subjugated the official apparatus of the church, but they had failed to uproot the popular Irish Catholicism, which was woven into the fabric of Irish distinctiveness, and perhaps resistance, as the Irish attempted to maintain their sense of peoplehood in the face of conquerors and over-lords. In the process, at least until the advent of the devotional revolution fostered by Bishop John McHale and Bishop Paul Cullen, Irish parish life deteriorated – at least, so it seemed if one viewed it from the perspective of the pulpit or the bishop's desk. Thus, on the Lower Canadian fron-tier, Michael Power encountered the idiosyncratic Catholicism of two Catholic peoples whose behaviour often seemed to fly in the face of all that he had been taught was good and proper about the Catholic faith, its liturgy, its moral discipline, and its sacramental rites.

Power's flock had only a lukewarm commitment to the responsibili-ties of Catholic practice, making his missionary work in the valley at times frustrating, unpleasant, and even soul-destroying. He was deeply troubled by the fact that so few of his parishioners availed themselves of the sacraments, particularly confession.[29] More serious, however, was his feeling of horror at the number of irregular marriages and living arrangements – that is, concubinage – that he discovered as he galloped from Drummondville to Shipton, Sherbrooke, Upton, and Grant. Less than one year into his mission, he reported twelve to fifteen cases of marriage irregularity, including several mixed marriages that had not been properly dispensed from impediments under canon law, and at least one marriage in which a Catholic was married to "une personne infidèle."[30] He also uncovered a case of common-law marriage between a widower, Ignace Levasseur, and his niece, Marie-Anne Desfosses. His predecessors, missionaries and bishops, had refused the couple the right to a church marriage because they were in violation of the rules of affinity prohibiting marriage to a relative within four degrees of separa-tion. The case was further complicated by the fact that the couple had two children. While such marital irregularities, cohabitation, and less restrained sexual behaviour were not uncommon among Lower Canadi-ans,[31] the importance of the context would be lost on a newly ordained priest like Power, who was building a library of Catholic periodicals and juridical texts in his rustic presbytery.[32] Although he may have been shocked by the Levasseur-Desfosses case, he nevertheless used his perspicacious reading of the canon law to convince the bishop that the proper dispensations could be granted. While the details of his efforts have been lost, on 3 May 1829, he married the couple at St-Frédéric Church.[33] During his tenure in Drummondville, Power officiated at forty-six marriages, almost evenly split between Catholics of French Canadian descent and those of Irish birth. In that time, Power officiated over no mixed marriages between Catholics and Protestants.[34]

He quickly learned that administering such sacraments was an important way of supplementing his income. As far as the finances of the mission were concerned, John Holmes's prognostications concerning the mission's wealth proved inaccurate. Power reported to his superiors that his penury was not due solely to the poverty of his flock; it was also caused by the fact that many members of his flock simply refused to pay the *dîme*. Within a year of his appointment, Power complained that his people were unable or unwilling to sustain him, and that it was impossible for any priest to carry out his mandate under such circumstances.[35] Observations made by Panet during his visit to the St-François Valley supported Power's assessment and indicated that Panet's idea that Odanak be added to the mission would not have been such a misguided one after all. The *dîme* collected at St François-du-Lac outstripped that of St-Frédéric in nearly every respect.[36] It is little wonder, in light of all the frustrations he was encountering on the frontier and the indignity of earning a pauper's income for his labours, that in 1831 Power informed his bishop that he "probably had the most difficult mission in Lower Canada."[37]

Some might consider such comments to be merely the whining of a young man who had previously lived a rather sheltered and privileged existence. But, to Power's credit, he had stuck it out in the St-François Valley for four years, a tenure that exceeded by eighteen months the average for a recently ordained man on his first pastoral assignment.[38] He had done his best to cover his territory on rough roads, and he had navigated his way through the canonical obstacles presented by unorthodox martial situations. He was not getting enough to eat (neither was his horse), and he began to comment that he was succumbing more easily to fatigue and illness. Worn out, Power asked for a change of appointment. His one positive piece of news for Panet was that St Columba's in Sherbrooke had been completed.[39] On 22 September 1831, Panet relieved Power of the Drummondville mission and assigned him to the mission of Notre-Dame-de-Bonsecours at Petite-Nation, the administrative centre of the Papineau seigneury in the lower Ottawa River Valley.[40]

With the removal of Power to Petite-Nation, Panet informed Jean-Jacques Lartigue, his episcopal vicar in Montreal, that he was offering him a priest whose "talents would be of great use" in the district.[41] The bishop's implication was that while Lartigue might be losing the popular Father Hugh Paisley, he was gaining a seasoned priest who knew what to expect of frontier pastoral work. Although Power never recorded his feelings about the transfer, he must have been relieved that his request to leave Drummondville had been granted, since, by his own assessment,

INCOME IN THE MISSIONS OF THE ST-FRANÇOIS RIVER VALLEY, 1830

Item		St-François-du-Lac	Drummondville
Population:	Canadian	1,450	500
	Native Peoples	150	–
Confirmations		288	59
Dîme	Wheat	300–400 pounds	8 minots
	Peas	100 pounds	1 pound
	Oats	500 pounds	–
	Rye	30 pounds	14 pounds
	Buckwheat	80 pounds	–
	Indian Corn	60 pounds	3 pounds
	Potatoes	–	15 pounds
	Sterling	£50	£3

Source: AAQ, Cahier des visites, vol. 8, 69 CD, p.59, 2 July 1830, 5–6 June 1830

any parish or mission in Lower Canada would be better. Still, when he arrived at Petite-Nation, it may have appeared to him as more of the same. The one exception was that Petite-Nation had remained under the auspices of the seigneurial system, and so he could expect some co-operation from the local seigneur. That seigneur was no less than Louis-Joseph Papineau.

The region in which the Petite-Nation River meets the Ottawa River was one of the last portions of seigneurial tenure to be settled after the conquest. Situated about forty miles southeast of Bytown (later Ottawa) and sixty miles northwest of Montreal, the seigneury was ideally located between Canada's commercial centre and the resource-rich upper Ottawa Valley. Its southern boundary lapped by the waters of the Ottawa, the seigneury was fifteen miles square. It was comprised mainly of the rocky and wooded terrain of the Canadian Shield, in this area part of the Laurentian highlands. The shield was not conducive to farming, and the region's only arable land was a thin strip wedged between the river and the Laurentian Mountains. The area thus held little interest for the inhabitants of the St Lawrence Valley, despite the overcrowding on the older seigneuries there. This meant that Petite-Nation was virtually unsettled by Euro-Canadians in 1800.[42] Although it was held for the Crown by the Seminary of Quebec, it was primarily a hunting and

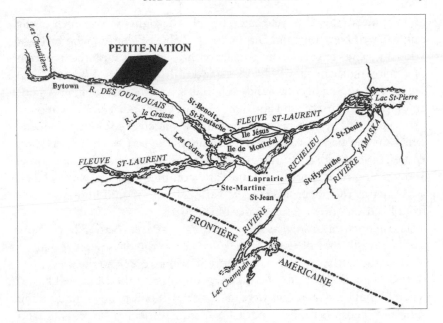

Map of Petite-Nation, the site of Power's second mission; also included are the locations of Power's subsequent appointments as pastor: Ste-Martine and Laprairie (from Claude Baribeau, *La seigneurie de la Petite-Nation, 1801–1854* [Hull: Éditions Asticou, 1983])

fishing reserve for the Algonquin people of the Ottawa Valley and the Iroquois people who lived on the reserve lands at nearby Kanesatake (Oka). Travel to the Petite-Nation seigneury was arduous. One could use the single bush road from Montreal, enduring its stumps, potholes, and mosquitoes, or one could voyage along the Ottawa River against the current, portaging past a series of rapids. All told, it was at least a week's trip from Montreal.

In 1801, the underdeveloped Petite-Nation seigneury was sold to Joseph Papineau, a well-known Montreal notary, a member of the Legislative Assembly, and, in time, patriarch of one of Lower Canada's most controversial families. The Papineaus viewed the Ottawa Valley as a region of potential agricultural settlement, and, perhaps more importantly, as a source of wood to fuel Britain's insatiable appetite for ships' masts and squared timber during the Napoleonic Wars.[43] In 1808, Joseph Papineau moved about one hundred settlers to the region, most of whom took up *rotures* of land between what is now the village of Montebello and Papineauville. One year later, he sold the rights to one-fifth of the seigneury to New England entrepreneur Robert Fletcher, who brought 160 Americans to the northwest part of the seigneury with the intention of employing them as woodworkers and mill labourers.[44] By 1810, the seigneury had roughly one hundred families, and they were either American Protestant or French Canadian Roman Catholic. Yet the economic promise of the region never materialized. Fletcher committed suicide when his lumbering ventures failed and his business went bankrupt. Petite-Nation, with its extremes of climate, poor soil, rough topography, and primitive transportation routes and communications, was as much a frontier as the upper St-François Valley. Power would find no respite from his difficulties on the shores of the Ottawa.

The seigneurial system as it was manifest at Petite-Nation bore many similarities to that of the older seigneuries in the St Lawrence Valley. Most of the settlers who came to Petite-Nation were from the previously settled seigneuries of Terrebonne, Argenteuil, and the Montreal basin, where population increases were making it difficult to keep subdividing *rotures*.[45] Petite-Nation's French Canadian settlers were tenants who acquired land from the Papineaus; title to the property could only be secured by *habitants* who had cleared at least six *arpents* of land.[46] The small farms protruded from the base of the Laurentians towards the Ottawa River in the familiar *rang*, or strip, fashion, as they did in the St Lawrence Valley seigneuries. The *rang* pattern was also in evidence along the Petite-Nation River and the creeks that fed into it. Like their French Canadian cousins elsewhere in the seigneurial lands, the *censitaires* (tenants) paid rent (*cens*) to their seigneurs, in this case the Papineaus, usually based on a portion of their annual harvest. The Papineaus preferred that the rent be paid in wheat, or its cash equivalent, since the value of this crop most accurately reflected market realities and inflation. When markets were high, wheat was among the most lucrative of all the grain crops.[47] Unlike their counterparts at other seigneuries, particularly those dating from the *ancien régime* (before the conquest of 1763), the *censitaires* at Petite-Nation were prohibited from cutting timber and milling for commercial purposes. Thus, the true wealth of the seigneury – its forests – were exploited exclusively by Joseph Papineau and his eldest surviving son, Louis-Joseph, who, in 1817, purchased the seigneury from his father.

As it was in other Lower Canadian seigneuries, the Catholic Church was accorded certain rights and had certain feudal obligations in Petite-Nation. From 1815 to 1828, Bishop Joseph-Octave Plessis of Quebec ensured that Petite-Nation was served by missionary priests from the nearby Sulpician seigneury at Oka.[48] As the Catholic population of the area grew, it became necessary to replace worship in private homes and the manse of seigneurial agent Denis-Benjamin Papineau,[49] younger brother of Louis-Joseph, with a more formal liturgy in a chapel setting. In 1818, Denis-Benjamin Papineau ceded two *arpents* of land in what is today the town of Montebello to be used as the site for a new church building, presbytery, and school.[50] Three years later, a chapel dedicated to Our Lady of Good Help (Notre-Dame-de-Bonsecours) was blessed and opened by the Sulpicians in the presence of Louis-Joseph Papineau, who was able to tear himself away from his political duties in Quebec City for the occasion. With its new chapel and population increase – due, in large part, to the clearing of new farms and the initiation of a canal project at Grenville, some fifteen miles southeast of Montebello on the Ottawa River – Petite-Nation was visited more regularly by missionary priests. Finally, in 1827, Sulpician priest Jean-Baptiste Roupe was given administrative responsibility for the entire Lower Canadian shore of the Ottawa, from Petite-Nation north to Buckingham, Aylmer, and Allumette Island.[51]

As the population grew, particularly because of increased Irish immigration to the region, Bishop Panet decided to appoint a permanent missionary to Montebello. In 1828, thirty-three-year-old Scotsman Hugh Paisley succeeded Roupe as the first resident priest at Petite-Nation. In his four years at the seigneury, the popular Paisley managed the completion of the sacristy and presbytery at Bonsecours, blessed and dedicated the chapel of Our Lady of the Seven Sorrows at Grenville, planned the financing of a Catholic school at Montebello, and enclosed the Catholic cemetery.[52] But what was perhaps Paisley's crowning achievement was formalized on 26 September 1831, when the episcopal vicar of Montreal raised Bonsecours to parish status.[53] Paisley had initiated the process in July, but he delayed his departure from the region until official notice of the canonical erection arrived from Montreal. He was severely criticized for this delay by both Panet and Lartigue, because Power had expected Paisley to assume the mission of Drummondville in early October.[54] It was not as though Paisley was reluctant to leave – he had actually asked to be relieved of the mission because it had not lived up to its tithing obligations, and he was unwilling to continue ministering to its people while living in poverty.[55]

At the new parish, Power would deal with the same *fabrique* as Paisley, and Paisley had suffered financial woes due to the attitude of the

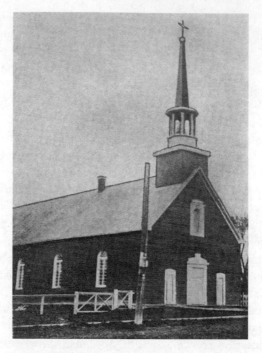

The Church of Notre-Dame-de-Bonsecours, Montebello,
Lower Canada, as it may have looked in Power's time (from
Abbé Michel Chamberland, *Histoire de Montebello, 1815–
1928* [Montreal: Imprimerie Sourds-Muets, 1929])

fabrique members. In the French Canadian tradition, as inherited from
late-medieval France,[56] parish temporal affairs were governed by a *fabrique* (committee) consisting of the *curé* (priest) and three *marguilliers*
(churchwardens), who were elected by the parishioners through secret
ballot every three years. The *fabrique* was the frontier's most important
administrative Catholic body, or expression of popular governance by
Catholics, until municipal governments were created.[57] It would build
and maintain the church, manage its properties, establish order during
religious ceremonies, secure tithes and bank them, and collect the pew
rents.[58] The tithes, or *dîme* (one twenty-sixth of annual farm yields),
supported the *curé's* household,[59] while the weekly pew rents would
sustain the needs of the church – its vessels, sacramentals, devotional
objects, physical maintenance, and sundry items. The *marguilliers* were
awarded special seats at the front of the nave and received Eucharist first

at Sunday Mass; they could receive candles and palm branches on Palm Sunday and venerate the cross in the sanctuary on Good Friday.[60]

Pew allotment in Bonsecours, as in any other Lower Canadian parish, provided a road map of local social groupings. Pews not held by the *marguilliers* were auctioned to the highest bidder, so the wealthier and more prominent parishioners sat at the front of the nave, closest to the most sacred place in the building – the tabernacle in the sanctuary – which was reserved for the "body of Christ" under the physical species of bread. The parish's less prominent and poorer families held pews in the middle and back of the nave. The poorest parishioners, as well as travellers or sojourners and the young and the restless, were placed farthest from the altar and tabernacle, near the doors of the church or on the steps leading to the gallery (the latter area was once described by Bishop Briand as the "gathering place for all libertines"[61]). When pews became vacant due to the death, departure, or forfeiture of the previous renters, they were auctioned off by the *fabrique*. The *marguilliers* were critical players at such times, as issues of parish income, peace between families, and social status came to the fore. Not surprisingly, due to the prestige and responsibility attached to the office of *marguillier*, the position was highly coveted by members of the more powerful families in the parish. Thus, when Power approached the altar at Bonsecours and looked out at his congregation, he would see assembled immediately before him the elite of the frontier community. He would make contact in liturgy with the less privileged members of his flock only at communion time or when they elected to receive the Eucharist. If he were to make enemies among the occupiers of the front pews, his income would suffer greatly, as would his ability to carry out his ministry in Petite-Nation. No doubt the success of Power's tenure was both of his own making and subject to the co-operation of such notables as seigneurial agent Denis-Benjamin Papineau and the *marguilliers*.

Power first set foot in the parish of Petite-Nation in mid-October 1831, and within days he had performed his first registered act – the burial of an unnamed two-day-old infant.[62] He would have noticed some similarities between his new parish on the Ottawa and his old mission on the St-François. For one thing, both had relatively small Catholic populations. Petite-Nation had as many as 666 Catholic faithful,[63] and this new flock was also predominantly French-Canadian, although the Irish Catholic presence in the region was growing, due primarily to increased immigration from Ireland, the attractiveness of the Ottawa Valley's canal projects and lumber camps, and the encouragement of

Louis-Joseph Papineau, who had discovered within the Irish Catholic communities potential allies for his battles for constitutional reform against the political oligarchy in Lower Canada.[64]

The numbers of Irish were increasingly noticeable in Buckingham, Grenville, and the southeast section of Power's mission, where young couples seeking Power's blessing on their nuptials hailed from a variety of Irish counties, including Mayo in the west, Donegal, Monaghan, and Tyrone in Ulster, and as far south as Wexford.[65] However, the Irish amounted to only about 10 per cent of Power's flock, and they resisted intermarriage with their French-Canadian co-religionists or with the remnants of Fletcher's Protestant settlers, with whom the Irish shared a common language (English was the first language of roughly 22.5 per cent of the seigneury).[66] The strong concentration of the Protestant population in Plaisance, in the northwest section of the seigneury, would offer Power the kind of multi-denominational environment that he had just experienced in Drummondville, Shipton, and Sherbrooke.

The similarities between the first pastoral duties in the St-François Valley and the new duties in the Ottawa Valley may have been unsettling for a young man already tired of ministering under frontier conditions. Petite-Nation, despite its more developed parochial institutions, was still the frontier. Parish business necessitated frequent travel to Buckingham, well beyond the northwest boundary of the seigneury, as well as to Plaisance, to Montebello and vicinity, and to the homes of an additional hundred families in the townships of Grenville and Chatham to the southeast.[67] The Catholic inhabitants, like most others, were spread thinly along the Ottawa River axis, so Power had to travel often if he was to see each community every few weeks.[68] Louis-Joseph Papineau had not helped matters much. Road building had not been one of his highest priorities, and he had left much of it to the *censitaires* themselves, most of whom were already far too busy trying to clear land and eke out an existence on their farms. Of particular concern to Power was the community served by the chapel of Our Lady of the Seven Sorrows at Grenville, a mission station that drew Catholics from nearby Chatham and from Hawkesbury and surrounding Prescott County on the Upper Canadian side of the river. In 1832 alone, Power made two trips to Upper Canada to administer the sacraments to Catholics in Plantagenet, Caledonia, Hawkesbury, and Nouveau Longueuil who had been without a priest from the Diocese of Kingston.[69] Meanwhile, back in Grenville, Power faced a formidable set of obstacles in trying to reach the local Catholic population. Newly arrived Catholics were mostly single young men – canal workers who had a penchant for working and drinking hard, and who had a greater affinity with the tavern than the tabernacle.[70] At times, the new pastor must have regretted his transfer from Drummondville to Petite-Nation – he was out of the frying pan and into the fire.

In addition to dealing with the familiar problems of the frontier, Power was called upon to minister to a community hit by the cholera epidemic of 1832. Having spread through eastern Europe in the 1820s, the highly infectious disease spread to the United Kingdom in 1831, and by 1832, the first cases were reported in British North America.[71] Geoffrey Bilson describes how the micro-organism responsible for the disease enters the body orally, with devastating results: "The disease's worst effects are caused by a toxin which makes the gut wall permeable to water. It causes vomiting and massive purging of liquid which quickly produces dehydration and upsets the chemical balance in the body. It produces ... severe spasms and cramps, a sunken face, blue colour, husky voice and further consequences, including kidney failure, as the bodily processes collapse."[72]

While today cholera can be treated with antibiotics, in the nineteenth century rudimentary treatments failed to prevent the deaths of hundreds of Canadians. In an effort to contain the epidemic, quarantine stations for immigrants were erected at Grosse Île in the St Lawrence. The arrival of cholera coincided with that of thousands of immigrants from Ireland and Britain, many of whom contracted the infection on board ship and transmitted it to others in port. Fleeing the ports of Montreal and Quebec proved to be no solution for the immigrants and their Canadian hosts. As early as 15 July, Michael Power went to Grenville to bless the grave of Michael O'Mara, who had died on 27 June of "a contagious malady" on the steamship *Sharron* from Montreal. Within the next forty-eight hours, he blessed the graves of three more victims, two of whom, a woman and an infant, could not be identified for his records – they were likely newcomers to his parish.[73] While hundreds died in the cities, many found their way to Power's parish. By November, he had returned to Grenville and blessed the graves of at least eighteen people, one-third of whom were of Irish origin; some had died just after his summer visit.[74] By year's end, cholera had claimed at least 10,000 lives in British North America,[75] and in Petite-Nation, it had placed far more stress on a situation that was already trying for Power.

Power also found the climate at Petite-Nation unbearable. When he arrived, in mid-October, the best weeks of the Ottawa Valley autumn

had already passed. Winds funnelled down the valley, sweeping the remaining red, yellow, and orange leaves from the trees. Winters in the
Outaouais were far more severe than winters in Drummondville and
Montreal. Bitterly cold winds and masses of snow made mockery of
Cornelius Krieghoff's romantic images of the Lower Canadian seigneury
in winter. Power, humbled by the elements, struggled through the snow
at least once a month to the Grenville mission to say Mass in the chapel,
baptize infants, marry couples, and bless the graves of those who had
died in his absence.[76] In December 1831, the weather conditions were
merciless. Power made the twelve-mile journey from Bonsecours to Grenville on foot, navigating a bush road clogged with snow and forest debris.
The chapel of Our Lady of the Seven Sorrows was aptly named. It had no
stove, and the glass in all of its windows was either broken or missing.
Less than a dozen congregants stood in the nave, wearing toques and fur
caps, which they only removed when Power consecrated the bread and
the wine. The young men jogged on the spot to stay warm – an observer
who did not know better might have thought they were dancing a jig.
Power, his back to the tiny assembly, wore his vestments over his winter
clothing. He had to interrupt the Mass periodically so he could thaw his
freezing fingers over a little heater that sat close to the altar. The sacramental wine turned to icy slush in the chalice. When the congregants
had received communion, they fled before Power could offer the final
blessing. He contracted a severe throat infection and begged Lartigue
to relieve him of saying Mass in Grenville until March.[77] In return,
he promised to visit the mission and administer the rites of baptism,
should the need arise. Lartigue left the decision to Power, who promptly
suspended services at Grenville.[78]

Power found the social climate at Petite-Nation equally inhospitable.
Paisley had been a popular pastor, and the local inhabitants greatly
resented his transfer. Hearing of his pending departure, his parishioners gathered at Bonsecours, and with the assistance of Denis-Benjamin
Papineau they issued a protest to Lartigue. The bishop received this
communication from the parish coldly, and he rebuked Papineau and the
others for questioning the decisions of his superior, the bishop of Quebec:
"In my opinion it would be a bad example to give to other parishes,
leading them to publicly pronounce themselves on the merits or faults of
their parsons or missionaries as well as insisting on their continuation or
their call to order, when they ignore the motives of the bishop's conduct
in this matter."[79] Lartigue would not countenance Congregationalist-
style behaviour on the frontier or in the diocese; the bishop and his

Papineau residence, Montebello, 1854. Although the house had not yet been constructed when Power was pastor on the seigneury, 1831–33, the painting exudes a sense of the region's ruggedness (NA, 1983-46-2)

curé were to be the supreme ecclesiastical authorities, provincially and locally. The fact that the parishioners and the *fabrique* were angry at, and somewhat humiliated by, their bishop put Power at a disadvantage before he had even met a soul at Petite-Nation. The parishioners made their indifference to him clear, and he became a convenient scapegoat for them in their conflict with Lartigue.

Furthermore, Power did little to advance his own cause, particularly when he became embroiled in a controversy over a Catholic school. Hugh Paisley had seen the need for a Catholic school at Bonsecours, and he had prompted the *fabrique* to accord six pounds and five shillings annually for the building and maintenance of a parish school at Montebello. The problem was that there was already a school at Plaisance, in the largely anglophone and Protestant section of Petite-Nation. The school was primarily an English-speaking and Protestant establishment, although Denis-Benjamin Papineau, who lived in the area, sent his children there.[80] Power, presumably instructed by Lartigue, refused to visit the school at Plaisance, invoking Papineau's ire. Power was eventually offered public support for his stance. This occurred in January 1833, when Lartigue addressed the parish at Petite-Nation during his pastoral visit. The bishop was upset that schools were being erected without his consent and took a swipe at the Plaisance institution: "We authorize the church's revenue to return to Mr. Papineau, if he gives satisfactory proof of his debt, the sum of five pounds and five shillings that would appear to have been advanced in good faith. We also disapprove that the above-mentioned syndic [school] was built without our permission on the church's property."[81] Lartigue threw his support behind Power's endeavour to construct a truly Catholic school, on church lands, at Montebello.

The new school was headed by Power and the French Canadian *marguilliers*, although the first registered pupils belonged to the parish's Irish Catholic minority: Arthur Crosbie, John Lee, and Lucinda Hayes.[82] This appeared to support Denis-Benjamin Papineau's contention that local anglophones were more interested in education than were their French-Canadian neighbours. The school episode, however, soured relations between Power and Papineau, and Papineau stopped overseeing the collection of money for his *curé*.[83]

Not to be outdone, Power accused Papineau of encouraging "all manners of indiscipline" among the *habitants* and endangering the pastor's livelihood. Within a year of his arrival at Petite-Nation, Power realized that the idea that the parish would support him was an illusion. He complained – albeit politely – to Lartigue that the promised one hundred pounds per year, as derived from the *dîme* and other fees, was really only about fifty pounds. In 1833, Power reported that he had collected only £115 since coming to the parish, but that his expenses had amounted to at least £120.[84] He could afford neither a horse nor a wagon and claimed to have insufficient funds to visit the sick in the farthest reaches of the parish.[85] He was penniless, and he felt hurt by his parishioners' refusal to support him. But what perplexed him most was the knowledge that some of his Catholic parishioners gave their hard-earned cash freely to the tavern keeper but were disinclined to slip any of it into the collection box on Sunday.[86] He was frank and emphatic about his predicament when writing to Lartigue: "I am very embarrassed in my means of living."[87] In little more than a year, he had been defeated by the seigneur and his parishioners, who resented his stand on the school question, preferred his predecessor, and seemed generally uninterested in the church.

Relying largely on the work of Montebello priest Michel Chamberland, historians have tended to blame Power's financial woes on the parsimony and the tavern culture of the inhabitants of Petite-Nation and Grenville. Chamberland, a priest-historian writing at a time when clergy enjoyed an elevated status in the eyes of most Quebec Catholics, was intent on defending one of his pastoral predecessors at Notre-Dame-de-Bonsecours. He evoked Power as "the future Bishop of Toronto" and "a martyr for religious zeal"; he also presented him as a man for whom parishioners should have shown a far greater respect.[88] This is more historical revision than investigative research. Chamberland essentially read Power backwards into the situation, attributing qualities to him then that he did not demonstrate until later. Power himself did not blame all of his problems on the indifference of the locals. He admitted that he had not arrived from Drummondville flush with cash and that he had had an initial disagreement with the *fabrique* at Petite-Nation over how much money he was entitled to draw from the parish accounts.[89] He also conceded that the parishioners were mostly farmers, labourers, and canal workers who did not own their land, suffered poor harvests, and earned so little that it was hard for them to pay the *dîme*.[90] Understandably, Power took delight in the promise of a good harvest, which occurred in the autumn of 1832. That year, his income increased by a whopping £57.[91] He also recognized that part of his income problem was due to the business interests of the *marguilliers*. These interests took them away from the seigneury in the nonwinter months, and so they were unable to convene meetings in the parish.[92] Thus, far from endorsing the interpretations of Chamberland, Power understood that his poor financial circumstances were caused by a number of factors, not just the parsimony of his flock.

As Power had observed, debt was indeed chronic on the seigneury of Petite-Nation. The six most prosperous farms were owned by Denis-Benjamin Papineau and five anglophone farmers. Elsewhere in Petite-Nation, the *rotures* were small, the soil was only marginally suited to agriculture, and crops were used mostly for subsistence. There were times when the Papineaus had to import wheat into the seigneury to keep the *habitants* alive. As a result, *censitaires* in fifty-one lots owed Louis-Joseph Papineau over £500 each, and some of them were in debt for over £1,000.[93] It appears that Papineau, although a firebrand of reform politics and visionary of a revolution in Lower Canada, was far less heroic when it came to taking care of his Petite-Nation *habitants* – he pressed his tenants hard for what they owed him. And most of Papineau's *censitaires* were also indebted to local merchants, primarily anglophone Protestants, who had extended them lines of credit in anticipation of a good harvest.[94] Thus, the empirical evidence supports Power's assessment that parsimony was only part of the reason why he lived hand-to-mouth in his own rectory. In fact, many members of his flock were simply reluctant to part with any penny or shilling that could go towards relieving them of a crushing financial burden.

Perhaps with an eye to easing the financial strain on his young pastor, Lartigue decided to officially expand Power's jurisdiction. When Power had first come to Petite-Nation, Lartigue had accorded him the title of vicar-general for the Diocese of Kingston, the eastern extremity of which lay across the Ottawa River from Petite-Nation and Argenteuil, where Grenville is located.[95] Such an appointment was not unusual on the frontier; bishops of adjoining dioceses often appointed one another vicar-general to enable a neighbouring bishop to cover the most remote territories of a diocese in times of need. Paisley, in fact, had been accorded the same status under the terms of an informal agreement between Bishop Alexander Macdonell of Kingston and Bishop Jean-Jacques Lartigue of the Montreal district. In a reciprocal fashion, Father John Cullen of Bytown, in Upper Canada, was named vicar-general for the Montreal district of the Diocese of Quebec so that he could address the needs of any Catholics who presented themselves in Hull or Gatineau or on the Lower Canadian side of the upper Ottawa River. The spirit of the position was an informal one – no direct or binding responsibilities accompanied the title, other than the responsibility for administering the sacraments or dispensing from two banns of marriage.[96] In 1833, however, Lartigue informed Power that he would now be directly responsible for the missions at Plantagenet, South Nation, L'Orignal, and Hawkesbury, all of which were on the opposite side of the Ottawa from Power, in Upper Canada.[97] Power would be required to cross the Ottawa River regularly to minister to an additional 1,400 persons who were technically in the Diocese of Kingston, with the assurance that he would be compensated to the tune of £50 per annum. For Power, this was the last straw. In two letters written in July 1833, he refused the appointment, requested to be removed from Petite-Nation, and made a veiled threat about leaving the diocese should his request be denied.[98]

Later chroniclers of Power's move from Petite-Nation have tended to gloss over details that could mar the image of the future "martyred bishop."[99] They describe the transfer from Petite-Nation as the act of a sympathetic bishop – Lartigue being charitable to an exhausted and financially strapped pastor who had served his first six years entirely on the frontier. While there may be some truth to this, it is by no means the whole story. Lartigue told Macdonell that he was "mortified" to hear of Power's refusal to serve Plantagenet and surrounding area but that he was almost powerless under canon law to force a priest to serve in another diocese against his will.[100] Power had argued that he could not in good conscience place himself under a diocesan ordinary who was not his own and, in essence, serve two masters. Moreover, he argued, crossing the Ottawa was hazardous, especially in winter, and the promise of increased income from service in Upper Canada was illusory; he knew that Upper Canadians were as debt-ridden as their brothers and sisters on the Lower Canadian side of the river.

Power had first-hand experience of the work awaiting him on the Upper Canadian side of the Ottawa. From 1 January to 7 October 1832, he made at least two trips to the Upper Canadian side, and of the 196 entries in his register of marriages, baptisms, and burials, sixty (or about 30 per cent) were Upper Canadian. In the same period the following year, without any service to the Upper Canadians (both before and after Lartigue's request), Power made only seventy-three entries.[101] Spending such a large portion of his time performing these voluntary tasks in Upper Canada, he was well aware that the Upper Canadians he was helping could contribute little to his maintenance. This, coupled with his problems with Denis-Benjamin Papineau at Bonsecours, convinced him that Lartigue's request meant more work and offered no guarantee that he would be able to dig his way out of debt. He knew he could not function in the proposed situation without further embarrassing himself and, by implication, the church. To Lartigue, he was frank but polite: should his situation not improve, he explained, he might have to seek his daily bread "outside of the diocese for which he had been ordained."[102]

Lartigue, himself embarrassed in the eyes of his episcopal colleague in Upper Canada, was not amused. His reply to Power was sharp. He pointed out that souls on one side of the Ottawa River "were every bit as precious in the eyes of God than those on the other," thus implying that Power should be more zealous and less preoccupied with money. "I also believe that a Priest," he continued, "zealously animated for God's glory and the salvation of souls can be content with what others would not consider to be an honest revenue, and, sufficient for their support; your predecessor at Petite-Nation ... and many of the Priests, in other countries and in less isolated areas than yours, have found a way to [live] honestly with less than £50 or £60."[103] Lartigue was even less impressed by Power's suggestion that he might leave the diocese in order to supplement his income, and he indicated to the priest that God would look unfavourably upon such a move.[104] Exasperated, Lartigue referred the matter to the new Bishop of Quebec, Joseph Signay, abandoning Power to deal with the guilt of leaving thousands of souls unattended.

Signay took charge of Power's case, but Lartigue attempted to influence his decision. The bishops disagreed over where Power should be sent. At first, Signay thought that Rigaud and its four townships would be appropriate. Lartigue, however, insisted that he needed another anglophone priest to serve the increasing numbers of Irish immigrants who were settling south of the St Lawrence River in lands adjacent to the old seigneurial tenure. Lartigue may have been outraged by Power's resistance, but he could not deny that Power and his linguistic skills were still needed in his episcopal district.[105] After taking a brief time to reflect, on 20 September 1833, Signay transferred Michael Power out of Petite-Nation and made him pastor of the Parish of Ste-Martine, in the seigneury of Beauharnois, in the Châteauguay River Valley.[106] After six years of saddlebag Christianity on the frontier, Power was entering a new phase of his career in a more settled agricultural area. He would have no permanent replacement at Petite-Nation – it seemed that its inhabitants were being punished for failing to support their priest. Father Thomas Moore was transferred to Nouveau Longueuil, and from there he would serve both Petite-Nation and Plantagenet as missions. Denis-Benjamin Papineau promised to support a successor to Power and pleaded for a new resident priest, but his pleas went unrequited.[107]

Michael Power was now ten days shy of his twenty-ninth birthday. He had been away from Halifax for seventeen years, six of which he had spent in two of the most underdeveloped regions in the diocese of Quebec. The frontier had frightened him. When he had first approached it, he was alone and young; he had barely left the sheltering confines of the seminary. Nothing was as he had expected it to be. He had needed a strategy to complete his mission, and he had been forced to draw often on his wellspring of patience. It has been all too tempting for writers, politicians, and historians to romanticize the frontier, infusing it with a determinism that cannot be sustained under historical scrutiny.[108] Indeed, the geography of the frontier – unnavigable rivers, hills, and mountains, vast expanses of woodland – made it difficult to replicate the church structures of Lower Canadian towns and their European antecedents. Difficult, but not impossible. No new religion was created on the frontier, despite the credit that a number of historians have given to Methodism, with its circuit riders and camp meetings; even the revival had to be enclosed within four walls when enthusiasm waned and cries for order, structure, and respectability were heard on the frontiers.[109] In fact, as populations grew in the hinterland, so did the possibility of re-creating the church in its familiar form. Many Catholics, despite their flexible applications of the canons, sexual morality, and pious discipline, sought out priests, built chapels, and even tried to support them. In time, the mission frontier became the settled frontier, and the churches of the old place were reconstructed in the new. The missionary needed patience and a plan.

Power, the newly minted priest in spiritual and cultural shock on the frontier, implemented the only kind of plan he knew. Instead of learning to move to the rhythm of frontier church life, he retreated behind rigorous church law. The law gave him a sense of security and purpose within a new reality that often seemed alien, threatening, and disordered. It provided him with a program to follow and a set of structures through which he could contain and corral the restless and chaotic elements he confronted. On Power's frontier, there would be banns for marriage, proper dispensations in canonically difficult cases, carefully completed registers, and correctly performed sacraments (even if it meant freezing his hands); children would be educated in a religious environment, not in a mixed school, where the Catholic faith would be ignored or watered down. Even when challenged by his bishop, Power would retort with a legalistic justification for his actions: a priest cannot serve two ordinaries at the same time.

But during his six years on the frontier Power also learned that by enforcing the laws, regulations, and disciplines of the church, he could neither compel people to pay him nor convince them to like him. At Petite-Nation, his failure to do both undermined his mission and perhaps his self-confidence. It is possible that the personal vocational struggle that he had faced in his final months at the minor seminary re-emerged. He had dealt with poverty before, but not while also coping with opposition to his views and having to do more work for less remuneration. Perhaps these external struggles caused him to question his life's work, as it had done before. He may have questioned whether he had the mental and physical stamina to continue, or asked himself if he should abandon the diocese. For Michael Power, the trials of Petite-Nation and the frontier were less catalysts of a crisis of faith than they were an opportunity to re-examine his conscience and his vocation. He emerged from his frontier experience tired, wounded, and spiritually unsettled. And, though Ste-Martine would offer him a new set of challenges, he would never leave the frontier behind completely.

CHAPTER FOUR

✲ "Clip the Gowns of the Clergy" ✲

STE-MARTINE PRESENTED MICHAEL POWER with the challenges of a new parish on a settlement frontier. For six years, a time equal to his service in missions on a more open frontier, Power undertook the day-to-day routines of a parish *curé*, a task for which the seminary had prepared him well. He traded in his saddle and paddle for a more ordered set of responsibilities: there were tithes to collect in the village and on the surrounding farms, *marguilliers* to supervise, pews to allocate, marriages to regularize, and buildings to maintain. Had this been all he had endeavoured on the south shore of the St Lawrence, this phase of his life would scarcely merit a full chapter. In most examinations of Power's life, Ste-Martine has been reduced to a phrase or even omitted entirely. Yet, upon closer scrutiny, and when placed within the context of the historical events of the day, Power's time in Ste-Martine was a crucial stage in his development.

Power was in search of peace when he left Petite-Nation, but he did not find it. Ironically, the Papineaus – in particular, Louis Joseph – whom Power had thought to escape with his transfer, would disrupt what might have otherwise been an uneventful tenure as pastor in the Châteauguay Valley. By 1838, the year he turned thirty-four, Power's life would be turned upside down by the second Lower Canadian rebellion and its aftermath. Soon after the cessation of the violence, he would be confronted by a second, quieter, revolution: the devotional reawakening of Catholicism that was sweeping Europe arrived with gale force in Lower Canada. In its own way, each revolution would have a formative effect on Power. The political revolution of the *patriotes* would solidify his political allegiance to the British Crown, and the Roman Catholic revolution would lead him to embrace the principles of ultramontanism.

At first appearance, the village of Ste-Martine, in the parish of the same name, seemed inviting. Although situated in a more recently settled region of the province, it boasted better-developed institutions than either of the parishes that Power had previously managed. The parish itself, shaped like a wedge of pie, was situated between the St Lawrence River and the American border. Nestled in the fertile Châteauguay Valley, the original mission of Ste-Martine was part of the seigneury of Beauharnois. It was held by Edward Ellice, a British settler and a Protestant. The ethnicity and religion of the seigneur was reflected in the first settlers of the underdeveloped southwest portion of the seigneury. During the great wave of British immigration after 1815, the upper Châteauguay Valley, with its rich soil, attracted hundreds of Scottish settlers. By 1823, when the registers for the mission of Ste-Martine were officially opened, the vast majority of the settlers in the region were English-speaking and Protestant. Ste-Martine's location – about ten miles from the St Lawrence and a little more than twenty from Montreal – made it possible for French Canadian and Irish Catholic settlers to enter the region at a rapid rate. Between 1823 and 1824, the Catholic population in the area (approximately 1,000[1]) increased at a rate of 11 per cent. Within the next five years, the rate of Catholic immigration increased by 15 per cent annually.[2]

By the time Power arrived, in October 1833, the parish of Ste-Martine was four years old and consisted of 3,356 souls.[3] The new parish compared favourably to Power's previous parishes in terms of size: it was vast. In addition to the village of Ste-Martine, Power was directed to serve areas to the south and east of the parish church, which included the future parishes of St-Jean-Chrysostom, St-Romain-de-Hemmingford, St-Malachie-d'Ormstown, and Lacolle.[4] Power was also in charge of the area's Irish Catholic immigrants, a responsibility that required him to travel extensively outside of his parish boundaries, particularly to the south shore of the St Lawrence River, where he would visit St-Anicet, Godmanchester, and the Crown lands adjoining the Mohawk territory at St-Regis, now Akwesasne. Perhaps as many as one in four of Power's own parishioners were Irish, presenting him once again with the Irish-French Canadian mix he had had in his previous pastoral charges. Attesting to Ste-Martine's bicultural reality was the number and type of marriages over which Power presided during his tenure as pastor, from October 1833 to October 1839. In that time, of 169 marriages, 120 (71 per cent) were endogamous French Canadian unions, whereas 44 (26 per cent) were endogamous Irish nuptials. Only four couples, or just over 2 per cent, were willing to bridge the parish's rigid French-Irish divide.[5]

Power was able to cover his large parochial and ethnic territories because he had assistant priests. Father Stephen Blythe covered the Irish frontier, while Father Joseph Marcoux, the missionary to the Iroquoian peoples, covered the territory adjacent to the parish. Marcoux, in fact, would maintain a lifelong friendship and an active correspondence with Power.[6] Power would never be without a curate at Ste-Martine – Lartigue kept him continuously supplied with help. In 1836, Lartigue sent Father Ryder of St-Jacques and, one year later, Father William Dolan, who had served briefly at Petite-Nation.[7] Ultimately, however, it was Power who had authority over the entire region; he was effectively the archpriest for all anglophone Catholics living south of the St Lawrence River and west of the island of Montreal.[8] This was a rather strange turn of events for Power, whose relationship with Lartigue was much in need of repair after Petite-Nation.

At Ste-Martine, Power gained valuable experience in the day-to-day operations of a settled parish and had the opportunity to hone his skills as a missionary priest on the frontiers of Lower Canada, where the St Lawrence disappeared into the upper province and the American republic. More importantly, his new circumstances helped to repair his self-esteem, which had been damaged by his experiences with the churchwardens and the seigneur at Bonsecours, as he made his mark as a careful and litigious manager of all aspects of parish life. His management efforts may have also helped to ease tensions with Lartigue and contributed to Lartigue's change of heart about Power's future in the diocese. The bishop had little choice, given the changing demography of the Châteauguay Valley and Beauharnois, other than to make this anglophone priest responsible for his own kind, but he would not have heaped greater responsibility and prestige on Power if he had thought that he was the same, perhaps weak, individual who had defied him in the Ottawa Valley.

And Power earned the bishop's trust. He quickly established most of the parish's essential foundations – for example, he had the cemetery, which was only a year old, enclosed.[9] He also spent considerable time addressing the sacramental needs and canonical disciplines of his rapidly growing congregation. At Ste-Martine, Power had less difficulty in collecting the pew rents and the *dîme*, and this freed him to seek reinvestment in the parish. In 1834, for instance, he oversaw the interest-free borrowing of £1,000 by the *fabrique* to install a heating system in the church (one suspects his memories of Grenville were still vivid), and, five years later, he arranged for general renovations to the church building.[10] For the first time, Power was able to cover his personal expenses and live in relative comfort. Regular payments of the tithe from his expanding congregation allowed him to subscribe to three major newspapers, purchase religious texts and other books for his library, and set a fine table – he indulged his special fondness for English cheeses.[11] At no time in his six years at Ste-Martine did he complain in his letters to Lartigue about a lack of income or parsimonious parishioners.

With Father Stephen Blythe doing much of the mission work in the hinterlands of the parish, Power was able to focus his efforts on the village of Ste-Martine and its immediate farm community. In doing so, he demonstrated an eye for the details of parish life and a litigiousness in applying church law that seemed to be a carry-over from his earlier postings on the frontier. Now, however, Power was dealing with a more settled community, a less transient population, and an established set of ecclesiastical structures. Shortly after his arrival, he made a complete inventory of the contents of the parish church, notably the sacristy, and forwarded it to Father Ignace Bourget, Lartigue's new secretary.[12]

But in his ongoing correspondence with Bourget and Lartigue, Power made it clear that not all was perfect in this parish. At the top of his list of administrative tangles was the issue of uncanonical marriages. He had to direct considerable energy towards regularizing marriages that had been contracted inappropriately; arranging for the mandated three announced marriage banns; and seeking dispensations for such things as mixed marriages, marriages between distant relations, and marriages involving girls under the age of sixteen. Power also found himself combatting the temptation of some parishioners to cohabit without any intention of marrying. Although navigating the shoals of marriage law would try the patience of most, Power seemed to enjoy the challenge of working with the canons to find a solution to a difficult case, in the process fine-tuning his skills as a canonist.[13] In most cases, Power took direct instructions from Lartigue, whose own resolve to uphold the canons of marriage and collect the necessary fees for dispensations was unequivocal. Power assured his superior that all was being done that could be done and referred the most difficult cases to him.[14] Later in life, Power would keep very few of the letters people sent him, including those from Lartigue, with whom he had a rich and sometimes torrid correspondence. However, he did retain letters discussing canonical questions related to marriage – it was as if he wanted to create a casebook of unusual circumstances, canonical interpretations, and plans of action for future use. He could refer to these letters when similar problems arose, or when he had to advise others on a prudent course to resolve legal entanglements involving marriages.

The parish also had its share of financial concerns. Shortly after his arrival, Power began to manage the pew-rental income, ensuring that the greatest possible number of parishioners was accommodated and that the rents were paid on time.[15] Close to the end of his tenure, the Irish Catholic farmers who dominated the northern section of his territory at Williamstown fell into arrears. When they had not paid their tithes for two consecutive years, Power bluntly reminded them that he had employed Father Blythe for a period of five years specifically to serve them, and that the assistant was owed compensation. In making his demand for payment to his local agent, Peter Maher, Power was adamant: "The farmers in your quarter can afford to pay now better than ever. Do not give them annoyance. If they refuse to pay quietly & peaceably, I will settle the business otherwise."[16] What "otherwise" means is not entirely clear, although Power did indicate that he was prepared to hire a lawyer to collect the unpaid tithes. When he left the parish, he took the ledger containing the names of the debtors with him. As far as he was concerned, these people were still on the hook for what they owed him – he even took the ledger with him when he went on to Toronto in 1842. While Power realized that the Williamstown farmers had suffered greatly during the crop failure of 1837, he also knew that they had had two good crop years, the earnings from which they could have used to pay their outstanding debts. Only two households on his list of forty paid a portion of their debts; most others deferred payment in the hope of negotiating a better deal with Power.

Over time, it appeared that Michael Power's diligence as a pastor had helped rebuild his relations with Lartigue. In fact, Lartigue began to seek Power's advice on how to manage certain aspects of Notre-Dame-de-Bonsecours, the parish that had seriously challenged Power's resolve to remain in the episcopal district of Montreal.[17] More was asked of Power. In November 1834, Lartigue and Bourget requested that Power take in a Father Keegan, who was to be employed as a schoolteacher until his canonical status as a priest was made clear. Evidently, Keegan, like many other foreign priests, had arrived in Lower Canada without the appropriate documentation – namely, the exeat from the bishop of his previous diocese. The reasons for the placement were explained to Power by Bourget, who told him that Lartigue had wanted Keegan placed "at the home of a good pastor" who would be able to watch over him carefully and assess his abilities.[18] Power, perhaps recognizing this as an opportunity to mend fences with Lartigue, and acknowledging his need for a Catholic schoolteacher, responded positively to the request, informing Bourget that a higher level of education was needed for the "poor country children" of the parish.[19] Although Keegan never took up the post – likely due to an early and unfavourable ruling on his previous activities in Ireland and New Orleans – Power had demonstrated himself to be co-operative.[20]

This precedent having been set, in 1835 Lartigue sent to Power a young man aspiring to the priesthood, Terrence Smith, whom he asked Power to mentor in dogmatic and moral theology, missals, liturgy, sacraments, and disciplines of the diocese. Lartigue added that Power and Smith were never to converse in English, because it was the bishop's desire that Smith become fluently bilingual.[21] The irony of this situation is too rich to ignore. This anglophone pastor who had earned Lartigue's disapproval two years earlier was now capable enough in the bishop's eyes to teach French and act as a theological and disciplinary mentor to a seminarian. Within six months, Power had informed his superior that Smith did not have what it took to be an Irish priest in Lower Canada. Although Power was unclear about which skills such a priest required, one suspects that given the bilingual functions essential to the ministries of other Irish priests in the province, Smith's French left much to be desired. Lartigue responded by offering Smith to Remi Gaulin, the coadjutor bishop of Kingston, which suggests that Smith's skills as a priest were not lacking – his failure to learn French was the only stumbling block.[22] Smith was ordained for Upper Canada and had a distinguished career in the Dioceses of Kingston and Bytown (Ottawa).[23] In the end, however, it was evident that Power had become one of Lartigue's principal "Irish" confidants.

Two issues confirmed Power's rising prominence in the episcopal district of Montreal and his emerging role as spokesperson for its anglophone priests. In 1835, he and Father Hyacinthe Hudon, who represented the francophone clergy, made a direct appeal to the Holy See for the division of the Diocese of Quebec and the establishment of the see of Montreal out of Quebec's western region.[24] Lartigue, both shrewd and cautious, did not make the petition himself but supported Power and Hudon as they made their plea to Signay and Pope Gregory XVI. Their reasons for wanting the new diocese were evident to those living in the Montreal district: the region was one of the fastest-growing in

British North America. In the 1830s, the natural increase in the French Canadian population, coupled with the steady stream of immigrants from Ireland, gave the Montreal district a total Catholic population of 245,000 – an increase of 83,000 (51.2 per cent) since the mid-1820s. This population explosion necessitated the creation of thirty-nine new parishes, the construction of new church buildings, and the renovation of outdated and smaller houses of worship.[25]

Despite the weight of the numbers and the commonsense view among locals that a self-governing Diocese of Montreal should exist, there were several formidable obstacles to be overcome. The Colonial Office and the British authorities in Lower Canada were reluctant to permit any new episcopal sees because they wanted to contain the spread of Catholicism in His Majesty's Protestant empire. Governors General in Lower Canada preferred to do business with a single representative of the "Romish" Church, and that person was the bishop of Quebec. The act of agreeing to the appointment of additional Catholic bishops to new episcopal sees was considered one that would complicate the current, more streamlined diplomatic channels between church and state. More-over, the relations between the Crown's representatives and the bishops of Quebec – from Briand, in 1766, to Signay – had been direct, gener-ally cordial, and mutually beneficial, with a few exceptions. Generally speaking, the bishop of Quebec had proven himself to be a reliable and loyal member of the colony's elite. A second bishop in the colony, or even a third, would potentially disrupt the efficient communications between the Crown and Quebec and give greater public prestige and voice to the Catholic Church in a province where the Church of England was meant to hold sway.[26]

There was also trouble within the world of the colony's ecclesiastical politics. The island of Montreal was still the seigneurial fief of the Société de St-Sulpice, which collected the seigneurial *lots et ventes* on the island and controlled the only parish church, Notre-Dame. Although Lartigue had been a member of the society, his appointment as the episcopal vicar of Montreal in 1826 had distanced him from his St-Sulpice confreres. The creation of a diocese at Montreal, where there had only been an episcopal district of the Diocese of Quebec, was considered by the Sulpi-cians to be an invasive measure with the potential to compromise their control over the island of Montreal. In an attempt to block it, they sent Jean-Baptiste Thavenet to Rome as their agent and lobbyist. Despite Thavenet's tremendous rearguard action, the attempt failed, and on 13

May 1836, with the consent of the Colonial Office, the pope created the Diocese of Montreal and promoted Lartigue to be its first bishop.[27]

For Hudon and Power, however, the creation of the diocese was only the first operation in a grand strategy hatched by the French Canadian hierarchy. For these two priests, as well as Lartigue and his secretary, Ignace Bourget, the elevation of Montreal to the status of diocese was an opportunity to reopen the issue of whether or not an ecclesiastical province could be created in British North America that would unite all of the existing dioceses and vicariates apostolic under the proposed archiepiscopal see of Quebec. In the fall and winter of 1835, Michael Power argued that the elevation of Montreal would help to bring to fruition the plan envisioned in Rome in 1819, when, without consulting the British government, Pope Pius VII raised Quebec to the status of archbishopric and made Joseph-Octave Plessis its first archbishop.[28] Because the Vatican made this move unilaterally, and since the Colonial Office protested it, Plessis never used his newly gained title publicly. British officials could not have expressed with greater clarity their reasons for refusing to approve Pius VII's action: this honour could not be conferred on the Roman Church in the colonies when no such honour existed for the Church of England in British North America. Fifteen years later, however, at the prompting of the young and energetic Ignace Bourget, Catholic leaders in French Canada revisited the issue from a different perspective. Quebec, Bourget and his supporters (including Power) insisted, could make its existing archiepiscopal powers effective over sees in Montreal, Upper Canada, Nova Scotia, Charlottetown, and Newfoundland. The British authorities, they added, need not fear a proliferation of Catholic power centres, because the supreme authority in the colonial church would still rest with the archbishop of Quebec. As had been the case in the past, the archbishop would be the exclusive and direct link with the British colonial administration. This argument would swirl within the hot-air currents of its own North Atlantic triangle (Rome-Quebec-London) for another decade, and a host of characters – Sulpicians, anglophone bishops, governors, popes, and clergy – would be sucked into its vortex.[29]

Power, who now appeared formally allied with Bourget, found himself drawn to the centre of Lower Canadian ecclesiastical politics. His role as spokesperson for priests of Irish, Scottish, and American backgrounds was firmly established by the time the Diocese of Montreal was created. He – instead of Lartigue, who wished to maintain a lower profile –

frequently entered the public sphere to articulate positions or negotiate questions. Lartigue rewarded Power by advancing his supervision in the Beauharnois and Châteauguay regions, keeping him well supplied with assistants, assigning him to mentor seminarians who aspired to positions in the district, and entrusting him to act as an investigator when trouble was brewing in adjoining parishes.[30] For Power, perhaps as important as regaining the trust of Lartigue was catching the eye of Bourget, with whom he shared a zest for order, ecclesiastical discipline, and the rule of church law. This was a fortuitous relationship for Power; as Lartigue's health waned in the late 1830s,[31] Bourget became a rising force in the French Canadian church.

The relatively peaceful rhythms of parish life at Ste-Martine would not last. As early as 1834, it appeared to most colonial observers of provincial politics that the conflict between the government and the Parti Canadien in the Legislative Assembly was approaching a crisis point. Their principal source of disagreement was the application of the Constitution Act of 1791, which had created the separate provinces of Upper and Lower Canada and accorded each a bicameral legislature that crudely mirrored the parliamentary arrangement in the United Kingdom. In Power's time, Lower Canada was ruled by a governor general, who represented the Crown. That governor appointed members of the Legislative Council, a poor facsimile of Britain's Upper Chamber, and members of the Executive Council, roughly equivalent to a cabinet but not responsible to the assembly, as would be the case today. The Legislative Assembly, inspired by the British House of Commons, was the only elected body, but the governor was not bound in any way to select his executive councillors from among the elected members of the assembly. Although the French Canadian majority in the assembly enjoyed electoral and franchise rights shared by few other Catholics in the British Empire, francophone leaders – Louis-Joseph Papineau, Denis-Benjamin Viger, and Louis-Hippolyte LaFontaine, to name only a few – became increasingly frustrated that the real power was in the Executive Council and the Legislative Council, and that neither of these was responsible to the popular will as expressed by the elected members of the assembly.[32]

The constitutional stalemate that arose between the assembly and the governor was exacerbated by changes taking place within French Canadian society. In the early nineteenth century, young French Canadian men who were educated, like Power, at the Petit Séminaire de Montréal, the Collège de St-Hyacinthe, or other classical colleges were filling positions in the province's law offices, medical clinics, accounting firms, and newspapers. Members of this new generation of liberal professionals were assertive, energetic, and ambitious. By the 1830s, they had become prominent members of the assembly and were speaking to the people from the pages of *Le canadien, La minerve,* and *L'avenir,* a publication whose very name ("the future") reflected the movement for change in European Catholicism by Félicité de Lamennais.[33] The young liberal professionals in the assembly desired access to the corridors of effective power, but they were denied because the governor resisted any form of ministerial responsibility. It was clear that regardless of the strength of the ruling party in the assembly, the governor would form the councils as he pleased. In 1834, the Parti Patriote, which became the reform voice of a new generation of French Canadians, issued ninety-two resolutions demanding constitutional reform, including ministerial responsibility, an elected legislative council, and greater liberties for the common people of Lower Canada.[34] When the administration rejected these demands, the Parti Patriote used the assembly's limited powers over the public purse to deny the governor his "supply." A deadlocked legislature, calls for broader democracy based on French and American models, and a cash-starved ministry created a political powder keg in Lower Canada.

This political crisis, which Power followed in the newspapers, was exacerbated by developments he observed among his parishioners. On the ground in Ste-Martine, Power would have witnessed a negative turn in the farm economy, a decline in the income of his parishioners, and a resultant social unrest in the region. A *curé* would notice a recession, particularly when it affected his income, gleaned through the *dîme,* and when the parish income decreased because of a decline in pew rents. The Lower Canadian agricultural economy had, in fact, been in trouble since the beginning of the century. Per-acre wheat yields were in decline, and export markets for wheat and flour were faltering. The drop in crop prices, or stagnation of prices in some regions, was most notable after 1823, but they were "violent" after 1830.[35] British imports of colonial wheat declined by 78 per cent between 1828 and 1837, while total exports of the wheat staple from Quebec City declined by 55 per cent over the same period.

To make matters worse, Upper Canadian wheat production was now challenging the former dominance of the Lower Canadian staple in the colonial wheat trade, leading to steady economic growth in the western colony and creeping recession in its eastern neighbour.[36] Historians have debated the origins and causes of this economic crisis for decades, citing such factors as the wheat fly plague, new competition, international depression, and the alleged inefficiencies of French Canadian farming techniques as the principal reasons for the economic distress and social unrest that had erupted in the province by 1837. In the midst of this crisis, *habitants* began to assert themselves in traditional group institutions, where they could flex their collective muscle: the *fabrique*, the local militia, and the festive *charivari* (a hazing ritual for newlyweds). They sought dramatic change – they wanted to overthrow existing social, political, and (in some cases) religious authorities who were deemed obstacles to liberty.[37] What became increasingly obvious to Power and others like him at the grassroots level was that farmers were in dire straits and barely able to meet their seigneurial *lots et ventes* obligations or keep up with their tithes.[38]

In fact, many farmers saw the seigneury system as part of the problem. Businessmen and merchants in towns and cities had already voiced their resistance to paying *lots et ventes*, and test cases had been fought against the Sulpicians by entrepreneurs in Montreal eager to shed their seigneurial obligations and witness the speedy growth of a capitalist economy.[39] In the seigneury of Beauharnois, where Power was *curé* at Ste-Martine, the local *censitaires* had grave reservations about their living situation, and particularly about the stringency of their feudal obligations. Edward "Bear" Ellice, the Anglo-Protestant absentee seigneur of Beauharnois, was one of the most notorious landlords in Lower Canada. As prospective *censitaires* left the overcrowded older seigneuries and moved into the parishes and missions of Ste-Martine, St-Timothée, St-Clément, and Châteauguay, they encountered two problems. Ellice was willing to open up the undeveloped lands in his seigneury and transfer grants to freehold tenure under the condition that settlers pay a fee of one hundred pounds, double the price of land in the Eastern Townships. Moreover, in the interim, Ellice jacked up his rents and charged those *censitaires* who violated their seigneurial agreements unreasonable fines.[40] It is little wonder that under such poor economic conditions, and considering the burden placed on them by landlords like Ellice, farmers became increasingly agitated in places like Beauharnois.

Signs of the strain on the social peace in rural Lower Canada began to appear in the Montreal region by the mid-1830s. In some parishes, radical *habitants* were successfully contesting the elections of the *marguilliers* and taking more direct control of parish affairs.[41] The liberal professional politicians made an effort to encourage this local democratization as early as 1831, when they sponsored a *fabrique* bill that would open elections to a greater number of *censitaires*.[42] Only the

"Wintering in Lower Canada, 1838–1841," by Philip John Bainbridge. Here we glimpse the Chatêauguay Valley, where Power encountered the *patriote* insurrection of 1838 (NA, 1983-47-66)

aggressive intervention of Lartigue and his political allies quashed this bill, which Lartigue regarded as a threat to the authority of the clergy in their parishes. The *habitants* continued to perform the traditional *charivari* to express their displeasure with certain transgressions of the unwritten rules of decorum in their community – particularly when the newlyweds involved were seen to have married for the wrong reasons (age, avarice, sensuality).[43] The *charivari* was enacted by a mob of young men, dressed in disguise, perhaps intoxicated, who created an unholy din for nights on end. It was easily adapted from its original purpose to serve political ends. In the 1830s, political enemies and members of the clergy became *charivari* targets as *habitants* expressed anger about rents, the *dîme*, and their social and economic circumstances.

The confluence of the agricultural crisis, a dysfunctional constitution, the rise of the liberal professional class, and social unrest in the seigneuries created an explosive situation in the Montreal district. By 1837, more fuel had been added to the fire: an international financial crisis; the failure of several major American banks and the subsequent withholding of cash payments; and the polarization of local politics between *patriote* politicians and those who supported Governor General Gosford. Louis-Joseph Papineau had emerged as the charismatic leader of an increasingly radicalized Parti Patriote. The movement took on a French Canadian nationalist character, and Papineau was joined by several prominent anglophones, in particular, Irish Catholic physician and politician Edmund Bailey O'Callaghan, who was also editor of the radical *Vindicator*, to which Power had briefly subscribed.[44] Gosford failed to break the deadlock between his administration and the assembly, and there was rampant hunger in the countryside,[45] compounded by a dramatic rise in food prices and a shortage of food and hard currency. Violence was in the air.

The urgency of the situation was not lost on the Catholic bishops and local clerical leaders like Power. In October 1837, Lartigue issued a carefully worded *mandement* ("mandate") forbidding any revolutionary activity against the legitimate government of the province. While much of his text was devoted to the pronouncements of Pope Gregory XVI's recent condemnations of revolution, he did make a final appeal to the heart: "Have you ever thought seriously about the horrors of civil war? Have you thought of the rivers of blood flooding your streets and your countryside and ... realized that, as experience proves it, almost without exception all popular revolutions are a bloodthirsty undertaking; and that the philosopher from Geneva, the author of the *Social Contract*, the great mistake of the People's sovereignty, says somewhere that a Revolution would be too expensive if it cost a single drop of blood?"[46] This pastoral letter was a public affirmation of what Lartigue had already told the 150 priests, including Power, who had gathered in July for the consecration of Ignace Bourget as the new coadjutor bishop of Montreal. Lartigue had told his priests in the strongest of terms that they were responsible for ensuring charity and unity within their parishes and that no transgressions of the law or dealings with contraband goods would be tolerated.[47] The church's position was clear: it was firmly allied with the British administration, and each priest's duty to the Crown was unequivocal. This policy was in keeping with views expressed by the Lower Canadian church in crises past and by the papacy; in Europe, the church had thrown in its lot with the Holy Alliance (the United Kingdom, Prussia, Russia, and Austria) in an effort to bury the residual effects of the French Revolution.

Power's response to Lartigue's predictable call for loyalty to the Crown was nuanced compared to those of some of his French Canadian colleagues. As an Irish Canadian priest, he was unlikely to harbour the strong nationalist feelings of men like Father A.M. Blanchet of St-Charles or Father Étienne Chartier of St-Benoît, both of whom had openly supported – and, in the case of the latter, died – for the *patriote* cause.[48] Power could not readily identify with that cause because he was bound by loyalty and pride to the two dominant forces in his life: the church and the Crown. This does not mean that he was uncritical of the factors that threatened the peace of his province and parish. On a daily basis, he witnessed the suffering of his parishioners, and he had also read widely in Irish constitutional history, particularly about the peaceful and popular initiatives of Daniel O'Connell, whose Catholic Association had successfully pressured the British government for the emancipation of Catholics in the realm.[49] In later years, Power's involvement in issues related to Irish politics and immigration would confirm his O'Connellite sympathies – he believed in political reform by peaceful and constitutional means. As a subscriber to the *Vindicator* during its radical phase of publication, 1833–34, he was familiar with O'Callaghan's rhetoric; he would have been aware of the similarities between the beliefs of local Irish patriots and those of O'Connell, and he would have seen where O'Callaghan's radicalism veered from the course charted by Ireland's "great liberator." Sifting through the pile of newspapers in his rectory parlour, Power would have noted the divergence between the *Vindicator* and the Montreal *Gazette* over such issues as the ninety-two resolutions, fiscal control by the people, an elected legislative council, and a free press.[50] O'Callaghan, however, would become increasingly radicalized, and when his paper was closed down, he would move towards advocating armed confrontation, a course that Power would have condemned.[51]

Power left no formal political manifestos and few written clues as to his explicit political allegiances or theories of governance. Nevertheless, one can review his correspondence and actions during the rebellion crisis and hypothesize that he was a political conservative with strong ties to the existing constitution, the reform of which, he believed, could be attained within existing legislative structures. There is no evidence to suggest that he was influenced by the anti-ministerial stance of the *Vindicator* when the crisis of 1837 and 1838 was underway. In fact, during the rebellion he subscribed to only two papers, both of which were loyal to the Gosford administration: the Montreal *Gazette* and *L'ami de peuple*, the only French-language paper allowed to publish in the Montreal district during the rebellion.[52] If he had sympathized with the rebellion, the frugal Power would not have wasted money on newspapers whose points of view he rejected. Moreover, since no *patriote*-oriented papers were available, he would likely have done as many rebellion sympathizers had and refused to take any paper at all. While one could argue that Power retained his subscriptions to protect himself from the recriminations of the loyalists, this too seems unlikely, since his district was marked by a strong sympathy for the *patriotes*.

Aspects of Power's thirty-year journey from Halifax to Ste-Martine also suggest that he would have been a staunch loyalist. When he was a child in the parish of St Peter's, Edmund Burke had instilled in him a strong respect for legitimate authority. Later, in Montreal, although many of his seminary classmates began to move towards joining the restless liberal professional class and jettisoning the political conservatism of their Suplician teachers, Power remained close to the Sulpicians, particularly Father Vincent Quiblier of Notre-Dame Basilica. The Sulpicians gave strong support to the government throughout the crisis of 1837–38 – so much so that they feared that their seminary would be attacked by the *patriotes*. As a precaution, they burned their papers.[53] Power's sense of loyalty to the government was also evident in his personal correspondence with Bourget, who instructed him to keep his eyes on a neighbouring priest who may have been encouraging dissent among the Irish immigrants in Beauharnois and surrounding area.[54] While such evidence is circumstantial, the case for Power's loyalty is strengthened by his actions when rebellion finally erupted in the Richelieu Valley to the east of his parish and in the Deux-Montagnes region north of Montreal.

In November 1837, mass meetings convened by the *patriotes* resulted in the formation of armed camps in the countryside. The bishop's *mandement* was ignored as the villages of the Richelieu Valley became weapons depots and marshalling areas for a *patriote* revolt. On 23 November 1837, British troops were repelled by a *patriote* force at St-Denis. Papineau, who had fled the area before the actual shooting began, found safe haven in the United States.[55] Two days later, Sir John Colborne's infantry crushed the *patriotes* in their stronghold of St-Charles, and later still, on 14 December, British regulars effectively broke the back of the insurrection when they destroyed the remains of the *patriote* army at St-Eustache. In this dramatic climax to the rebellion, the *patriotes* made a last desperate stand, taking up a defensive posture in the parish church. British Lieutenant Colonel George A. Wetherall ordered the church torched, and the remaining defenders were either burned alive or shot as they jumped from the flaming holes where stained glass had once been.[56] With the *patriote* army vanquished and the town reduced to a smouldering ruin, the rebellion was effectively over.

Ste-Martine had been spared the military engagements of 1837, but threats to peace still menaced the Montreal district. In 1838, the British government had sent parliamentarian John "Radical Jack" Lambton, Earl of Durham, to assume governorship of the two Canadas and to conduct an investigation of the causes of the rebellions in both provinces.[57] In an effort to curb any further violence, Durham issued a blanket pardon to most of the rank-and-file insurgents. Church leaders were quick to reiterate their loyalty to the new queen, Victoria, and in a declaration released in December, the Catholic clergy distanced themselves from the rebels: "That the clergy has seen with an extreme affection the state of political division, agitation and insubordination in which a part of this province has found itself plunged, and particularly the district of Montreal, where despite the efforts of Catholic Pastors and the other loyal subjects of Your Majesty, we have had to deplore the insurrection of a portion of six or seven counties of twenty-one in this district."[58] On 16 January, Power, his assistant William Dolan, Father Labelle of neighbouring Châteauguay, and missionary priest Joseph Marcoux added their signatures to this loyalty manifesto.[59] Shortly before this, on 8 January, Lartigue had issued a second *mandement* restating his abhorrence for the rebellion and calling for reparation and penitence in his diocese.[60]

Amid these professions of loyalty and calls for the restoration of peace and harmony, the insurrection was still alive, though it had moved underground. After the defeat in 1837, the surviving *patriote* leaders, in conjunction with sympathizers in Upper Canada and the United States, formed a clandestine society known as the Frères Chasseurs (or the "Hunters' Lodges"). With his parish strategically located in the border country between the United States and Montreal, Power found himself at the epicentre of the new guerrilla movement. The recruitment efforts of the officers of the Frères Chasseurs in Ste-Martine and the seigneuries of Châteauguay and Beauharnois were meeting with some success. Despite higher crop yields in the smaller parishes close to Ste-Martine – St-Timothée and St-Clément – there was still much dissatisfaction over the draconian policies of Edward Ellice and his seigneurial agents. And there was increasing resentment of the tithe. According to James Perrigo, one of Power's parishioners, he and his fellow Frères Chasseurs intended to "abolish the *lots et ventes*, make the country free, do away with the rents, and clip the gowns of the clergy."[61]

To this end, throughout the summer of 1838, another of Power's parishioners, Joseph Dumouchel, busily inducted other parishioners into the Frères Chasseurs. As an Eagle,[62] or local commander, Dumouchel would have his subalterns blindfold the inductee and, under cover of darkness in some secret hideout, make him swear his loyalty to the revolution and promise to die rather than betray a compatriot.[63] As the Frères Chasseurs network expanded from Quebec City to Beauharnois, so did anticipation among its members that the exiled *patriote* leaders – Papineau, O'Callaghan, and Robert Nelson – would return from the United States and, leading a combined force of Americans and expatriate Canadians, link up with the Frères Chasseurs to capture Canada. Frères Chasseurs living under Power's nose at Ste-Martine were responsible for cutting the transportation links from Upper Canada to Montreal and clearing the way for an invading army that would enter the region from the American frontier.[64]

Whether Power had any indication of what was transpiring beneath his nose is unknown. In the flurry of letters exchanged by Power, Bourget, and Lartigue, there is no mention of rebellion brewing in Ste-Martine. This signals either Power's fear that his correspondence would be intercepted or his sense that such topics were not germane to discussions of official church matters; it could also indicate that he did not know a thing, given the heavy veil of secrecy that shrouded the activities of the Frères Chasseurs. Nevertheless, whether he knew it or not, Power was sitting on a time bomb, which by November 1838 was ready to explode.

On the evening of Saturday, 3 November 1838, Power would have readied himself for the Masses to be celebrated at the parish church the following morning. The weather was miserable, and Power likely went to bed to stay warm.[65] All night, Ste-Martine was pelted by a cold, driving rain – there was little incentive for any creature to venture outdoors. As Power and many of his 3,558 parishioners slept and dreamed, the Frères Chasseurs mobilized. In the wee hours of Sunday, 4 November, dozens of men armed with muskets, pikes, and pitchforks moved from farmhouse to farmhouse on both sides of the Châteauguay River, which bisected the parish. Bleary-eyed occupants who responded to the knock on their doors knew instantly that these night visitors were not there to invite them to a *charivari*. When they testified later before British military authorities, many of the incarcerated rebels claimed that they were not members of the Frères Chasseurs and had been unwilling participants in the uprising. At Ste-Martine, shoemaker Paul Barré, bailiff Gédéon

Neveu, and farmers Vital St-Onge Payant, Louis Thibault, Michel Trem-blay, Louis Turcot, and François Vallée all claimed that they had been pressed into service against their will.[66] While the investigations of the military court and some contemporary historians have cast doubt upon such professions of innocence, Power suspected that some of these people had, in fact, been coerced by press gangs.[67] Regardless of their disposi-tion, willing or unwilling, 300 men set off from Ste-Martine in the rain and headed for the manor house at Beauharnois, where they hoped to seize an alleged cachet of arms and cannons.[68] At the head of the column were Ste-Martine's youngest physician, Jean-Baptiste-Henri Brien, and the local Eagle, farmer turned recruitment officer Joseph Dumouchel.[69] They left behind their pastor, snug in his bed, unaware of the unfold-ing drama.

Before dawn, the Ste-Martine detachment of Frères Chasseurs was joined by units from other parts of the seigneury. Led by Dumouchel, rallied by his calls to end the seigneury system and the tithe forever, the mob attacked the Beauharnois manor house, captured Ellice's son and daughter-in-law; two of his nieces; the seigneurial agent, John Ross; and Lieutenant Colonel Laurence George Brown of the Beauharnois Loyal Volunteers. In one sweeping move, the rebels had decapitated the local leadership, seized enemy headquarters, and sent their prisoners under Brien and heavy guard to Châteauguay, already in the hands of the Frères Chasseurs.[70] But at this point the attack seemed to stall. The rebels decided to consolidate their positions: half the force would defend the manor; half would go to the farm of George Washington Baker, where they would drill while awaiting orders to join the main invasion in the border country near Napierville.[71]

By the morning of Monday, 5 November, it was clear to the remaining parishioners at Ste-Martine that something was wrong. In his testimony to British military officials, Joseph Dumouchel admitted, "our parish was in great agitation."[72] While eyewitness records are fragmentary and at times contradictory, it appears that the insurgents controlled the roads in and out of town. They were attempting to protect Camp Baker, as they now called Baker's farm, which was several miles to the west of Power's rectory and further separated from the village by the Châteauguay River.[73] The base of operations at Camp Baker linked rebel forces at several nearby villages and parishes. Thirty-year-old François-Xavier Touchette, blacksmith at Ste-Martine, had spent weeks making pikes for the insurgents, while Louis Dumouchel, local hotel keeper and brother of the Eagle, had provided a safe haven for insurgent leaders. Also, shopkeeper Joseph Brazeau had acted as Joseph Dumouchel's assistant during the recruitment drive in the spring and summer.[74] The village was firmly in the hands of the Frères Chasseurs, and the leaders and members of this occupying army were well known to Power, who had married at least four of the Frères in the previous three years.[75]

The pastor urged calm, and he was later credited with maintaining a semblance of order in the village during the crisis, despite some debilitating personal problems.[76] Since he was the local representative of the church, which had opposed the insurrection, and a man known for his personal loyalty to the Crown and the colonial administration, it comes as little surprise that the Frères Chasseurs allegedly imprisoned him in the rectory for a short time. The evidence of this incarceration is sketchy, at best, and Power did not leave written testimony of the incident. In 1840, however, on a personal visit to Halifax, he shared the details with the editor of the Cross, who published the tale after Power died, seven years later.[77] But during the rebellions it was not unusual for the patriotes to place curés who were government sympathizers under house arrest. During the Beauharnois uprising, Power's colleague Father Michel Quintal was placed under house arrest, and his rectory was used by the insurgents as a holding area for the prisoners captured at the seigneurial manor.[78] If Power had, in fact, been held prisoner, the experience would have enabled him to account for the actions of at least forty of the men who were eventually taken into custody by the loyalist forces.

The rebellion of 1838 was short-lived. On 9 November, loyalist volunteers exchanged fire briefly with the Frères Chasseurs outside Camp Baker, but they withdrew when they recognized the superior force of the rebels. However, knowing that the loyalists were closing in on them – including recently arrived troops from Glengarry in Upper Canada and volunteers from nearby Huntington – the insurgents slipped out of the base camp and headed off to link up with the remaining rebel forces near the border. Meanwhile, Wolfred Nelson's main force of Frères Chasseurs had failed, as had a group of insurgents who had tried to recruit the Mohawks of Kanawake to their cause. The Mohawks turned the tables on the intruders, took them prisoner, and awaited the arrival of government forces.[79] When loyalist volunteers under Major John Campbell arrived at Camp Baker and discovered it abandoned, they lost no time in torching Baker's house and barns and those of Baker's brother-in-law, James Perrigo, who lived nearby. Perrigo was well known to Power, because only two years before, Power had officiated at the Baker-Perrigo nuptials in the parish church.[80] With the rebel farms a smouldering ruin, the volunteer force entered the village, took control of the streets, and promptly set fire to Brazeau's store.[81] Scattered, frightened, and beaten, the remnants of the rebel forces scurried home to hide, fled across the border, or were captured by militia, regular troops, or volunteers.

We know little about what Power did during the occupation and the events immediately following the liberation of Ste-Martine by armed loyalists. From the fragmentary evidence available, however, we can deduce that Power was faced with two serious problems: the Glengarry troops and volunteers had wreaked considerable damage on local property, and over three dozen of his parishioners had been incarcerated by the military and transferred to Montreal jails. Power indicated to Bourget and Lartigue the extent of the damage that had been inflicted on farmsteads, private homes, and commercial establishments; he also suggested that some church property might have been damaged during the crisis.[82] There is no other evidence to substantiate the destruction of church property, nor were any claims filed by the church for compensation, either at the time or after the passage, in 1849, of the *Rebellion Losses Bill*. In fact, the military authorities lauded themselves for the restraint demonstrated by loyalist forces in pacifying the Ste-Martine area.[83] Nevertheless, Lartigue requested an account of property pillaged during the insurrection.

Perhaps the more pressing problem for Power was the fact that so many of his parishioners were sitting in Montreal jail cells. While it may have been of some comfort that the approximately 300 loyalist volunteers raised in the parish offset the roughly equal number of insurgents, the fact remained that farms were left unworked and families were deprived of fathers and sons. In November, Power drafted a list of forty incarcerated parishioners of whom nearly half were married; ten had children. Some fifty-one children in the parish were without a father due to the incarceration of these insurgents.[84] Official lists from Ste-Martine also include an additional seven men and one woman who were never brought to trial. Of these, for example, Joseph Brazeau, whose shop had been razed, had fled to the United States, eluding prosecution. The first three men on Power's list were the acknowledged kingpins of the local insurrection: Jean-Baptiste-Henri Brien, Joseph Dumouchel, and Charles Bergevin Sr.[85] Also included were four men at whose weddings he had officiated: Charles Bergevin Jr, Godfoi Chaloux, Jean-Marie Lefebvre, and James Perrigo, all of whom were local farmers. Perrigo was charged with being a leader of the rebellion.[86] Despite strong circumstantial evidence that Perrigo was guilty of high treason, the conflicting testimony of witnesses called before the military court made it impossible for the prosecutors to secure his conviction, and he was acquitted.[87] Power made no attempt to defend Perrigo, although on 24 January 1839 he did intercede on behalf of six other parishioners – Gédéon Brazeau (shopkeeper and relative of the notorious Frères Chasseurs organizer Joseph Brazeau), Jean Laberge, Augustin Legault, Louis Gédéon Neveu (bailiff), Vital St-Onge Payant (farmer), Michel Primeau (farmer), and François Vallée (farmer) – all of whom were subsequently released. They returned to their lives in the parish.[88]

Power's intercession may have saved Vallée's life. The man faced a court martial on 8 April 1839, and he was found guilty of all charges, including associating with the Frères Chasseurs and bearing arms against the Crown. Vallée was sentenced to death by hanging, but the decision was reversed, his release was secured with bail, and he was eventually pardoned.[89] He was thirty years old, married with no children. All that the remaining records indicate is that he knew several of the convicted Frères Chasseurs well. One of these men, Louis Turcot, claimed that Vallée had ordered him to go to Beauharnois on the first night of the insurrection.[90] Neither Power nor the court believed this, so, instead of dying with a noose around his neck, Vallée died of natural causes in 1841.[91] Another man whose release was secured by Power, Louis Gédéon Neveu, claimed that he had been at Camp Baker under protest, although there were accusations that he had helped to supply the Frères Chasseurs with whisky.[92] Upon his release, he returned to his modest *cens* in the parish, which he retained in 1854, when the seigneurial system was finally abolished.[93]

Other members of Power's congregation were not as fortunate. Of the forty men arrested, most were tried in military court, beginning in January 1839. Brien – the young doctor with whom Power may have had only a passing acquaintance, since he had only lived in Ste-Martine a short time – was effectively banished from the province, as he was forbidden to come within a 600-mile radius of his home. Brien had been a principal Frères Chasseurs operative, and he avoided execution by volunteering evidence against his compatriots.[94] Eight of the Ste-Martine prisoners had their death sentences commuted but were shipped to the penal colony of New South Wales, Australia, where they were assigned to work details at Longbottom, west of Sydney. For six years, they had only intermittent contact, by mail, with their loved ones in Ste-Martine.[95] In 1840, Louis Dumouchel, the unhappy innkeeper and brother of the Eagle, contracted a stomach illness and died, as did fellow prisoner Ignace-Gabriel Chèvrefils, one year later.[96] By 1845, after community leaders had spent years petitioning the colonial authorities – Bishop Bourget offered some help, as did politician Denis-Benjamin Viger and Governor General Charles Metcalfe – the remaining Frères Chasseurs returned to Canada. Six of them – Charles Bergevin Sr. (*dit* Langevin), Constant Buisson, Joseph Dumouchel, Jean Laberge, François-Xavier Touchette, and Louis Turcot – returned to Ste-Martine. Several of these men moved on with their families and established homes elsewhere in the province. Their lives had been shattered and their property destroyed; their children had grown in their absence, and their home had become part of the strange and threatening creation called "the Province of Canada."[97] Power was not in Ste-Martine to greet them. By the time of their homecoming, he had departed the Diocese of Montreal for good.

The rebellions had cemented Power's loyalty to the British Crown and its representatives in British North America. His confidence in the empire became more evident as he rose in prominence in the Diocese of Montreal, drawing ever closer to Bourget, who succeeded Lartigue as bishop in 1840. Disturbed by Catholic participation in the rebellions, Power wrote a strongly worded letter to Lord Stanley at the Colonial Office advocating the extension of Catholic institutions to the western Canadian frontier. He believed that establishing such institutions in what had been the hinterland of Upper Canada would help to quell "the spirits of insubordination and fierce democratic spirit which unhappily exists in a formidable degree."[98] This letter, perhaps Power's most boldly political statement to that point in his life, tells us a great deal about the man who emerged from the 1830s tumult of provincial politics and society.

The letter reveals three things. First, by writing to Stanley, Power was clearly advancing Bourget's plan to create an archiepiscopal see in Quebec, with suffragan dioceses from the Atlantic to the interior of the continent. The fact that he wrote the letter while he was in London, England, serving as Bouget's aid during the bishop's European tour indicates just how close the young priest had come to Bourget, the rising star of the Canadian church. Second, the letter shows the depths of Power's political conservatism – or, at the very least, his ability to use the potential of political instability to justify extending the Catholic Church, an institution he regarded as a bulwark against fierce, unbridled democratic forces. In his mind, the church was an instrument for quelling dissent against the state. Third, the very language of the letter hearkens back to Power's identification of the frontier as a wild and undisciplined Babylon in need of order and strong moral leadership. Thus it appears that by the end of his tenure at Ste-Martine, Power's ideas regarding the mutually beneficial reciprocity of church and state had deepened, as had his allegiance to the empire.

At this time, others began to see these qualities in Power. Upon his consecration as bishop of Toronto in May 1842, the Montreal *Gazette* celebrated him by pointing to his loyalty to the Crown, particularly during the insurrection at Ste-Martine.[99] Governor Charles Poulet Thompson, Baron Sydenham, and Sydenham's successor, Sir Charles Bagot, held Power in very high esteem. None of these men wanted to see the proliferation of Catholic bishops in British North America, but if such appointments were necessary, Michael Power was the kind of cleric they wanted. Bagot wrote, "Of Mr. Power I have received a very favourable account. He is a man of enlarged views – of mild temper combined with firmness – and of undoubted loyalty. I believe it would have been scarcely possible to select a better man for the office or one more harmoniously to act with the government."[100]

While the political revolutions of the 1830s had confirmed Power's patriotism and sense of duty to the state, Bourget would lead him in directions that would have a similar effect on his sense of being a Catholic cleric.

CHAPTER FIVE

∿ The Ultramontane Revolution ∿

NO SOONER HAD ONE REVOLUTION ENDED in Lower Canada than another one began stirring. Michael Power would have little time to help repair the damage wreaked by the insurrection and trials of 1838 and 1839 before he was called to serve the diocese in a new way. On 15 September 1839, nearly six years after Power's appointment to Ste-Martine, the sickly and frail Jean-Jacques Lartigue transferred him to the Parish of La Nativité de Très Sainte-Vièrge at Laprairie. Power had only about two weeks to pack his things, complete his unfinished business, and say farewell to his parishioners.[1]

La Nativité, where he reported on 6 October, was of comparable size to Ste-Martine, numbering about 3,835 souls.[2] Unlike Ste-Martine, however, La Nativité was one of the oldest parishes in the diocese, with a well-settled farming population dating back to the late seventeenth century. In 1670, the Jesuits had erected a modest chapel on their seigneurial grant at Laprairie with the primary intention of serving the local Native peoples, particularly the Mohawks who had settled at Sault-St-Louis, now Kanawake, on the banks of the St Lawrence. By 1687, the Jesuits had found that they were too absorbed in this apostolate, so they ceded the day-to-day operations of the parish to the Sulpicians, who renovated the original church structure to better accommodate the growing French-Canadian population on the south shore.[3] In 1705, the Sulpicians had constructed a stone church on the site to replace the earlier wooden structures. Nearly all the male religious orders left the colony after the 1760 conquest, and the remaining Jesuits were disbanded by the Vatican in 1773, but the Sulpicians continued to serve the parish until they were replaced by diocesan clergy.

Laprairie was one of the most strategically placed parishes in the diocese in terms of its proximity to episcopal power. Situated directly across the river from Montreal, it was also a transportation hub. Its ferry was the principal conveyance for farmers, merchants, traders, and the military between the south shore and Montreal. In 1836, this transportation link was augmented when Laprairie became the northern terminus for the Lake Champlain-St Lawrence Railway, the first steam-train line built in Canada. Drained by the St-Jacques and Montreal Rivers, and providing links to the St Lawrence for the Tortue and Portage Rivers to the west, the seigneury offered not only excellent possibilities for agriculture but also many access routes to the interior beyond the St Lawrence flood plain.[4] It is little wonder, then, that between 1821 and 1840, Laprairie's parish population grew by over one-third.[5]

The reasons for Power's transfer to Laprairie were never clearly articulated by the ordinary. Unlike the transfers from St-Frédéric and Notre-Dame-de-Bonsecours, this one did not seem to be the result of a request by Power, because when it came about he was preoccupied with the rebuilding of his parish community, which was suffering the social and economic fallout of the rebellion. Nor is there any evidence that scandal or incompetence caused the cessation of his pastoral duties at Ste-Martine. In fact, the record fragments that survive from the period indicate that the opposite was true. In his six years there, Power had rehabilitated his image as a complainer in Lartigue's eyes and emerged as an articulate spokesperson on matters germane to diocesan politics, particularly as they affected the small group of anglophone priests serving linguistically and culturally mixed communities. Lartigue had bestowed upon Power the honour of archpriest and entrusted him with the responsibility of promoting the establishment of the Diocese of Montreal. Power had also won the respect of Lartigue's "bishop-in-waiting," Ignace Bourget. And because Power had distinguished himself at Ste-Martine during the rebellions, he was now generally considered to be trustworthy, courageous, and loyal. If anything, the transfer could be interpreted as a reward for faithful service to the diocese. Living on the south shore, he could be more easily summoned by his superiors in Montreal when they needed him. His appointment could also have been a formal response to the inhabitants of Laprairie, who were among the most independent-minded people in the region. Since 1800, and particularly during the years immediately before the insurrection, Laprairie had been viewed as an unruly parish; its laypeople had a history of voicing their discontent and insulting *curés*.[6] In light of this, Laprairie's stipendiary magistrate commented that the influence of the parish clergy in the

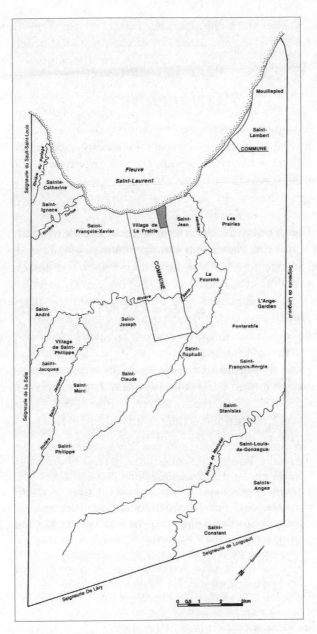

Map of the Laprairie seigneury at the end of the
French regime (from Louis Lavalée, *Laprairie en
Nouvelle-France* [Montreal and Kingston:
McGill-Queen's University Press, 1992])

area was weaker than "in any other Catholic country."[7] Bourget and Lartigue might have considered Power to be the kind of self-contained law-and-order clergyman who could control the tempestuous parishioners of La Nativité.

The bishop's plan to employ Power beyond the parish boundaries was in evidence early in Power's tenure at Laprairie. His day-to-day work there was frequently interrupted by requests to investigate problems, to visit Montreal, or to undertake special missions outside the diocese. In fact, of all Power's pastoral appointments, Laprairie was the shortest in real terms, given the amount of time he spent outside the parish on the bishop's business. In the official history of La Nativité, Chanoine Chevalier describes Power in respectful, yet oddly affectionate terms: "It was thus under the clever and wise direction of their priest Mr. Michael Power that the church had risen. A man of cold disposition, but mild and affable none the less, he had known how to insinuate himself imperceptibly into the heart and soul of his parishioners."[8]

It is hard to understand how Chevalier could say that Power was cold yet able to penetrate the hearts and souls of his parishioners. His appraisal comes a century after Power's departure from the parish and in light of the fact that he had gone on to become a bishop and die in selfless service to the most vulnerable in his community. But we must bear in mind that most parish histories would not criticize the character of a former pastor considered a martyr of the faith, so it makes sense that Chevalier's description is polite and respectful to a man whom few parishioners ever got to know intimately.

Although there were occasionally problems in Laprairie during Power's tenure, his short term there is remembered chiefly for the manner in which he rallied the congregation to build a new church.[9] The stone church that stood in the parish when he arrived there had been commissioned in 1705 by the Sulpicians. Nearly 135 years later, it had become far too small for Laprairie's Catholic population, and it was in serious need of repair and renovation. Having secured the necessary permission from Bourget (who was by then bishop), Power initiated the construction in May 1840.[10] It took parishioners and workmen months to demolish the old structure and cart away the stone, wood, and debris, during which time Mass was celebrated in a makeshift chapel in the old sacristy. In October 1840, Power's friend and mentor Father Vincent Quiblier, rector of the Seminary of St-Sulpice and one of Bourget's vicars-general, blessed the cornerstone of the new church. More than a year later, on 18 November 1841 – and after £24,000 had been spent on the project – a team of workers led by Antoine Bourdon put the finishing touches on the new church building. It was consecrated by Bourget himself,[11] who placed within the main altar the relics of St Clément and St Quinten, which he and Power had acquired on their recent trip to Rome.[12]

The building of this house of worship was something of a landmark in Power's career as a pastor. He had never before managed a construction project of such magnitude. The new parish church of La Nativité de la Très Sainte-Vierge measured 160 feet long by 62 feet wide, and it had a sacristy of 1,200 square feet. Because the pews were not ready in time for Bourget's visit, Power instructed that the old pews, which had been salvaged for the temporary chapel, be placed in the new nave. For the time being, no pew rent would be charged, and this meant that for a short period the parish elite could not lay claim to the best seats in the house. Power had private meetings with those who objected to these egalitarian arrangements, advising them to demonstrate their public spirit until the new pews were ready for installation. Few other details of this incident are available, but, given the politics of pew renting, one can imagine the excitement of the local farmers and labourers who, for no fee, could enjoy choice seats in the new church and the chagrin of the local elite. Power had thus skilfully treated one of the open sores of the rebellion by allowing the less fortunate a small window of opportunity to put aside the issue of social standing. Perhaps it was incidents like these that spawned affectionate memories of Power, but what is certain is that any affection he inspired was reciprocated. His friend and colleague Father Joseph Marcoux once commented that Power's attachment to Laprairie was so deep that he had wished to remain there for the rest of his life.[13]

Although he loved his new parish, Power could spend little time there. His close involvement with Bourget's agenda, particularly his master plan for the Catholic Church in Canada, kept him away from the parish during much of the church construction period, from 1840 to 1841. In 1840, he was absent from the parish for much of the autumn, and in 1841, he spent more than five months in Europe. Laprairie may very well have been his long-awaited ideal parish appointment, but he was now too involved in episcopal politics to immerse himself in parish life. His reputation as a leader of the anglophone priests in the diocese, the respect accorded him by government officials, and Bourget's increasing awareness of his legal expertise kept Power on the move. Bourget sought his opinion on difficult cases in canon law, and Power responded in detail, citing case studies from canon law, magisterial documents, and

"View of the Village of Laprairie," by Henry R.S. Bunnett
(NA, C-034157)

the pronouncements of popes past and present.[14] He was being drawn
more closely into Bourget's inner circle, and the bishop was grooming
him to be his protégé.

In the autumn of 1840, Bourget sent Power to Nova Scotia. While it
was Power's first recorded return to Halifax since his departure in 1816,
Bourget had not intended it to be a social visit. He wanted Power to
use the trip to advance the plan to establish an ecclesiastical province
of Quebec and to form suffragan sees from the Atlantic to the Great
Lakes. As an anglophone and a native of the eastern colonies, Power
was charged with the task of selling the plan to the bishops at Charlottetown, Halifax, and St John's. The interior and western sees were already
in line. The new bishop of Kingston, Remi Gaulin, was in full support of
Bourget, his former superior, as were Bishop Signay and Bishop Turgeon,
his coadjutor, in Quebec City. Bourget had further strengthened his position by seeding the areas west of the Ottawa River with some of his own
priests, ensuring that, at a bare minimum, all the sees and the territories
in the Province of Canada were solidly behind the new plan. Bourget's
argument to the Colonial Office and to the governors general of the time,
whose approval was critical to the plan's success, was twofold: first, as
the Catholic Church expanded in British North America, it would be far
easier for the Crown to liase with a single archbishop at Quebec than
with a plethora of mitred heads from St John's to the Red River; second,
the creation of a metropolitan see would mirror the developments and
the benefits of the Archdiocese of Baltimore. Bourget also envisioned his
plan as a means of enhancing the presence of the church and strengthen-
ing its social control over the new frontiers while facilitating the work
of British authorities in these regions.[15]

But Power was soon to discover that the eastern bishops would not be easily convinced of the merits of Bourget's plan. In August, he conferred with Governor General Sydenham and Bishop Turgeon about the establishment of the ecclesiastical province before proceeding down the St Lawrence, through the gulf, to Pictou, Nova Scotia.[16] Over the next few weeks, he would meet with Bishop Bernard MacDonald of Charlottetown[17] and Bishop William Fraser, the vicar apostolic of Nova Scotia, whom Power met in Antigonish. Neither bishop seemed willing to endorse the scheme to elevate Quebec to the status of a metropolitan see, despite Power's arguments that such a move would enhance the status of the church and give British North Americans the administrative structures enjoyed by Catholics in the rest of the world. Bishop Michael Anthony Fleming, vicar apostolic of Newfoundland, was in Ireland, making it impossible for Power to present his case directly to all potential suffragans. It was fairly evident, however, from gossip circulating in Nova Scotia, that Fleming had absolutely no interest in cementing a relationship with the Diocese of Quebec. His focus was eastward, towards Ireland and Europe. Later, Fleming mused to Signay that nature itself discouraged formal ties between Newfoundland and Quebec: "the dreary shores of Cape Gaspé ... are regarded by our most experienced mariners as pregnant with perils," and "the wrecks of hundreds of European and Canadian Traders, that strew the southern part of our Island and the bones of thousands that blanch upon its shores testify to the dangers that must be surmounted before that Gulf or Great River can be reached."[18] Given the cultural and historical differences between Quebec and the Atlantic colonies, the fact that those colonies tended to look towards the North Atlantic world, and the fact that it took a great deal of time to travel or communicate between these regions in the early nineteenth century, it was predictable that the Maritime bishops would refuse to surrender their autonomy. Power's mission ended in failure.[19]

For Power, the silver lining to all of this was his twelve-day sojourn in Halifax.[20] He retraced the meanderings of his youth, strolled through the woods at Point Pleasant,[21] and visited the graves of his father and brothers in the churchyard of St Peter's. He met the sisters he had never before laid eyes upon because they had been born after he went to Montreal. He celebrated Mass at St Mary's, the new stone church on Spring Garden Road that Burke had built to replace the older chapel. He made the acquaintance of Father John Carroll, who had officiated at the burials of his father and brother James. Carroll would later move to Toronto to become one of Power's most trusted priests. But most important, Power saw his mother, for years his primary source of family news.

Though the effort to create an ecclesiastical province had stalled, Power could at least take some time to relax, reflect, and put some physical and mental distance between himself and the events that had consumed him at Ste-Martine and Laprairie.

When Power returned to Laprairie, later that autumn, he found himself in the middle of another revolution. This one however, did not involve pikes and manifestos; instead, its proponents grabbed their rosary beads and scapulars. The European Catholic revival, known variously as the ultramontane revolution or the renewal of Tridentine Catholicism, had hit the Montreal district with force, but it was neither new to Lower Canada nor monolithic in character.[22] The movement began in Europe shortly after the fall of Napoleon, as the survivors of the *ancien régime* struggled to restore the monarchies and dynasties of the pre-revolutionary period. Within the Roman Catholic Church, this period of restoration witnessed the convergence of unlikely and diverse Catholic interest groups bitten by the bug of medieval nostalgia; among them were the *zelanti* in the Roman Curia, who advocated the creation of a strong papacy in order to avoid a repeat of the humiliation of Pius VI and Pius VII at the hands of Emperor Joseph II of Austria and later Napoleon. A second group of conservative thinkers, including layman Joseph de Maistre, envisioned the abandonment of the principles of the revolution and the redirection of Catholic energies towards rebuilding the papacy and the church and extending Catholic missionary endeavours.[23] Yet another group, which embraced the arguments of Father Félicité de Lamennais and his newspaper, *L'avenir*, sought to baptize the revolution and separate church from state, enabling the papacy to emerge as the uncontested power of European Catholicism. In the leadership vacuum following the revolution, the ultramontane reformers foresaw the rise of a strong papacy released from its bondage to the crowned heads of Europe to act as an independent moral force in world affairs.[24]

In the 1830s and 1840s, the *zelanti*-inspired Pope Gregory XVI was the living embodiment of a cautious, conservative – but revived – sense of papal authority in both the temporal and spiritual realms. True to their medieval name, the nineteenth-century ultramontanes literally and figuratively sought direction and inspiration ecclesially and politically by "looking over the mountains" to Rome. They had a deep and abiding devotion to authority, stability, and structure, which had been informed by the recent revolutionary crisis. They eschewed the new liberalism of European politics and condemned the radical and revolutionary forces that persisted beneath the surface of restored world order.[25] In Lower

Canada, the ideas of Lamennais had been enormously popular, especially with Bishop Lartigue, and they had been taught in several schools and seminaries.[26] The practice of disseminating Mennaisian ideas came to an abrupt end in 1834, however, when, in a second encyclical on the matter, "Singulari Nos," Gregory XVI condemned the liberal thought of Lamennais, a man who had openly criticized the pope for his failure to support Catholic Poland when it rebelled against its Russian overlords. Although Lartigue ordered the withdrawal of Lamennais's writings from the school curricula in his district, the Mennaisian ideal of enhanced papal authority and international leadership, albeit recast in a more conservative mould, took hold among some French Canadian clerical leaders. Such ideas were opportune at a time when the liberal professional leaders of the Lower Canadian rebellion had been defeated, demoralized, and dispersed. Lower Canada had a leadership vacuum of its own, which a revitalized clergy would be ready and willing to fill.[27]

The ultramontane revolution also had a significant influence on the resurgence of popular piety and religious life. The charismatic Pope Pius IX (1846–78) encouraged the growth and renewal of such traditional devotional practices and prayers as the Rosary, the Forty Hours, the devotion to the Sacred Heart of Jesus, and the veneration of the Blessed Virgin Mary.[28] Older religious sodalities flourished among the laity, and new confraternities with a focus on prayer and service emerged. Such organizations as the Apostleship of Prayer, the Sodality of the Blessed Virgin Mary, and the St Vincent de Paul Society drew the laity into the ultramontane revolution, allowing them to practise a devotional life as individuals while remaining rooted in communities that were parish-based and that operated in vernacular languages.[29] Similarly, the grassroots devotional revolution was complemented, supported, and amplified by the revival of vocations to existing religious orders and by the creation of new orders of men and women dedicated to social service and missionary activity. In Canada, rejuvenated orders like the Congregation of the Sisters of St Joseph and the Society of Jesus, in addition to new orders like the Oblates of Mary Immaculate and the Soeurs de Ste-Anne, would become vital to the evangelization and formal education of Canadian Catholics in the nineteenth and early twentieth centuries.[30]

While Lartigue had clearly tapped into the ultramontane stream in the 1830s, the political troubles in Lower Canada impeded his promotion of a Canadian version of the Catholic revival.[31] But his successor, Ignace Bourget, facing the devastation of French Canadian leadership in the wake of the rebellions, embraced the ultramontane vision of restored papal authority, the primacy of church teaching in civil matters, the renewal of religious orders, and the popularization of devotions and sodalities.[32] No clearer a statement of Bourget's appreciation of the church's renewed structures of authority, order, and discipline can match this famous assertion: "Let each say in his heart, I hear my *curé*, my *curé* hears the bishop, the bishop hears the Pope, and the Pope hears our Lord Jesus Christ."[33] Bourget would put the stamp of the ultramontane revolution on nearly every aspect of his episcopate. With the temporary eclipse of the liberal professionals, and with the two former colonies of Upper and Lower Canada joined in an unholy union of Catholic and Protestant cultures, Bourget and his followers applied their confidence, energy, and vision to defending the interests of the church, particularly its French Canadian majority. The church became more than the guardian of the faith – it became a haven for French Canadians' sense of peoplehood.

Power, now securely within the bishop's inner circle, was by no means immune to the revolution swirling about him. Conservative and legalistic by nature, as well as orderly and disciplined in his personal habits, he appreciated the clarity, confidence, deference to authority, and attention to hierarchical structures that characterized ultramontanism. What he considered to be the moral and spiritual laxity of the frontier had been a source of frustration for him, as had the contempt for authority expressed by the rebels in 1837 and 1838. It is not surprising, then, that he took to heart a vision of the church that offered clear structures for prayer and devotion and sound religious authority in the face of the rampant "isms" unleashed by the revolutions of the early nineteenth century. In 1840, Bourget confirmed his appreciation of this attitude by appointing Power vicar-general of the Diocese of Montreal.[34]

That year, Bourget also mandated a series of parish missions throughout the diocese. In an effort to create even more interest in the missions, he recruited the exiled Bishop of Nancy and Toul, Charles-Auguste-Marie-Joseph Comte de Forbin-Janson, a charismatic speaker and a passionate agent of the Catholic revival. Forbin-Janson appeared at a retreat held at Notre-Dame Cathedral in Quebec; he then embarked on a whirlwind tour of the Montreal region, which concluded in September 1842.[35] Over this two-year period, Forbin-Janson swept into parishes that Bourget had identified as in need of serious renewal, and into places where he was likely to attract a gargantuan crowd – notably, Notre-Dame Basilica in Montreal.[36] Forbin-Janson's mode of operation was similar whether he was preaching in the chapels of villages like L'Acadie and Terrebonne or in Montreal. The mission would begin with evening vespers, and then Forbin-Janson would arrive in a procession of as many local priests as he could muster. After hymns and prayers, he would ascend the sculpted pulpit and deliver a thundering oration, calling people back to God and the church. He warned of hellfire and damnation and encouraged the faithful to embrace a life of prayer and penance.[37] God loved them and wanted them to be his children: "I bring you peace, the true peace of the soul, the peace that angels announced to earth at the moment of the saviour's birth. The peace in which all men of goodwill participate. *Gloria in excelsis Deo, et in terra pax hominebus bonae voluntatis* ... Join us, my brothers, no matter who you are, rich or poor, young or old, no matter what your condition, you all need shelter."[38] The evening would also be flavoured with the ringing of bells, the lighting of candles, the distribution of devotional medals, and the reception of the Eucharist. Forbin-Janson would prescribe devotional practices (other than the Eucharist) in which the laity could engage on a daily basis in order to remain strong in their faith long after his mission had ended.

The mark of the mission's success, however, would be measured by the degree to which Forbin-Janson drew the faithful to confessional stations manned by the army of priests in his entourage. These confessors were given powers of absolution often reserved for bishops alone, including the power to absolve sins relating to sexual transgressions.[39] Like the Methodist camp meeting, which reached a crescendo when the preacher's passionate oration provoked "awakenings" among the assembled, the Catholic confession peaked with the cleansing of sins and the opportunity to begin life anew.[40] The crush of the faithful at the confessionals required a large complement of priests. At Forbin-Janson's mission at Notre-Dame, for instance, seventeen priests were required to meet the needs of the capacity crowd of 17,000 communicants and an additional 1,200 seeking the sacrament of confirmation. Even at the smaller mission of St-Scholastique (in January 1841), a dozen priests were needed.[41] Forbin-Janson set the diocese ablaze with religious activity, and although he managed to carry his message to only 42 of the diocese's 105 parishes, the small churches at the mission sites were always full to busting because pilgrims from outside the parish thronged to them to hear the bishop.

The results of Forbin-Janson's tour were impressive, and in two short years the Catholic revival had changed the focus of Catholic life in Quebec for generations to come. At some parishes, such as Notre-Dame in Montreal, the number of Easter communicants – Catholics required by canon law to make their Easter duty – increased by 50 per cent immediately after the mission. Meanwhile, parishioners across the diocese who frequented the communion rail at Sunday Mass increased from 60.3 per cent of the parish population in the 1836–40 period to 75.4 per cent by 1845. This was just the beginning of an upward trajectory of reception of the Eucharist that would peak at 95 per cent by the 1870s.[42] The effect of bringing male Catholics back into the fold and inspiring them to participate in weekly liturgies obviously outlived the period of enthusiasm that followed the missions. Forbin-Janson's revivalist tour of 1842 launched Lower Canadian Catholics into a new state of religious consciousness. They would embrace the ultramontanism of the day, including its devotional practices, sodalities, fraternal associations, and enhanced parish participation. Clergy who had slogged their way through the dog days of the rebellion and the time of religious indifference that had preceded them must have seen the movement as a dream come true.

The Roman religious revolution was exploding all around Power, although Laprairie had not been on Forbin-Janson's itinerary. It could have been that under Power the parish had no pressing need for Forbin-Janson's ministrations, or it could have been that the parish church was under construction for much of Forbin-Janson's visit and therefore unusable – for whatever reason, Bourget excluded Laprairie from the tour. Nevertheless, Power's parishioners would have had the opportunity to hear the spellbinding oratory of the French exile at L'Acadie, Châteauguay, or Chambly, all of which were within easy travelling distance of Laprairie. Although Power was too ill with a cold to attend the great rally at Notre-Dame in December of 1840, it is difficult to believe that as Bourget's protégé, soon to be vicar-general, he would have had no contact with Forbin-Janson's mission.[43] The imperatives of Forbin-Janson's conversion message were integral to Power's sense of his own priestly ministry. Forbin-Janson's ultramontane vision harmonized with Power's already well-formulated sense of obedience, truth, and discipline in matters of the body and soul. And if Power's mind had been elsewhere during this period, he would not have made such a speedy ascent to Bourget's inner circle.

Power's visit to Rome in 1841 completed his absorption of the ultramontane revolution. In April of that year, Bourget began to make plans to visit the United Kingdom, France, and the Papal States. He had four principal objectives for a journey that would take nearly five months. First, in order to nurture the Catholic revival in his own diocese, he wanted to recruit members of several reconstituted and revitalized European religious orders. He had his sights set on the recently restored Society of Jesus (Jesuits), the Oblates of Mary Immaculate and a new missionary order of men founded by Eugène de Mazenod in Marseilles, and several orders of women who could assist with schooling, health care, and social services.[44] Bourget's second objective was to petition Rome, with the co-operation and consent of Remi Gaulin, the bishop of Kingston, for the division of the Upper Canadian diocese; he also intended to secure an appointment of a bishop for its new western section. If Bourget failed to accomplish these things, then Gaulin wanted him to secure a coadjutor bishop to assist him in administrating a growing diocese that extended from the Ottawa River to the head of Lake Superior.[45] Bourget's third, and perhaps most crucial, objective was to lobby Rome and the Colonial Office in London for the creation of an ecclesiastical province of British North America, anchored by an archiepiscopal see at Quebec. While this plan was rather ambitious, Bourget believed that he had enough support from his brother bishops in Canada and Governor General Sydenham to pull off the creation of North America's second archbishopric (after Baltimore).[46] Bourget's fourth objective was to fulfill a request that Bishop Signay had made of him to ask Rome to give the British Columbia mission independent status or reporting responsibility to another jurisdiction. The sheer difficulty of communicating with the St Lawrence Valley from the Pacific coast, in addition to the shortage of clergy in Quebec, made it nearly impossible for Signay to continue the missions in BC.[47]

When Bourget left Montreal on 3 May 1841, he was accompanied by a canon from St James Cathedral, Joseph-Octave Paré, who would serve as his secretary, and Michael Power.[48] To the lay observer, Power's presence in the travel party would seem logical enough. He was a trusted advisor, a vicar-general, a skilled canonist, and an anglophone – which was an advantage not to be underestimated in dealing with British authorities. But what everyone – perhaps even Power – did not know was that Bourget had special plans for him. Not only could Bourget rely on Power's notable skills, but he could also showcase the *curé* of Laprairie as the obvious choice for bishop of the proposed diocese of western Upper Canada. Among Bourget's many expectations of the European tour was that Gregory XVI would agree to divide Kingston and create a new diocese of western Upper Canada and that he would appoint and consecrate Power as bishop while they were still in Rome. This way, Power would be able to use the trip to collect resources and personnel for the home church, as Bourget would do for Montreal. A flurry of correspondence between Bourget and his colleagues confirms that Power was being taken to Rome to "be seen."[49] One month before the voyage, Gaulin had designated Power as his choice for bishop of the new see – or, in the very least, his coadjutor – and Bourget asked Signay to write a glowing testimonial for Power. Signay agreed, describing Power to the pope as a man of pure faith, great virtue, *zelum pruden-tiae moderatum*, and diligence in observing his religion.[50] Bourget also carried with him a letter signed by ten priests of the Diocese of Montreal endorsing Power as a future bishop.[51] The plan was set.

Power may have sensed that something was afoot, but he appeared uninterested in, or perhaps naïve about, Bourget's intentions. One of his friends, Father Joseph Marcoux, the missionary priest among the Iroquois at St-Regis, claimed that he had told Power that he would be an excellent candidate for bishop of the new diocese of western Upper Canada and lamented that Power had rejected the very idea of it. According to Marcoux, Power was satisfied to remain at La Nativité, where he had figuratively "built his tomb."[52] There is nothing else in Power's correspondence or that of his friends to suggest that he was aware of Bourget's specific plan for Upper Canada.

After spending the night at St-Jean-sur-Richelieu, Bourget, Paré, and Power headed south to New York. En route, they stopped at Iberville (St-Athanase), where they celebrated Mass for the Confraternity of the Blessed and Immaculate Heart of Mary; they then visited several enclaves of expatriate French Canadians living in Burlington, Vermont, and upper New York State. By 6 May, they had arrived in New York City, where they were greeted by Bishop John Hughes and their old colleague Forbin-Janson, whom Bourget invited to make a return visit to Lower Canada. In New York, the trio made a change in plan that Bourget would later interpret as "providential."[53] Acting upon the advice of Hughes and Forbin-Janson, Bourget abandoned the idea of sailing to Liverpool via Boston aboard the *Britannia* and instead booked passage on the *Albany*, sailing directly to Le Havre, France. This would necessitate a postpone-ment of their meeting at the Colonial Office, but they would be able to launch their recruitment effort in France and their diplomatic endeav-ours in Rome sooner than anticipated. The change in plan would also allow them to get to Rome before late July, which was advantageous, because due to the intense summer heat, the city was virtually shut down between then and the end of August. The *Albany* made the crossing in a record twenty-three and a half days – some thirty-seven days less than its previous crossing to New York. The *Britannia* had an accident at sea and was stranded in Saint John, New Brunswick. For Bourget and company, the £48 fee for cancelling passage on the *Britannia* turned out to be money well spent.[54]

Exactly one month after their departure from Montreal, Bourget, Paré, and Power were in Paris. They lodged at the Séminaire des Missions Etrangères,[55] which they also used as a base of operations for recruiting members of French religious orders for the Diocese of Montreal. After less than two weeks, with the assurances of the Sisters of St-Vincent de Paul that they would extend their ministry to Montreal, Bourget's party moved on to Lyons. There were many reasons to visit this ancient centre of French Christianity and martyrdom, not the least of which was that it was the birthplace of Father Quiblier, the rector of Notre-Dame and one of Power's closest friends and supporters. Most important, however, the headquarters for the Society for the Propagation of the Faith (SPF), a key source of funds for the Canadian mission field, was in Lyons. After thanking their SPF benefactors and delivering their reports, the trio headed south to Marseilles to recruit the Oblates of Mary Immaculate.

Their short stay in that port city was profitable. Bourget met with the Bishop of Marseilles and founder of the Oblates, Eugène de Mazenod, and he presented Mazenod with a plan that would see the Oblates step into the role of missionaries on the western frontier of the Diocese of Montreal, notably among the First Nations peoples of Lake Temiskaming. Within thirty-two hours of their meeting, Mazenod sent word to Bourget that he would assist the Diocese of Montreal. The first Oblates would land in Montreal later that year, on 2 December, and they not only assumed missionary duties on the frontier, but they also assumed control of the parish missions established by Forbin-Janson.[56] The recruitment of the Oblates in 1841 marked the beginning of a frenzy of missionary activity west of the Ottawa River. Within fifty years, Oblate missions would dot the map of Canada, from Victoria to Moosonee, and from Montreal to the Arctic Ocean.[57]

But Bourget did not remain in Marseilles savouring his success for long. He hoped for a speedy passage to Rome, arriving by 29 June, in time for the Feast of St Peter and St Paul, one of the four great festivals in the Roman calendar.[58] There were two possible ways to get to Rome from Marseilles: a scenic coach ride through Liguria and Tuscany, or a voyage through the Mediterranean, Tyrrhenian, and Ligurian seas.[59] Bourget chose the latter option, which was faster. The Canadians sailed out of Marseilles harbour, past the infamous prison island of Château d'Iff, into open waters. After that, it is uncertain which of three routes they took. They perhaps rounded the north coast of Corsica and headed through the northern reaches of the Tyrrhenian, aiming for the Italian coast; or they passed between Corsica and Sardinia and then crossed the Tyrrhenian to Civita Vecchia; or they followed the longer trade route through Malta and Sicily.[60] Their port of call was not recorded, although had they landed at Civita Vecchia on 22 June,[61] they would have covered the short distance to Rome by coach. There, they would have entered the "eternal city" by the Flaminian Gate at the Piazza de Popolo in the northwest section of the old city enclosed by the Aurelian Walls.

For the thirty-six-year-old Power, this journey to the centre of the Catholic world was the experience of a lifetime. He would have snatched his first glimpses of Rome from the window of the coach as it bumped down the Corso, central Rome's principal artery, once described by Stendhal as the most "beautiful street in the world."[62] Linking the Piazza de Popolo in the north and the ruins of the Forum in the city's heart, the Corso was the stage for Rome's festivals – in particular, the Mardi Gras costume spectacle, which was held immediately prior to the penitential season of Lent. Such scenes must have impressed author Alexandre Dumas when he visited the city six years before Power, because he set part of his novel *The Count of Monte Cristo* on the Corso during the pre-Lenten festival in the time of Gregory XVI. Similarly, three years later, in 1844, American historian Francis Parkman visited Rome during Mardi Gras and described the Corso as "a noble street, of a most grand and solemn architecture."[63] Passing the ruins of the Roman Forum, the coach in which the Canadians travelled lurched to the left, bumped down two narrow side streets, and stopped before the Convent of the Holy Apostles, where Bourget had reserved rooms.

Although they inhabited a city of between 135,000 and 140,000 people, the vast majority of Romans still lived within the ancient Aurelian Walls.[64] Rome lacked many of the amenities that Power would have noted in Paris. Leo XII and Gregory XVI had shunned such French innovations as gas lighting for streets and the new steam railways, which Gregory XVI referred to as "les chemins d'enfer."[65] It appeared that the passion of the *zelanti* popes and their supporters for stamping out the evil legacy of the French Revolution extended to technological innovations. Despite the developments that survived the Napoleonic occupation earlier in the century, Rome was home to some curious juxtapositions – sixteenth- and seventeenth-century buildings bordered ancient

St Peter's Basilica and the Vatican in the early nineteenth century

ruins that were slowly being engulfed by overgrown vegetation. Settling into this unique environment, Power discovered the convenience of his situation. From his lodgings, he was within easy walking distance of sites that were critical to his mission and others that would nourish his burgeoning ultramontanism and natural intellectual curiosity. In fifteen minutes, he could walk to the Propaganda Fide in the Piazza d'Espagna, or the Quirinal Palace, where the popes conducted their business in summer, or the ruins of the Colosseum and the Forum. St Peter's Basilica, a half-hour's trot to the east, sat on the opposite bank of the Tiber River flanked by the working-class district of Trastevere to the south and farmlands to the north. Save for the small district of Borgo, which lay outside its northern wall, the Vatican occupied the outskirts of early-nineteenth-century Rome.[66]

Bourget, Paré, and Power had to conduct most of their official business in the morning. The oppressive heat of the Roman summer and the omnipresent mosquitoes, which bred with impunity on the Tiber, forced residents to close their shops and businesses and flee the city; those who could afford it retreated to the Appenine Mountains, Sorrento, or the coast of Campagna. Before Bourget himself went on retreat, in mid-July, he and Power spent hours mapping out their agenda for meetings at the Propaganda Fide and presentations to Gregory XVI. Bourget and the pope had several audiences, although there are only fragmentary records relating to their discussions, none of which indicate the success or failure of Bourget's master plan. It is reasonably clear, however, that Gregory's determination to assert the prerogatives of the church above the "isms" of the modern world fortified Bourget's efforts to revitalize the French Canadian church in accord with ultramontane piety and ecclesiology.[67]

Bourget and Power's meetings at Propaganda Fide are far better documented. After the Feast of St Peter and St Paul, Bourget, Power, and Paré began in earnest to implement the four critical elements of Bourget's master plan: the division of the Diocese of Kingston; the appointment of a bishop for the newly created Upper Canadian diocese (or, at the very least, a coadjutor for the ailing Gaulin); the erection of a metropolitan see for British North America at Quebec; and the removal of the British Columbia mission from the direct control of the bishop of Quebec.[68] Power made several visits on his own to the Propaganda Fide and established a good working relationship with Monsignor Giovanni Corboli, consultor to Bishop Ignazio Giovanni Cadolini, secretary of the Propaganda Fide. As Power laid out the plan for Corboli and his colleague Padre Castruccio Castracane, it must have become increasingly obvious to him that Bourget had had his reasons for including him in the travel party, beyond the fact that he spoke English and was a trusted advisor.

Bourget was presenting Power in person as the only possible candidate for bishop of the proposed Upper Canadian diocese. He had brought the *curé* of Laprairie to Europe to impress the officials authorized to suggest candidates to the pope. With supporting documentation from Gaulin himself, Bourget asserted the necessity of relieving the sickly Gaulin of the task of administering the western portion of his diocese, where the Catholic population was growing due mainly to an increase in Irish Catholic immigration. Should the division of Kingston take place, insisted Bourget, the new bishop of the western territory had to be fluent in English and fluent in the culture of the Irish pioneers. In a menacing tone, Bourget also suggested that if such moves were not made, particularly the appointment of an anglophone bishop, the new Catholic immigrants in the region would fall victim to the clergy of the Protestant majority: the Catholic Church, he maintained, needed to "prevent the rape [of Catholics] by Protestant ministers."[69] Such strong language was calculated to infuse the proposed plan with a sense of urgency at a time when the Catholic Church, under Gregory XVI, was afflicted with paranoia about clandestine movements afoot in the Papal States – the Carbonari, the Masons, the liberals, and the Protestants. Having thus established the urgency of his case, Bourget found it much easier to promote Power. He bolstered his argument with the testimonials from Gaulin, Signay, Turgeon, and the ten Montreal priests, all of whom named Power as the best possible choice for the new frontier diocese. Gaulin added that none of his priests in Upper Canada possessed the necessary linguistic attributes for the appointment. When Corboli made his own summary of Bourget's proposal, he duly noted that Power's supporters used glowing terms to describe his character and faithfulness.[70] Evidently, Power was the Canadians' unanimous choice.

Throughout his month-long Roman sojourn, suffering in the heat and swatting insects, Power weighed the implications of creating a new Upper Canadian diocese. Much of the time, he was alone with his thoughts. On 15 July, Bourget left for an eight-day retreat under the direction of Jesuit Superior General Jan Roothan, with whom he had much business to discuss. Bourget then rushed off to make a pilgrimage to the shrine of Loreto, the alleged site of Jesus's childhood, miraculously transported to Italy.[71] This gave Power considerable time to think about the plan to make him bishop, and the more he thought about it, the more he resisted the idea.

On 28 July, just prior to his departure for Paris, where he was to set up Bourget's France itinerary, Power penned a lengthy epistle to Bishop Ignazio Giovanni Cadolini, secretary of the Propaganda Fide, in which he as much as asked that the "cup" be taken from him. True to form, he executed his request to be passed over for bishop in a legalistic, factual, and unemotional manner. Without questioning the judgment of his nominators, he raised what he considered serious canonical questions about the nomination process. He was most concerned that his nomination was made without the submission of a *terna* – a list of three nominees ranked in descending order from "most dignified" to "dignified" – a procedure that was well established in Canadian ecclesiastical tradition. He viewed this abandonment of the norms as a dangerous precedent that could compromise his legitimacy as a bishop and, ultimately, "the authority and rule" of the church in Canada.[72] That Power would take such a legalistic approach to the matter was to be expected, although one suspects that it masked his basic fear of assuming the leadership of the proposed frontier diocese. He believed that he would not measure up physically or morally to the demands of the appointment, and he was brutally frank to Cadolini about it, referring to "Obstacles of all kind that one would have to necessarily meet, the difficulties that would have to assume a clergy, hardly formed and composed of ecclesiastic many of which hardly knowing the ecclesiastic rules and disciplines, I do not even have the physical force, never mind the moral force, to be able to resist it. Although it would seem that I have a fairly strong temperament, I am nevertheless naturally very feeble, and it is only by attention and very particular care that I succeed in fulfilling my duties even in my own parish."[73]

Power discussed the problem of dealing with itinerant and perhaps unruly clergy on the frontier far more forcefully in an earlier draft of this letter, wherein he also referred to the priests of Upper Canada as "poorly formed and poorly disciplined."[74] The fact that an early draft of the letter exists is testament to how strongly the proposed elevation to the episcopacy preyed on his fears and evoked memories of his frontier service. The hardships of life in the St-François Valley and at Petite-Nation must have flooded back to him. Marcoux was not far off the mark when he said that Power was anxious to put down roots in a well-settled parish like Laprairie. Feeling incapable of facing the frontier again, Power begged Cadolini to relieve him of the appointment before it became official or to at least put his name at the bottom of the *terna*.

Power's plea went unanswered. Bourget returned from his pilgrimage and dispatched him to Paris, partially in an effort to keep him out of the negotiations surrounding his appointment. In the final days of his Roman trip, Bourget responded to Power's anxiety about the lack of a *terna* by hastily cobbling one together. On this list of three candidates, Power was the *dignissimus*, at the top. Joining him were François Demers and Hyacinthe Hudon, both of whom had appeared on the 1836 *terna* that had advanced Bourget to the position of Lartigue's coadjutor. These two candidates had already been vetted by Bourget's episcopal colleagues in Canada as priests suitable for the office of bishop. In presenting this list, a brilliant sleight of hand within accepted canonical limits, Bourget laid to rest Power's fear, and perhaps that of others, that Power's nomination was somehow questionable. Bourget was in a hurry to get the deed done, and he had neither the time nor the patience to await supporting documents from Canada. He knew that the Propaganda Fide had the dossier for his own *terna* on file, including letters of recommendation for Hudon and Demers.[75] With one simple move, Bourget had met his own deadline and addressed arguments about the canonicity of Power's elevation to the episcopate.

Bourget left Rome in August with no firm commitment from the Roman Curia regarding any facet of his master plan. While the division of the Diocese of Kingston appeared inevitable and both the appointment of Power to the new Upper Canadian diocese [76] and the separation of the British Columbia mission from Quebec (which actually did take place in 1843) seemed probable,[77] the creation of the ecclesiastical Province of Quebec still required more study and some judicious negotiation with the Colonial Office. It appeared certain to the Canadians that the Vatican would not move on the issue until the Colonial Office had approved the scheme. Canada was still a part of the Protestant British Empire, and the potential threat to the good relations between church and state throughout the growing empire was motivation enough for prudence. Curial officials had copies of recent correspondence between Lord Glenelg and the Earl of Gosford indicating that the British were reluctant to "pursue any course in this matter which might appear to be unprecedented or unusual." [78] While Cadolini and others found the American model of the archiepiscopal see at Baltimore a compelling incentive for action in the northern half of the continent, the Vatican required more British support than Governor General Sydenham's endorsement of the plan. Bourget departed for Paris, leaving Paré in Rome to continue the negotiations.[79]

In Paris, Bourget met up with Power, and they resumed their efforts to recruit French religious orders to serve in the Diocese of Montreal. During these weeks, Bourget kept in close contact with the Vatican, reminding Cadolini of the necessity of making a quick decision.[80] Time was running out for Bourget. He had been away from Montreal for nearly four months, his funds were running low, and he had failed to realize several of the principal objectives of his trip. By the end of August, Paré had joined them in Paris, and to begin the last leg of their tour, the trio headed to the United Kingdom. Bourget was confident that the necessary groundwork for his plan had already been laid with the British authorities. He had forewarned Prime Minister Lord John Russell that he wanted to discuss with him a "new ecclesiastical" arrangement for Canada.[81] But Bourget's timing could not have been worse. By the time he got to London, the Russell administration had fallen from power, and the Canadians had to start anew with the government of Lord Stanley.[82] Facing delays in securing British approval of several aspects of his master plan, Bourget left London in September, travelled to Liverpool, and from there sailed to Boston, leaving Europe with only a few promises from religious orders and some hazy commitments to some portions of his vision of redrawing the ecclesiastical map of Canada.[83] He left Power and Paré behind in London to continue talks with British officials, hoping that they would win the necessary British approval and forward the documentation to the Vatican with due speed.[84] He also instructed Power and Paré to make a brief trip to Ireland to recruit English-speaking clergy for Canada and discuss with church leaders "diverse points of discipline."[85]

Given his linguistic skills, Power was critical to the success of Bourget's London mission. Little is known about Power's sojourn in the empire's capital other than that he was billeted at the Sablonière Hotel in Leicester Square, off Piccadilly. Here, he would have been close to some of London's most noted public buildings and historic monuments and just west of its most notorious slums. This was the largest city he had ever visited, and it stood in striking contrast architecturally and socially to Paris and Rome. His daily routine was focused on early morning Mass and sorties to key government buildings and the Whitehall office complex occupied by the Colonial Office. While he would have seen the impressive monuments to the British Empire – Westminster Abbey, the Houses of Parliament, and Buckingham Palace – Power would also have travelled the back alleys that fed into the main thoroughfares, parks, and monuments of the great city. He knew the squalid areas of working-class Montreal and the rough sections of Halifax south of Fort George, but these would pale in comparison to London's sordid underbelly, which had inspired the novels of Charles Dickens.[86] Power would have been confronted with the worst of the new urban frontier as he passed near St Giles parish:

> This was the time of the rookeries, an island of cellars and tenements roughly bounded by St Giles High Street, Bainbridge Street and Dyott Street. Within this unfortunate triangle, before New Oxford Street was constructed to lay waste the slums, were ... a congregation of yards and courts and alleys which turned the area into a maze used both as a refuge and as a hiding place for those who dwelt there ... there were thieves, coiners, prostitutes and vagrants as well as labourers, road sweepers and street sellers. The lanes were narrow and dirty, windows of decaying tenements were stuffed with rags and paper, while interiors were damp and unwholesome. The walls were sagging, the floors covered in dirt, the low ceilings were discoloured by mould; their smell was altogether indescribable.[87]

In reflecting upon his travels to friends, Power never mentioned London with fondness, and he ranked England far behind Ireland and Italy in terms of his favourite places to visit.

Although Power was determined to make headway with the task Bourget had assigned him, he found that Lord Stanley was far too busy in his new position to meet with him. The prime minister instructed him to make any presentations in writing.[88] Historians ought to be thankful for this, because it forced Power to map out the entire Bourget proposal in longhand, thus committing to paper one of the most articulate expressions of the Canadian argument for the creation of an ecclesiastical province at Quebec. On 27 September 1841, Power issued this lengthy communiqué requesting that the Colonial Office approve the division of the Diocese of Kingston, the appointment of a bishop for the proposed new diocese in western Upper Canada, and the creation of a metropolitan see at Quebec.[89] Arguments for the first request were relatively simple – the region was growing, and the church needed a more effective means of managing the spiritual affairs of the new settlers. Recognizing British trepidation about political stability in Upper Canada in the wake of the recent rebellions, Power added, "Your Lordship will likewise feel that a Catholic Bishop in a case of emergency will possess more authority over those committed to his care than an ordinary clergyman; his presence and his advice might also prove highly serviceable to Her Majesty's Government in quelling that spirit of insubordination and fierce democratic spirit which unhappily exist in a formidable degree on many parts of the Frontier Line."[90]

As it turned out, the Colonial Office approved the division of Kingston, and later, once Rome had endorsed Power for the position, it consented to the appointment of an additional Catholic bishop in British North America. In a letter confirming Power's selection, Lord Stanley informed the Canadian governor general, Sir Charles Bagot, "In deference to the concurrent opinion of Lord Sydenham and yourself, and averting to the high character for piety, for moral conduct, and for loyalty to the British Crown which is attributed to the Reverend Mr. Power, I have the pleasure of conveying to you Her Majesty's Authority for recognizing him in the character of Roman Catholic Bishop of Toronto."[91] Thus, on the first two objectives of Bourget's master plan, Rome and London were of one mind.[92]

However, this was not the case with the question of the proposed ecclesiastical province, which would consume most of Power's energies while in London. He argued that the creation of the metropolitan see of

Quebec with several suffragan dioceses would parallel church structures already in place in the United States and the rest of the hemisphere. It would also provide for a "greater harmony and uniformity of conduct" from which both church and state would benefit.[93] Playing the card of the church's role as agent of social control, Power asserted that this "harmony" would give the church "much greater authority against the principles of disaffected men" and allow her to enforce "submission to the law, loyalty to Her Majesty, and above all, unbounded attachment to the mother country."[94] Again, he crafted his arguments to respond to political uncertainty arising from the rebellions and the disaffection over the forced union of Upper and Lower Canada, which had been recommended by Lord Durham. Also, adding a practical dimension to the plan, he maintained that the appointment of an archbishop at Quebec would provide the state with a more effective point of communication with the entire Canadian church. It would permit colonial officials to deal with one centre of power that would effectively bind the whole episcopal system instead of dealing with each Catholic bishop individually. While Power's missive merely outlined Bourget's intentions, he tailored the facts with a sensitivity to British concerns; in particular, he offered assurances about Catholic loyalty and administrative efficiency. If anything, the quest for an ecclesiastical province revealed Power to be adept at political persuasion.

Power received no immediate response to his report other than notification that Her Majesty's government would consider it in due time, although it was not high on the new prime minister's list of priorities. But Stanley's staff were true to their word, and they began to compile an impressive sheaf of documents on the subject in order to ascertain the legal, religious, historical, and constitutional implications of establishing a Roman Catholic metropolitan see in British North America. Their search for answers uncovered problems that were well beyond Power's control or his ability to resolve through argument. First, although bishops had been appointed episcopal vicars to the Diocese of Quebec after 1819, the government had never formally recognized them as bishops. Second, the Church of England in Canada would deeply resent the Catholic prelate of Quebec receiving the title of archbishop if no similar honour was bestowed upon the Anglican bishop of Quebec.[95] While the documents were being gathered and debated, Stanley, as minister of state for the colonies, received a communiqué from the cardinal prefect of the Propaganda Fide regarding the proposed metropolitan see of Quebec. Since the Papal States had no formal diplomatic ties with the United Kingdom, the letter was conveyed to Stanley by Bishop Nicholas

Wiseman, the titular bishop of Melipotamus and resident at St Mary's College, Birmingham.[96] Rome indicated that it approved of Bourget's proposal for the archdiocese but would enact it only if "Her Majesty's Government had no objection to the measure."[97] Wiseman informed Stanley that Lord John Russell had been open to the proposition and had been prepared to meet with Bourget during the latter's European tour of 1841; only the change in administration had prevented the meeting. Echoing many benefits of the plan already voiced by Bourget and Power, Wiseman offered to act as liaison between the Vatican and Whitehall on the matter.

Deliberations too detailed to mention dragged this matter well into 1842, long after Bourget, Power, and Paré had returned to Canada. In April, law officers of the Colonial Office ruled that the Crown could make changes to the ecclesiastical establishments in the conquered territories of Canada, but it could not do so in the "provinces not conquered in which there are no stipulations respecting the maintenance of the Roman Catholic Religion either by Treaty or Act of Parliament."[98] This ruling was heartily applauded by the Catholic bishops in the Atlantic colonies, who opposed their inclusion in any metropolitan province centred in Quebec and resisted surrendering their authority to a jurisdiction with which they had little in common, pastorally or culturally.[99] In May 1844, the question was finally settled in accord with the law officers' opinion: Quebec was raised to the status of archiepiscopal see, with only Montreal, Kingston, and Toronto as suffragans – in essence, the dioceses of the "conquered" territory where Catholic rights were established by treaty and act. The bishops in the Atlantic colonies were only obliged to attend meetings of the provincial synod.[100] Ultimately, the success of this part of Bourget's plan was contingent on an interpretation by Governor General Bagot of Power's argument. If, Bagot reasoned, you could not eliminate or slow the proliferation of Catholic dioceses and bishops in the colonies, then the Crown should render them subordinate to one man upon whom it could prevail. In 1845, Bagot's successor, Sir Charles Metcalfe, formally recognized Signay as archbishop.[101]

However, this protracted affair was not resolved until long after Power had brushed the dirt of London's inner city from his shoes. In November 1841, he arrived in Laprairie. The only consolation he could offer Bourget was that Stanley was deliberating on the matter.[102] He also had little good news to relate to his bishop concerning his side trip to Ireland, during which he had interviewed the bishops of Dublin, Kilkenny, Waterford, and Carlow and visited the superior of the Brothers of Christian Schools. Despite his best efforts, he had returned home without any promises of Irish clergy for the Diocese of Montreal.[103] That meant that none of the four religious orders from which the Canadians had recruited during their European tour were of Irish origin. They had failed to acquire new leaders and service providers for the anglophone Catholics in their diocese and surrounding areas. One month after Power's return to Laprairie, however, the first contingent of the Oblates of Mary Immaculate arrived from France. They were followed in May 1842 by six priests of the Society of Jesus accompanied by four secular priests and three Jesuit lay brothers. In December of that year, the Ladies of the Sacred Heart disembarked at Montreal. By 1844, the last of Bourget's recruits, the Sisters of the Good Shepherd, had arrived.[104]

So, although they had been forced to endure frustrating and at times infuriating delays,[105] within three years the Montreal trio had achieved all of the principal objectives of their 1841 European tour: the recruits were in place; the metropolitan see was a fact; Kingston had been divided; and a new bishop had been appointed for western Upper Canada. But Power had done his work for Bourget too effectively – he was having trouble reconciling himself with the success of that fourth objective.

On 17 December 1841, Pope Gregory XVI created a new diocese in western Upper Canada and Power was appointed its first bishop.[106] The word travelled slowly across the Atlantic to Canada. On 9 January 1842, still unaware of the official appointment, Power wrote to the pope suggesting that the new diocese be dedicated to the Sacred Heart of Jesus, an increasingly popular devotion.[107] While the bulls had not yet been dropped, the fact that Power still wrote to Gregory XVI regarding this matter shows that he was waiting for the inevitable to happen. The loose talk and private assurances concerning diocesan division and the effectiveness of Bourget's *terna* gambit made it clear that Power was about to be promoted. The waiting game had begun – in fact, it took three months for the bulls to arrive in British North America. On 20 March 1842, Bishop Gaulin of Kingston reported that he had received the bull dividing his diocese but was perplexed that the new boundaries and the actual seat of the new diocese had not been indicated in the Roman correspondence. Gaulin was relieved, however, that Power had been chosen as bishop, noting that he would be able to "stop much of the badness" that had transpired in the diocese. "The Good God," Gaulin exclaimed, "in this news has given proof of the grand mercy bestowed upon the church of Canada." He also thanked Bourget for all he had done.[108]

Power was left in the dark about the appointment until 6 April, when Bourget, still his ordinary, had finished making his episcopal visitations.

Bourget, who was well aware of his priest's efforts to remove himself from the running, presented the bulls to Power personally. Bourget confided to Gaulin that he had convinced Power to accept the appointment, although as events unfolded, it appeared that Bourget might have been deluding himself.[109] Four days later, on 10 April, after considerable thought and prayer, Power informed Bourget that he still doubted his ability to be a bishop and had not yet responded to Rome. "The more I reflect," he confessed, "the more I am convinced that the choice that has been made of me, is poor, and I will not make good in the new bishopric that has been erected by the Holy See ... I am keenly aware that I am not strong enough to face the obstacles and the difficulties that present themselves in the administration of such a vast and poorly organised diocese."[110] Power was also concerned about his poor financial situation and about the fact that much remained for him to do in Laprairie, given his long absences during the previous two years.

We know little about what transpired between Bourget and Power over the next few days, but Bourget finally prevailed. On 15 April, Bourget's weekly newspaper, *Mélanges religieux*, the official organ of the Diocese of Montreal, announced that Power had been made bishop of western Upper Canada, and four days later the bishop-elect instructed Bishop Gaulin to continue to exercise his authority over the territory soon to become the Diocese of Toronto.[111] Evidently, Bourget, acting on Gaulin's advice, had convinced Power to select the former Upper Canadian capital as his seat.[112] Toronto was the commercial centre of the former colony and the political and social nerve centre of the western territories. Power would have to wait until September, however, to finalize the boundaries for the new diocese with Gaulin.[113] Until the proposed ecclesiastical province was created, Power's new jurisdiction would remain under the direct authority of the Propaganda Fide. Questions persist as to why Power, plagued by self-doubt, changed his mind and accepted the position. The pressure applied by Bourget cannot be discounted, nor can Power's strong sense of obedience to church leaders, which was strengthened by his reading of Thomas à Kempis's *The Imitation of Christ*, the devotional classic that taught humility, self-sacrifice, obedience, and finding peace in suffering.[114] In his explanation to Bishop Turgeon, Power strongly hints that this form of spirituality ultimately opened him to a task that he did not want. He told Turgeon that he would accept this "cross," hoping that God would give him the strength of "heart" and the "grace necessary to carry it with dignity."[115]

On 8 May 1842 – the Feast of the Appearance of St Michael, his patron saint – Michael Power was consecrated bishop in his parish church at

Laprairie. The day began in Montreal with much fanfare, as Bishops Bourget, Gaulin, and Turgeon, accompanied by a legion of priests, left the seminary building and walked in procession to the docks, where they boarded a steamship for the south shore.[116] An hour later, the party was greeted by a crowd of well-wishers as large as the one that had cheered them as they left Montreal. Led by the marching band of the Seventy-fourth Regiment, the parade of clergy and enthused locals snaked its way through the streets to the new parish church of La Nativité de la Très Sainte-Vierge. As the procession approached, Power appeared on the balcony of the church, and the crowd gave a deafening roar. In the throes of the Catholic revival, these people did not need to be told that there was a hero in their midst. The scions of Laprairie could now boast that their village had given the world a bishop. This was all a little much for the shy and retiring Power, who had never craved the limelight, let alone such unbridled adulation.

The procession entered the church, and the solemn ceremony began with a sung Mass, followed by the Rite of Consecration. In addition to the three bishops, who were required to be present to validate the conse-cration, thirty priests were in attendance, including many of Power's colleagues from the Diocese of Montreal. There were also priests from Québec and Kingston, including Father William Peter MacDonald, a vicar-general and the highest-ranking cleric in the territory that would soon be Power's diocese. Vincent Quiblier delivered a stirring homily on the dignity of the episcopate. At one point in a discourse that could have been a standard treatise on the origins, duties, and sanctity of the office of bishop, Quiblier added a personal note. He reminded his audi-ence that Power's given name tied him to the mission of his archangelic patron. Like St Michael, said Quiblier, Bishop Power would do battle, and his "new mandate called henceforth to fight more intrepidly against the rebel angel."[117] Quiblier then looked at Power and called upon him to go forth with the blessings of his colleagues and the prayers of his people: "Leave, go fight against the Dragon, in keeping with the Arch-angel your patron saint, go preach the true word to the people of your vast diocese; go bring light to where darkness would have reigned, force back, make noise before the errors, the schisms and the heresies."[118] This homily reinforced Power's consternation about what lay ahead – he faced a battle of celestial proportions.

The consecration event, as animated by Quiblier and reported by *Mélanges religieux*, seemed to mark something much greater than one man's elevation to the episcopate. It was a public acknowledgment of the revived ultramontane church and an assertion that rejuvenated Catholicism would spread across the continent. The message was clear: the frontier would be conquered in Christ's name. To some observers, Power was no mere bishop – he was an affirmation of a church "militant and triumphant" that would establish itself in every corner of British North America. The *Mélanges* enthusiastically pontificated:

> Catholicism was going to receive a new force; a new leader was going to give to his saintly army; this great vocation of Canada, of which one of our correspondents spoke a few days ago, was going to begin to fulfill itself on a grand scale. Indeed, a new and immense diocese has been formed in the western part of Canada, and adds an additional ring to this chain of Episcopal seats that one day must reach, we hope, from sea to sea: *a mare usque ad mare*. Catholic teaching in British America will carry even further its camp and establish sentinels even further in the vast countries of which it covets, and of which its missionaries were the first to take possession. The new bishopric will become the centre of an ardent activity; a more vigorous combat will be fought on our interior oceans where the voice of Catholicism will enter more powerful than ever: *vos Domini super aquas*.[119]

Michael Power was not only part of the great Catholic drama unfolding in Canada, but he and his new diocese were also perceived as central to the success of the drive to extend the reach of the Catholic Church across the continent.

Power's episcopal colleagues and the new cohort of ultramontane enthusiasts had high expectations of the new bishop. Having blessed the cornerstone for the new House of Providence in Montreal, Power hurriedly settled his personal affairs, attended to urgent matters relating to the establishment of the new diocese, and girded himself for the challenge he wished had not been his.[120] Likely with his trials at Drummondville and Montebello in mind, he faced the task of realizing the ultramontane vision in a frontier region with a poor reputation for religious practice.

CHAPTER SIX

✌ At the Edge of Civilization ✍

MICHAEL POWER DID NOT KNOW very much about Upper Canada, which in 1841 was Canada West in the new Province of Canada. He had been there only on short missions to Hawkesbury and Plantagenet while serving at Petite-Nation a decade before. Then, he had had little enthusiasm for that type of mission, but it paled in comparison to the one awaiting him beyond Toronto. In June 1842, as he waited on the dock at Lachine for his steamship, he prepared himself, yet again, to make a great leap into the unknown.

What he did know about Upper Canada he had gleaned from Remi Gaulin, several priests, and letters from other colleagues, and it was daunting. The diocese was larger than the entire land mass of Great Britain and Ireland, with a Catholic population thinly stretched along rivers, lakes, and rough roads from Toronto to Sandwich (Windsor). As a priest of Lower Canada (now Canada East), Power was accustomed to the sense of social, cultural, and political weight that came from being a member of the province's majority. He felt comfortable in an environment filled with the signs of Catholic presence: roadside crosses, shrines, and large village churches. In Canada West, his new flock would be a tiny minority in a powerful Anglican and Protestant ascendancy, and he would find little physical evidence of the Catholic Church in public life. Catholic feasts, liturgical celebrations, and public spectacles of the faith did not mark the passage of the seasons. Here, life would be different.

Despite his misgivings about what he was facing, Power displayed a new confidence, likely derived from the support shown him in Rome as well as at home. Cardinal Fransoni at the Propaganda Fide gave him enthusiastic affirmation, and Ignace Bourget was clearly proud of him. Power was enlivened by the ultramontane revolution, and his ordination to the episcopacy seemed to be a kind of mandate to carry the tenets of that revolution to his new diocese and beyond. The revival had made a lasting impression on his spirituality, and he had begun to speak of his complete surrender to the merciful God, whose gift of grace would sustain his leadership in even the most difficult moments. In a self-deprecating manner reminiscent of the *Imitatio Christi*, Power maintained that his personal weakness would be compensated for by God's protection and blessings, which would be divinely accorded in proportion to his spiritual and physical frailty.[1]

Power would often refer to his dependence on the "merciful God" as he faced challenge after challenge in the newly created Diocese of Toronto. He would also rely upon his frontier experience, his adherence to the devotional revolution fostered by Forbin-Janson and Bourget, and his knowledge of the regulations, customs, and church laws exercised in the Diocese of Montreal. With these three tools, Power would attempt to shape a new diocese. He decided that the first step in taming the Upper Canadian frontier was to impose a strong, centralized clerical authority, and the spirit of the ultramontane revolution and his experience of Bourget's early episcopate would be his most valuable guides. He could also review the challenges he had confronted in the Ottawa and St-François River Valleys if he wanted to reassure himself that strong leadership and the steady application of church law were the key to ensuring that church life conformed to the practices and devotion expected by the magisterium. In his few years as bishop of Toronto, Power would become known for his efforts to affirm episcopal authority, establish clerical discipline, command uniform adherence to local church regulations and canon law, and create an institutional infrastructure that would serve as a framework for a healthy and disciplined diocese.

Although Power was aware of the work that his predecessor – the late pioneer bishop Alexander Macdonell – had already done in the region, almost everything else about his new home was a mystery. A voluminous reader of history, law, and theology, Power was determined to educate himself about the geography, politics, and personalities of Canada West. The first leg of his journey – a steamboat ride from Lachine over the rapids to Les Cèdres, where he would catch another boat to Cornwall and then one to Prescott, all of which would take two full days[2] – gave him immediate insight into the primitive and cumbersome transportation system in the oldest settled portion of the western province. Given this state of affairs in the developed part of the province, he would have felt some trepidation about what awaited him in the remote, virgin part. At Prescott, Power caught a steamer that made direct runs to key western centres: Kingston, Toronto, and Niagara-on-the-Lake (formerly Newark).[3] He opted for a private cabin and his supper served on a china plate, complete with a glass of fine wine, eschewing the less expensive stagecoach option, a bump-a-minute ride along potholed roads.[4] But even though he chose the marine route, Power still furthered his education. He watched the shoreline become less and less developed as he moved west and noted Durham boats and sailing craft filled to the gunnels with Irish, Scottish, German, and English immigrants. Each port of call along the St Lawrence and the north shore of Lake Ontario bustled with newly disembarked settlers, and the wharves and the lanes leading away from these places were clogged with crates, hogsheads, and animals ready for loading onto boats or onto wagons heading inland. Within three days, Power was in Kingston. Bishop Remi Gaulin, his old colleague from the Diocese of Montreal, was there to meet him, and together they travelled on to Toronto, an overnight voyage.[5]

Power's new diocese was a study in contrasts. Although it contained Toronto, the former capital of the province and its most important commercial centre,[6] it also encompassed some of Canada's most rugged and sparsely settled terrain. His jurisdiction began in the east, at the boundary of the Newcastle district and the township of Whitby, on whose eastern frontier was the village of Oshawa; it then extended westward to the town of Sandwich, which lay east of the Detroit River, directly across from the United States. In the south, Power's dominion was bordered by Lake Ontario, the Niagara River, and Lake Erie; moving northwards, it embraced the lakes and rivers of the watersheds of Lake Huron and Georgian Bay and the lands above Lake Superior.[7] Given the vastness of the territory, it is evident why the Vatican simply created the diocese as western Upper Canada and left it to Power to name the location of the official seat of ecclesiastical authority. While arguments could have been made for selecting Sandwich as the see – it had a large Catholic population and served as an entrepôt to the upper country – Toronto was the more obvious choice due to its established reputation and influence in the former province.

Nevertheless, Toronto did not possess the charm or the Old World flavour to which Power had become accustomed in Montreal and Quebec. Known as York until 1834, it was nothing more than a muddy colonial backwater just twenty-five years before Power's arrival. And outsiders in his own day would argue that precious little had changed. Just prior to Power's arrival, visitor Anna Brownell Jameson described

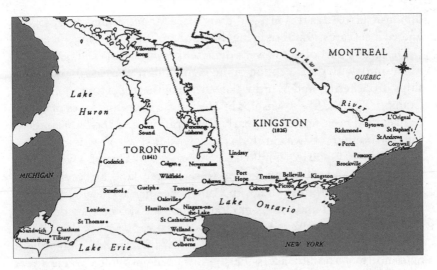

Map of the Dioceses of Toronto and Kingston, 1841 (courtesy of the
Canadian Catholic Historical Association)

Toronto as "strangely mean and melancholy ... a little ill-built town on
low land at the bottom of a frozen bay, with one very ugly church ...
some government offices, built of staring brick, in the most tasteless and
vulgar style imaginable."[8] Its brief history as a town had been equally
undistinguished. Shortly after the cessation of the 1812–14 hostilities
between Britain and the United States, during which it had been burned
and looted by American troops, York had a population of just 1,200.
It was the hub of a farming hinterland, and its watershed and estuary
lands at the mouth of the Don River were the breeding grounds for
mosquitoes, which brought disease to the town.

When Power got there, in 1842, the mosquitoes were still fierce, but the
agricultural frontier had been conquered and was prospering.[9] Toronto
had emerged as Upper Canada's leading market town, possessing the
province's key financial institutions and port facilities for commercial
navigation. Although the mud and wet weather were still a problem – as
one commentator noted, "fatal to the thin shoes of the ladies"[10] – the
ramshackle wooden structures had given way to monuments of brick and
stone, fully modernized and serviced by gas lines. Toronto's population
had reached 15,000, no doubt as a result of the area's growing prosperity
and political importance.[11] With the union of the Canadas in February
1841, Toronto had to surrender its status as capital, but this did not

diminish its role as a regional gathering place for politicians, magistrates, and civil servants responsible for the affairs of Canada West.

The largest portions of Power's diocese sprawled to the north and west of Toronto, with the exception of the farmlands to the east in the townships of Pickering and Whitby (later the southern portion of Ontario County). By 1842, the townships bordering the rivers and lakes of Upper Canada had been settled for nearly a generation, and the only land left for new immigrants was in the back townships, which would eventually comprise Ontario's landlocked counties.[12] In Guelph (Wellington County), for instance, immigrants were offered land at between two shillings and thirteen shillings and ninepence per acre, with no down payment required and only a modest annual fee should they decide to rent instead of purchase.[13] And, shortly after Power's arrival, the Canada Company began promoting settlement in Tiny Township, eighty-eight miles north of Toronto, accessible by the heavily potholed Yonge Street and by steamers crossing Lake Simcoe. In 1842, this corner of Power's diocese, on the tip of the Penetanguishene Peninsula, had a population of only 266, and only 643 acres under cultivation.[14] Clearly, the wilderness frontier was still close at hand for the new bishop.

The province's primitive road system linked Toronto with most of the major areas of settlement to the west, east, and north. In addition, by 1842, these roads and the regular steamship service linked Power's episcopal see with important centres of Catholic population in Hamilton and on the Niagara Peninsula.[15] Elsewhere, crude, stump-riddled roads had been hacked from the dense bush in order to connect the former capital with Dundas, Brantford, Woodstock, London, Chatham, and, finally, Sandwich and its surrounding villages. Although a few toll roads still existed on which travellers paid directly for improvements, most public roads in the province were in desperate need of maintenance and repair.[16] As a result, "highway" travel required stamina and strong stomach and buttock muscles, as carts and coaches careened over stumps, roots, ruts, and rocks like tubs in a tempest. In the spring, these roads to the reaches of the diocese streamed with water and muck, making travel slow, filthy, and frustrating.[17] One exception was the route that paralleled the Lake Erie shore. Colonel Thomas Talbot, who had been responsible for much of the settlement in the region, had insisted on building passable roads to link farm settlements and towns to the frontier.[18]

Those wishing to traverse the diocese quickly came to rely on steamships and sailing craft. The former not only expedited travel across

The road between Kingston and York, 1830 (NA, C-012632)

Lakes Erie and Ontario and up major river systems like the Grand, but they also offered the swiftest means of communication between the major towns of the province and between the province and the outside world.[19] Bishops, politicians, merchants, and newspaper editors came to depend heavily on receiving news via the "mail packets" powered by steam. Power could expect to get messages from Europe via steamships connecting with stagecoaches and sailboats in about twenty days.[20]

Beyond these networks of travel and communication lay the more remote regions of the diocese, which Power had to find a way to access. In 1827, construction had begun on the Huron Road linking Guelph with the port of Goderich, on Lake Huron.[21] This road became an important colonization route for Irish Catholic immigrants, who carved out farmsteads in the counties of Perth, Huron, Waterloo, and Wellington. Ten years later, work began on a roadbed that would link Oakville, on Lake Ontario, to Owen Sound, on Georgian Bay, thereby facilitating settlement in what would eventually become the counties of Bruce, Grey, and Simcoe.[22] Between Owen Sound and Goderich lay millions of acres of lakes, trees, and beaver meadows, which were only accessible by canoe or lake boat. The upper lakes could be traversed by sailing craft, and later by steamboat. Power's new diocese was truly a great and lonely land. By day, its dense forests shut out the light of the sun; by night, its skies were a panorama of stars (a sight that today is rendered invisible in many places by the glare of city lights). This was a wilderness where one could see through crystal-clear water to a lakebed,[23] and where the roar of the wind through stands of white pine was almost deafening. Compared with a pastoral tour of his diocese, Power's steamship journey from Lachine would seem a mere excursion.

For Power, the social frontiers of his diocese would pose as many challenges as the physical ones. Despite its facade of Anglo-Protestant ascendancy, the province was a rich tapestry of cultural groups, languages, and varieties of Christianity. As Power would discover on his summer rambles through the diocese, there were great numbers of First Nations peoples – the Odawa, Ojibwa, Mississauga, Saugeen, Potawatomi, Chippewa, and the six nations of the Iroquois Confederacy – in the northern and western portions of Upper Canada.[24] Segregated by reserves and non-ceded territorial lands around the upper lakes and areas beyond the pale of European settlement, members of the Algonquin linguistic family were the dominant peoples of the northern region of the diocese.[25] In the southern areas, closer to the farms, towns, and cities of the Euro-Canadians, lived a mixture of Iroquoian- and Algonquin-speaking peoples, the largest concentration of which was on the Six Nations Reserve, a huge tract of land straddling the Grand River, ceded by the British Crown to the Iroquois who had supported the British during the American Revolution. Power had few religious concerns in these parts, principally because Anglican or Methodist missionaries served the few Native people who had embraced Christianity in Six Nations territory.[26]

The diocese also contained a variety of non-English Europeans, some of whom were Roman Catholic, but the majority of whom were not. The largest Catholic group was the French Canadians who had come to live in the Detroit River and Lake St Clair region long before the conquest of 1760. They were the descendants of the trappers, voyageurs, farmers, and artisans who had ventured to Detroit in 1701, when the Sieur de Cadillac had established the hub of the New France fur trade in the "pays en haut." By the 1840s, these French Canadians had formed thriving parish communities in Sandwich (where the church of Our Lady of the Assumption was founded in 1767, Upper Canada's oldest parish), Amherstburg, Maidstone, and Belle Rivière.[27] There were also pockets of French Canadian settlement on the Penetanguishene Peninsula, 150 kilometres north of Toronto, and the remnant of a colony of exiles from the French Revolution at Windham, near the present town of Aurora, also north of Toronto.

As Power's gaze shifted to the west, he would discover numerous pockets of Catholics interspersed among the British, Scottish, German, Dutch, and American farmers.[28] And there were nearly as many Irish Catholics as French Canadian ones. In townships like Kincardine, Hibbert, Biddulph, Adjala, and Adelaide, to name only a few, Irish Catholic immigrants toiled alongside their Protestant neighbours, carving farmsteads out of the bush at a rate of two to three acres per year.[29] These were not the "exiles of Erin" of popular history, who had fled their homes as a result of famine or eviction. Power's Irish flock in western Upper Canada were primarily pre-famine Irish immigrants, small farmers, cottiers, and labourers who could afford to abandon Ireland's antiquated landholding system and purchase farms freehold in the interior colonies.[30] Unlike the stereotypical urban Irish underclass, these Catholics adhered to the province's rural farm settlement patterns, labouring like other farmers to raise livestock, plant orchards, and cultivate wheat – the one crop that in a good year could yield a handsome income.[31] Many of these farmers in the recently settled Huron Tract were still engaged in setting up their farms, and by 1842 they were not yet able to generate sufficient income to support a priest or build a church.[32]

Closer to Toronto, in Wellington and Waterloo Counties, Power would be faced with a small community of German-speaking Catholics. Like their Lutheran and Mennonite neighbours, they hailed from Alsace, Lorraine, and Baden-Wurttemberg, and they were spread thinly through four townships. Power would also be responsible for a pocket of German Catholic settlers on the Niagara Peninsula who were temporarily being served by a German-speaking priest stationed at Buffalo, New York.[33] The bishop would still need to find more permanent pastoral solutions for German-speakers, especially in the township of Wilmot, near Waterloo – he would have to recruit German-speaking priests from the United States, the German States, or the Austro-Hungarian Empire.[34]

Power would quickly come to understand that the church in western Upper Canada was concentrated primarily in the urban areas, upon which the rural areas were heavily dependent for personnel and services. The major centres of Toronto, Hamilton, Niagara, Brantford, London, St Thomas, and Sandwich were catch basins for Catholics of a variety of ethnic origins. In 1842, however, the bishop would note the increasing presence of Irish Catholic men in the provincial towns that acted as magnets for those engaged in the building trades, day labourers, and transportation workers. They saved their wages to buy land or support the families they had left behind on the frontier. Many found employment in the ports of entry like Toronto or Hamilton, but others were forced to wander from town to town in search of work.[35]

It would wrong to categorize the urban portion of Power's new flock – including the Irish – as a faceless, feckless urban proletariat. Catholic communities in Upper Canadian cities and towns harboured all of the class divisions, petty politics, and social hierarchies that existed in non-Catholic communities. The difference between Catholics and Protestants was really a matter of scale, as the Catholics had a much smaller presence in the province as a whole. Catholic booksellers, grocers, lawyers, dentists, and haberdashers flogged their goods and services in the local weeklies.[36] In 1840, there were even some Catholic weeklies, including the *Catholic* in Hamilton, and Charles Donlevy's the *Mirror* in Toronto. So Power's Catholic flock cultivated the land, pulled teeth, cut stone, reported the news, framed windows, collected Toronto's garbage, drank in local taverns, and sued each other in the courts.[37] It spanned both the social spectrum and the settlement frontier.

What was clear to Catholics in the province was that they were a minority. In all of what had been Upper Canada, now technically Canada West, there were 476,000 people, of whom roughly 65,000 were Catholic. As a religious group, they ranked fourth behind Anglicans (120,000), Presbyterians (114,000), and Methodists (100,000). In his own diocese, Power overestimated that he was shepherd to 40,000 to 50,000 Catholics; the accuracy of this estimate is suspect since it was difficult to enumerate frontier settlers and those who were constantly on the move.[38] Power reported that the minority status of his Catholic flock was all the more precarious because that flock was divided into forty parishes and had two chapels served by nineteen clergy, only four of whom had been born in Canada.[39] Even these figures were deceptive, as the parishes with mission stations inflated the number of areas served to fifty-seven, which, in theory, meant that each serving priest was responsible for administering the sacraments at approximately three stations.[40] Furthermore, the burden placed on individual priests would increase should one of their rank elect to return to the Diocese of Kingston, which was an option open to priests in the new diocese after the division. Not surprisingly, the tone Power used when he begged the Society for the Propagation of the Faith for financial aid was urgent. He argued that Catholic bishops on the frontier were poor, with neither religious establishments nor the means to supply themselves with the resources they needed.[41]

When Power disembarked in Toronto on 25 June 1842, the greatest problems awaiting him were an impoverished church infrastructure, a lack of strong local leadership, a scarcity of funds, and a very fragile unity among believers. The latter point was not to be underestimated. Six years earlier, Power's predecessor, Alexander Macdonell, had placed Toronto under interdict when local priest William O'Grady and a large portion of his mostly Irish congregation publicly criticized the bishop's Tory political ties and locked him out of the church when he attempted to discipline the "malcontents" of St Paul's parish.[42] Prior to the 1837 rebellion, O'Grady left the active priesthood and threw in his lot with radical reformer William Lyon MacKenzie, for whom he served as a writer and clerk. Toronto's Catholic community was torn asunder along political lines, which was symptomatic of deeper divisions between Catholic haves and have-nots – Catholics who had an in with the provincial government and those who existed on the periphery. There were also tensions between the Irish and the French Canadians, between Irish and Scottish church leaders, and among the Irish themselves. These troubles continued long after the conclusion of the rebellion and the deaths of both Macdonell and O'Grady.[43] Catholic notables John Elmsley and Dr. John King came to loggerheads with O'Grady's successor, Father Patrick McDonagh, when the two took up a collection for the construction of a new church. McDonagh, angry at what he considered his rude treatment at the hands of these laymen, protested to Bishop Gaulin that the money would be better used to construct a Catholic school for the poor. Other parishioners also had complaints about McDonagh, whose popularity paled next to that of his flamboyant predecessor.[44]

As Power and Gaulin steamed across Lake Ontario towards Toronto, Gaulin may have revealed to the new bishop that his diocese was a mess. Priests were complaining that the subscriptions for their support were inadequate, accusing their parishioners – including leading citizens – of parsimony. They also voiced their unhappiness with the bishop of Kingston for not paying them their government allowance of ten pounds per year.[45] Facing poverty on the frontier, several of the priests whom Power would desperately need were considering leaving Upper Canada for good.[46] Even William Peter MacDonald, Gaulin's vicar-general in Hamilton, was angry and embittered. His newspaper, the *Catholic*, was in financial trouble because it had too few subscribers, and some of them had failed to pay their subscription fees. Part of MacDonald's problem was that many members of his Catholic flock were on the move, seeking more lucrative employment in the United States or beyond the head of Lake Ontario. In addition, MacDonald believed that local Catholics were in danger of being engulfed by the Protestant majority. The mobility of his flock and their reluctance to part with a shilling had forced him to pay for vestments, chalices, and the services of his assistant out of his own pocket.[47] Tired, frustrated, and somewhat paranoid, MacDonald claimed that "all is Dead in our Diocese,"[48] and he generated a stream of protest that flowed from Burlington Bay to the banks of the Tiber: "I have written to Rome complaining of the inefficient state of the Diocese. It was thought that when a Canadian bishop was chosen, the rich Canadians would have assisted us. What have they done for us? Nothing. Could not my Rev'd friend Angus MacDonald [Macdonell] look into, and ascertain how things are carried on, and what has become of the monies paid for our support? What might not a proper Bishop have obtained from Government for the erection of a Seminary ... when the vile Methodists have obtained some thousands to erect their Victoria College at Cobourg? And lately the Presbyterians?"[49] Stepping off the gangplank in Toronto, Power may well have felt as though he was actually walking the plank.

There was only a small crowd on hand to greet the new bishop, and perhaps, given his shyness, that was just as he preferred it.[50] St Paul's parish had no rectory, so he and Gaulin took rooms at the North American Hotel, which would serve as Power's episcopal palace until he could rent a house in the neighbourhood of the new cathedral of St Paul's.[51] The following day, 26 June, Power met with Toronto Catholics for the first time. On Sunday morning, close to 1,500 of them either jammed into St Paul's, whose tiny nave of 4,140 square feet could barely hold half that number,[52] or spilled out onto the surrounding grounds and streets. Prior to the morning Mass, the men and children of the parish went to the residence of the pastor, Father McDonagh, where the bulls declaring Power as the pope's designated bishop were read and Bishop Gaulin formally relinquished his authority over western Upper Canada.[53] The crowd then returned to the church, with both bishops in tow. Gaulin later commented on the unusual nature of the proceedings, but Power's thoughts and words concerning the event have not been recorded. Journalists who attended the morning Mass and the evening service commented that his remarks were affecting and conciliatory, although the throng of believers, crammed like sardines into St Paul's, may have been more appreciative of Power's brevity.

The more attentive and literate members of the diocese would already have known some of the new bishop's intentions. In May, while still at Laprairie, Power had issued his first pastoral letter and ordered that it be read during the first High Mass. For those who were hearing impaired or who suffered from an attention deficit during liturgies, William Peter MacDonald reprinted Power's words in the *Catholic* two weeks before his arrival.[54] The letter's tone and content confirm that Power was aware of some of the challenges facing the diocese, and that he had not ignored the missives sent by an angry MacDonald, whom he had retained as vicar-general. After relating a brief history of the creation of the diocese, Power launched into a discussion of the most serious problem facing the church in the region: disunity. Drawing from Paul's Epistle to the Ephesians, he tipped his hand as to how he would shepherd the renewal of the diocese: "With all humility and mildness, with patience supporting one another in charity, careful to keep unity of the spirit in the land of peace ... One body and one spirit ... Let therefore all bitterness and anger, and indignation and clamour, be put away, be put away from you with all malice. And be ye kind to one another, merciful, forgiving one another, even hath forgiven you in Christ."[55] Built upon additional scriptural foundations, the pastoral sent a gentle yet forceful message to the priests and laity that peace and unity would be demanded of them.

Power believed that peace and unity could be secured through the holy leadership of the priests and the example of upright, moral living set by the laity. He called upon his priests to be pure of heart, shining examples to their flocks, and mild towards all. He further instructed them to eschew all wealth, warning that "the desire of money is the root of all evils."[56] He was equally as forthright with the laity, whom he instructed to live in charity and avoid schism – perhaps a veiled reference to the troubles deriving from the O'Grady problem. Moreover, with a sense of how religious practice could vary widely when applied on the frontier, Power made it clear that laypersons should guard themselves against the carnal desires that make "war" on the soul.[57] As a text, his first pastoral letter illuminated his intention to strengthen Catholic unity in the province by means of strong leadership from a holy, disciplined, and uniform priesthood presiding over an upright, obedient, and devout laity.

But Power was not finished. He added a reminder to the laity that their duty was not only to serve the church but also to be good citizens. As a pastor during the rebellions in Lower Canada, he was well aware that questions of loyalty and liberty were still fresh in the minds of the members of his new flock, who had also been exposed to rebellion, albeit of a less widespread nature. Once again leaning on the scriptures – specifically, Peter and Paul's first letter to Timothy – Power forcefully explained that Catholics in his diocese must be loyal to the Crown: "Honor all men. Love the Brotherhood. Fear God. Honor the King." He insisted that his laypersons were duty-bound not only to obey their priests but also to serve the British Crown and its representatives in Canada. Employing a political theology akin to that of one of his mentors, Joseph-Octave Plessis, he maintained that such loyalty was the will of God. Moreover, in a less than subtle critique of the radical reform movement, he stated that a strong show of loyalty to the Crown "would silence the ignorance of foolish men; as free, and not as making liberty a cloak for malice but as servants of God."[58] He thus set the two benchmarks of his episcopate: ecclesiastical discipline and order in the diocese, and unimpeachable loyalty of the church to the state.

With his installation complete, Power began to establish his residence and make a first-hand assessment of religion in the diocese. The latter task was not easy, and it did it not produce positive results. Two days after the installation, Power and Gaulin travelled by steamer to Hamilton, where they met with William Peter MacDonald, who, true to character, offered them a graphic description of the state of the church in the upper country.[59] After two days of gathering information from the vicar-general, Gaulin departed for Kingston, while Power, with his newly appointed secretary, James J. Hay, returned to Toronto. He spent the next two weeks making arrangements concerning his rented quarters and the administrative infrastructure of the diocese. It was a baptism of fire. After less than two weeks in office, on 14 July, Power learned that Father Alexander Kernan of Niagara had been struck down and killed by a runaway horse and carriage. The bishop now had one less priest to help him minister to a diocese in a state of religious crisis.[60] On top of this, he and Hay were knee-deep in the mundane task of setting up housekeeping (ordering dishes, glassware, and basins) – a nuisance, and a drain on his precious time.[61]

And time was not something that the new bishop was prepared to waste. In the middle of July, with the news of Kiernan's death still weighing on him, he visited the northern section of his diocese. On 21 July, he travelled to Manitoulin Island to attend an annual event at which the British authorities presented gifts to the First Nation's peoples of the upper lakes. By the end of August, Power had sailed as far north as Sault Ste Marie, headed back south via Manitoulin, landed at Penetanguishene, journeyed overland by cart to the village of Coldwater, and continued south by foot, canoe, and wagon to Toronto. Not yet finished his summer rambles, he boarded a steamer for Kingston to confer with Gaulin once again.[62] In only two and a half months of his formal episcopacy, Power had covered over 600 miles, but he had still only seen a small portion of his vast diocese. In addition to learning about the peoples of its northern reaches, he had set the precedent of summer visitations, which he would maintain throughout his tenure. These visits gave him the authority to claim that his diocese was truly at the "outside edge of the civilized world."[63]

What he discovered on these first journeys disturbed him and confirmed many of his fears about the state of the faith in western Upper Canada. He had witnessed non-Catholic missionary endeavours in the north, and he had ascertained that Catholic missionary priests were urgently needed there.[64] People lived too far from the nearest Catholic church or chapel, and they needed more priests to serve them. Even in the established and well-staffed parishes, Power noted that improvements were needed in administration, physical structures, liturgical practices, and the discipline of pastors.[65] On 10 September 1842, Power took the first step in creating a strong priestly leadership by ordering all of his priests to attend a retreat in Toronto, which would be immediately followed by a diocesan synod. All priests were "strictly enjoined to attend"; there would be no excuses.[66] Power's friend Jesuit Pierre

Chazelle, to whom he had handed his parish at Laprairie, was scheduled to direct the retreat. All priests were required to bring with them copies of the Decrees of the Council of Trent and the New Testament, as well as Thomas à Kempis's *The Imitation of Christ*. In addition, those priests who had been ordained outside of Canada were instructed to bring their official dismissal letters and any other documents attesting to the fact that their transfers to Upper Canada had been executed according to canon law. The cassock was mandatory dress. Within days, it became public knowledge that the new bishop intended to use the synod to "adopt a uniform system of ecclesiastical discipline" and bring the frontier diocese into accord with the conciliar decrees issued during the Counter-Reformation.[67] Michael Power's own ultramontane revolution was now underway.

The retreat began on 29 September, the feast of St Michael the Archangel, Power's patron saint and the saint he had chosen to be patron of his diocese. Few facts about the retreat are known, other than that several priests missed it. Chazelle, the retreat's director, was a highly respected theologian and teacher. A native of Montbrison, near Lyons, Chazelle taught dogmatic theology at the Jesuit residence on Paris's Rue de Sevres from 1822 to 1823 and until 1828 at the diocesan seminary at Montmorillon, near Poitiers. Having been expelled from France following the revolution, in 1830, Chazelle became the first superior of the Jesuit mission at Bardstown, Kentucky, where he also served as rector of St Mary's College.[68] He and Power may have met in 1839, when Chazelle preached at a Montreal clergy retreat, but it is clear that the two established a close relationship when Chazelle arrived in Montreal in 1842 as the head of the newly erected Canadian Jesuit mission, the fruit of Bourget and Power's labours in Europe. Steeped in the ultramontane spirituality of the day, Chazelle emphasized religious order, authority, obedience, and harmony in the church, which Power would have considered a tonic for his ailing diocese. By including *The Imitation of Christ*, a favourite of the Jesuits, Power hoped to direct his priests' focus to the inner sanctity, sacrifice, and personal holiness required of them and to offer strength to those of their number facing the challenge of maintaining spiritual health on the frontier.[69] Although only fifteen of Power's priests attended the retreat, Chazelle left Toronto feeling enthusiastic about the possibility of the Jesuits returning to Toronto to resume their mission work, which they had been forced to abandon in the dying days of the *ancien régime*.[70] He and the new bishop likely discussed this possibility, given Power's overtures to the Jesuit general in Rome later in 1842. Power was very pleased with the retreat: he had managed to gather the priests of the region together for the first time in their history, and he was optimistic that Chazelle would give him some much-needed help on the frontier.

When the retreat ended, on 6 October, the four-day synod of the diocese commenced. Power had well-defined goals for the synod: with the Decrees of the Council of Trent in hand and the precedents set by the Diocese of Montreal and the American church during the Council of Baltimore in mind, he would conduct a general discussion of the rules and norms for the diocese and the codification of the approved regulations. With his expertise in canon law and legalistic approach to ecclesiastical discipline, Power was the synod's driving force.[71] His interest in the reforms and the devotional revolution instituted by Bourget had never flagged, and he read and reread the circulars and other documents pertaining to the regulations and disciplines in Montreal that Bourget sent to him.[72] He was also armed with a modest but helpful library, which he had brought with him from Montreal and to which he would add numerous volumes over the next five years, ordering texts on canon law, church history, theology, devotional tracts, and magisterial documents from booksellers in Montreal, Buffalo, and New York.[73] He also relied heavily on his thirty-two-volume set of papal bulls, his *Compendium juris canonici*, and a seven-volume edition of the *Sacred Ritual* (recently purchased) in conducting the synod.[74]

After several days of discussion and prayer with his priests, Power proudly informed Bourget that they had prepared new diocesan constitutions incorporating "the disciplinary rules that had always been observed for a long time in Lower Canada." These new constitutions, he added, would provide the blueprint for the development of the diocese, offer guidelines for his priests, and create "perfect uniformity."[75] Within days, Bourget responded that he was most pleased with the way Power had established discipline in the new diocese. The approval of such an influential mentor undoubtedly buoyed Power's spirits and bolstered his resolve to impose the rule of church law over all Catholics and their priests on the frontier.[76]

The twenty-two constitutions promulgated by the synod covered a variety of things, including norms for sacramental and liturgical life, church construction, lay responsibilities in parish life, and parish finances. Confessional boxes and baptismal fonts were mandated in all churches. Proposed marriages had to conform strictly to the directives of canon law, particularly those involving members of the Catholic Church who would marry members of other Christian denominations. In such cases, Power wanted the *Tametsi* decrees of the Council of Trent to serve as guidelines, even though the French Canadian church had not formally promulgated them.[77] No marriage ceremonies could be conducted in private homes; this would curtail clandestine marriages and those officiated by non-Catholic clergy. In addition, all parish priests had to keep accurate and up-to-date registers of baptisms, confirmations, marriages, and burials. The constitutions even went so far as to authorize *Butler's Catechism* as the official teaching text for Catholic schools and for catechism classes, although the *Catechism of Quebec* could be used in areas where francophone Catholics were the majority. It is not surprising that each of the constitutions that Power set forth was cross-referenced to a council that had set the precedent on the matter or to interpretations of scripture, canon law, pronouncements of popes, or the Decrees of the Council of Trent.[78] In sum, the new constitutions demonstrated the breadth of Power's knowledge of the church and his reliance on the ecclesiastical jurisdictions in which he had been trained.

But perhaps the scope and rigidity of the constitutions regarding priestly life are the most revealing of the bishop's drive to tame the frontier. Power provided touchstones for his priests in the form of regulations governing clerical life in the diocese. His general intent was to rein in the undisciplined members of his clerical team, those whose reputations he had known about long before he left Laprairie. At the heart of his system of rules was an implicit prime directive: his priests must always defer to the authority of their bishop; he was in charge, whether they liked it or not. Priests were prohibited from crossing parish boundaries to collect money or administer the sacraments unless he authorized them to do so. This constitution was designed to end the practice of frontier priests poaching each other's stipends for marriages, baptisms, and other church-related services. It was accompanied by a regulation that forbade pastors to leave their parishes or drop their assigned duties without the bishop's consent. Moreover, they had to refer to the collection of monies as the acceptance of alms, lest it appear that they were engaged in simony – selling the services of the church.[79] In a more controversial move, Power mandated that priests look like priests and decreed that they wear cassocks in their rectories and in public (there was a special provision for wearing black garments while travelling). Power thought that priests should always be recognizable as members of an ecclesiastical order, and to this end the constitutions declared, "the Collar, suitable to presbyters, is called by Benedict XIV 'the badge of priests' [and] is worn by all everywhere."[80] In order to avoid scandal and to arrest a practice engaged in by some frontier priests, it was expressly forbidden for a woman to live in a rectory, even if she was a housekeeper. In fact, priests were not to have any "intimate association with women"[81] – not even with female family members. Housekeepers had to be women of "advanced age."[82] Power's fifteen priests assented to these rules, and in so doing acknowledged that they would themselves be to blame if they were caught violating them. Having thus established his authority over his priests, Power ordered that one hundred copies of the synod's proceedings be printed and distributed widely within the diocese.

In the months and years to follow, Power would learn that it is one thing to inscribe regulations on paper and another to enforce them in daily life. In the five remaining years of his episcopate, priests and laity alike openly flouted the constitutions he had forged as the cornerstone of his work in the Diocese of Toronto. Of particular concern to him was the continued lack of discipline among church leaders on the frontier. The state of the priesthood in the diocese was an ongoing and weighty concern. He had few priests and many churches and missions requiring pastoral leadership. He was increasingly frustrated not only by this numbers game but also by the quality of the priests he did have. Many of those recruited from Europe brought their Old World problems with them, and their former bishops were delighted to be rid of them. Others entered the diocese without official papers, and others still, schemers who had never been ordained, used their priestly status to extract money from unsuspecting frontiersmen. In a two-year span, from 1843 to 1844, Power refused fifteen itinerant priests who entered the diocese in search of a post. He believed that these men would bring nothing but "scandal" to the church, and he complained to Turgeon, "The good priests here are lacking!"[83]

In searching for new priests and trying to retain those of good quality, Power was often forced to make tough decisions with regard to the spiritual needs of parishes and missions. When, for instance, Father Flouet of Amherstberg left his station and was excommunicated, Power had no one to take his place, and that parish was left without a pastor.[84] Compounding the severe shortage of priests was the fact that two other local priests who served in what is now Essex County, the highly talented Angus Macdonell and a local francophone priest, Father Antoine Vervais, departed the diocese within a year of the new bishop's arrival in order to serve in their dioceses of origin – Kingston and Montreal, respectively.[85] Power resolved that if he could not secure a good and faithful priest for a parish and its missions, then he would leave the post vacant. As he told his confidants several times, better no priest at all than a bad one.[86] The heavy burden this placed upon the shoulders of those priests remaining in the region was akin to what Power himself had experienced in the St-François and Ottawa Valleys.

Coping with defections from the diocese and clerics in need of stern discipline, Power found that he had few priests in whom to place his trust. Out of his small cadre of pastors, he came to depend most heavily on seven men: John J. Hay, his hand-picked secretary; William Peter MacDonald, his outspoken vicar-general in Hamilton; the very popular Edward Gordon in Niagara; the German-speaking Redemptorist Simon Sanderl, who served in the Wilmot and Waterloo areas; James Quinlan, who anchored church life in the north, at Newmarket; Louis Boué, a young and promising priest recruited from the Diocese of New Orleans; and the Irish-born John Carroll, who had served Power's family in Halifax and who had moved west to join his fellow Haligonian in Upper Canada.[87] It was evident, however, that this core group of trusted individuals was not large enough, and this made Power even more determined to create a strong priesthood like that envisioned by the ultramontanists.

By November 1842, Power had become very discouraged by the quality of clerical leadership and the state of parish life, which he had witnessed on his tour of the western frontiers of the diocese. His pessimism was so profound that he withdrew his support for Bourget's grand plan to make the Upper Canadian dioceses suffragans of the proposed archbishop of Quebec. He told Monsignor Giovanni Corboli, consultor to the secretary of the Propaganda Fide, that given the distinct frontier character, the poverty, and the underdevelopment of his dioceses of Toronto and Kingston, these dioceses should continue to report directly to Rome for the time being. He had come to see the Upper Canadian church as very different from those of Montreal and Quebec, where institutions were well established, discipline was more uniform, and parish churches were notable for their "richness and beauty." In fact, Power suggested that these two French Canadian dioceses were more naturally suited to forming an ecclesiastical province. As for the Upper Canadian dioceses, Power thought that they still had "need of direct surveillance from the Holy See" and maintained that an archbishop in Quebec City would be too remote to speak effectively for the fledgling dioceses on the Canadian frontier.[88] Ironically, Power now sounded like the Maritime bishops whom he had lobbied to support the Bourget plan only a year before. His reversal, however, came too late in the game; the wheels were already in motion to create the archiepiscopal see in Quebec.

Although disappointed at the state of his diocese, Power was by no means defeated. Two days before penning the letter to Corboli, he had begun one of the most important initiatives of his episcopate: recruiting priests from the Society of Jesus. He had made his initial contact with the Jesuits in 1841, when he was in Rome with Bourget. He had opened Laprairie to them, thus allowing them to return to the seigneury they had once held for the French Crown. This had endeared him to the Society of Jesus,[89] paving the way for a mutually beneficial relationship between the diocese and the Jesuits. Later, he had invited Jesuit Pierre Chazelle to direct his first priests' retreat, thus solidifying his relations with the Jesuits who were already in Canada. Then, on 12 November 1842, Power formally invited the Jesuit general in Rome, Father Jan Roothan, to send a company of his order to Upper Canada. Power's plan for the Jesuits was twofold: first, he wanted them to act as missionaries to the province's Native peoples; second, he wanted them to help educate the children of Irish immigrants, who were increasing in numbers every year.[90] He explained to Roothan that during his pastoral visitation to the upper lakes the previous summer, he had noted about 6,500 Natives, of whom he reckoned about 2,500 were Roman Catholic and some 600 were "fervent Christians" living on Manitoulin Island. He had only one missionary in the region, Jean-Baptiste Proulx, and the Native peoples themselves had asked for more.[91]

In the eyes of Power, Proulx, and the Catholic Native peoples, the Catholic Church in the region was at a near crisis point due to the increased presence of Anglican and Methodist ministers. So Power sounded the alarm. He insisted that if the church did not mount a more effective effort on the mission frontier, then the Protestants, who were supported by the state, would prevail. In his closing remarks to Roothan, Power even employed nostalgia, tugging on the Jesuits' heartstrings and appealing to their pride, insinuating that the work that they had started in the seventeenth century had not been completed: "This country has already been watered by the sweat of your veteran fathers, the Brébeufs, the Lallements, the Jogues."[92] The bishop also laid out the financial arrangements, assuring Roothan that the generous Society for the Propagation of the Faith (SPF) in Lyons and Paris would assist in this mission. In fact, that week Power sent letters to the SPF employing the same arguments and much of the same language as the letter to Roothan.[93]

The Jesuits took little convincing, although Roothan was uncertain as to the availability of the personnel serving in the French province.[94] Pierre Chazelle was Power's most enthusiastic ally, and he assured Roothan of the advantages of Power's proposal. Although they had been in Montreal less than a year, Chazelle and his compatriots were openly upset with Bourget, who had asked them to take over a heavily indebted school in Chambly. The Jesuits were willing to establish a school, but they wanted to start their own institution at Laprairie, their base of operations in Lower Canada. Bourget refused to permit it, and Chazelle confided to Roothan that the bishop had bowed to pressure from the Sulpicians, who did not want to see their competitors set themselves up so close to Sulpician educational operations in Montreal (later, in 1848, the Jesuits would plant themselves firmly in Montreal, establishing Collège Ste-Marie).[95] Thus, in light of the Jesuits' temporary setbacks in Lower Canada, Chazelle regarded Power's invitation as a wonderful opportunity to work with Natives peoples in "this magnificent colony." He reminded Roothan that he had conducted the retreat for the priests of the diocese and had found Power to be a man of "elevated and wise views ... filled with zeal and activity."[96] In Chazelle's eyes, this project merited Jesuit preference, and he urged Roothan to grant Power's request, particularly since the bishop had promised SPF funding.[97] By May 1843, Roothan had agreed to the plan, and so had the superior of the French Jesuits in Paris. On 30 July, Fathers Jean-Pierre Choné and Pierre Point assumed control of the parish at Sandwich, soon to become the base of Jesuit operations in the northwest.[98]

While Power now had much to celebrate, he still had some fences to mend. Bourget was not pleased by what he might have seen as Power poaching his Jesuits. Before inviting the Jesuits to Upper Canada, Power had acknowledged to his mentor that he desperately needed priests; he also pointed out that Bourget had a wealth of clergy with the recent arrival of both the Jesuits and the Oblates, and that he would willingly take recruits from Montreal if Bourget offered them.[99] None were forthcoming. Power's invitation to Roothan must have been a poorly kept secret, however, because within days of writing to the Jesuit, Power was obliged to defend himself to Bourget. He assured his mentor that he had never intended to steal his Jesuits, and that he would never accept Jesuits in Upper Canada who "were already employed" in Lower Canada.[100] What Power actually meant by this could be understood in two ways: either he meant that he would not attempt to recruit any Jesuit from Lower Canada, or he meant that he would try to lure away

any Jesuit who had no assigned duties – one such Jesuit was Dominique du Ranquet, who was learning the Algonquin language at Deux-
Montagnes.[101] But whatever Power meant, Bourget had no intention
of losing a single priest.[102] The matter seemed to complicate relations
between the two friends; they even began to haggle over whether or not
Power should be reimbursed for all the expenses he had incurred during
their European tour of 1841. Bourget said that he had never agreed to
cover all of Power's costs, and he also pointed out that the tour had been
of inestimable benefit to Power since it had provided him with an opportunity to make connections that could help his new diocese. Bourget also
implied that since his diocese had paid the passage of several members
of religious orders who had come from France and were now employed
elsewhere, those who had employed them should consider reimbursing
the Diocese of Montreal. After all, he told Power, the Diocese of Quebec
had reimbursed Montreal £150 for the passage of Oblates who had gone
to work in the Saguenay region of Signay's diocese.[103] At this point in
their argument, Power decided to let the money issues drop.

In the summer of 1843, Power assigned the Jesuits to the western
flank of his diocese. Once Point and Choné had arrived at Sandwich,
Father Angus Macdonell – who had elected to go back to Kingston but
was staying on until a replacement could be found – was free to leave.
Power saw Macdonell's departure as a serious blow to the diocese, and
he continued to make the priest offers, all of which Macdonell declined;
Gaulin was ill, and Macdonell believed that his home diocese needed his
services and had the greatest claim upon him.[104] Soon, the Jesuits were
in control of the western frontier of the diocese, and it appeared that
Power's plan to secure the frontiers of his vast diocese was meeting with
some success. While there were some missteps – in 1844, for example,
du Ranquet was dispatched to Walpole Island northwest of Sandwich
to establish a mission among the predominantly animist and Protestant First Peoples of the area, and his ill-fated mission would generate
considerable controversy[105] – overall, Power was making progress. In
1845, the Jesuits replaced the secular Proulx on Manitoulin, employing
the island as their bridgehead for missions in Penetanguishene and the
north shore of Lake Huron. With this move into the upper lakes, the
Jesuits established a presence in what is now Sault Ste Marie. By 1848,
they had founded the mission of Immaculate Conception among the
Ojibwa near Fort William, at the head of Lake Superior.[106] At that point,
Pierre Point was the dean of the entire western territory, including all
francophone Catholics, a position given to him by Power in 1847, prior

to the bishop's departure for Europe.[107] Power even expanded the Jesuit administration beyond First Peoples missions. In 1847, he appointed a Jesuit to serve the Germans in Wilmot and Waterloo.[108] Delighted with how well his plan for the west had unfolded, a jubilant Power told du Ranquet and Choné that he never ceased praying for God's blessings on their mission "for the glory and interest of the Church."[109]

While that plan was in progress, Power worked assiduously to provide a living wage for the priests who had decided to remain in the Diocese of Toronto. Of particular concern to him was the fact that William Peter MacDonald had been ignored when he complained that the semi-annual government allowance (ten pounds to eleven pounds, five shillings) promised to Catholic priests at the time of the union had not been paid to eligible priests in Canada West.[110] In 1843, Francis Hincks, the inspector general of public accounts for Canada West, altered the method of payment of the allowance, adding the requirement that clergy with an entitlement (those who were serving in Upper Canada at the time of the union in 1840–41) would have to apply to the legislature directly for their stipend.[111] Power considered this alteration problematic in two ways. First, it deprived his priests of their promised income. Second, compelling priests to apply directly to the legislature undermined the authority of the bishop. Power made his first venture into the realm of provincial politics by petitioning Robert Baldwin, Francis Hincks, and Receiver General John H. Dunn to ensure the continued payment of the allowance to entitled veteran priests. Moreover, he insisted that these payments be made directly to the bishops of Toronto and Kingston, who would then distribute them to their priests.[112]

While Power's intervention worked from a political point of view – the principal political players acquiesced to his wishes – not all of his colleagues were pleased with it.[113] After his appointment as the coadjutor bishop of Kingston, in 1844, Patrick Phelan insinuated that Power had interfered in the affairs of the Diocese of Kingston. Power's response to his old friend was blunt. Had he not intervened, he said, neither the priests of Phelan's diocese nor Phelan himself would have received the monies that were owed them by the government.[114] Although the stipend was relatively small – an average of twenty-five pounds per recipient annually – the loss of it would be devastating to men who constantly had to prod their congregations for a salary and housekeeping money. In fact, Power's efforts appeared even more altruistic because only ten of his priests were eligible for support compared to fifteen of Phelan's.[115]

Power had managed to get some much-needed cash for his fieldworkers while preserving the authority of bishop over priest.

But despite his efforts to reinforce the authority of the local bishop, Power still found it difficult to convince many of his priests to change their ways. Nearly a dozen of them received frequent stinging epistles from Power, usually prompted by what the bishop considered their "unpriestly" or outright scandalous behaviour. Between his arrival in Toronto in 1842 and his untimely death in 1847, Power dealt with forms of clergy misconduct that fell into three broad categories: public scandal, neglect of duty or financial impropriety, and open violation of the diocesan constitutions. Throughout history, clergy have displayed human failings. Early councils of the Christian church routinely issued canons to control, censure, and discipline violent, unruly, greedy, or overly amorous priests and monks.[116] On the Canadian frontier, where there were great distances between missions and parishes and centres of authority, and limited communications and transportation, clergy stretched the rules or ignored them entirely. Loneliness, overwork, exhaustion, or even paranoia arising from being a Catholic leader in a sea of Protestantism could easily lead a man into temptation.[117] Power had experienced this temptation himself in his early years as a priest, and although he had not always complied with the wishes of Bishop Lartigue, he had remained disciplined and ever mindful of the rules and regulations governing clerical behaviour in the Diocese of Montreal. As a pastor at Ste Martine, he had proven himself a reliable judge of the young priests placed under his mentorship, and as vicar-general, he had been called upon by Bourget to enforce church discipline. As he revealed later to mentor Vincent Quiblier of the Sulpicians, he had high expectations of his own priestly life and lived his life rigidly according to the disciplines of the church.[118]

Power demanded that his own priests keep the same high standards. In the first pastoral letter he issued upon arriving in the diocese, he was very clear about their duties: "The servants of the Lord, priests must not wrangle but be mild towards all men, apt to teach with morality, admonishing them to respect the truth. Be prudent, therefore, and watch in prayers but before all things, have a mutual charity among yourselves for charity covereth a multitude of sins. Be you an example to the faithful in word, conversation and in chastity."[119] Power insisted that his priests use *The Imitation of Christ* to rediscover and strengthen their deference to authority – as Thomas à Kempis wrote, "No matter where you go, here or there, you will not find rest except in humbly subjecting yourself to the authority of a superior."[120] The seeds that had been planted in the Diocese of Montreal and nurtured during the devotional revolution of Bourget had now germinated in the new soil of the Diocese of Toronto.

Power's Montreal roots would also be relevant to his pursuit of new recruits for his diocese and his efforts to inspire a homegrown priesthood. He arranged for all prospective Diocese of Toronto priests to receive their formation at the Grand Séminaire in Montreal under the supervision of Quiblier, whom Power appointed vicar-general for his diocese in 1845. In this role, Quiblier was empowered to administer the tonsure and minor orders and to recommend to the subdiaconate and diaconate the students he deemed ready for the priesthood. Power also instructed Quiblier have each candidate for Holy Orders take the oath for being a missionary, as missionary status was essential for all who served in Power's diocese. Fresh recruits who did not bear the title of pastor or curate would be aware of their subordination to the bishop, and they would be less tempted to conduct themselves as independent pastors, as did some priests who asserted their ancient Gallican rights and did what they pleased in their parishes.[121]

Power's intentions did not play out neatly in the reality of diocesan life. The scandals among the clergy to which Power had to respond were similar to those that had already occurred on settlement frontiers in Nova Scotia, Newfoundland, New Brunswick, Lower Canada, and the Diocese of Kingston.[122] On these frontiers, priests experienced the same distance from authority, loneliness, penchant for the bottle, and lack of intimacy that many of Power's priests would experience in the 1840s. Knowing that the authorities could not respond quickly to an infraction or perhaps never even find out about it, a number of frontier priests tested the boundaries set for them by their bishops.

They fought with parishioners, and they waged turf wars with one another over revenues derived from parishioners who frequently crossed parish boundaries – boundaries that meant little to those in search of better farmsteads, woodlots, or pastures. These battles often erupted in public fits of vitriol, and the source of conflict was often related to money. Power admonished Father William P. McDonagh for rough behaviour, warning him that "great scandal is taken when the people see a Priest flying into such fits of anger and passion."[123] Such behaviour convinced Power to transfer McDonagh out of Toronto, where he had been threatened with legal action by members of his own flock. Power regularly received reports of drunken priests, priests who had women living with them in their rectories, and priests who inflicted verbal or physical on their parishioners.[124] To Power, it was shocking enough that some priests were behaving in such a manner, but it was truly horrifying that their deeds were discrediting the Catholic Church as a whole. Womanizing and intoxication would only validate the "calumnies" circulating about the church among Upper Canada's Protestant majority.[125] Not even Power's stern warnings and threats of dismissal and excommunication could curtail the bad behaviour of some clergy. In Adjala, north of Toronto, Father James O'Flynn provoked not only disciplinary action on Power's part but also the intervention of civil authorities and the courts when he had an "altercation with parishioners."[126]

Others earned Power's wrath for their unauthorized dabbling in civil matters. Clergy who could not account for their spending habits, or who spent an inordinate amount of time maintaining their own properties at the expense of their parishes, received speedy and heated missives from their bishop.[127] Pastors who attempted to transform their church buildings into political assembly halls were threatened with suspension if they continued to ignore Power's directive that churches were to be used solely for divine worship.[128] Power severely reprimanded a priest who had a rather fulsome record of offences for selling trees that he had cut down on church property.[129] He accused another of not being "what a priest should be" because he spent more time on his farm near Maidstone than in his parish. Worse still was the fact that this priest had incurred an embarrassing personal debt.[130] A repeat offender, Father O'Flynn of Adjala, stretched the bounds of credulity – Power discovered that he had been running his hogs in the parish "burying ground." "This manner of acting," wrote an agitated Power, "has shocked many of those who witnessed the fact beyond all expressed."[131]

While all scandals and breaches of discipline involving his priests disturbed Power, transgressions of the constitutions of 1842, to which the priests of the diocese had assented, cut him most deeply. After all, these rules had been Power's means of instituting order, structure, and discipline where precious little had existed, and it dismayed him to see them ignored and sometimes flouted. A number of priests were still poaching pew rents in neighbouring parishes and collecting donations for sacraments they had no legal right to administer.[132] Others remained absent from their parishes without Power's permission, a violation of constitution X of the synod.[133] Power's anxiety about lack of priestly discipline in the diocese was enhanced by reports that many of his clerics were simply ignoring the diocesan regulations and universal canons regarding the administration of the sacrament of holy matrimony. Mixed marriages were being blessed without proper dispensations; there were problems of consanguinity when cousins married; and minors were marrying without parental consent.[134]

Yet of all of the constitutional violations, none upset Power more that those involving clerical dress. His desire to see Catholic priests dress according to their vocation, both in public and in private, had been enshrined in constitution XVII. The cassock not only made a symbolic statement about the dignity, distinctiveness, and holiness of the priestly estate, but it also provided priests with a means of modelling Catholic leadership at a time when the church was in the throes of the ultramontane revolution. For Power, the wearing of the cassock was a visible expression of the church's presence in society and a practice to which he had become accustomed in Lower Canada. For priests in Upper Canada, however, such public statements of priestly office were not customary. It was one thing for a priest to wear a cassock on the streets of Catholic Montreal or Quebec, where it would prompt little more than a respectful tip of the hat. It was quite another thing in the Protestant towns of Toronto, Hamilton, Goderich, or London, where such a sartorial display could provoke a hurled snowball, a snide comment, or an insult. Moreover, priests of Scottish and Irish origin, who predominated in Upper Canada, knew that in their homelands cassock-wearing clergy were subjected to intimidation and persecution. For them, donning the cassock would have been unthinkable prior to the Catholic emancipation of 1829; and even after that date it was still unadvisable, given the sense of religious propriety and the anti-Catholic sentiment among some Protestants.[135] The overwhelming presence of Protestants in Upper Canada, and the manner in which Protestant culture permeated the social life and political institutions of the province, discouraged most Catholic priests from being ostentatious in their clerical dress.[136] Power's inability to enforce constitution XVII indicated both the persistence of local tradition and the bishop's unwillingness to acknowledge that different Catholic cultures were emerging on either side of the Ottawa River.

Nevertheless, in this as in all things, Power demanded unquestioning obedience from his priests. When Father Patrick O'Dwyer, a popular temperance preacher and the pastor of the London parish, refused to abide by the diocesan dress code, Power warned him that if he refused to conform to constitution XVII he would be denied absolution. "I hope that you will not compel me to have recourse to the censures of the

Church for the enforcing of regulations," wrote Power, "but whatever may be the consequences, *they shall be observed*."[137] Although he was popular among the laity, O'Dwyer had been in Power's bad books before, and the bishop was not about to grant an exemption from constitution XVII to any priest, regardless of his reputation. Power had even severely remanded his vicar-general, William Peter MacDonald, for not adopting the dress code as "a rule of conduct." MacDonald annoyed Power further by reminding his bishop that not even the priests in Rome were subject to such strict regulations regarding clerical dress. Power's retort was swift and to the point: "We are not here, Rev'd Sir either in Rome or Spain. Out in the Diocese of Toronto ... You are therefore hereby commanded under penalty of suspension to wear habitually after the 12th day of this month, the *sutan* (sic) *vestum talarem* in the town of Hamilton and in your own house. You must moreover adopt the whole article [XVII] as a rule of conduct."[138] Power also criticized MacDonald for making flippant remarks on the subject in the *Catholic*, of which MacDonald was editor, and for directing disrespectful comments at Power himself in their correspondence. The aged MacDonald was still smarting because Power had taken away his principal responsibilities as vicar-general, allowing him only to retain the dignity of the title.[139] It would have been very difficult for MacDonald to forego the Scottish custom of wearing street clothes, and this difficulty was compounded by the fact that in the *Catholic* he had been less than charitable towards local Protestant leaders – wearing the cassock would make him more readily identifiable to those who had scores to settle with him.

Power's unequivocal defense of the constitutions, his sharpness of tone, and his frequent missives to offenders in which he discriminated by neither age, rank, nor reputation, revealed a side of him that few had ever glimpsed before his episcopacy. His manner of dealing with offending priests during his five years as bishop took on a predictable pattern. Upon first hearing of an infraction, he would write a strongly worded letter rebuking the priest in question and reminding him of the importance of uniform obedience to the canons of the church or the constitutions of the diocese, depending on the case. He would then warn the priest that if he did not discipline himself and abide by the rules, then he would face a penalty relative to the transgression – suspension of his priestly faculties, removal from his parish, removal from the diocese, or excommunication.[140] Power delivered these warnings in a stinging invective, telling a priest that he was "bad," untruthful, or deceitful; he declared to one transgressor, "the only thing I regret, in the pres-

ence of God, is ever having employed you in the Holy Ministry."[141] He
suspended another priest, placing his church under the supervision of the
lay churchwardens, and refused to correspond with him any further.[142]
After clashing repeatedly with Power, some priests were suspended or left
the diocese of their own volition. A few fought back. Patrick O'Dwyer
of St Thomas, for example, allegedly spoke improperly of his bishop
from the pulpit.

There is no doubt that Power's short episcopate was a stormy one in
terms of his relations with a majority of his priests. The confrontations
can be accounted for in several ways. Certainly, the realities of life for
priests on the settlement and missionary frontiers undermined Power's
efforts to instill strong episcopal authority in the region and implant
in Upper Canada the principal elements of the ultramontane revolution. But some of Power's contemporaries saw the bishop's battle royals
as resulting from his severe personality and heightened sense of self-
discipline. Power's seemingly endless trouble with Father Michael Mills
of Brantford (after 1843, of St Thomas) is a case in point. Lay observers
in 1842 might have assumed that the two men were natural allies. The
popular Mills had been honoured with a request to preach the Sunday
homily for the Pontifical Mass of the Holy Ghost during the first synod
of Toronto, singled out as worthy of preaching to his peers and the laity
in the nave of St Paul's.[143] Eventually, however, they would engage in a
conflict that would illuminate some of Power's personality flaws.

Mills was no model priest. He had violated practically ever major
constitution of the synod, and more: he interfered with the affairs of
other parishes; he used abusive language in speaking to parishioners;
he permitted women to reside in his presbytery; he drank to excess; he
completely disregarded the clerical dress code; and he failed to enforce
the canons pertaining to marriage in his parish. Power had charged
him generally with "unpriestly and un-Christian conduct."[144] One can
understand Power's exasperation and, perhaps, the harsh tone of his
language: "No clergyman has ever shown more bitterness and violence
than you, when other priests, *even your superiors*, thought themselves
authorized to interfere with those committed to your charge."[145] Mills's
activities in Brantford so dismayed and disgusted his flock that they
demanded that Power remove him and send them a new pastor.[146] In a
rare display of episcopal acquiescence to the petitions of the laity, Power
moved Mills to St Thomas in 1843, although the new surroundings
did little to discourage Mills's inappropriate behaviour. In fact, Mills

became an even worse problem for the Catholic faithful of the area and for Power.[147]

What makes the Mills case remarkable is not just the manner in which it confirmed Power's observation that the church in Upper Canada was mired in "scandal." The explosive relationship between Power and Mills reveals that Power's efforts to order the frontier diocese were complicated by his preoccupation with the letter of church law and episcopal authority. When his directives were ignored, he would often erupt in a fury that, according to Mills, put his ability to lead in question. Power kept very few of the letters written to him by his priests, although one poignant and lengthy missive from Mills is held with Power's personal papers. In it, Mills gently picks apart the bishop's personality, and, with a flare and an audacity not in evidence among his peers, he accuses Power of being a tyrant: "You seem to me, My Lord, easily excited, and when angry, your voice & your face are very severe indeed. Several lay persons have spoken to me of you: all acknowledge that you are a good Bishop, but you have been accused of tyranny in governing your priests. I have even defended you ... But what could I say when two different persons at two different times & places said to me: 'Did not yr. Bishop raise his hand to you twice in the same morning in his own house and say to you "take care"' ... Several persons say ... Mr Mills it is useless to defend yr. Bishop, he is a true tyrant. He suspended Rev'd McDonagh without any reason or cause, he commanded your silence in the presence of his priests, he governs you with a rod of *Iron*." Mills goes on to explain that he does not intend his words to offend; he is merely imploring the bishop "to govern yr. priests as a father would govern his child."[149]

One could simply dismiss this letter as a rogue's last defense, given Mills's track record and the fact that Power had removed his faculties "forever," telling him he was "altogether unfit to serve at the Altar." One could also view it as the attempt of a desperate man to regain what he had lost by claiming to be his accuser's defender against those who were calling him a tyrant. Although it is a blend of manipulation and contrition, Mills's letter does recall the style and tone of Power's letters to those who failed to measure up. Power perhaps kept the letter as a reminder – like *The Imitation of Christ* – of his own imperfections. Moreover, Mills's missive seems to have worked, prompting Power to demonstrate a remarkable degree of forgiveness towards a man who had surely made his work, at times, seem like purgatory on earth. In December 1846, Mills travelled to Toronto "in tears" to request absolution.

Power not only forgave him and lifted the penalty of excommunication from him, but he also provided him with a fresh start by transferring him to Adjala.[150] As peevish, impatient, and harsh as Power could be, he was not without mercy.

The Mills case, however, did not deter Power from imposing episcopal authority in the diocese. Within a week of Mills's transfer, Power issued his tenth pastoral letter, in which he reasserted the constitutions of 1842 and strengthened their force. He had been ill and therefore unable to call additional synods to discuss diocesan matters, but with this pastoral letter he sent a clear message to his clergy that he would act unilaterally to ensure that diocesan rules were followed, that discipline was the order of the day in the diocese, and that his entire territory was controlled by men who accepted his vision. In the six deaneries of the diocese, he placed loyal priests like Edward Gordon and James Hay. The two frontier deaneries – in the west and the upper lakes – he placed under the control of Jesuit Fathers Point and Choné, respectively. He strengthened the prohibitions against priests visiting from outside the diocese and against his own priests crossing parish boundaries without his express permission – permission that would remain valid for only a limited time. For Power, "the 15th article of the Diocesan Statutes [was] perfectly clear, and in accordance with the rules of the Church." Similarly, in another attempt to impress upon his priests that they had to report to him first, he forbade, "Under penalty of excommunication," the acceptance of a government salary or "any stipend or salary, or ... any place or profit or emolument for the performance of ecclesiastical function, from the Government, or any Civil, Military, or other Department."[151] Power was not rejecting the idea of priests serving the state – far from it. He was insisting that he alone, as bishop, had the authority to approve any assumption of civil duties on the part of his priests.

One reason that Power was reiterating his demand for obedience from his cadre of priests was that he would soon be leaving the diocese in their hands. He planned to travel to Europe, where he would try to re-establish and strengthen contacts with those who could help finance and provide personnel for his mission to build a church at the "edge of civilization."

CHAPTER SEVEN

◞ The Fifth Age ◟

IT WAS BECOMING INCREASINGLY evident to his priests and to the laity that Michael Power had been seized by the spirit of the church "militant and triumphant" that had marked his consecration ceremonies at Laprairie. With the 1842 appointment of William Dollard as bishop of New Brunswick, Power understood that the Catholic conquest of North America was well underway. Knowing that his vision was shared by many of the colleagues he had left behind in Lower Canada, Power wrote with passion to his old friend Joseph Marcoux, "I hope that soon we will have an unbroken chain of Bishops and Missionaries from Halifax to Columbia, and from the Hudson Bay to Cape Horn, including all isles and inlets in this great area. You admire as I do the Church's rapid conquests and divine Providence's admirable ways: I will convert the infidels, but will the heretics enter the Church's bosom? The poor; the ignorant; the common people; one must hope that God will have mercy on them."[1]

Power's belief that he and his new diocese were part of a world Catholic revolution was not surprising, given the explosion of ultramontane enthusiasm among Catholics during the mid-nineteenth century. Many of Power's contemporaries, and particularly his mentor Ignace Bourget, had already been transported by the idea that the "true" faith would triumph through the re-energized agency of priests and bishops. It is surprising, however, that Power saw this Catholic conquest of the continent as a means to an even greater end. He asked Marcoux if he thought there were more important signs to be read in the progress of the ultramontane movement, particularly in the conversion of the "infidels," the "heretics," and the poor. He suggested to his friend that perhaps they were standing at the end of an era – a "fifth age" – poised to enter the final dispensation, as prophesied in the Book of Revelation.

Quoting the *Vulgate*, Power said that he believed the end of time was near, "But the strong, the powerful, the learned, who among them will repent? It is said in chapter XVI of the Apocalypse, speaking of those that live in this time that some see as the end of the fifth age of the Church: *factum est regnum eius tenebrosum et commanducaverunt linguas suas prae dolore et blasphamaverunt.*"[2] The Revelation passage in question depicted the Fifth Angel of the Apocalypse, who poured out his bowl on the "beast, whereupon his kingdom was thrust into darkness" and "the people gnawed their tongues in agony." Instead of being contrite and repentant, these people remained obdurate and cursed God. Power recognized the same type of obduracy on the frontier – among Protestants, non-Christians, and even Catholics – and he saw it as a sign that the end of time was at hand.

Where, or from whom, Power got such ideas is a mystery. Explicit references to the Apocalypse appear neither in his public statements nor in his other private letters. Yet his early experiences on the frontier and the challenges of his new diocese prompted him to suggest to Marcoux that his work was part of a plan that transcended the dreams of the Canadian hierarchy, and even the wishes of the papacy. Perhaps the references to fourth-century Christian apologist Lactantius included in remarks made at Power's consecration had tapped a far greater vein of apocalyptic thought than that which Power had already explored. In the seventh book of *The Divine Institutes*, Lactantius discusses the "last times of the world" in terms of six ages: "since all of the works of God were completed in six days, the world must continue in its present state through six ages, that is six thousand years."[3] If Power had not actually read Lactantius, he would have been exposed to his ideas through the writings of Félicité de Lamennais, which were on the curriculum of Lower Canadian seminaries and colleges until 1834, when the priest-philosopher was condemned by Gregory XVI. Before the Vatican prohibition, Lamennais had been a favourite of Jean-Jacques Lartigue, Power's bishop and the force behind the ultramontane movement in Canada. Lamennais had significant influence in Quebec, and Power had written his name in the margins of a cahier of aphorisms by "an old author" dating from his Montreal school days.[4] In addition to being a pioneer of the ultramontane movement, Lamennais was a fervent Millenarian, who, in his famous *Paroles d'un croyant* (1834), wrote, "the times were drawing near."[5] Whatever his sources, Power had begun to see his episcopal work as serving a much higher purpose than he had once thought: it was a means of ushering out the Fifth Age, at the conclusion of which the unfaithful would either be converted or doomed to perish.

The conversion of the continent depended upon the strict discipline of the clergy, but there was more to it than that. Power and other church leaders also had to ensure the appropriate behaviour of the laity, discipline and order in the parishes, and the acceptance on the part of all Catholics of the authority of the bishop. In Power's vision, the frontier would become a model of holiness, not just for the sake of the church but also of the entire province. As early as 1842, his parish visitations were making him aware of the pressing need to reform the religious life of the laity and restructure the administration of parishes and missions. When he actually came face to face with members of his flock, Power had to relinquish any hope that he might have inherited from his predecessor, Alexander Macdonell, for a pious frontier laity.[6] The tavern culture, perpetuated by the many grog shops and watering holes along the province's trails and major roads,[7] served as a constant reminder to Power of how difficult it would be to transform the frontier. Itinerant priests, however, were already taking to the stump and pulpit, emulating Ireland's Father Theobald Mathew in their crusade to rescue the faithful from the demons of drink and drunkenness.[8] In the first few years after Power's arrival in the diocese, priests and editors alike had come to see intoxication as the principal cause of crime, disease, poverty, and "spiritual wretchedness" in Upper Canada.[9] In Power's day, there was a general belief in a correlation between sobriety and religious diligence, which entailed regular appearances at the altar rail for Eucharist. Father James O'Flynn of Adjala boasted that 2,000 people had taken the "pledge" in his parish, and thirty to forty persons of "both sexes approach holy communion every Sunday."[10]

While alcohol abuse was all too common on the frontier, Power was also disturbed by a number of other moral abuses he had witnessed on his visits to frontier parishes – clandestine marriages, incest, extramarital sex, infanticide, and, in one case, abortion.[11] Power also noted that Catholic burial grounds were poorly maintained, or the regulations governing them were ignored; particularly upsetting to him were cases in which Catholics were interred with non-Catholic spouses or family members. Furthermore, bodies were being exhumed and reburied without the church's consent.[12] Church buildings were neglected, altars were not maintained, confessional booths were missing, religious articles had been stolen, and the record systems of the lay trustees were in disarray.[13] Some Catholics were joining secret societies akin to Masonic lodges, a practice condemned by the church – for example, Irish workers on the Welland Canal had reportedly been drawn into clandestine worker associations or loosely knit labour fraternities.[14] The sum of these conditions, no doubt solidified Power's conviction that the laity needed reforming at least as badly as the priests.[15] Power's episcopal colleague Pierre Paul of Detroit had told him about problems with Catholic discipline and worship in his part of the world, but the bishop took little consolation in the fact that his problems were not unique.[16]

His program to reshape the Catholic Church on the frontier took three distinct forms: education and lay formation, strict application of sacramental and disciplinary regulations, and administrative reform that would centralize control of the parishes with the bishop. To make certain that his reforms took hold, Power travelled to as many regions of the diocese as he could in order to make his presence felt. Beginning with his pastoral visit of 1842, every summer and autumn thereafter, barring illness, Power took to the roads, lakes, and rivers of his diocese on a mission to assess the development of his parishes and implement necessary reforms.[17] To assert the aims of the church and defend it more broadly, he supported William Peter MacDonald's editorship of the *Catholic*, digested each issue carefully, and made suggestions to the editor when he thought there was a need to address public insults directed at the church by individuals or the secular or religious press.[18] Until it ceased publication in April 1844 due to a lack of funds and MacDonald's advanced age, the *Catholic* was a valuable resource for literate Catholics from Upper Canada to Nova Scotia who wanted news of the church and the world, essays on sacraments and piety, calendars of church observances and feasts, and political commentary supportive of the reform benches in the assembly.[19]

But Power's educational program did more than just maintain a newspaper or mandate annual personal visitations. Since the reformations of the sixteenth century, both Catholics and Protestants had used catechisms to bridge the gap between what churches preached and what the faithful were supposed to believe and practice. Larger volumes by Luther, Calvin (for Protestants), or Pius V (for Catholics) were distilled into abridged manuals written in the vernacular. Power was anxious that his reforms penetrate to the youngest and most vulnerable members of his flock, so, in 1843, he and Remi Gaulin published their own version of *Butler's Catechism*, an English-language question-and-answer-style catechism popular among British Empire Catholics. There are few remaining copies of this uniquely Upper Canadian catechism, although its publisher, Charles Donlevy of Toronto, printed at least one hundred of them. With the Power-Gaulin *Butler's Catechism*, which had been authorized by the first Toronto synod, Power attempted to reach his flock by means of a simple and direct instructional tool.[20]

In another effort to reach the greatest possible numbers of Catholics
in his diocese, Power tapped into the devotional streams emanating from
the ultramontane revolution in Europe and Lower Canada. His most
significant effort in this regard was introducing lay confraternities and
public devotions to the Diocese of Toronto. Power's intentions were little
different from those of ultramontane bishops elsewhere. He wanted to
inculcate a greater degree of piety among laypersons; to enhance individual spirituality through group prayer and fraternal organizations; and to
bind Catholics at the parish and diocesan level to international Catholic
organizations of prayer and devotion. He had not forgotten the efforts
of Forbin-Janson in the Montreal district, and he maintained contact
with the French bishop. In 1844, following Forbin-Janson's handwritten
instructions, Power established the Holy Childhood Association for the
conversion and evangelization of the youth of the world, particularly
"dans les pays infidèles."[21] The involvement of the children of his diocese
in such a cause would in itself be a form of domestic evangelization;
these children would be immersed in the spirituality of the day, as it
underpinned the mission of the association.

Similarly, in 1843, Power had instituted the Confraternity of the Immaculate Heart of Mary, thereby linking the francophone members of
the western portion of his diocese with francophone parishes internationally, particularly the parent organization established at the Basilica of
Notre-Dame-de-Victoires in Paris.[22] Members of the confraternity were
rewarded for their attendance by an indulgence of 500 days.[23] Later, in
1845, Power gave the recently arrived Jesuits permission to promote the
Confraternity of the Holy Scapular, a sodality that emphasized Mary's
role in assisting the souls in purgatory.[24] Those who wore the scapular – two pieces of cloth adorned with pictorial representations, joined
together by a long cord, and worn around the neck – were promised
speedy release from purgatory into heaven after death. Power encouraged
other Marian devotions in the spirit of his age, including the celebration
of the Feasts of the Assumption and the Annunciation.[25]

Implanting these devotional societies in the diocese was one of the
ways that Power tried to bring the ultramontane revolution to Toronto
and thereby imprint the rhythms of daily life with a sense of the sacred.
Those who learned to follow the church calendar would have a saint
or a feast upon which to focus their prayers. Power also mandated that
certain feasts celebrated internationally be celebrated in the Diocese of
Toronto: the Feast of the Circumcision, Epiphany, Ascension, Corpus
Christi, Annunciation, and Assumption. Catholics were obliged, as
well, to abstain from eating meat on the vigil of the Feast of Saints

Peter and Paul.[26] But while Power attempted to bring his diocese into conformity with the calendar of feasts and holy days followed in the neighbouring dioceses of Detroit, New York, Cincinnati, and Milwaukee – aiding this effort was the fact that there was considerable human traffic between these dioceses and his own – his brother bishops in Lower Canada insisted on upholding their previously established calendars.[27] At times, enforcing the various regulations and religious practices among his Upper Canadian flock was difficult, owing to the distinct circumstances of Catholics living on the frontier. At Lent, for instance, Power would publish liturgical and dietary obligations in the form of a standard letter, which was often reprinted in the press. In 1844, however, acknowledging the problems of frontier life and the "difficulties under which you [the laity] labour," Power permitted Catholics to consume meat more frequently.[28] His pastoral education plan also extended to church artifacts. In an effort to remind his flock of the Paschal Mystery, the Passion, the death of Jesus, and the Resurrection, Power instructed every congregation to erect the fourteen stations of the cross wherever possible.[29] He intended the imposition of these disciplines, devotions, and displays of public piety to encourage a life of holiness on the frontier and active participation in the devotional revolution that was sweeping Catholic Europe. For Power and his contemporaries, sacred spaces, sacred times, and devotions to sacred persons would demarcate the line between the communion of the faithful and the profane world. Such spiritual segregation could also resolve the problem of the frontier, where the wild environment was a great temptation for the wayward, the weak, or the lost Christian.

Power's promotion of adult faith formation was complemented by the series of diocesan regulations promulgated by the first synod of Toronto. The disciplines imposed upon priests were simply a taste of the detailed and sweeping rules designed to define moral behaviour, sacramental life, and worship in the new diocese. Early in his episcopal mandate, Power imposed regulations covering the stages of pastoral life extending from newborn babies to those ready to be laid in their graves. On the frontier, newborns whose lives were in danger were often baptized by midwives or non-Catholics attending the birth. In 1843, Power issued a formulary for the rite of baptism and instructed that those children baptized in "emergency" situations be rebaptized by a priest as soon as possible, because the validity of the original baptism was "highly doubtful."[30] Infants who succumbed to death would require, like any other Catholic in good standing, burial in Catholic burial grounds, which were also a target of strict regulation by the bishop. These sacred spaces were no longer to be used as grazing areas for livestock; a cemetery had to be enclosed by a fence, and a cross had to be erected at its centre to mark it as consecrated ground.[31] Power was adamant that only Catholics in good standing be interred in these places: "no person who is not a member of the Church can be buried in a Catholic burying ground. Let the Protestant who is so anxious to be buried at the side of his late Catholic wife *follow her faith* and then he can become a partaker in the rights and privileges of the Church of God, but not otherwise."[32] Power reacted sharply to laypersons who, due to frontier conditions and their distance from church authorities, felt that they could do as they pleased in this regard.[33]

The frustration Power felt over the freewheeling practices of many laypersons was most evident when it came to the sacrament of matrimony, which was considered an entry to one of the highest vocations for Catholics. A valid Catholic marriage symbolized the mystical union between Christ and his church. A man and a woman conferred this sacrament upon themselves in the presence of a priest and at least two witnesses, and in so doing they bound themselves to each other in a covenant of love and faith, pledging to bring forth children whom they would educate in the faith. For Catholics and other nineteenth-century Christians, the family was the bedrock of a civil, orderly, harmonious, and peaceful society. Given the importance of the marital estate, the magisterium of the church issued a series of regulations protecting the sacrament of matrimony and upholding the sanctity of marriage. In 1563, for example, the Council of Trent had issued the *Tametsi* decrees, which not only clarified the criteria for valid marriage but also placed the entire institution under the watchful eye of the clergy.[34] Power sought to promulgate these decrees as widely as possible. He had learned while he was in Lower Canada that missions, as opposed to formal parishes, were not subject to the marriage regulations, so, after first consulting with Rome, he ensured that as each parish of his new diocese was created, it adopted the *Tametsi* decrees.[35] These regulations were reiterated over and over again in terms a layperson could understand in the verses of the catechism that Catholics were required to memorize.[36] For those who knew their catechism, the nature and purpose of marriage would be clear, as would the penalties for transgressing the regulations.

Still, many laypersons in Power's frontier diocese continued to behave as though the marriage regulations did not exist. Underage women married older men without the written consent of their parents.[37] Many marriages were performed without the appropriate number of witnesses or the blessing of the parish priest. This often occurred among Irish immigrants, who claimed to have been "married" before leaving Ireland and then admitted in the confessional after arriving in Upper Canada that the union lacked validity.[38] One of the most common violations that Power discovered was the high incidence of marriage between blood relatives, an overt transgression of the canons covering consanguinity and "degrees of affinity."[39] None of this came as a complete surprise to Power, given his previous pastoral work on the Lower Canadian frontier, but the fact that such disregard for church authority was so widespread in his new diocese was very disconcerting to him, partly because it indicated a lack of leadership on the part of his priests. Local pastors failed to publish banns of marriage or charged exorbitant fees for their services, thus driving Catholic couples to seek blessing from civil magistrates, Protestant ministers, or, worse, no one at all.[40] In the Niagara region, couples who wanted to circumvent Power's crackdown on marital irregularities simply crossed the border and were married by the parish priest at Buffalo, no questions asked.[41]

By far the most troubling marriage-related issue was the high instance of unions between Catholics and non-Catholics. Such unions were discouraged because they were viewed by the clergy as potentially hazardous to the faith of the Catholic partner and harmful to the children they produced, as these children would likely be raised outside of the church. The institution of marriage and the rules governing matrimony provided strong boundaries between Catholic and "the other," thereby creating a zone of comfort for the development of faithful families, the basis for healthy parish life. While church officials considered mixed marriages a threat to the Catholic family, they did acknowledge that interfaith marriages were sometimes a necessary evil. Better to tolerate a mixed marriage, they argued, than to risk losing a Catholic soul who was physically or emotionally compelled to embrace a Protestant or non-baptized partner out of wedlock. The canons of the church permitted "mixed" couples to seek a dispensation from the local bishop – in essence, a relaxation of the marriage regulations. For a small donation, the Catholic partner could procure a dispensation *mixtae religionis* to marry a non-Catholic Christian or a dispensation on the grounds of *disparitas cultus* in order to marry a non-Christian.[42] In order to qualify for such a dispensation, the contracting partners had to accept certain conditions: the non-Catholic partner would not interfere with the religious practice of the Catholic spouse; the non-Catholic partner would agree to raise the children as Catholics; and the Catholic partner would try to influence the non-Catholic spouse to convert. Once this agreement was made, the couple would be married in a simple private ceremony in the parish rectory, and, if they could afford it, they would make a small donation to the parish.[43]

In the Diocese of Toronto, these details and formalities were generally ignored. As early as 1842, shortly after he took possession of his see, Power noted that clergy officiated at mixed marriages without the required dispensations. Owing to the size of the original Diocese of Kingston, geography and transportation made the dispensation process a bother, and it was more convenient for priest and betrothed to dispense with the formalities. Priests also worried that if a wedding was delayed by ecclesiastical red tape, then the couple would opt to be joined by the nearest Protestant minister. Power had never lost his dislike for mixed marriages, but he realized that due to the nature of frontier society and the vastness of the Protestant majority, they had to be tolerated. There were risks involved, he thought – in particular, such unions could cause some Catholics to leave the faith. He was resentful that all responsibility for this had been "thrown on Bishops' shoulders," making them "answerable to God and the Church for the evil consequences that may follow from unions of that description."[44] Nevertheless, given the daily interaction between Protestants and Catholics in the towns, cities, workplaces, markets, and associations of the province, the odds were great that Cupid's arrow would strike young men and women without regard to religious affiliation – or canon law, for that matter. In an effort to ward off greater evils, Power issued dispensations but constantly reasserted the necessity for couples to honour the conditions attached to these exceptions to canonical norms.

He counselled his priests to refer all mixed-marriage cases to him, and he treated these cases very seriously. He advised one priest who had to deal with a Catholic who wanted to return to the fold after leaving it due to a mixed marriage, "I hope that you will take the greatest care not to give the slightest offense. Be guarded in your expressions from the altar or the pulpit. It will never answer the purpose of Religion to speak too severely and moreover people in general will not bear with it ... You know my feelings towards separated brethren; it is my desire that they should always be treated with kindness and that we should overlook many little acts of non-Conformity in the Church, if they believe in other aspects with reverence and propriety."[45] This reveals a great deal about Power and his ministry on the frontier. While signalling that marital regulations must be respected in his diocese, he was also saying that the regulations should be relaxed when the relevant parties could agree to the terms of the dispensations.[46] Moreover, he was suggesting that tolerance, gentleness, and forbearance towards non-Catholics could mute their hostility, and perhaps now that the Fifth Age was drawing to a close, it could ease their conversion to Catholicism.

If Power's correspondence is any indication, marriage questions dominated his pastoral agenda. The ninth article of the synod of 1842 afforded him the opportunity to implant the *Tametsi* decrees in the corpus of diocesan law, despite the fact that the decrees set by the Council of Trent had never been formally promulgated in Upper Canada. Since, in 1842, no congregation aside from St Paul's in Toronto had canonical status as an official parish, *Tametsi* had not been applied.[47] The diocesan synod changed this when Power demanded that all of his priests apply the decrees in their churches or be subject to a severe penance.[48] Marriage banns were to be published, the affinity of the partners assessed, clandestine marriages prevented, and mixed marriages referred to the bishop.[49] Although there existed extraordinary provisions for Catholics to be married by Protestant ministers in Upper Canada at a time when the Church of England had the legal monopoly over such rites, and Catholics in Protestant European countries often exercised a similar provision known as the Dutch Precedent, Power forbade Catholics to be married by Protestant clergy under any circumstances.[50]

He even attempted to thwart cross-border marriages. Invoking his authority as a vicar-general for the Diocese of New York, he ordered Father William Whelan of Buffalo to refuse to officiate at any marriages involving residents of the Diocese of Toronto. Should Whelan ignore this directive, Power warned, then he would report the rebellious priest to his superior, who happened to be Power's friend Bishop John Hughes.[51] Any Canadian couple attempting cross-border nuptials would be excommunicated.[52] Under such ecclesiastical pressure, Whelan complied. Power included the entire lesson XXI on marriage in his revised version of *The General Catechism (Butler's)* and instructed the literate laity on marital matters in the pages of the *Catholic*, but there is no recorded evidence to demonstrate the success or failure of his campaign to regularize marriage in the diocese.[53] Even in the last few weeks of his life, marriage questions still permeated his correspondence. The freedom afforded young Catholics on the frontier remained a powerful countervailing force to the orderly implementation of church law.

Driven by his intention to assert episcopal authority over the diocese, Power aggressively challenged lay control over parish property and local church administration. As a priest of Lower Canada, he had been accustomed to working with the churchwardens, or *marguilliers*, who held title to the church's properties and managed its temporal affairs. This practice of administering the parish by means of a *fabrique* had existed in various forms in the British colonies, as Power well knew from his childhood in Halifax and from his correspondence with American bishops who had stymied the practice of lay trusteeship in the United States.[54] Long before the creation of Upper Canada, French Canadian Catholics inhabiting the farmlands near the Detroit River and Lake St Clair had permitted the laity to own parish properties, collect rents and tithes, and keep the parish books; they had also elected their churchwardens. This system empowered them to take the initiative in constructing the churches they needed, maintaining them, and requesting the services of a priest, first from the Bishop of Quebec and later from the Bishop of Kingston. Similarly, the Irish Catholics of St Mary's Church in Hamilton elected a committee of five wardens to collect pew rents, offertory donations, and other gifts in order to pay parish bills and offset debts.[55] In a very real sense, these practices gave francophone and anglophone Catholics a rare opportunity to excercise some control within their church.

As Power knew, particularly from his experiences at Montebello and Ste-Martine, such lay initiatives gave rise to certain problems, especially for the clergy. In Lower Canada, they fuelled notions of sovereignty at the grassroots level, inspiring some Lower Canadians to take up arms against their government in 1837 and 1838.[56] In Newfoundland, the Maritimes, and the American colonies, elected lay churchwardens had clashed openly with pastors, either because these pastors were attempting to take control of parish funds or they simply disliked them. They also fought with bishops who had contrary notions of local church governance. In Toronto, local trustees had clashed at St Paul's with Father William O'Grady and his successor, W.P. McDonagh. In light of his own experiences, and reading the signs of the times, Power was wary of the power of trustees, especially because the ultramontanists were now promoting episcopal authority over all diocesan activities.

What Power witnessed during his pastoral visits of 1842 and 1843 caused him to worry about the widespread popularity of trusteeism, so much so that he moved quickly to regulate parish governance. He

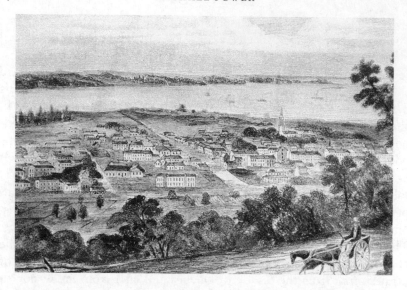

Hamilton, circa 1845–52 (John Ross Robertson Collection, Toronto
Public Library, JRR1437)

discovered that French Canadian parishes at Maidstone, Sandwich, and
Amherstburg were controlled by *marguilliers* in the Lower Canadian
fashion. Irish and Scottish migrants in townships such as Adelaide, in
the Huron Tract, elected trustees, built structures intended for worship,
and then petitioned the bishop for a priest, just as trustees had long done
in the old country and in other colonies.[57] Even the German Catholic settlers in Waterloo, in the township of Wilmot, and in Preston
elected trustees to manage the construction of places of worship and
local temporal affairs. In Amherstburg, Power learned, the pastor and
the wardens were at loggerheads over church finances, specifically the
origins of the mission's debt. After scrutinizing the books, Power discovered many irregularities in the *marguillier's* accounting methods.[58] He
warned the trustees at St Thomas who had asked permission to select
their own priest that he alone had the right to do that.[59]

Matters were far graver for Power in other parts of the diocese. In
Preston, for example, he once again flexed his episcopal muscles, prohibiting local Catholics from electing a Protestant to their board of trustees.
He impressed upon them that trustees were subject to their bishop, and
that they should consider themselves merely a building committee. He
outlined his ideas about episcopal authority and how that authority

should be exercised. Trustees, he insisted, must be "guided by their Bishop and their pastor under him. I would rather allow them to remain forever without a priest and see their churches fall into ruin than admit them in any other quality than that temporary committee interested merely with the collections of money and the building of a church for the use of a people among whom they live: the church once built, it becomes the property and falls under the jurisdiction of the Bishop, the sole proprietor of the ground plot, on which the church is erected."[60]

By 1844, Power's bid to centralize episcopal control over parishes and assume control of their properties began to gather momentum. He started by issuing regulations for trustees and pastors,[61] and then he made a dramatic move – one that was unprecedented in the history of the Catholic Church in British North America. Making the best of a situation he considered intolerable, Power worked to regulate parish affairs without completely overhauling parish governance; biding his time, he simply demanded that the existing system be made to work in an effective manner. Once church buildings were erected and a priest appointed, trustees were mandated to bank the parish income, pay the pastor (from fees for baptisms and marriages, and from Sunday offerings), and manage the parish properties.[62] Principal sources of revenue – such as Sunday collections and pew rents – had to be monitored carefully. Power declared that all revenues were for the exclusive use of the parish, and that "all parishioners must enjoy equal advantages."[63] He would not permit any family to have an "exclusive seat" in their parish church; consequently, all vacant pews were put up for open auction. However, he did concede to the familiar Lower Canadian practice of charging higher rents for pews closest to the altar.[64] Parishioners were permitted to construct pews and occupy them exclusively until the costs of the pew had been paid, at which point the pew was auctioned.[65] Visitors were exempt from paying pew rent, although Power insisted that their hosts make a donation for them, sometimes at a rate of one dollar per person.[66]

Such regulations were part of a more sweeping plan to bring uniformity to parish life on the frontier and assert episcopal micromanagement of all parishes and missions in the diocese. After each of his visitations, Power issued a series of ordinances to parish trustees and pastors. He demanded that they keep registers for burials, marriages, and baptisms perspicaciously, and that they purchase and care for altar linens and vestments. Tabernacles were to be reserved exclusively for the Eucharist, leading one to wonder what had been stored in tabernacle boxes before

Power's arrival.[67] Power also demanded complete inventories of church property, both real estate and chattels.[68] During his visits, Power poured over the parish books, checking to see whether the accounts were in good order and whether the churchwardens and the local pastor were abiding by his regulations.[69] In his effort to assert his authority, he was typical of his age. His brother bishops Ignace Bourget in Montreal, Michael Anthony Fleming in St John's, and John Hughes in New York were all active agents of ultramontanism, with its emphasis on episcopal control. What makes Power's introduction of ultramontanism to Upper Canada notable is the fact that he was undaunted by the size of his diocese and, in an intrepid fashion, he travelled in person to the frontier outposts of his diocese to ensure the success of his vision.

In an effort to assert his episcopal prerogatives and legalize his take-over of parish properties, Power entered the political arena of the United Province of Canada. On 16 December 1844, dragging Bishop Patrick Phelan of Kingston kicking and screaming behind him, he petitioned the legislative assembly to "severely endo[w]" the Roman Catholic bishops of Upper Canada "with corporate powers, to enable them to acquire and hold real estate for religious purposes."[70] On 24 January 1845, the bill to create episcopal corporations was introduced to the House, and, although the titles of the ordinaries of Kingston and Toronto were mentioned specifically in the bill, it was Michael Power who had spear-headed this action. At its root was the question of who would control church properties in his diocese: the bishop or the laity. As early as 1842, disputes over church properties at Belle Rivière and Chatham had convinced Power that the only solution was to put all church lands under the ownership of the bishop himself, thereby creating an episcopal corporation "for the purposes of the Catholic Religion."[71]

Power was well read on the mechanics of episcopal corporations. Earlier in the year he had written to his contacts in the Archdiocese of Baltimore to ask them to send him copies of similar legislation in Maryland.[72] The following year, 1843, he travelled to Kingston, the first of several capitals of the Province of Canada, to connect with the politicians who would make it possible for him and his colleague in that city to keep the church independent from the "whims of men."[73] Power spent two weeks in Kingston, hoping that his request for episcopal corpora-tion would win the approval of the executive council. The records of the Parliament of the Union are slim, and Power kept no record of the progress of his proposal through the secular institutions. Facing a full agenda, Canadian politicians shelved the proposal until the next legislative session. It is certain, however, that Power had made up his mind at an early stage in his episcopal career to use civil law to attain control over church property.

In 1844, he did not travel to the new capital, Montreal, to promote his petition. Confident that he had already made the appropriate political connections, he entrusted his former vicar-general, Angus Macdonell, with overseeing the initiative. The bill itself was introduced by Colonel John Prince (MLA, Essex), a Protestant who was considered friendly to Catholic interests, and it moved speedily through two readings in the Legislative Assembly. By 6 March 1845, it had been passed on to the non-elected legislative council for amendment. Macdonell sensed that there was no great enthusiasm for the bill, but "sheer shame prevented many to vote against it."[74] Evidently, the members from Lower Canada (Canada East), who had been supportive of their own parish institutions, were hostile to the bill, and their hostility abated only when the concluding clauses of the bill were omitted. On 29 March 1845, royal assent was given to An Act to Incorporate the Roman Catholic Bishops of Toronto and Kingston in Canada, in Each Diocese.[75] Bishop Power and the ailing Bishop Remi Gaulin (actually, Gaulin's coadjutor, Patrick Phelan) were now corporate persons who could purchase, have, and hold property for the Catholic Church. These rights to soil and freehold included the right to construct tenements, burial grounds, churches, and chapels. Most important, however, they could be enjoyed by Power's and Gaulin's successors, including those who would become bishops of dioceses created in the future. Expressing his delight, Power reported to Rome that there had been little resistance to this incorporation, and that Protestant legislators had assisted a bill that guaranteed "the advancement of Catholicism" in Canada.[76]

Power lost little time in exercising his newly accorded rights. Angus Macdonell remained his agent in Montreal, and he instructed him to pursue the title to the church at Sandwich, lands in the township of Adelaide, near London, and church properties in and around Toronto.[77] Once he had taken control of existing parishes and missions, Power set out strict guidelines for the establishment of parishes he would ultimately own. The construction of a new parish church in Caledonia was a case in point. Power told the local building committee that the selection of a site for the new church building was exclusively the prerogative of the bishop or his delegate. He then informed the trustees, "The property once acquired must be made over *forever* to the Right Rev's Michael Power, Bishop of Toronto and his successors in office ... when the deed is executed and is registered, then I should allow the inhabitants to commence building the Church."[78] Nothing was to happen in Caledonia without his approval; the powers accorded him through episcopal corporation gave him and other bishops in Canada West the kind of leverage they would need over parishes should either the laity or the clergy become unruly or disobedient. In the short term, Power's bold foray into the public sphere to secure property rights was evidence of his rigour and his demanding personality, and it revealed how thoroughly he had come to embody the push for episcopal control, a hallmark of the ultramontane revolution. Through Power, ultramontanism had come to Upper Canada well in advance of any European bishop. In the long term, his achievement of corporate status for bishops set the pattern of episcopal governance in parish temporal affairs and the subordination of the laity to clerical control at the local level, and this pattern would endure in Ontario for generations. Episcopal corporation might well be Power's most lasting and important contribution to the church in Canada.

Unlike their fellow Catholics in Nova Scotia, Newfoundland, New York, and Pennsylvania, Upper Canadian Catholics could not even muster feeble resistance to Power's takeover of parish properties. In fact, their silence was deafening. Those who opposed episcopal corporation either said nothing publicly or left their parishes. The oldest parish in the diocese, Our Lady of the Assumption in Sandwich, had been placed under the control of the Jesuits, who were completely loyal to Power. From their headquarters on the Detroit River, they oversaw missions throughout the upper country. Under Pierre Chazelle, and later Pierre Point, the Catholic inhabitants of this region of the diocese acquiesced to Power, although their fulfillment of his directives took more time than Power had anticipated. These francophone regions contained the diocese's oldest church buildings, oldest parishes, deepest roots, and most entrenched tradition of lay governance. Power put his request bluntly, informing prominent layman Charles Baby, scion of one of Upper Canada's most prominent Catholic families, that until church properties were handed over to him, he would not "sanction any measure" for the local church.[79]

Power was equally blunt with the German Catholics near Preston: if they did not turn over the land for the new church to him "on [his] conditions" and continued to use the church, then he would instruct their pastor, Redemptorist Father Simon Sanderl, to refuse them the sacraments and rites of Christian burial.[80] In time, all of the parishes and missions in the diocese submitted to Power, a transition that was relatively calm compared to similar transitions in other parts of English-speaking North America.[81] Perhaps the roots of the Irish and Scottish settlers in western Upper Canada were not yet deep enough. Their communities were still fragile, they had limited experience in local trusteeship politics, their energies had been drained by frontier life, and they had too great a need for the services of a priest to do battle with this young, energetic bishop.

Power's episcopal colleagues elsewhere in British North America could not boast such a noiseless transition to episcopal corporation. In his native parish of St Peter's (now St Mary's), in Halifax, the lay trustees were in open revolt against William Walsh, the coadjutor of the apostolic vicariate of Nova Scotia. It was not until 1849 that Walsh could claim ownership of the parish through episcopal corporation, which became normative in his new diocese of Halifax. Two years earlier, Michael Anthony Fleming, the vicar apostolic of St John's, Newfoundland, consolidated his control over the new diocese of St John's by manipulating a deep factionalism within the majority Irish community.[82] In New Brunswick, the new bishop, William Dollard, was intent on establishing an episcopal corporation in his new diocese of Saint John. As had been the case in Canada, in New Brunswick the legislature had balked at the initial legislation because time was short, but the bill was reintroduced the following year, 1845. Due to the considerable sectarian division over the incorporation issue in the New Brunswick Legislative Assembly, Dollard did not receive his desired status until 1846. Power also set the course for his former Lower Canadian colleague Bishop Norbert Blanchet, who, upon his election to the new Archdiocese of Portland, Oregon Territory, instituted church ownership by means of an episcopal corporation.

Power's achievement made expansion of the diocesan building program far easier. At a time when there was increased Catholic immigration to western Upper Canada and a natural increase of the previously settled population, there were also demands for new churches and additional priests.[83] Consequently, during his very short term as bishop, Power created nine new parishes in the diocese; of these, only two had been approved prior to 1845. This is not an insignificant detail, because until he had the legal and financial affairs of parishes firmly in hand, he was reticent to establish new congregations – this is supported by the fact that he established seven parishes in the final two years of his episcopate. Of course, other factors slowed parish growth and building initiatives, not the least of which was the inability of local farmers to raise the capital to construct new churches or replace original log structures with more durable monuments of stone.[84] Power was frank with the Society for the Propagation of the Faith (SPF), from which he received considerable financial assistance, explaining that his highest priority was to construct a network of parish churches on the frontier, although this was difficult because his frontier diocese was certainly among the poorest in North America.[85] Given the scarcity of funds and his concern that existing funds be carefully managed, Power demanded of building committees meticulous bookkeeping and complete transparency in every transaction involving a new church. As soon as a church was built, he tried to bless it in person and ensure that it was ready for public worship.[86]

The most ambitious of Power's building projects was reserved for Toronto: an episcopal residence and a new cathedral. He undoubtedly needed both. Since 1843, he had been living in a private home that he owned in St David's ward, and St Paul's Church, the only Catholic place of worship in the city and Power's temporary cathedral, was much too small for Toronto's growing Catholic population. However, a cathedral was far more than a permanent seat for the local bishop – it was a bold testament to the faith and a forceful reminder to the Protestant majority of the Roman Catholics in their midst. Power was aware of the public role of the cathedral as a focus of worship for the entire Catholic community, regardless of parish, region, or class. In requesting funds for the cathedral's construction, he reminded his flock of its spiritual and public importance: "it is well known to you all, that the Cathedral Church belongs properly to no peculiar Parish, but that it is the Mother Church of the whole Diocese, and it is but just that such a temple should be built in a manner and style suitable to the Greatness and Majesty of Our Holy Religion."[87] Thus, the vision of a cathedral, a cathedral that Power had already dedicated to his own patron saint and that of the diocese, was not just a practical necessity for a new diocese; it was a permanent reminder to Catholic and non-Catholic alike that the Catholic Church was a presence in the life of Upper Canada.

The construction project was an enormous undertaking. Immediately upon his arrival in Toronto, in 1842, Power had used personal funds and donations from the SPF to purchase land from Peter McGill in the vicinity of what is now Bond and Church Streets for £1,800.[88] The cathedral was to be complemented by a brick house on the west side of Church Street that would serve as the episcopal residence (often termed

St Paul's Parish, Power Street, Toronto (Reverend Edward Kelly, *The Story of St Paul's Parish, 1822–1922* [Toronto, 1922])

"palace"). Some locals considered the proposed site to be too far out on the margins of the city, and thus too far from St Paul's, a twenty-minute walk. In April 1845, however, Power's building committee was in place and accepting tenders for construction.[89]

Within days of the first public notice of excavation, on 5 April, a mob of Torontonians, both Catholic and Protestant, armed with picks, shovels, and baskets, descended upon the new site. A week later, they had succeeded in digging a pit for the cathedral's foundations and a crypt for their honoured dead. The project took on a carnival atmosphere. Citizens laboured happily in the hole, and when they were finished they dined on roasted ox, donated by a local butcher. Writers at the *Mirror* were truly impressed by the way the community had pooled its resources, describing the undertaking as "an agreeable instance of the solid benefits to society in general when persons disconnected by religious creed can cordially assist each other in mutual undertakings."[90] Although perceived by Catholics as hostile to their cause, the Methodist *Christian Guardian* expressed grudging admiration for the "spirit" of the diggers. The staid Wesleyan organ was astonished that even "gentlemen" had rolled up their sleeves to hack away at the ground and cart off baskets of earth. "We suppose," the *Guardian* concluded, that "no other Church in Toronto would achieve" such a feat – "the worst object has sometimes the best supporters."[91]

The excavation had been done at virtually no cost. The volunteers had dug and hauled 95,000 cubic feet of earth and clay to create the five-foot-deep pit.[92] Once this phase of the building project was complete, Power ordered that a cross be erected on the site as a reminder of what was to come. On 8 May 1845 – coincidentally, the third anniversary of Power's ordination – 4,000 spectators representing a cross-section of Toronto's Christian denominations huddled around the pit as Bishop Power blessed the cornerstone of his new cathedral.[93] The brass plate affixed to the stone bore an inscription that embodied the two foci of Power's personal loyalty: the name of Pope Gregory XVI, followed by those of Queen Victoria and the current governor general, Charles Theophilius, Baron Metcalfe. The plate also indicated that the cathedral was dedicated to St Michael the Archangel. Power's name and those of the architect and contractor were the only others included on the cornerstone.[94] The bishop placed within the stone several rather poignant religious and secular symbols, which once again reflected his own strong sense of a Catholic Church in a British context. He chose some British and Canadian coins, and a fragment of the oak roof over the nave of

England's York Cathedral, an architectural inspiration for St Michael's. The ceremony concluded in typical Catholic fashion with the passing of the collection basket, all proceeds earmarked for the new cathedral.

Power would not live to see the fruit of architect William Thomas's vision. Designed in an early Gothic style germane to fourteenth-century England, St Michael's was, by Toronto standards, vast – it measured 190 feet by 115 feet, with a nave soaring to 66 feet between the piers and central arches and 45 feet in the side aisles.[95] The tower and spire rose over 200 feet, making the cathedral the tallest religious monument in the city. This alone would create the sense of Catholic presence that Power desired, although the edifice was not completed until the 1860s, during the tenure of Bishop John Joseph Lynch.[96] The stones required to build the walls of this massive structure were carried to Toronto from elsewhere, elevating construction costs. By January 1846, Power had reported to the SPF in Lyons that the church was only completed to its windows and had already cost 100,000 francs.[97] One year later, he made a special plea for funds to the SPF, claiming that although the cathedral was his highest priority, he had been forced to spend the society's donations on a variety of projects, including establishing missions to First Peoples, building churches in rural areas, and educating priests.[98] At the local level, in December 1846, Power instituted a subscription to help defray the costs of the cathedral project. He told all of his priests to post loan proposals on the doors of every church in the diocese. Each parish was to strike a committee, consisting of the pastor and two laypersons, to draw up a subscription list and make collections. All monies would be forwarded to Archdeacon Hay or layman S.G. Lynn, who would apply them to the cathedral expenses.[99]

Despite Power's fundraising efforts, solicitations for the cathedral building fund continued after his death, when church authorities realized that an additional 60,000 francs were required to complete the structure.[100] In 1850, Power's successor, Armand de Charbonnel, informed the SPF that at the time of Power's death, the accumulated debt for the cathedral and the episcopal palace stood at 250,000 francs.[101] The new bishop was impressed that local Catholics and Protestants were able to clear this debt, despite a typhus epidemic and a horrific 1849 fire that had destroyed the city's core. While Charbonnel likely overestimated the importance of the latter calamity, which occurred after the dedication of the cathedral, Catholic philanthropists John Elmsley and Dr. John King made personal contributions to ensure that the cathedral was debt-free so that it could be blessed.[102] It was only fitting that on the feast of

St Michael, 29 September 1848, Power's mentor Ignace Bourget dedicated the cathedral.[103]

Power did, however, live to see his episcopal palace completed, in 1846. The brick building, though furnished in a Spartan manner, accommodated Power, J.J. Hay, and any visiting priest who wanted to stay the night in Toronto.[104] It also contained a small chapel, dedicated to the Blessed Virgin Mary but placed under the patronage of the famed bishop of Milan, St Ambrose.[105] Power's selection of Ambrose is hardly surprising, given the saint's reputation as a pastor, homilist, and doctor of Christian thought. With his penchant for church history, Power liked to create physical memorials. He memorialized St Ambrose and Thomas à Beckett in sacred spaces built of stone and wood, enduring reminders of the life to which he had been called. Beckett, for whom two chapels were named, also represented Power's love of the Catholic Church as it had existed in England and his fervent hope for a Catholic restoration there – perhaps one that would come to pass at the end of the Fifth Age. Such monuments, however, came at a price, and this was one reason why the episcopal palace was still carrying a considerable debt load at the time of Power's death.[106]

Having undertaken to centralize control of the parishes and their properties, and having initiated programs to offer structures of stone and wood to new congregations on the frontier, Power was hard pressed to find priests for his expanding diocese. He clearly wanted to organize a cadre of disciplined and obedient pastors, but recruiting them was a challenge. The climate in his diocese, the rustic surroundings, and the lack of amenities in the bush country were severe deterrents. At the end of 1846, Power had only twenty-eight priests to cover forty-four churches and forty-nine chapels.[107] Worse still, many priests passed through the province, and the bishop had to monitor them. Some were simply heading for other destinations, but others were intent on "freelancing," like the itinerants Power had locked horns with as a young priest in the St-François Valley.[108]

In some ways, Power was his own worst enemy when it came to recruiting new men for the priesthood. If his correspondence with Father Michael Mills is any indication, he cultivated a reputation for sternness, legalism, and impatience. He insisted that all clergy be able to produce the proper paperwork – formal exeats and letters of reference from bishops – but most European priests would not be carrying such items with them when they came to British North America to make a fresh start. As well, Power frowned upon priests taking on supplementary work – moonlighting, so to speak – as chaplains to militia units and hospitals, or to workers on mega-projects like the Welland Canal, unless the assignment met with his approval and the stipend was channelled through his office. What for Power was an assertion of episcopal authority over priests and pastoral life some clergy in the field viewed as an annoyance or even undue interference. To impress upon his priests that he alone, not civil or business leaders, was their superior, he threatened any moonlighting pastor with excommunication.[109] Such threats and actions on the part of the bishop would certainly have discouraged many priests from taking posts in the Diocese of Toronto.

Instead of waiting for priests to come to him, Power instituted a twofold policy of local recruitment and "appointment by invitation." To enact the former, he sponsored the education of local young men, as he had in Montreal.[110] In 1844, he ordained Charles Kileen, the first to be ordained to the priesthood expressly for the Diocese of Toronto. Two years later, John O'Reilly became the second.[111] As exciting as the prospect of producing a generation of homegrown priests was, their training and preparation would be costly and unpredictable (some might choose not to complete the program); it was a long-term project, and it would demand patience of the bishop and his people. Too often, as had been the case in the Lower Canadian church, young men were hurried through training and thrust into pastoral assignments before they had completed their studies or found solid pastoral mentorship.

In the short term, as he waited for the local men, Power borrowed priests from neighbouring dioceses.[112] Kileen himself had come from Cincinnati to train with the intention of settling in Canada.[113] In the township of Whitby, situated at the extreme east of the diocese, Power acknowledged the "spiritual wants" of parishioners and the "miserable manner in which these poor people [had] heretofore been attended to." Without a priest to serve the largely Irish population of what is today Whitby and Oshawa, Power borrowed the services of the priest at Cobourg, in the neighbouring Diocese of Kingston.[114] Power incardinated Whitby's new pastor, Father Hugh Fitzpatrick, into the diocese when Fitzpatrick decided to leave the Diocese of Kingston permanently.[115] In a similar move in the west end of the diocese, Power asked neighbouring American bishops at Detroit and the upper Great Lakes to send their missionary priests to cover areas between Fort William and Sault Ste Marie until he could get priests or Jesuits to the Lake Superior country.[116]

However, Jesuits were not always welcomed by the First Peoples or the Anglican and Methodist clergy on the mission frontier. Power was soon facing troubles on Walpole Island at Lake St Clair and at Wikwemikong on Manitoulin Island. In each case, the Jesuits, whom he had hoped would have a pacifying effect on the frontier, were at the centre of conflicts involving Native factions, rival Christian denominations, and the Indian Department. Factions with vested interests in the situation offered different versions of what had transpired on Walpole Island, but pitted against one another, they generated a protracted storm that would eventually destroy Power's plan to extend the influence of the church along the St Clair River. In April 1844, Pierre Chazelle sent Father Dominique du Ranquet, who had been studying the Algonquin language, to Walpole Island in response to a request from local First Peoples for a priest.[117] There were over 1,000 Native people in the area, and this had prompted the Methodists and the Anglicans to send missionaries, but they were discouraged by the number of conversions they had managed to make.[118] Chazelle, Power, and du Ranquet believed that because there were four Catholic families on the island who wanted a priest, they should go there. Their trip was approved by the local superintendent of the Indian Department, John Keating.[119] In fact, as early as March, Chief Superintendent Samuel Jarvis told Keating, "it would not be right to prevent [the island's Catholics from] having a priest."[120]

Du Ranquet had been given an extremely difficult mission, but the young French priest damaged his own cause. The local Anglican missionary and several Ojibwa accused du Ranquet of denouncing the Church of England, of cutting down an ancient grove of oaks, and of erecting his cabin on land the Natives claimed was "the place where the bones of our fore fathers and Fathers ... are buried."[121] Asserting that the Jesuit had not been invited there in the first place, the Ojibwa council declared that he should be removed from Walpole. The Ojibwa also maintained that any right a Catholic might have to preach on Walpole was null and void, since the three or four Catholic families were "strangers on the Island" – they were natives of Michigan and "two half Frenchman."[122] When asked to ban Catholic missionaries from the island, the Indian Department replied that Catholics had a right to be there, but it conceded that they had no right to cut timber or build without the permission of the Ojibwa council. The fact that du Ranquet had broken these prohibitions the department blamed on Keating, because he had failed to tell the Jesuit of the restrictions.[123] In response, du Ranquet and the Jesuits claimed that they had Keating's permission to live on the island and establish a house, a school, and a chapel.[124] After meeting with the council on 31 July 1844, Jesuit superior Pierre Chazelle won a temporary stay of the expulsion of his missionaries.[125] The battle, however, was by no means over, and a debate ensued between Jesuits and civil authorities over the future of the Walpole Island Catholic mission.

As bishop, and as the one who had commissioned the Jesuits to evangelize the First Peoples in the west of the diocese, Power supported the Jesuit interpretation of the incident. He insisted that since 1763 the Catholic Church had enjoyed the right to evangelize and practice its faith freely in Canada. The charges directed at du Ranquet and the "incredible persecution" to which he was being subjected on Walpole Island were, to Power's mind, a violation of this right.[126] Power also believed that the Walpole Island case called into question the Crown's ability to treat the Christian churches equally and fairly; evidence presented to him suggested a clear bias in favour of the Anglicans, Methodists, and Presbyterians. Sensing a conspiracy, he insinuated that local Protestant missionaries had incited the controversy in the first place and had told Natives that they would be denied government presents if they attended the priest.[127] As he wrote to Father Hudon, "We do not demand a single favour: but we want to preach the Gospel to the Infidels without the Government having the right to interfere."[128]

The bishop also consulted with his political friend Dominick Daly, and the governor general's door was opened to him. In August 1845, armed with documents from S.P. Jarvis, secretary of the Indian Department, declaring that Catholics were at liberty to preach on Walpole provided that there were Catholics among the island's Native population and bearing du Ranquet's testimony that he had acted with the department's permission, Power met with Sir Charles Metcalfe. The governor general reassured the bishop that he had had nothing to do with attempts to force the Jesuits from the island, and he restated their right to be there on the condition that they took no Native land without the permission of the Ojibwa council.[129] However, Metcalfe was dying of cancer, so he was unable to resolve the issue. Power had to petition his successor, Charles Murray Cathcart, to ensure the continued Catholic presence on Walpole. But in October 1846, Cathcart ordered du Ranquet "to quit the Island." With a vehemence he rarely expressed in his dealings with the state – although he maintained that he had spoken his mind in a "positive and solemn manner" – Power described Cathcart's action as an "open act of persecution and gross violation of the rights of ministers and members of the Catholic Church."[130] His patience worn thin, Power remarked to Daly that given the turnover rate among Her Majesty's governors in Canada, it would take three years for anything to be done about the matter.[131]

In 1847, Cathcart's ruling on Power's petition did not satisfy the bishop at all. In a tersely written statement, the governor general sided with the Walpole Natives: "A very large majority of Indians *professing the Christian faith* has hitherto uniformly declared themselves to be thoroughly opposed to the interference of the Roman Catholic Missionary in their spiritual affairs and have urgently and repeatedly requested his removal from the Island."[132] Power was livid. Later that year, he travelled to England, en route to Rome for his *ad limina* visit (all bishops were required to make these visits every five years in order to present their reports on the state of their dioceses). In London, he met with Earl Grey. He insisted that du Ranquet's good name be restored and demanded assurances that Catholic missionaries would be unmolested in their work. Power also told Earl Grey that he wanted the matter settled privately, as he did not want the fact that there had been a "misunderstanding" between "civil and ecclesiastical authorities" to be made public.[133] As incensed as he was over this issue, Power held fast to the belief that Catholicism and the British Empire were not at odds and that the parties involved could work co-operatively for their mutual benefit. But he did not know that on 30 March, a provincial enquiry headed by J.B. Clench had ruled that du Ranquet was guilty of all charges and had ordered the mission closed and the property returned to the Natives.[134] The matter was still festering when Power returned to Toronto, and he died without knowing the final outcome. As late as 1848, Walpole Island Catholic Natives, caught up in political skirmishes and conflicts between church and state, were still protesting the treatment accorded du Ranquet and objecting to his removal,[135] but the majority faction had the final word. In 1849, the locals burned du Ranquet's abandoned chapel to the ground.

More trouble awaited Power on the mission frontier at Wikwemikong, where the Jesuits competed against the Church of England and the Indian Department. The Manitoulin Island mission predated Power's appointment, having been established in 1836 by Bishops Macdonell and Gaulin in response to a formal request from First Peoples living near Coldwater, on the mainland between Lake Simcoe and Georgian Bay.[136] The first missionary, secular priest Jean-Baptiste Proulx, arrived on the island while civil and Anglican authorities were engaged in a two-pronged effort to subdue the Ojibwa peoples of the area. In 1835, Lieutenant-Governor John Colborne had envisioned Manitoulin Island as one big reserve, and his successor, Francis Bond Head, had ordered all bands on Manitoulin to cede their land to the Crown.[137] At Manitowaning, the government financed an Anglican mission centre, workshops, and a school with the aim of indoctrinating the local Ojibwa in Anglicanism and Protestantism and teaching them farming techniques and skilled trades.

Most Catholic Ojibwa refused to attend the Church of England mission. Even worse for Indian agent Captain Thomas Anderson, they also refused to cede their territory, and it remains unceded to this day.[138] Instead, they formed their own centre with Proulx at the village of Wikwemikong, southeast of Manitowaning. In 1838, Proulx erected the first mission church, Holy Cross, and proceeded to encourage his Native flock to stay independent from government programs. He worked with the Ojibwa in their own language, a method of evangelization that was not employed in the English-only Church of England mission.[139] Thus, Power assumed spiritual responsibility for a growing Catholic Ojibwa community– close to 1,500 strong when he visited in August 1842 – but the Manitoulin mission was also a hotbed of sectarian discord and the site of a frontier standoff between the Catholic Church and the Canadian government.[140]

During a visit to Manitoulin, Power identified several problems. Although he had questions about Proulx's lax record-keeping, he was much more concerned about the status of the missionary's housekeeper. He feared that the young woman's presence in the rectory might engender scandal, and Protestant rivals in the region would use any indiscretion to discredit the Catholic mission. He asked George Gordon, the pastor at Penetanguishene, to "secretly and confidentially" monitor the situation, and he recalled Proulx to Toronto for the winter, where he shared quarters with Power and Hay. For Power, scandal in this volatile region was to be avoided at all costs, even if it meant making the hard decision to leave the local First Peoples without the services of a priest.[141]

After Proulx returned to the island in the spring, Power became increasingly concerned that the Indian Department was not only aiding the Anglican mission at Manitowaning but also discriminating against Proulx and the Catholic First Peoples at Wikwemikong. Proulx reported that Catholic Natives were prohibited from living near Manitowaning, the Catholic mission was receiving no financial aid from the government for education, and the government was not paying him a salary as it was the Anglican missionary.[142] The fact that the Ojibwa of Wikwemikong had refused to cede their lands likely prompted this inequitable treatment from civil authorities. Given Proulx's defence of Native claims and the rivalry between his mission and the Anglican one, Power interpreted the government's parsimony as a means of coercing Proulx into obeying the department's directives. To Power, this was yet another instance of persecution by government agents on the frontier, and in 1845, he added the handling of Manitoulin to the list of complaints he delivered in person to Governor General Metcalfe. The government, he maintained, was interfering with the work of the Church; by proffering money, the state could direct or influence the affairs of the church. He confided to Ignace Bourget that if this was indeed the case, then he would refuse all government money: "La pauvreté et l'indépéndence de l'Église seront toujours préférables a cette boue qu'on appele or, et a l'esclavage." [143]

In 1844, aware of the stress under which Proulx was working, Power relieved his priest of Wikwemikong and replaced him with two men: Ferdinand Roque, a translator, and Jean-Pierre Choné, a Jesuit. [144] The latter served as superior of the mission from 1844 to 1848 and effectively became Power's front-line officer in the ongoing war between this mission among the Catholic Ojibwa and the Anglican mission at Manitowaning under Reverend Frederick O'Meara, who had his own Ojibwa allies and the support of the state. Over time, Choné noted that the Anglican hold over Manitowaning was weakening, as was the resolve of the government to keep pouring money into a failing venture. The Jesuits, who were fluent in the Algonquin languages and who had invested considerable time in studying and recording the stories and rituals of Native spirituality, reported that they were slowly adding Catholic neophytes to the one chief and twenty-six other Catholics who had originally formed the minority in the Anglican mission. [145] In the unceded territory, Choné established his own industrial school to serve the 327 residents of Wikwemikong, and by 1846, he had acquired the services of Jean Véroneau, a Jesuit brother who was skilled in the building trades and blacksmithing in addition to possessing some culinary skills. [146] In 1848, under the new superior, Father Nicholas Point, the Jesuits constructed storehouses to facilitate Ojibwa trade and agricultural work in the region. [147]

Recognizing Manitoulin as a bridgehead from which to expand the northern missions, Power requested that the Jesuits extend their operations to include First Peoples and Euro-Canadians living along the shores of Georgian Bay. In what was tantamount to a Power offensive into Protestant-held territory, Choné established a mission at Owen Sound with the expressed purpose of converting the resident Methodist First Peoples to Catholicism. [148] Similarly, the Holy Cross (St-Croix) mission became the Jesuit base of operations for additional missions to

Roman Catholic mission, Kaministiquia River, Fort William. Using
their bases of operations at Sandwich and Wikwemikong, the Jesuits
established this mission at the head of Lake Superior shortly after the
death of Power (Lakehead University Library and the Thunder Bay
Historical Museum Society)

the north shore of Lake Huron, the Parry Sound district, and Sault Ste
Marie. In 1846, Fathers Choné and Clément Boulanger (who had been
instrumental in convincing Jan Roothan to re-establish the Jesuits in
Canada) visited the Hudson's Bay Company post at Fort William and
commenced evangelizing 2,000 Native peoples to the west of the lakehead. Power mistakenly thought that this region beyond the lakehead,
in what is now northwestern Ontario, was part of his diocese, but it
actually came under the jurisdiction of Norbert Provencher, the bishop
of Red River.[149] By 1847, the moderate success of the Jesuits in the upper
lakes region transformed Power's attitude towards the mission frontier
from defensiveness to assertion.

The Walpole and Manitoulin episodes demonstrated how difficult it
was for Power to claim the frontier as Catholic territory. On the settlement frontier inhabited by Euro-Canadian Catholics, where there were
existing parishes or parishes in the planning stages, Power could exert
control through his pastoral visitations – he could enforce church discipline among the laity and the clergy and take ownership of local church
real estate. On the margins of the diocese, however, the circumstances
were quite different. There, First Peoples were either uninterested in

converting to Christianity or already allied with non-Catholic missionaries, and they put up significant resistance to Power's dream of marking the end of the Fifth Age with mass conversions. While Protestant-
Catholic relations in the more settled areas were peaceful, in the country
stalked by the "black robes" – as the Jesuits were called – a sylvan re-
enactment of the Reformation of the sixteenth century was underway.
Anglican, Methodist (new to the fight), and Jesuit fought one another
for the souls of aboriginal peoples, who were reluctant to embrace the
white man's creed. Just as he was affronted by anti-Catholicism on
the mission frontier, Power was stung by the manner in which government bureaucracy, cronyism, and favouritism hampered the work of
his priests in the upper country. This, compounded by the runaround
he had been given concerning several issues during a visit to London
in 1847 and his experiences with petty bureaucrats, Indian agents, and
civil servants during the Walpole and Wikwemikong troubles, made him
question British fair play when it came to religious rights. This conflict
between the faith he loved and the Crown he respected disturbed him:
"Your Lordship [Bourget] knows my sincere and inviolable attachment
to the Majesty's government and that there is only the most intimate
conviction, founded on incontestable facts, that force me to place myself,
even momentarily, in opposition to the views of the administration. For
18 months, I have been patient and I hoped that I would never be forced
to give publicity to the most iniquitous persecution that has ever taken
place in the country. The only opposition that has been given to all
of their scheming is that of passive Resistance and silence."[150] Power
believed that Sydenham had broken his promise to allow the Catholic
Church to evangelize the frontier. His faith in the British colonial apparatus was shaken, though not destroyed.

Desperate times, however, demand desperate measures. The Catholic
population of Power's diocese was growing steadily, the difficulties of
parish and frontier mission life persisted, and the need for more priests
remained acute. Power sought to recruit secular and religious priests
directly from European bishops. Targeting specific European dioceses,
Power hoped to avoid feeling pressured to incardinate priests who arrived
on the scene without official papers and, perhaps, with something to
hide. Petrified at the thought of importing scandal into the diocese, he
demanded proof of a canonical exeat from each priest seeking employment.[151] "Upper Canada," he lamented, "has been the scene of too many
scandals already and in this part of the world we cannot wait untill
[sic] the Church be again and again dishonoured."[152] Thus, Power's

strategy was to appeal directly to the source – Ireland, France, Austria, the German States, the Irish Christian Brothers, the Society of Jesus, the Institute of the Blessed Virgin Mary, the Presentation Sisters – in staffing his parishes, missions, and schools. He crafted his requests with the particular interests of each group in mind. He told the Irish seminary of All Hallows that he had "neither Colleges, Schools, nor men"; he informed Archbishop Milde of Vienna that he was "situated at one of the earth's extremities," trying to nurture a small group of poor German Catholics.[153] He continued to lure Jesuits with the idea that they could resume the original missionary endeavours of Brébeuf, Lalement, and Jogues.

By January 1847, Power was barely managing to provide priests for existing parishes and missions. In the previous fifteen months, four of his priests had died, Jesuit superior Pierre Chazelle had died while visiting Green Bay, and his only German-speaking priest, Redemptorist Simon Sanderl, had injured his leg and was forced to withdraw from the diocese.[154] While Power dedicated his six-month visit to Europe in early 1847 primarily to making his *ad limina* report to the pope, he also conducted a recruitment drive, knocking on doors in France, the Italian States, Ireland, and the Papal States in search of new blood for his diocese. In Paris on 8 May 1847, he fired off pleas for funds and personnel to the Leopoldine Association and the Archbishops of Munich and Vienna, desperately seeking help from any source he could think of. The immediate results of his trip were very disappointing. His only consolation was that he managed to enlist the services of the Institute of the Blessed Virgin Mary (IBVM), or the Ladies of Loretto (in Europe, "Loreto"), a teaching order of sisters headquartered at Rathfarnham, outside of Dublin. The sisters' task would be to establish schools for young women in the Diocese of Toronto. The IBVM was the only religious order – besides the Jesuits, who had already been at work in the diocese for four years – that Power had succeeded in bringing to Toronto. By the time of his death, in October 1847, he had enlisted the services of four sisters and thirty-three priests, of whom fifteen were members of the Society of Jesus.[155] When one considers how many clergy were serving in the region prior to his arrival, Power could claim a moderate success: the number of active priests had increased by 50 per cent since 1842.

By 1847, it would have been clear to anyone who had anticipated it that the end of the Fifth Age had not come. In five short years, however, Michael Power had imposed a structure upon an unruly and independent-minded frontier clergy and laity. He had laid the groundwork for priestly and parish discipline in the synod of 1842, an event that he was never able to mount again. Although he had intended to hold a second synod in 1845, ill health prevented him from gathering his priests together to tighten and review the diocesan constitutions.[156] He had divided the diocese into manageable districts and deaneries to be co-ordinated by his most trusted priests. He had curbed local control and ownership of parishes and church properties by embedding the principle of episcopal corporation in provincial law. At the very least, by the time he died, Michael Power could be credited with creating structures of diocesan governance, promoting a policy of clerical discipline and lay adherence to canon law and ecclesiastical regulations, centralizing ownership of church property, fostering missions to convert non-Christians, and building positive relations between his office and the province's Protestant political and religious leaders. This was not the Sixth Age of which he had dreamed, but the framework of an ultramontane pastoral plan had taken root.

CHAPTER EIGHT

∴ Virtually a Canadian ∾

IN THE HISTORY OF THE western Christian Church, there is often a fine line between the duties of a bishop as a pastor and as a politician. Some bishops have natural political instincts; they enjoy the thrust and parry of public debate, sometimes venturing freely into the public sphere to defend positions or to assert issues of great import to the church. At times, these men cross the boundary between the sacred and the profane. They display a near insatiable appetite to be the centre of public attention, often in relation to matters only tangential to their ordained role as shepherds of the Christian Church. Catholics in early-nineteenth-century North America could readily identify such political animals in episcopal garb: John Hughes of New York, Michael Anthony Fleming of Newfoundland, Alexander Macdonell of Upper Canada, and Ignace Bourget of Montreal, just to name a few.[1] These men were filled with certitude, imbued with strong loyalties to the institutional church, and graced with fearless natures. They did not hesitate to express the righteousness of their cause in a public and often partisan fashion.

There were other bishops, however, who, when left to their own devices, shunned unnecessary political engagements. Such men had as much conviction and as much loyalty to the church as their assertive episcopal colleagues, but due to shyness, detachment, humility, or perhaps even fear, they avoided confrontation within the church and did not attempt to gain prominence in political circles. Few, however, ever completely succeeded in insulating themselves from the social, economic, and partisan forces that conspired to turn them into politicians. Like their more assertive colleagues, bishops who had politics thrust upon them tasted both success and failure as they navigated the shoals of public life. At times, they were compelled to work behind the scenes in religious and political contexts; on other occasions, they had to operate in full view of pundits, politicos, and a volatile public. Rare was the bishop – and perhaps little has changed in this respect – who managed to elude this reality.

Had he ever been asked, Michael Power would likely have categorized himself as the second, more passive type of bishop. Given the extent of his library and the number of secular newspapers to which he subscribed, there is little doubt that he was well attuned to the major political and social events of his time, particularly after the rebellions of 1837 and 1838. Nevertheless, the young bishop practised a quiet diplomacy, his correspondence with politicians was minimal, and his interventions in the major political debates of the day were infrequent. His undertakings in Lower and Upper Canada indicate that his natural political instincts were to lie low and keep his powder dry, only emerging when a situation could be turned to his advantage or the health of the local church was at stake. While he read the newspapers, he rarely wrote to them. He acknowledged the temporal duties of those in public service and elected office, but he never pandered to them by offering them the Catholic vote. He tolerated his non-Catholic neighbours, co-operated with them whenever possible (while praying for their conversion), but he avoided public confrontation with the leaders of other Christian churches. One can attribute this to many factors: his political shrewdness; his introverted personality; or perhaps his spirituality, which he had cultivated from his close reading of Thomas à Kempis's *The Imitation of Christ*. It is possible that from this Christian classic he imbibed personal ideals of humility and forbearance and a suspicion of familiarity. He seems to have taken to heart the writer's advice, "It is vanity to pursue honours and to set yourself up on a pedestal."[2] Kempis's writings were so important to him that he ordered his own priests to read them, and he had intended to use them at the failed diocesan synod planned for 1845.[3]

In Canada West, Michael Power was thrust into political discourse, whether he wanted it or not. Several issues of importance to the Catholic faith would transform the retiring "Dr. Power," to whom Pope Gregory XVI awarded a Doctor of Theology in 1845, into one of the most respected Catholic clergymen in the province.[4] Of particular concern to him was the minority status of Catholics in Upper Canada and the manner in which Protestant-Catholic relations were imbedded in local and provincial politics. Questions regarding denominational education and civil liberties for the Catholic minority would draw him into the world of politics. The most pressing of these questions concerned the status of Upper Canada's fledgling publicly funded Catholic schools.

In his five years of service, Power managed to establish these schools and initiate a policy of staffing them with laymen and teachers from European religious orders. He also managed to keep a lid on the sectarian rivalry that often accompanied the debate over the establishment of Catholic denominational schools in British North America. By 1847, he had emerged as a voice of moderation and a humble man whom Protestant leaders believed would deal with them fairly. Eulogizing Power, Egerton Ryerson, Methodist minister, editor, and founder of public education in the province, paid the deceased bishop the highest compliment he could; Power, he remarked, although born in Nova Scotia, was "virtually a Canadian."[5]

In estimating the Catholic population of the western portion of Upper Canada, Power determined that Catholics accounted for less than one-fifth of the entire population. His flock was scattered across all of the districts of the western peninsula and had a measure of numerical strength only in francophone settlements in the Sandwich area, in the German enclave in the Wellington district, and in the urban centres of Hamilton and Toronto. In his see of Toronto, for instance, Catholics constituted about one-quarter of the population the year he arrived, and due to the influx of potato-famine refugees, this figure increased to 27 per cent shortly after his death.[6] In other pockets of the diocese, Catholics were not so numerous. In 1842, for instance, there were 65,203 Roman Catholics in the entire province (including the Diocese of Kingston), comprising only 13 per cent of the total population of Upper Canada.[7] In Power's diocese, however, Catholics numbered only 24,956 – less than 10 per cent of the total population west of the township of Whitby.[8] With the exception of the areas already mentioned, in practically every district in Upper Canada, Catholics were a minority of 6 per cent. The fact that his province was overwhelmingly Protestant and Catholics were weak in numbers and concentration justified Power's prudent approach to politics and public life. By the same token, due to the relative weakness of Catholic representation in Upper Canada, Protestants thought that they had little to fear from the pope's minions on the west bank of the Ottawa River.[9]

Perhaps it was the numerical insignificance of Catholics in the upper portion of the Province of Canada that facilitated toleration between Protestants and Catholics in the 1840s. But the fact that they coexisted peacefully did not necessarily imply that each group accepted the belief system of the other; rather, each acknowledged the differences of the other and respected the other's right to practice their faith.[10] In 1841, for example, Irishmen of all creeds joined the St Patrick's Benevolent Society to "afford advice and assistance to their distressed fellow countrymen," to celebrate their Irish heritage, and to accomplish all of this without "treading on ... forbidden ground – colonial politics."[11] Similarly, Catholic politicians and civil servants had made notable contributions to public life in the colony well in advance of the Act of Union of 1840. The Honourable John MacDonell (Aberchalder), speaker of Canada's first assembly; Alexander Macdonell (Collachie); Sheriff Donald MacDonell, a former member of the assembly; and Charles Baby were all respected Catholic leaders before Power ever set foot in Toronto.[12]

Even Power's predecessor as bishop of the territory, Alexander Macdonell, had forged convenient political alliances with Ogle Gowan, the grand master of the Orange Order, and John Strachan, the Anglican bishop of Toronto and a man with whom Macdonell shared a friendship and a conservative political ideology. Strachan asked Macdonell to keep an eye on his son when the younger Strachan went to study in Kingston, where the Catholic bishop resided.[13] Moreover, as late as 1846, Catholic and Protestant laymen agreed that King's College (an Anglican institution founded by Strachan and precursor of the University of Toronto) would be open to "all classes of the community, without distinction of creed, of national origin, or of party denomination."[14] While Strachan's supporters would oppose the concept of an open university whose terms and curricula would not be set by the Church of England, the issue of higher education provided Catholics and Protestant dissenters with a mutual concern and an opportunity to co-operate in order to produce benefits for both communities.

The private relations between Catholics and Protestants in Power's early years as bishop are much harder to track. Yet there is some evidence to suggest that various Christian groups lived, worked, and played together in relative peace. In 1842, a correspondent to William P. MacDonald's the *Catholic* gleefully reported that 150 Protestants in Chippewa (near Niagara) had responded warmly to a talk given by local priest Constantine Lee.[15] Power himself would remark on how many members of his flock would fall in love with Protestants and marry them,[16] but he would soon discover that such unions often served to augment Upper Canada's Protestant population rather than its Catholic one. When mixed marriages occurred among the wealthy, it was not uncommon for husbands and wives to attend one another's churches on Sunday morning. It could be somewhat unnerving for a Toronto priest, satisfied at early-morning Mass to see a Catholic wife seated next to

Toronto, Canada West, 1854, by E. Whitfield. Although in 1848
Toronto suffered a fire in its downtown core that prompted a massive
reconstruction project, this lithograph depicts a busy metropolitan
center shortly after Power's death; notable to the east are St James
Anglican Cathedral and Power's St Michael's Cathedral (NA, Coverdale
Collection of Canadiana, no. 1970-188-1478 C)

her Protestant husband, to learn that shortly thereafter the couple had
occupied a front pew at St James Anglican Cathedral, or Knox Presbyterian, or the Methodist church.[17] Even the most tolerant of Power's
priests were likely shocked to discover that in some eastern parts of the
province, Catholics and Protestants shared houses of worship to avoid
having to build too many expensive churches.[18] Such co-operation was
evident, to a lesser degree, in Toronto: Power reported that several Protestants had given generously to his cathedral-building fund.[19] Indeed,
there were isolated church-burning incidents and sporadic violence in
the Bathurst district, now eastern Ontario, but there was also strong
evidence of Protestant-Catholic co-operation in the region, particularly
in 1837–38, when the denominations worked together to quell a rebellion
outside of Bytown.[20] Thus, in the 1830s and the early 1840s, far from
being a province torn asunder by sectarian conflict, Upper Canada was
the site of peaceful coexistence between Catholics and Protestants at
home, in public, and in provincial institutions.

Occasionally, a short-lived incident would disrupt the peace and
demonstrate that denominational relations could be volatile if a certain
issue – an issue concerning loyalty, education, or public policy, for exam-

ple – was at stake. Rhetoric on religious rights or theological matters exchanged between individuals sometimes sparked debate in the press, in the church, or in political forums. In 1832, for instance, Power's friend and ally John Elmsley converted from Anglicanism to Roman Catholicism. Actions of this kind would not normally attract public attention, but Elmsley was a notable Toronto landholder, a naval officer, and a prominent member of the Executive Council of Upper Canada. Also, he had become so zealous about his newfound faith that in celebration of his conversion he had financed the printing of 5,000 copies of *The Bishop of Strasbourg's Observations on the Sixth Chapter of St John's Gospel* and had them distributed throughout the province.[21] One unappreciative recipient of this tract was John Strachan, Elmsley's former bishop, who attacked the convert from his pulpit and the pages of the local newspapers, decrying Elmsley's apostasy and denouncing the doctrine and ritual of the "Romish" church. Strachan's public tirade in his official organ, the *Church*, led to an extended public debate in Toronto and prompted Father William Peter MacDonald to rise to the defence of Roman Catholicism.[22]

Just prior to Power's arrival in the city, MacDonald's rejuvenated *Catholic* staked out its position as the official voice of Catholic thought and theological argument. The weekly was ready to engage its principal rivals – the heavily subscribed *Church* and Egerton Ryerson's Methodist *Christian Guardian* – whenever the opportunity arose.[23] "We would tell the editors of the Toronto *Church*," wrote MacDonald, "that the dark age of Protestant imposition on the public mind is fast drawing to a close. There is freedom now in the British dominions for Catholics to speak and write in their own confidence." He compared opening a copy of the *Church* to "turning up a dunghill to notice all the hodge podge of filth it contains."[24] Although peace prevailed between Protestants and Catholics in the era leading up to Power's arrival and during his early tenure as bishop, if sectarian bitterness raised its ugly head the Catholic community could count on MacDonald, with his magisterial turn of phrase and flare for verbal recklessness, to defend their church. Power, though appreciative of MacDonald's determination to defend the church from "virulent attacks ... by the non-Catholic media,"[25] read the paper carefully and coached the editor when he thought that his language or tone warranted correction.

Though the papers of each church were spicy on some occasions and downright nasty on others, the rhetorical flourishes of the religious pundits of the 1830s and early 1840s rarely sparked acts of public mischief or open hostility among Upper Canada's Christians. But if this war of words in the weekly press did not reflect the day-to-day reality, then how does one account for it? The answer is certainly more complex than the fact that early-nineteenth-century Canadians were more keenly interested in religious issues. Three developments in Upper Canadian society might explain this heightened awareness of sectarian differences in the press, religious and secular. First, international movements within the Catholic Church in the late 1830s and early 1840s made Upper Canadian Protestants uneasy about the growth of Catholic influence and power in continental Europe and potentially in Great Britain. The editors of John Strachan's the *Church* expressed alarm at the growth of the tractarian movement at Oxford University, where Anglicans were rediscovering their medieval and Catholic traditions. By 1843, these editors were decrying the ideas of Anglican professor John Henry Newman, who would soon convert to the Church of Rome; they also warned that the Church of England was being eaten away from the inside by the reintroduction of Catholic doctrine and tradition.[26] The existence of an aggressive Roman Catholic revival was confirmed domestically by Forbin-Janson's crusade in Lower Canada and the subsequent rise of the ultramontane movement in French Canadian dioceses.[27] Second, and equally unsettling, by the mid-1840s, Roman Catholic Irish immigration to Upper Canada was increasing, and this gave rise to the fear that the religious balance was shifting. Third, the organization of governance in the new Province of Canada was giving Upper Canadians cause for concern. Since representation in the assembly was equal between Canada East (Lower Canada) and Canada West (Upper Canada), French Canadian Catholics now had a powerful vote in the only elected body of the Canadian Parliament.

Fear of a Catholic resurgence based on both domestic and foreign developments grew as Upper Canadians came to see the practice of religion as voluntary. While there was a tolerance of the other, though not necessarily an acceptance of the other's value system, there was also a sense that no one group ought to assert its own dogmas or distinctive spirituality to the exclusion or detriment of other religious cohorts. The attempt to implant an established church had failed, and Christian Upper Canadians of Power's age were slowly stripping away the vestiges of Anglican particularism. Anglican control over marriage had already ceased.[28] In time, the clergy reserves, the Anglican rectories, and the denominational foundation of King's College would also pass away.[29] New political movements in Upper Canada and their supporters in the press advocated a voluntary approach to religion that could be formally recognized by all faiths before the law.[30] Egerton Ryerson was formulating a plan to ensure that no denomination had an exclusive hold on education in the province; denominationalism in schools was not to be supplanted by agnosticism or secularism, but rather by a common set of Christian principles – in essence, there would be generic Christian-based education. As denominational life was separated from public institutions and the ties between a specific church and the state were loosened, the religious press became the obvious forum for religious discussion, and its editors and those of the secular press became watchful and protective of the voluntary principle: equal rights for all, special privileges for none.

In a free market of Christian faith groups, jealousy over the perceived rights of other groups inflamed sectarian passions that had always been close to the surface. Unscrupulous politicians curried favour with certain religious groups by criticizing their rivals. By the mid-1840s, the *Mirror* was suggesting that both the *Examiner* and the *Banner* were attempting to woo Protestant voters to the cause of reform by means of anti-Catholic statements.[31] In 1844, people in Power's diocese and adjoining areas worried about thefts from Catholic churches, but no one named Protestants as the culprits.[32] More troubling, however, was the burning of two churches, one in St Catharine's in 1842, and the other in Guelph one year later.[33] While investigators suspected arson in both cases, neither Power nor the Catholic journalists made any accusations. Instead, Catholic leaders swiftly arranged to rebuild the churches and celebrated the blessing and dedication of the cornerstones.[34] Local authorities in Guelph, however, did offer a reward of fifty pounds for information leading to the arrest and conviction of the arsonists. Catholics considered the fires indignities committed against them, but they did not appear alarmed that justice had not been served or that the crimes had been committed in the first place.

If Catholic leaders had fingered anyone for the arsons, it would likely have been members of the Loyal Orange Order. Gone were the days of sectarian rapprochement, when Bishop Macdonell and the Orange Lodge had combined forces, in 1836, to re-elect a Tory majority in the Assembly of Upper Canada. By the mid-1840s, relations between Catholics and the order were glacial, to say the least. In 1795, the order had been revived in Ulster to defend the interests of Irish Protestants amid the resurgence of Irish Catholic nationalism and United Irish republicanism that seemed to gain strength in the wake of the French Revolution.

The Loyal Orange Order sought to maintain Ireland's ties to Britain, to defend such Protestant principles as the open Bible, and to thwart any political or social advances made by the Catholic minority in the north of Ireland. In the early nineteenth century, the Loyal Orange Order was transplanted to North America by means of Irish Protestant immigration and the British military units serving in North America.[35] Just prior to Power's arrival in Upper Canada, one priest reported to Bishop Gaulin that the members of the Eighty-third Regiment, stationed in London, possessed "a horrible Orange spirit."[36]

In 1830, Wexford native Ogle Gowan founded the Grand Lodge of British North America. Two years later, this new branch of the Loyal Orange Order was recognized by the parent organization as a separate jurisdiction.[37] The order quickly spread from its birthplaces, Perth and Brockville in eastern Upper Canada, to nearly every part of the province where Protestants could be found. Although the order still identified with its original loyalist and sectarian aims and engaged in political action, on the frontier it also offered its members a sense of community, fraternity, and an agency for mutual benefits, such as some insurance and death benefits.[38] Nevertheless, Catholics viewed the Loyal Orange Order at the very least with suspicion; some, like William Peter MacDonald, identified it as an "outlandish hate-stirring, broil-making and insolent over-bearing institution."[39] Thus, in 1846, when Irish Catholic settlers' homes and shops in the nearby Newcastle district were torched by "the Blazers," Catholic editors knew that the Orange Order was to blame.[40] The sectarian peace that had marked much of Power's tenure was fast coming to an end.

Power skilfully piloted his church through the shoals of sectarian agitation. Although his personal letters do not indicate a vigorous correspondence with local Protestant leaders, the documents that do survive show that he had excellent relations with John Strachan and Egerton Ryerson. In fact, it was Strachan who recommended to Ryerson that Power be appointed in 1846 to the first school board in Canada West. Ryerson was deeply shaken by Power's sudden death, and he eulogized the bishop in the warmest and most familiar terms when the board opened the province's first normal school for teacher training.[41] He lauded Power for his moderate approach to public affairs and his evident desire to transcend denominational barriers in order to "elevate the Roman Catholic population of the country" and mix all religions in the province's public schools.[42] In public, Power had been quick to praise the "peace and harmony" that existed between Catholics and "other religious sects," particularly in regions where historically there had been minor sectarian incidents.[43] It is possible that, in the context of his own millenarian ideas, Power was using kindness as a first step towards conversion at the end of the Fifth Age, but the impression of him put forward by the secular media and community leaders was that of an exceptional Catholic bishop who was willing to work for peace among all groups.[44]

Applying balm to the acrimonious relations between competing Christian denominations was only part of Power's public mission. He pursued other activities discreetly, he selected his interventions judiciously, and he conducted himself patiently and in the spirit of compromise. While in camera, instructing his priests and other members of the Catholic community, his view of his Protestant neighbours varied little from the view expressed by the Council of Trent during the Reformation. In his first pastoral letter, written prior to his arrival in the diocese, Power gently extolled the virtues of Christian unity under the pastoral leadership of the Holy See. Citing the Gospel of John (10:16), he hinted that his mandate would be focused on gathering the separated brethren into one flock, perhaps a sign that his declarations to Marcoux about the end of the Fifth Age were part of his pastoral plan: "for we acknowledge with grief ... other sheep we have who are not in this fold; and those we must bring, and they shall hear our voice; and there shall be one fold and one shepherd."[45] Power's upbringing in Halifax and ecclesiastical training in Lower Canada had impressed upon him the notion that there was one true flock and one earthly pastor of that flock, who resided in Rome. Accordingly, he exhorted the faithful to pray "for the conversion of those who do not belong to the one fold of the one shepherd."[46] His expectation was that Catholics would do their utmost to evangelize the Diocese of Toronto and England – a nation to which Power had a very strong sentimental attachment.[47] He would repeat his instruction to lift "the veil of prejudice" from the eyes of those "who are without" in most of his pastoral letters.[48] This evangelizing impulse coupled with a moderate approach to public affairs resulted in a strategy for conversion characterized by peace and gentleness.

When Power did intervene in public affairs, he often did so with the intention of putting an end to sectarian troubles, protecting the Catholic community from "error" and "apostasy," or promoting Catholic rights in education.[49] At times, he argued that Catholic distinctiveness must be respected, as he did in 1845, when he requested that a separate Catholic chapel be built in Toronto's insane asylum. "It is a settled and unchangeable principle among Catholics," asserted Power, "not to join in public or private devotions with those of any other denominations or attend any other place of worship but their own."[50] He would make a similar case for educating Catholic children in their own schools. Thus, while Power maintained cordial relations with the local Protestant population, he insisted that the special needs of Catholic worship and education be respected in a civil society.

In order to stake out the necessary ground to protect Catholic distinctiveness, Power would have to negotiate the political partisanship that had fractured Upper Canadian society and his own flock and address public concerns about Catholic loyalty to the Crown. The wounds created by the rebellions of 1837 and 1838 and the associated cleavages between reformers and Tories survived into the 1840s, as each faction of Canadians put its own spin on the recommendations of Lord Durham's 1839 report. Two features of that report – the union of the Canadas and the institution of responsible government – were the focus of political discourse. On 23 July 1840, the unification of Upper and Lower Canada was effected by an act of the British Parliament. Few in the Anglo-Protestant minority objected to the union, which came into effect on 5 February 1841. Upper Canadian merchants eyed trading advantages, since Montreal would become part of a single trading network under one government with jurisdiction stretching from the upper Great Lakes to the Gulf of St Lawrence. The establishment of a unilingual English legislature with equal representation from both parent colonies foretold the cultural assimilation of the French Canadian people. Even the selection of Kingston as the capital of the union fed the hegemonic ambitions of the citizens of what had been Upper Canada. Power would have to deal with a cadre of politicians who were increasingly confident that the 1840s would see an English-speaking, Protestant ascendancy in British North America.[51]

However, the second feature of Durham's report, the institution of responsible government – that is, the principle that the executive government should be responsible to the legislature – would shatter the prediction that French Canadians and Canadian Catholics would face assimilation and therefore annihilation. Durham failed to anticipate the fact that members of the legislative assembly would not vote along linguistic lines (and thereby swamp the French Canadian Catholic minority); instead, they chose to vote with those members who shared their political convictions or who would cut political deals with them. Debate over the question of whether the governor general's executive council should be responsible to the legislative assembly resulted in the formation of ideological rather than linguistic camps. Tories from both sides of the Ottawa River, most of them anglophone, tended to support the interpretation of ministerial responsibility espoused by Governor General Sydenham, who believed that he could ensure responsibility by effectively making himself his own first minister and forming an executive council of members whom he had personally selected from the assembly; among these conservatives, loyalty was measured by the strength of one's support of the governor general's position.[52] The Orange Order exploited this idea of loyalty, moving swiftly to align itself with the conservatives of the assembly.[53] A coalition of Robert Baldwin's Upper Canadian reformers and moderate French Canadian reformers led by Power's former classmate Louis-Hyppolyte LaFontaine supported the union but argued that Sydenham's executive council should be subordinate to the assembly. They characterized themselves as a loyal opposition to distinguish themselves from those who had made more radical pronouncements in the 1830s and had finally taken up arms. Another faction, comprised mainly of French Canadians, rejected the union as injurious to French Canadian liberty. If Power was to assert the interests of the Catholic minority in the western portion of the province, he would have to satisfy the Tory criteria for loyalty while convincing the house majority, which in his time was usually the reform coalition of Baldwin and LaFontaine.

Power waded into these dangerous waters alone. His predecessor, Alexander Macdonell, had been unabashedly Tory and had thus allied himself with the province's elite; acting for the Family Compact (the small but powerful Tory clique that had then dominated the government of Upper Canada), he became the agent of political patronage for his clansmen and supporters in Glengarry and other eastern districts of Upper Canada. While he had ensconced himself within the power circles of York, he had also made many enemies in the reform and radical camps, some of whom were Catholic. Power neither sought nor acquired the salaried civil appointment of his predecessor, nor did he consider it prudent to run roughshod over the many Catholics who had aligned themselves with the moderates and the reformers. In fact, Power's two unofficial organs – William P. MacDonald's the *Catholic* and C.P O'Dwyer and Charles Donlevy's the *Mirror* – were openly sympathetic to the reform movement and its proponents' interpretation of responsible government.[54] Power had been greatly influenced by

Irish Catholic constitutional reformer and liberal Daniel O'Connell, whose writings he had collected in his personal library. In fact, he let the *Catholic* openly espouse reform politics, and even though he kept a close eye on the religious content of the paper, there is no evidence to suggest that he censored its ongoing political commentary or its pointed attacks on the Orange Order.[55] Power could afford to keep MacDonald on a long leash, as there was no official tie between the diocese and the paper, and the bishop's reputation for being loyal to the Crown was unassailable.[56] Moreover, his admiration for England, its history, and the legacy of English saints such as Thomas à Beckett and Edward the Confessor was well known.

Power's incursions into the political arena tended to involve forging personal relationships rather than constructing partisan deals. In his short career as bishop, he cultivated close and beneficial friendships with politicians and public servants from across the political spectrum. His friend John Elmsley had strong ties with reformers, conservative politicians, and even remnants of the Family Compact. At the same time, Power relied heavily on the advice and co-operation of reform leader and Torontonian Robert Baldwin, whom he held in very high regard. Baldwin, an Anglican, had sent two of his daughters to Quebec City to be educated by the Ursulines.[57] Power and Baldwin were so close that when Baldwin's daughter Maria decided to become a Catholic, the Ursuline superior asked Power to break the news to her father.[58] Baldwin consistently supported Power's plans for education and episcopal corporation, easing legislation concerning both through the assembly. Even more of an asset to Power was his friendship with Dominick Daly, a non-aligned Irish Catholic member from Canada East. Nicknamed "the perpetual secretary," Daly served both reform and Tory administrations as provincial secretary from the early years of the union until 1848, when he was dumped from the executive council.[59] Daly and Power were in frequent contact when the church required the assistance of the assembly, and Daly was the only politician whom Power ever formally congratulated on record – in 1844, Daly earned the bishop's approval for remaining in the cabinet after his colleagues had resigned en masse.[60] The congratulatory letter, however, was private. Power would make no public statement that could jeopardize the goodwill he had cultivated among the reformers, who had resigned, or with Governor General Metcalfe, whose policies had prompted their resignation. If he wanted to present a public face, he sent Angus Macdonell, who served as the bishop's unofficial envoy to the politicians when it came to separate schools, land acquisition, or other church matters. Power pulled the strings from offstage, away from the centre of the action.

Public officials, however, came to regard him as the voice of Catholicism in Canada West. This was odd, given that in 1842 the thirty-eight-year-old Power was inexperienced as a bishop. Moreover, Remi Gaulin, Macdonell's successor in Kingston, was the senior prelate west of Montreal, or so it first appeared. Gaulin, however, was not well; by contemporary diagnosis, he was suffering from mental illness or dementia. On one occasion, Power noted, Gaulin thought that he was in the Holy Land and was impressed that his midday bowl of soup had been brought to him all the way from Kingston! Power visited Kingston several times and witnessed the steady deterioration of his colleague. It was becoming more and more urgent that church officials appoint a coadjutor bishop who had the right to succeed Gaulin.[61] Until Patrick Phelan was installed as titular bishop of Carrhae and coadjutor of Kingston, Gaulin directed Michael Power to serve as the administrator of the diocese – this over and above his duties as bishop of Toronto.[62] Thus, within a year of his appointment, Power had assumed responsibility for all Catholics from the Ottawa Valley to the lakehead. And this responsibility did not necessarily terminate on 20 August 1843,[63] when Phelan was formally consecrated for Kingston, because Gaulin did not go peacefully into his planned retirement and refused Power's invitation to take up residence in Niagara.[64] Furthermore, Phelan stumbled out of the gate, and Power noted to Pierre-Flavien Turgeon, coadjutor bishop of Quebec, that the new coadjutor of Kingston had quickly become very unpopular with his priests.[65] Outsiders would have seen Phelan as merely a titular bishop, and this could have made Power seem the Catholic leader of choice to politicians seeking the support of the Catholic Church or ecclesiastical advice. Power's loyalist credentials, private networking, quiet diplomacy, and perceived ecclesiastical clout in Upper Canada made him the most sought-after Catholic Church official west of the Ottawa.

No political issue preoccupied Power more than that of Catholic separate schools. From 1842 until his death in 1847, his political agenda would be dominated by the push for public funding for Catholic schools. During the same period, the common – or public – schools were experiencing tremendous growth, both in structure and in numbers. There has been considerable disagreement and confusion over what Michael Power really wanted in terms of education for Catholic children, resulting in two very different interpretations of his intentions. The first, originating within the Catholic community, is that Power sought the establishment of Catholic schools as a matter of principle. Proponents of this interpretation rely heavily on the comments of John Elmsley, Power's close friend and a former chair of the trustees of Toronto's first Catholic school. In 1856, in response to statements to the contrary, Elmsley argued that Power earnestly believed that Catholics had a right to publicly funded separate schools, and had Power lived, he would have made as vigorous a defence of this right as had his successor, Bishop Armand de Charbonnel.[66] Likewise, Catholic historians have long maintained that Catholic leaders since early settlement days have demanded government support for separate Catholic schools.[67]

The second interpretation of Power's educational intentions, originating with a group of historians, leans heavily on the testimony of Egerton Ryerson, Upper Canada's second superintendent of education and arguably the architect of Ontario's public school system. Ryerson claimed to have had a special relationship with Power, remarking that they had enjoyed "full and frequent conversations ... on subjects of public instructions, and on the scrupulous regard in which [Power] ever manifested, for the views and rights and wishes of Protestants."[68] Ryerson regarded Power as the most progressive member of the Roman Catholic clergy in his support for a common school system in which all of Upper Canada's children could learn together in an atmosphere of peace and tolerance. Power, Ryerson pointed out, not only agreed to sit on the first board of education, in 1846, but he also served as the board's first chair. Ryerson's secretary, J. George Hodgins, and a host of other respectable historians have come to accept Ryerson's view that Power was an enlightened prelate who preferred a common non-sectarian school system to separate denominational schools.[69] These historians regard Charbonnel, who succeeded Power in the 1850s, as the principal advocate of Catholic separate schools. The implication here is that denominational schools were a product of the ultramontane revolution imposed upon Upper Canada by foreign-born French and Irish bishops after Power's death.

In a nutshell, the historical interpretation of Power's vision for Catholic education hinges on the contrary opinions of two Victorian gentlemen. But both Ryerson and Elmsley had their personal agendas, and, consciously or unconsciously, they remembered their dead friend in ways that bolstered their respective views on the subject of schools. Elmsley, Power's trusted advisor and the diocese's leading Catholic philanthropist, was a zealous convert, perhaps more Roman than Rome. He was determined to stop those whom he saw as bent on imposing a common system that would prove injurious to the faith. Ryerson was equally passionate. His vision of a common, progressive, free, non-denominational though generically Christian public school system would be compromised by a proliferation of denominational schools, whether they be Catholic or Protestant.[70] He smarted from Charbonnel's unceasing criticism of those who promoted "godless" education. His nostalgia was unmistakable as he imagined what could have been if the moderate Power had lived.[71] Both Ryerson and Elmsley tended to see Power through the tinted lenses of their own ideals, but it is highly unlikely that these men, pillars of the community with deep religious convictions, would lie about Power, whom they both greatly admired. We are thus left with a standoff, so we must look more closely at Power's writings and actions on the subject of education and again try to determine his intentions for Catholic children. Despite the paucity of his correspondence on the issue and the scant attention accorded him by the press, there are some indications that neither Elmsley nor Ryerson had Power pegged.

Power's approach to the question of denominational schools was characterized by his resolve to honour the precepts of his faith while upholding his duty as a citizen of the British Empire. In balancing his faithfulness to church teachings and his loyalty to the Crown, he demonstrated an astute sense of timing and a great judiciousness, particularly when addressing issues of the family, the school, and morality in the public sphere. Dealing with committees and negotiating with public officials, most of whom were Protestant, he gauged the public mood before he strategically asserted Catholic rights. He believed that state-funded Catholic separate schools, as established in law, had a rightful place in society; like most Upper Canadians of his time, he did not think that common schools should be the exclusive deliverers of education, let alone religious education.[72] In Power's opinion, the Catholic curriculum could be delivered to wealthy and disadvantaged children alike by several means: common schools employing Catholic teachers in which Catholics dominated in numbers; mixed common schools supplemented by parish-based catechetical programs; publicly funded Catholic separate schools; publicly funded separate schools operated by members of religious orders; and tuition-based superior schools. Power's approach to the schools question, like his approach to most issues, was more nuanced that even his friends and co-workers realized.

Michael Power's arrival in Upper Canada coincided with a virtual revolution in the colony's administration of education. The annual increase in population due to immigration was accompanied by a growth in industry in towns and cities, and the last of the primeval forests were hacked down to make way for new farms. Upper Canadians demanded a modern education system. Common schools had been established in all districts, local trustees were hiring their own teachers, and communities began to build permanent schoolhouses. The Province of Canada and its two distinctive sections had always been characterized by a religious balance, and legislators knew that provision would have to be made for religious minorities. In 1841, the assembly approved the creation of separate schools for the Protestant minority in Lower Canada and the Roman Catholic minority in Upper Canada. They hoped that this would afford some security to members of minority groups who felt threatened with assimilation by the local religious majority.

When Power arrived in Toronto, in June 1842, provisions for the creation of separate denominational schools were already in place within his diocese. In 1841, section XI of the Common School Act (Day Act) permitted the establishment of denominational schools where "any number of inhabitants ... professing a Religious faith different from that of the majority of the Inhabitants" requested them.[73] Section XVI of the act also provided for Catholic representation on local boards of examiners, so that where a Catholic school existed, its pupils could be examined exclusively by Catholics. In the case of mixed schools, a denominationally mixed board would administer examinations. In 1843, three of Power's priests and John Elmsley were on the board of examiners.[74] When, in 1843, Francis Hincks introduced new legislation to correct problems with applying the Day Act in Upper Canada, Power lobbied his friends in the assembly to ensure that Catholic rights granted by the act remained secure.[75] Until this point, few Catholics in the diocese had taken advantage of the provisions to create separate schools. In fact, only one such school existed in the province, and it was in the township of Kingston; there were none at all in Power's diocese. In 1843, Power and Elmsley secured Toronto's and the diocese's first separate school under section XI of the Day Act.[76]

The Hincks Act became law in December 1843, and in sections 54 through 56 were provisions for ten Catholic or Protestant freeholders in each district to petition the municipality for the creation of a separate school, on condition that the local common-school teacher was of the "other" faith.[77] The religion of the teacher was critical to the legislation, because if the teacher of the local common school was Catholic, then there was no danger to the faith of the school's Catholic students, since it was assumed that such a teacher would not employ anti-Catholic texts or introduce topics that were offensive to the church.[78] The new legislation also entitled Catholics to elect trustees, whom both the government and Power considered to be chiefly responsible for the operation and maintenance of the schools.[79] Power travelled to Kingston to lobby the politicians to retain all of the clauses relating to Catholic rights in the earlier legislation. He confided to his colleague Pierre-Flavien Turgeon that he wanted to prevent the "Orangistes" from tampering with those rights. He was successful, and he commissioned his former vicar-general, Angus Macdonell, who was now residing in the capital, to keep an eye on the assembly and let him know if any other education bills were added to the order paper.[80]

Between 1843 and 1847, with separate-school rights confirmed by law, the number of Catholic schools in the Diocese of Toronto increased dramatically. By the time of his death, Power had overseen the establishment of eight publicly funded Catholic schools where there had been none at all. In addition to the Toronto school, there were new Catholic schools in Etobicoke (York County), Wellesley (Waterloo County), Wilmot (Waterloo County), Easthope South (Perth County), Westminster (Middlesex County), and the village of Preston. In 1847, these would be augmented by a second school in Toronto and, one year later, another in Hamilton, where there was a burgeoning Irish Catholic community.[81]

Despite indications to the contrary in the pronouncements of Ryerson and his supporters, Power was instrumental in the creation of Catholic schools. True to the spirit of the religious revival that had influenced his formation in Lower Canada, Power envisioned the establishment of separate Catholic schools wherever and whenever possible. He charged his priests with the task of building this vision as they built the infrastructure of the church on the frontier. In a revealing letter to Michael Mills, pastor at St Thomas and one of his least favourite co-workers, Power gave instructions on how to deliver Catholic education most effectively. He reminded Mills that his decisions as bishop were final and confidential, and not subject to the scrutiny of the laity:

> You ought to know that the Bible cannot be made use of as a mere class book and that no Catholic child can attend the reading of a chapter from a protestant [sic] version of the Holy Scriptures. The Catholic children should be allowed to remain in a separate room until the usual lesson from the Holy Scriptures shall have

been read; they can read themselves a chapter from the authorized Catholic version of the New Testament. It would be preferable in every way if the parents of Catholic children could have a separate school of their own; but this must depend in great measure on the number of Catholics in each locality. You must not communicate any part of my letter to any person: You have no right to force me to communicate even indirectly with any gentleman. You have asked my advice; I have given you my instructions and you must act in accordance with them without bringing your superior forward, as if you wished to get rid of all responsibility.[82]

Here, Power acknowledges that mixed schools were a reality, but one that could be made acceptable with certain alterations to the Catholic children's curriculum. Yet one senses that Mills was reluctant to accept the concept of separate schools, probably because of the costs involved – elevated costs might have made him more unpopular among his parishioners. He had apparently tried to pass the buck to his bishop to avoid looking like the enforcer of an unpopular policy, but Power clearly saw through his scheme.

On several occasions, to at least two other priests, Power reiterated his belief that publicly funded separate schools were preferable for Catholic children. He repeated the advice he gave Mills to the pastor at Belle Rivière and to Simon Sanderl, the Redemptorist priest responsible for the German Catholic missions at Wilmot and Waterloo.[83] "Catholics," Power wrote, "have a right to a school of their own and this ought to be the case in every school district when practicable."[84] Sanderl and the Germans responded positively to their bishop's directive, having already established two separate schools – separate schools were not only a way for them to preserve their faith but also their language. If Power's letters to clergy in Waterloo County, Belle Rivière, and St Thomas are any indication, he was willing to support the option of Catholics attending common schools as long as the local Catholic population was small and there was no threat to the faith development of the children in those schools. It is clear, however, that he preferred separate Catholic schools. He made that preference known to his priests, instructing them to take advantage of the provisions of the Hincks Act whenever circumstances permitted.[85]

Power, his clergy, and lay leaders soon learned that the legal right to establish separate Catholic schools did not ensure that such institutions would function smoothly or for an indefinite period. The Hincks

Act stipulated that separate schools were permissible only if a group of parents forming the local religious minority objected to the fact that the local common-school teacher shared the faith of the local religious majority. This provision created institutional instability, financial headaches, and social tensions at the grassroots level. For instance, if the local common school hired a Catholic teacher, then the local separate Catholic school would lose its grant and be forced either to close or to draw on property taxes. If no Catholic school existed, then none could be established if there was a Catholic teacher in the common school, because Catholic students would face no threat of Protestant proselytizing. So Ryerson encouraged trustees to hire Catholic teachers, thereby limiting the proliferation of Catholic schools.

Those Catholic schools that were created under the Hincks Act often found it difficult to obtain the government monies owed them, and some waited years for funding that had been guaranteed by legislation.[86] Some Protestants accused Catholics of padding the voter lists for separate-school-trustee elections with "vagrants" from outside the municipality or by using common-school funds to sustain both a separate school and a "nunnery school."[87] Finally, there were also questions raised on both sides regarding how large a share of the common-school fund should be awarded to a separate school. Teachers were uncertain about whether the funding was pegged to the total number of children in attendance or just those between the ages of five and sixteen. Questions were also raised as to whether funding was contingent on a teacher having been hired for a full year.[88] Uncertainty, conflict, acrimony, and ill will reigned wherever separate and common schools competed for students and funding.

Certainly, the most frustrating aspect of the Hincks Act was its stipulation that the creation of any separate school was contingent on the faith of the common-school teacher. A fiasco in Markham Village, York County, was a vivid example of the kind of problem that Power had to face. On 4 October 1845, a teaching vacancy in Markham's common school was filled by a Roman Catholic. Two days later, the local Protestant majority opted to establish its own separate school under section 55 of the Hincks Act. By 8 October, that school had opened. All went well until several months later, when the Catholic teacher at the common school resigned and was replaced by a Protestant.[89] Now Markham had two schools with Protestant teachers competing for a single financial entitlement. The rigidity of the act, the transience of teachers, and the general lack of knowledge among trustees about the act's finer points made the implementation of the Hincks Act problematic and, in some areas of the diocese, unstable.[90] Even Ryerson's own statistics reflect this confusion. In 1847, he claimed to have forty-one separate schools, Protestant and Catholic, and he delighted in what seemed to be their decline. However, his updated statistics, published in 1855, showed that there had been only twelve separate schools in 1847. This either called into doubt the manner in which his department gathered data or attested to the brief life of schools like the one in Markham.[91] Separate schools appeared to be even more labile than the superintendent had anticipated.

For Bishop Power, the glitches that occurred when applying the separate-school sections of the act were compounded by basic problems in the local management of Catholic schools. In Toronto, right under his nose, unresolved issues relating to teachers' salaries created what one columnist referred to as a "confused state" in school affairs.[92] Toronto's Catholic school, located at the corner of Richmond and Jarvis Streets (then Nelson and New), began in 1839 as a private school under schoolmaster Denis Heffernan. The pupils were mostly young Catholic men, although there were some non-Catholics among them. In 1841, John Elmsley donated land for the school, and the institution took on a more Catholic curriculum, although it was not formally recognized as separate until 1843, when it claimed funds under the terms of the Hincks Act.[93] Heffernan assumed teaching duties at the new school, and the student body consisted of about forty boys, most between the ages of seven and sixteen.[94] The trustees had promised Heffernan a salary of ninety pounds, which, unfortunately, went unpaid because the local superintendent, George A. Barber, refused to recognize the validity of Heffernan's certification. The trustees petitioned Ryerson, and one of their number, Charles Donlevy, editor of the *Mirror*, made public issue of Barber's "indiscretion and petty tyranny on this and other educational matters."[95] Barber consented to pay Heffernan thirty-three pounds, but he claimed that he was unable to pay the full salary because the trustees had failed to file a report before the deadline for the "apportionment of school funds."[96] Heffernan appealed to Ryerson and even threatened to sue the trustees for the remainder of his wages. Ryerson replied that since Heffernan had accepted the thirty-three pounds, he had effectively accepted compensation for his lost wages and should not expect another penny.[97] Heffernan relinquished his post to Timothy McCarthy.[98] Throughout the entire affair, Power kept his distance, allowing the trustees to manage a crisis that, through a lack of attention to detail and a disregard for deadlines, they had brought upon themselves. Moreover, in the heat of the crisis, Power was in Montreal attending to business with the Quebec bishops and Governor General Metcalfe. Upon his return, he was busy with pastoral visits to Sandwich and the western portion of the diocese.[99]

However, Power's disengagement from this affair did not indicate a lack of concern for Catholic education. In fact, he was very concerned. Between 1842 and 1847, he actively sought money and real estate in order to expand Catholic educational opportunities in western Upper Canada. In the first two years of his episcopate, he lobbied Governor General Metcalfe to release to his diocese lands promised by the government for the erection of a Catholic school in west Toronto.[100] In a similar frame of mind, he issued a protest to civil authorities and to his episcopal colleagues in Lower Canada when Bishops Bourget, Signay, and Turgeon requested that the government hand over funds derived from the Jesuits' estates to the French Canadian hierarchy. Although the Jesuits were officially expelled from New France at the time of the conquest of 1760 and disbanded by the church ten years later, some continued to live and serve in the province. When Joseph Casot, the last Jesuit, died in 1800, the British Crown assumed control of the properties of the former Society of Jesus.[101] In 1832, the Lower Canadian assembly gained control of the estates and mandated that revenues from these properties be used exclusively for educational purposes.[102] When the rejuvenated and restored Jesuits returned to Canada, in 1842, the bishops of Canada East, strengthened by the legal opinion of the noted French jurist Count Vatismesnil of the court of Charles X, petitioned for the revenues from the estates to be returned to the church.[103] The prelates considered this to be the right course of action, since the properties had been seized from the Jesuits and ecclesiastical control over them should be restored, particularly since the Jesuits needed resources to carry out the missionary work that Bourget had mandated of them.

Power was incensed. He insisted to Metcalfe and his brother bishops that the revenues be divided among all of Canada's bishops, since the Jesuits had been given missionary jurisdiction in territories that were now part of his diocese and that of Patrick Phelan.[104] Power had planned to use some of these funds to finance the Jesuit missions in the upper lakes,[105] but the earlier legislation stated that the money could only be used for educational purposes. With this in mind, Power was prepared to continue his fight for his share of the funds and then apply them to the establishment of higher education in his diocese. His Lower Canadian colleagues did not receive his proposals warmly; they envisioned their own share diminishing by the amount accorded to the Upper Canadians.[106] In the end, however, the hopes of Power and his episcopal partners went unrequited. Other issues clogged the agenda of the assembly, and the estates remained in the hands of the government until 1888, when they were dispersed for educational purposes in Quebec's public Catholic and public Protestant school systems. Although Power failed to achieve his ends, the episode does add credibility to the notion that whenever the opportunity arose, Power tried to promote Catholic education in his diocese, even if his endeavours ran afoul of the plans of other, sometimes more powerful, prelates.

Although Power required his priests to facilitate the establishment of Catholic schools wherever possible, he knew that dancing through the denominational details of the Hincks Act – which passed into the School Act of 1846 without significantly altering the terms relating to separate schools – was not the only way to tackle the problem. Like other religious leaders of his day, he tried to deliver religion-based education in a number of ways. In the 1840s, there was little unanimity as to how a child ought to be educated, or whether formal schooling was even necessary for everyone. Common schools, grammar schools, and private schools were merely several acceptable options for offering education to the "classes and the masses."[107] Under Ryerson's leadership, the Upper Canadian state assumed a greater responsibility for providing money, structure, governance, and curricula to public schools. These local institutions were set up to provide boys and girls from a broad range of social backgounds with basic literacy and numeracy without burdening their parents with school fees. Middle- and upper-class families could elect to send their children to private institutions for a "superior" education. This diversity of educational institutions underscored class distinctions between schools rather than differences between primary and secondary curricula, which would become more important later.[108] Thus, the 1840s produced not only the embryonic form of Ontario's public school system but the decade was also distinguished by a high degree of heterogeneity in the way education was structured and delivered.

By recruiting men and women from religious teaching orders to Upper Canada, Power confirmed that he, like Strachan and Ryerson, wanted to provide several types or levels of schooling. Members of the Institute of the Blessed Virgin Mary – the Ladies of Loretto – whom he had brought from Ireland in 1847, established a tuition-based school for girls, emulating a Catholic variant of the superior schools available to children from wealthy families. The Ladies of Loretto advertised a program that included curriculum basics like reading, arithmetic, foreign languages, and history, along with painting, ornamental needlework, and music.[109] Even in his correspondence with Mother Teresa Ball, the institute's superior in Ireland, Power clearly stated that the sisters must charge fees that were competitive with those charged by a comparable Protestant school for young women.[110] Contemporaries of Power would find nothing unusual in a school charging tuition and advertising its excellence. In fact, in the 1840s, Ryerson's idea of free schools was a radical one to those involved in school promotion.[111] Yet Power was not content with just the Lorettos and the Jesuits. He designed his European tour of 1847 as a recruitment venture; he would use it to encourage more religious to come to his diocese to staff parishes, assist with missions, and build schools.[112]

Power's plan for the religious orders in the field of education, however, was multipurpose. In his letters to the Loretto Sisters, for example, he asked that they not dedicate their mission in Canada exclusively to running tuition-based schools. In 1847, he told Mother Teresa Ball that her delegation to Canada ought to involve itself in two different types of school: a day school and a common school – both of which, he hoped, would be "numerously attended."[113] He acknowledged that the sisters would "have as much as they can do," but he promised to supply them with everything they needed. Power's request of the Lorettos suggests that in educational terms, he was a creature of his times – he promoted the superior type of education while advocating state-assisted basic education for the general population of Catholic children. He had explored, in total, five different ways of delivering Catholic education in the diocese: separate denominational schools as mandated by legislation; parish-based catechism classes in areas where the weakness of Catholic settlement precluded separate schools; superior schools for children whose families could afford the fees; separate schools operated by religious orders as opposed to lay schoolmasters; and common schools with a Catholic ambiance in places where Catholics constituted the overwhelming majority of the population. The last possibility was certainly the most realistic in francophone areas such as the township of Sandwich, where, in 1845, local Protestants formed a separate school, thereby abandoning the common school to the Catholics. Since common schools were far better funded, Sandwich's "Catholic" common school received more financial support than any school conforming to the Catholic-school models suggested by Power.[114] In 1850, Protestants in the township of Medonte, Simcoe County, would do the same, beginning a tradition of Protestant separate schools in the Penetanguishene area that continued to the 1990s.[115]

Thus, John Elmsley's contention that Power was committed to the establishment of separate schools reflected only part of the bishop's broader vision of how a Catholic education could be delivered in a Protestant province. Power had the advantage of living in a time when educational policy was not graven in stone and there was no strong movement for homogeneous schooling. This advantage coupled with his prudent approach to asserting Catholic rights and prerogatives in the face of a non-Catholic majority opened the door to many options in the realm of education.

Under the circumstances, Power's willingness to serve on the first board of education for Canada West is quite understandable. Ryerson's magnum opus in education, the School Act of 1846, did not substantially alter the rights accorded to Catholic and Protestant minorities concerning separate denominational schools. However, the superintendent had hoped that the majority of Upper Canadians would be attracted to the new common schools, institutions that would incorporate "the Christianity of the Bible, regardless of the peculiarities of sects or parties," which would form "the basis of public instruction." Ryerson saw no need for separate schools, but he allowed them, hoping that they would die a natural death.[116] The act's one pertinent innovation was the creation of a board of education for Canada West. This new administrative body was mandated to supervise the selection of texts for common schools, create and manage a normal school for the training of teachers, and advise the superintendent of schools. Ryerson and Attorney General William Henry Draper (chief minister of the government) had wanted the first board to reflect the religious diversity of Canada West without seeming "too clerical." In 1846, on the glowing recommendation of John Strachan, Ryerson appointed Michael Power to the seven-member board as Roman Catholic spokesperson. Power and five others would have voting privileges, while Ryerson would sit as an ex officio member.[117] At the first board meeting, in July 1846, Power was elected chair of the board, a post that he held until his death.[118] He oversaw the adoption of Irish readers for Canada West's common schools, the conversion of the old legislative building in Toronto into the new normal school, and the hiring of its first master, but Power's tenure as an educational public servant passed without controversy.[119] Ryerson remarked upon Power's seriousness in performing the job, claiming that he could set his watch according to the punctual arrival of the bishop at each board meeting.[120]

Power's board membership provided the Catholic clergy with important representation in Ryerson's inner circle and gave the church a strong presence during the formulation of educational policy. From his vantage point on the board, Power could watch over the delivery of Catholic education and ensure that Catholic rights were preserved. Those supporters of Ryerson's later depiction of Power's views on education might have asked themselves why the bishop, if he was so committed to Catholic separate schools, did not try to prevent the board's Amendment to the School Act (1847), which permitted each incorporated town and city in Canada West to appoint its own board of trustees to control and manage common schools. Did this not remove the right of Catholics to elect their own trustees for their separate schools? [121] Under section V of the amended act, these new boards of appointed trustees would have the power "To determine the Number, Sites and Description of Schools, which shall be established and Maintained in such City or Town aforesaid, and whether such School, or Schools shall be Denominational or Mixed." [122]

The same board of trustees would appoint a committee "of not more than three persons" for each school. In denominational schools, these committees would be "of the religious persuasion to which such schools belong." [123] There were several reasons for these amendments, not the least of which was to make available to urban communities a variety of schools – common schools and "schools of a higher order." [124] Ryerson also proposed these amendments on the urging of Anglican bishop John Strachan, who was perplexed that Anglicans did not have the right to establish separate schools distinct from those of other Protestants, who possessed rights equal to those of Catholics in this regard under the 1843 and 1846 acts. [125] Strachan was confident that the large Anglican populations in the cities and towns would be able to convince local counsellors and their appointed trustees to erect Anglican separate schools. Conversely, Roman Catholics, who constituted less than 17 per cent of the population, would be at the mercy of municipal councils dominated by Protestants and Anglicans.

The question looms: Faced with this threat to Catholic education, how could Power, as chair of the board, have consented to the amendments? Moreover, why did it take Power's episcopal colleague in Kingston, Patrick Phelan, nearly ten months to protest the amended School Act? [126] There are several possible explanations, each of which is consistent with Power's previous political engagement in the area of separate schools. First, from January to June 1847, Power was again travelling in Europe; he was not in Canada when the amendments were drafted and passed in first reading or under discussion in second reading. [127] Furthermore, when he returned, the school year was nearly over, and there would be no new applications for separate schools until the autumn. But even if he had been conversant with the amendments, he would have understood that the legislation would not touch rural schools and, given the reasonably good relations between Catholics and Protestants in his diocese, municipal bodies would give Catholics their due. In the summer of 1847, however, one matter eclipsed all others for Upper Canadian leaders, regardless of their religious or political stripe: the influx of thousands of refugees from the Irish potato famine. The priority of prelates and politicians was to assist the immigrants and arrest the mass panic caused by the outbreak of typhus in major Canadian cities. For Power and others, the school legislation became a secondary concern in light of the horrors of "Black '47."

There are some indications that the number of Catholic separate schools had peaked by the time of the legislation. In 1847, Ryerson reported that there was a marked decline in the number of separate schools, and he anticipated, with some satisfaction, that this downward trend would continue.[128] There is no reliable evidence to suggest that even Catholics made requests for new separate schools that year, although Ryerson admitted that he had not received reports from either Toronto or Kingston regarding schools. Yet subsequent reports from the superintendent's own department indicate that Catholics in the Toronto area had attained their long-desired second school, and that new separate schools had appeared in Preston and Hamilton in 1847 and 1848, respectively.[129] Despite the amendments, and with a crush of new children to educate – the offspring of famine immigrants – there was continued pressure to establish Catholic separate schools in Power's diocese. We can only speculate as to how Power would have reacted to the situation had he lived past the famine immigration period. All we know is that there was a delay in the clergy's public response to the amendments. Then, in November 1847, with the number of new school registrations on the rise, Phelan denounced the sections of the act that placed the establishment of new separate schools in the hands of the Protestant municipal politicians.

Throughout his episcopate, Power had been on excellent terms with his Protestant colleagues when it came to education. After 1847, he was no longer around to help balance the interests of the Catholic Church with those of the Protestant majority. When Armand de Charbonnel arrived to replace him, in 1850, the social, political, and economic climate of Canada West was in the throes of change. The 1850s would be marked by bitter sectarian passions, alleged papal aggression, and episodic

violence. Perceived aggression by Pope Pius IX in Europe, deadlock
between the French- and English-speaking members of the Assembly of
Canada, and the visibility of unemployed famine refugees in the cities of
Canada West provoked a high degree of cultural and religious tension,
rarely experienced in Power's time.[130] This charged social and political
climate, when combined with Charbonnel's more volatile temperament
and more overt ultramontanism, lead to explosive relations between
Power's successor and Ryerson,[131] who likely yearned for the days when
he worked with judicious, soft-spoken, and calculating Power.

Power's view of Catholic education in a Protestant province had been
broadly conceived – much more so than either Ryerson or Elmsley and
their followers had imagined. The memories the two men harboured
of the bishop were quickly coloured by their respective ideological and
religious biases and tainted by the developments of the turbulent 1850s.
Elmsley and Ryerson could only offer a limited perspective on Power's
vision of how Catholic education could be provided for his diocese and
how Catholics could participate in a large and powerful non-Catholic
country. Power had been a model contributor to a decade of moderation, the 1840s, when Protestant and Catholic leaders did a yeoman's
job of keeping the lid on sectarian passions that could have torn the
Province of Canada apart. In so doing, Power managed to respond to
the needs of Catholics and co-operate effectively with Protestant leaders of church and state. In his public life, he was able to promote the
idea that there were several means by which a Catholic catechesis could
be delivered, independent of how the state supported denominational
education, while not compromising his belief in publicly funded Catholic
common schools. In some ways, Bishop Joseph-Octave Plessis was his
true political mentor. Plessis had been a spiritual guide to the younger
Power, and he had perhaps passed on his artfulness in politics to the
future bishop of Toronto. After all, in the early 1800s, Plessis had skilfully navigated the treacherous waters between the imperial ambitions
of the British conquerors and the urgent necessities of a growing church
on the Canadian frontier. By co-operating with the Crown, Plessis had
won concessions and gained advantages for the church. It appears that
Power learned his lessons well.

ᴠ: The Year of the Irish ᴠ

ON NEW YEAR'S DAY 1847, the *Mirror* published a sombre message to its readers. Editor Charles Donlevy wrote that while the "blessings of Providence" had been "profusely bestowed" upon Canadians in 1846, this had not been the case elsewhere in the world. Cholera had crippled India, claiming tens of thousands of lives each day; some members of the British military stationed there had been reduced to "mere skeletons." The "plains of Mexico [were] crimson with gore" and her churches desecrated by "the Army of a Nation, calling itself *Christian*." Donlevy also reviled this "Nation," the United States, for enslaving millions of blacks, whom it "held as chattels." But Donlevy reserved his most venomous rhetoric for the United Kingdom – and Whitehall, in particular, for its failure to relieve the Irish potato famine: "In the bloody war of extermination waged against the unhappy people of Ireland, by the Sovereigns of England, millions were swept out of existence by starvation ... Thousands perishing of want amidst surrounding plenty."[1] Donlevy urged Irish Catholic *Mirror* readers to give thanks for their blessings but also to remember their brothers and sisters in the homeland and raise their voices in protest against such suffering.

Canadians, however, would have little time to count their blessings. They would long remember 1847 as the year of the Irish. The insulation of the Canadas from the calamities of Ireland would come to an abrupt end in the spring, when the shipping season opened on the St Lawrence and the sails of the first Irish coffin ships were sighted from the heights of Grosse Île. In the coming months, close to 80,000 Irish migrants would pass through the Grosse Île quarantine station, conveniently situated in the middle of the St Lawrence, about forty-five kilometres downriver from Quebec City.[2] Thousands of migrants on apparently disease-free ships were permitted to bypass the island, but thousands more – the sick and their healthy fellow travellers – were forced to stop at Grosse Île, where they filled the makeshift medical facilities, primitive decontamination centres, and fever sheds. Some 5,424 persons found their final repose in the graveyards at the southern and northern extremities of what contemporary writer Robert Whyte terms "the island of pestilence."[3]

Many of Grosse Île's survivors unknowingly carried the deadly typhus bacteria with them as they pushed inland to Quebec City, Montreal, Bytown, Kingston, and Toronto. By the time the *Mirror* published its next New Year's Day editorial, one out of every five Irish migrants who set sail for British North America in 1847 were dead.[4] Survivors found their kinfolk on the farmsteads of the Canadian interior or huddled in the major centres of Hamilton, Toronto, St Catharine's, or London waiting for an opportunity to earn a living. But instead of finding employment, many encountered hunger, sickness, and poverty; many also faced discrimination from those who considered them carriers of disease, or worse. Most of the Irish immigrants who arrived in Toronto in the spring and summer of Black '47 just kept on going. Only 2,000 of the nearly 38,000 who landed in the city remained there, and 1,100 of them died and were buried in Toronto before the church bells could ring in the new year.[5]

Among the dead was Michael Power, who had contracted typhus while working among the thousands of sick and dying on Toronto's waterfront. Power's parents had been part of the first, pre-famine wave of Irish immigrants to the Atlantic colonies, and his first pastoral charge had been among the Irish immigrants who came in subsequent waves and settled Lower Canada's eastern townships or toiled as canal navvies and woodworkers in the Ottawa Valley. His assignment to the new western Upper Canada diocese had been prompted by the fact that the newly arrived Irish Catholics there required a spiritual leader who was familiar with their culture and traditions. Other bishops and political leaders looked to him for help when Irish Catholic communities were in crisis. He was called to intervene between Bishops Walsh and Fraser when relations between the Highland Scots of eastern Nova Scotia and the Irish of Halifax soured. So closely was his career associated with the Irish that after his death some thought that he had actually been born in Ireland and brought to Halifax as an infant.[6]

The famine and Black '47 amplified the popular notion that Power was essentially an "Irish" bishop. In the winter and spring of 1847, he made his second trip to Europe. After his *ad limina* visit to the newly elected Pope Pius IX, he went to Ireland in search of priests and religious for

Upper Canada, and what he discovered was a land devastated by hunger, poverty, and civil unrest. Prior to his Irish visit, having read horrific reports on the famine in the London papers, he wrote a pastoral letter about it and sent it ahead to Toronto. His plea for prayers and assistance for the hungry and dying of Ireland set in motion four months of advocacy for famine victims. His passion to alleviate the suffering seemed to transcend all other priorities in what would prove to be the final weeks of his life. It is therefore not surprising that in popular memory, Power would endure as the "martyr" of the Irish potato famine. Furthermore, the "famine moment" would become the prism through which future generations of Canadians and many historians would read the entire Irish Canadian experience. Yet, however poignant this memory of Power might be, it does not do justice to his longstanding commitment to the Irish in British North America.[7]

It is important to remember that most of the Irish settlers in Power's diocese were not "famine" Irish. Whether they wielded pick and spade at Thorold, fished for pike and perch on Lake Huron, or tilled the soil near Elmbank in Peel County, most of the Irish whom Power served had left their homeland long before the first tubers began rotting in Irish potato patches. Since the end of the Napoleonic Wars, in 1815, and the corresponding collapse of the British economy, the Irish had been setting out for Britain's colonies in North America and for the American republic. From 1815 to 1845, close to half a million Irish Protestants and Catholics entered Upper and Lower Canada.[8] Some remained in the principal ports of call, but most pushed on into the interior and hacked out farmsteads in newly surveyed back-country townships from Glengarry to Goderich.[9] An undetermined number – in the thousands – either fulfilling their original intent or dissatisfied with what they found in Upper Canada, crossed into the United States at the Niagara or Detroit frontiers, never to return.

In this pre-famine period of immigration to Upper Canada, Irish Protestants tended to outnumber Irish Catholics two-to-one.[10] Except in the Catholic block settlements established by Peter Robinson near Almonte (1823) and Peterborough (1825), most Catholics from Ireland were well interspersed among their Protestant cousins and non-Catholic fellow travellers in the colony.[11] When Power arrived, in 1842, if he had commissioned an enumerator to take stock of his Irish flock, he would have learned that most of the Irish actually resided in the sections of Remi Gaulin's diocese not ceded to the new Diocese of Toronto. The enumerator would have told Power that Irish Catholic farms, churches, and families were scattered through the Ottawa Valley, Lanark County, and the rocky lands of the Canadian Shield that dipped into Frontenac County; they were to be found, as well, in the township of Tyendinaga near the Bay of Quinte and in the two Robinson settlements. He would also have reported to the new bishop that there were sizeable Irish communities in Kingston, Belleville, Bytown, and the villages that would become part of Renfrew County.[12]

Power's enumerator would report some modest Irish settlement within the new diocese. Concentrations of pre-famine Irish settlers could be found in the township of Adjala north of Toronto in Simcoe County, the townships of Hibbert and Biddulph in the London district, and in the villages dotting the banks of the canal projects in the Niagara district, where Power would soon meet some of his most troublesome countrymen.[13] In the first week after his installation, in June 1842, Power would visit the Irish Catholic enclaves in Toronto, Hamilton, and St Catharine's. He would come to realize that in the home district – Toronto and the surrounding bits of what would become York County – the local Irish Catholic population constituted about 40 per cent of the total Irish population, thereby exceeding the ratio of Irish Catholics to Irish Protestants in the remainder of the diocese.[14] As he travelled more extensively in his diocese, he would become increasingly aware that with the exception of the First Nations Peoples of the upper Great Lakes and the French Canadians of Essex County, the Irish were the most prominent Catholic group. They were the fastest-growing ethnic group in his care, and Power would share in their joys and their disasters.

The life of Power's Irish flock was by no means easy. Although those Irish who ventured as far inland as Upper Canada were people with sufficient means to make such a long journey – and not the stereotypical Irish migrants who had been subsidized by their former landlords – they still found it difficult to establish themselves.[15] Many had exhausted their liquid capital by the time they made it to their final destination. They were physically exhausted too. In 1842, even Governor General Bagot took note of the infractions against the navigation laws committed by the captains of the ships on which the Irish travelled. These captains offered such a minimal standard of human comfort to their passengers that many disembarked in Canada malnourished and sick.[16] Earlier, in 1840, the *Mirror* had lashed out at the immigration agents who lured Irish families with promises of excellent farms, only to leave them on marginal lands and swamps, where many were doomed to die "in a most destitute state" and be buried "without a coffin."[17] Much of the criticism of the poor treatment of Irish immigrants and the lack of state support for settlement was directed at Thomas Rolph, the Canadian government's commissioner for immigration and the founder of the Canada Emigration Association.[18] The *Mirror* blasted Rolph for promoting trans-Atlantic migration without arranging adequate support for the settlers once they arrived. This situation was exacerbated by Orange politicians and municipal workers, who refused Irish Catholics employment.[19] While the census shows that many of the Irish Catholics in Power's diocese established themselves on farmsteads with relative degrees of success, these people for whom migration had been such a misery remained an isolated group within Upper Canadian society.

Although physically separated from Ireland, Power's Irish retained strong ties to their homeland. Some Irish Catholics in Upper Canada regarded themselves as "exiles."[20] Such a notion appeared to be on the mind of Charles Donlevy when, in 1842, he pulled the heartstrings of *Mirror* readers by relating the story of a dying Irish migrant: "Farewell, said he, you fertile hills, on whose sunlit summits brouze (*sic*) the sportive herds in wanton luxuriance, farewell to that spot on which I first drew breath ... I, a poor disconsolate Exile am doomed never more to behold you, I wish from the bottom of my heart that I had never left my native land, thus roved the poor exile, and thus ended the colloquy."[21] The *Mirror* employed the theme of exile periodically; its editors saw it as a useful motif to describe the relationship between the Irish migrant and the homeland. "Ireland, the 'great difficulty' of the mountebank premier of England, the object of the world's sympathies, the 'Cushla ma chree' of her exiled sons who now find themselves scattered across the globe, and still feel the vibrations of that chord of mysterious sympathy, which links the heart of the patriot to the fortunes of his native land."[22]

Such rhetoric was of great use to *Mirror* editors as they attempted to tie the problems of the colonies to a more general malaise within the empire. Donlevy's support for responsible government and its Upper Canadian patrons, Robert Baldwin and Francis Hincks, could be viewed as a reaction to what he regarded as the abject failure of the Act of Union, which had been imposed upon Ireland in 1800, and to the dissolution of representative government wherein the Catholic majority could participate. In Donlevy's opinion, the union served to keep the Irish as the "starving and uncared for millions; ye care-worn, rent-racked, tillers of the soil, who elaborate from a teaming land ... who toil amidst a land of plenty, and dare to taste the fruits of their labour."[23] Donlevy linked the repeal of the Act of Union in Ireland and the quest for ministerial responsibility in Canada, and while such rhetorical flourishes and turns of phrase raised the political awareness of those in Power's flock who could read, they also alerted non-Catholics to the fact that Old World political battles could soon become Canada's problem as well.[24] While we do not know how deeply the motif of exile and alienation affected Power's Irish Catholic flock, we can be certain that Irish Catholic immigrants remained bound up in homeland issues.

In fact, Irish Catholic Upper Canadians held on tightly to the social and spiritual traditions of Ireland. Irish Catholic parishes retained their calendar of feasts and saints days. Across the diocese, pre-famine immigrants celebrated St Patrick's Day, marking the feast of Ireland's patron saint with parades, banquets, and liturgies.[25] The feasting was usually punctuated by speeches and toasts, the latter often to the health of political hero Daniel O'Connell or, ironically, Father Theobald Mathew, Ireland's intrepid temperance crusader.[26] Power's own priests actively fused the spiritual and the nationalist. In Brantford, for instance, three priests – Quinlan, Gibney, and Mills – were important guests at the 1846 St Patrick's Day banquet. The chair, Dr William Murphy, noted, "The Irish people have ever been proverbial for their attachment to the clergy and very justly so, for they are the real soothers of afflictions and sincere friends in the trying hour of need."[27] As Murphy spoke of the centrality of church and clergy to the sense of Irish peoplehood, the crowd responded with wild cheering. The presence of the clergy at such events not only confirmed Murphy's claims, but it also served to moderate the tone of the festivities and dampen the easily inflamed passions between the Irish and their neighbours. In Hamilton, Father Edward Gordon delivered a keynote address to an 1847 gathering of the St Patrick's, St George's, and St Andrew's Societies, advancing the argument that "in this country of their adoption, their religious dissensions which had been the *curse* of Ireland would not find place, but the spirit of charity would prevail."[28] That year, the processions of each society ended without a banquet, because it was considered inappropriate to feast while Ireland starved.

As the Hamilton episode suggests, the nature of Irishness in Power's diocese was not narrowly sectarian. In Toronto, Irish Catholics and Protestants formed the St Patrick's Benevolent Society (SPBS), a virtual who's who of the municipality's leading Irishmen. Provincial reform leader and Anglican Robert Baldwin served as president for a time, and Roman Catholic priest Eugene O'Reilly was appointed chaplain, with Power's approval.[29] Although local Tories sometimes criticized it for being an opposition or reform association, the local Irish paper defended the SPBS as an organization "based on broad and liberal principles."[30] The society's most ardent defender, the *Mirror*, was unabashedly reform in its editorial policies, but the ecumenism of the SPBS was undeniable, as was its fraternal and charitable mandate.[31]

The Irish community Power inherited, however, was not without its tensions. Even in the St Patrick's Benevolent Society, explosive feelings lay below a calm surface of trust, co-operation, and fraternity. In 1841, for example, the 200 original members of the SPBS left the society when it was discovered that the parent organization was tied too closely to members of the Loyal Orange Order. This separation, which occurred amid some heated rhetorical exchanges between the *Patriot* and the *Mirror*, eventually caused the dissolution of the older society, leaving no middle ground between the new society and the Orange Order and polarizing the Irish community. On one side were Catholics and their moderate Protestant colleagues; on the other were hard-line Protestant Irish. Tensions heightened with the arrival of the primarily Catholic famine migrants.[32] By the 1850s, the SPBS would have a more Protestant flavour as Catholics began to form parish-based associations, sodalities, and clubs. By 1870, the St Patrick's Benevolent Society would be renamed the Irish Protestant Benevolent Society of Toronto, a title that more accurately reflected its membership.[33]

During Power's tenure as bishop, Irish Catholics in the diocese became more actively engaged in the movement to repeal the Act of Union affecting Ireland and Great Britain. Once O'Connell and his Catholic Association had secured Catholic emancipation, in 1829, his movement refocused its efforts to repeal the union and restore an autonomous Irish Parliament in Dublin. O'Connell almost reached the status of a saint in 1843, when he was arrested for his political beliefs and the constitutional agitation perpetrated his movement. The effect of this in the Diocese of Toronto was the rapid growth of the Repeal Association. It is hard to gauge to what extent Power had a hand in these developments. He had read O'Connell's constitutional reform policies and was supportive enough of grassroots Irish politics that he subscribed to O'Callaghan's *Vindicator* while he was a priest at Ste-Martine. As was his practice in all things political, Power made no public statements on the issue, but he gave his priests considerable latitude to participate in the repeal movement. Given the firm control he exerted over them in almost every pastoral matter, this speaks volumes about his sympathy for repeal. Moreover, in Power's own weekly paper, the *Catholic*, William Peter

MacDonald boldly stated that if repeal was not granted, then the United Kingdom could face civil war.[34] Without censure from Power, MacDonald used the paper to promote the repeal movement, report on repeal developments in Ireland, and publish the minutes of meetings of local repeal associations.

Repeal associations appeared in the townships of Oshawa, Toronto, Hamilton, Dundas, Adjala, Tecumseh, and King, as well as in Thorold and Newmarket.[35] In 1844, the Brantford Repeal Association had sixty members; in Oshawa, association members raised eighty-eight dollars in "repeal rent," adding it to the Toronto Repeal Association's $630 collection for O'Connell's movement.[36] Financial commitments were usually encouraged with fiery rhetoric about "liberty" for Ireland modelled on that enjoyed by the colonies of British North America. In 1843, for example, at a meeting of the Hamilton Repeal Association, speakers urged the British government to grant Ireland the self-government that had already been "allowed to Canada, New Brunswick, Nova Scotia, Jamaica, and Newfoundland, the whole of which taken collectively in point of numbers, wealth, and politics, would fall far short of Ireland."[37] Irish Canadians demanded just one thing of the Crown: that it ensure that the "rights of Irishmen ... be on par with that of the Englishmen."[38] Such comparison-based arguments were not unique to Power's time – they would be repeated by moderate Irish nationalists in Canada until 1921, when the Irish Free State was created.

Due to the increase in Irish Catholic immigration and settlement in Upper Canada and the rise of the repeal movement, the fragile sectarian entente was at risk. In 1843, Power reported that although Toronto was "perfectly tranquil," trouble was brewing between Catholics and Orangemen in several sections of the diocese.[39] Earlier that year, Orangemen in Amherstburg had hung an Irishman in effigy from the mast of a schooner moored near the site of local St Patrick's Day festivities. To the east, in St Catharine's, the Anglican Church was burned to the ground, possibly in retribution "for that diabolical act of depravity which was committed against the Catholic Church in August [1842]."[40] Power attributed the trouble principally to the strength of the Orange Order in the province, the increase in Catholic immigration to Upper Canada, and the subsequent rise in prominence of the church. He regarded these factors as having created a spirit of anti-Catholicism with few parallels elsewhere in North America.[41] The Niagara Peninsula, in particular, was a powder keg, and the person who would strike the match would

not necessarily be an Orangeman. All along the ditch stretching from
Lake Ontario to Lake Erie, soon to be transformed into the second Welland Canal, gangs of Irish Catholic labourers fought among themselves
for better wages, improved working conditions, or control of the Irish
labour market.

These "foolish riots" occurred regularly.[42] Between 1842 and 1849,
there were as many as forty-seven clashes. There were twenty-six strikes;
Irish workers rioted for higher wages; navvies from Cork and their rivals
from Connaught even resorted to street brawling and stone throwing.
When Irish Catholics were not pounding each other senseless, they were
smashing their fists into the faces of local Orangemen, usually when
the latter decided to disrupt St Patrick's Day celebrations. Drunk or
sober, the Irish also clashed with their contractors and periodically skir-
mished with American sailors.[43] Disgusted by this behaviour, the *Mirror*
demanded order: "The disgrace that they have brought upon themselves
will scarcely be wiped away. Irishmen forbear, and be united, love one
another, and you will reap the reward."[44] Whether one defines this
behaviour as "ritualized violence" or the result of creating an all-male
working-class culture on the frontier,[45] local leaders still faced serious
problems with the Irish in the Niagara region.

Soon after Power's arrival in the diocese, the problem of the Irish
Welland Canal labourers landed in his lap. In the fall of 1842, he dispatched Father William P. McDonagh to St Catharine's to replace the
deceased Father Constantine Lee.[46] Immediately, McDonagh set out
to quell the squabbling between the Irish Catholic factions, presenting
himself as a mediator and an Irish Catholic advocate for fair wages.[47]
He insisted that peace in the region depended upon "strangers" keeping
out of the business of the Irish Catholic canal workers, thus appearing
to confirm the claims of the Catholic press that the Loyal Orange Order
was behind much of the trouble. The *Catholic*, for example, had asserted
that the provincial government had hired a riot-prevention squad that
was essentially a posse of local Orangemen.[48] Moreover, exposing their
own racism, Irish Catholics claimed to be humiliated by the fact that
the government had hired a "corps of blacks" to preside over the canal
workers – "an insult offered on any white population."[49] McDonagh
was praised for establishing control over warring factions from Munster
and Connaught, but, as a Catholic priest, he had little hope of keeping
the "strangers" at bay. Area Orange lodges were growing in number
and strength, and this increased the possibility of sectarian violence.[50]
The strong presence of the repeal associations and McDonagh's open

support for the movement ensured that peace along the canal would be hard-won.

Although Power did not intercede directly in the canal workers' affairs, he did send a capable priest who was fluent in the Irish language, a bonus when dealing with migrants from the west of Ireland.[51] His decision not to intervene was both judicious and necessary. The weather in Upper Canada made travel difficult except in summer and early autumn, and he knew that it would be a poor use of his time to remain at the head of Lake Ontario for four months waiting to see what would happen to the Irish workers on the Welland Canal. During the summer of 1842, he spent his time wisely, exploring the northwestern section of his vast diocese by sailboat and canoe, covering territory between Toronto and Sault Ste Marie. He was reassured by the fact that Father Lee was monitoring the situation in St Catharine's, and his vicar-general, William Peter MacDonald, was doing the same in nearby Hamilton.

This in no way indicates that Power was indifferent to the Irish in the diocese or unaware of the issues facing them. His library was replete with Irish monographs and pamphlets, particularly those of O'Connell, and he had a subscription to the Boston *Pilot*, an important mouthpiece for Irish Americans. Power's chief supplier of reading materials was Patrick Casserly, a New York bookseller with strong Irish nationalist ties.[52] And at Toronto's St Patrick's Day celebrations, Bishop Power was a familiar figure. In 1844, he initiated citywide festivities by officiating at early-morning Mass at St Paul's, where he treated a capacity crowd to an "eloquent sermon" and then called upon the assembled to give generously to the SPBS.[53] Power's penchant for crisp oratory kept him on the St Patrick's Day program for two more years (in 1847, however, he was absent because he was still in Europe on his *ad limina* visit).

In 1846, the crowds that gathered at St Paul's to hear the bishop overflowed the church. When the liturgy concluded, Power mesmerized the congregation with what one correspondent described as "one of the most eloquent and earnest appeals" on behalf of Ireland that he had ever heard: "with simple and unaffected, but originally nervous and powerful language, he displayed the history, and the devotion and the success of Ireland's Saint in the cause of Ireland's conversion and regeneration; dwelling on the happy fruits that resulted to Ireland in the union and education and enlightenment of her people ... We have never heard patriotic aspiration and proud historical reminiscence more happily blended with the subdued and pure spirit of Christian piety." Power also took the opportunity to remind the faithful of Ireland's economic distress but offered hope that happier days would soon come. "Providence," he remarked, had already begun to regenerate Ireland, particularly from the "degrading stain of intemperance." Here, Power's hopeful note was laced with a caveat: God's "displeasure" could be linked to Ireland's "national disgrace" of alcohol abuse.[54]

In public, Power kept his distance from the repeal movement lest it drag him into the political fights of Canada, in which the repealers had a substantial stake. Nevertheless, he gave wide latitude to his lay leaders and priests as they engaged with the repeal associations to lobby Westminster to repeal the Act of Union and thereby restore an Irish Parliament in Dublin. However, Power did become involved when certain incidents in Ireland called into question Catholic rights as they existed elsewhere in the empire. In 1844, for example, British authorities left Catholics off jury lists, effectively prohibiting their participation in jury trials, including those of repealers facing criminal charges. Catholics in Upper Canada were outraged, describing this action as "an injustice to the people of Ireland and ... [an] insult ... to every Catholic of the British Empire." On 15 April 1844, at the Catholic school on Richmond Street, Power chaired a meeting of Toronto's Catholic leaders called to articulate a loud protest against this instance of discrimination against their religion in the British courts. Power chaired the meeting with a firm hand; he knew that things could get out of hand if the rhetoric became overheated and the anger spilled out into the streets. He was flanked by several of his lay allies in the community: Dr John King, Michael Hayes, M.J. O'Beirne, Edward McSherry, James Fitzgerald, Samuel MacDonald, and John Elmsley.

The bishop's eloquence and sense of balance were reported to have been key factors in shaping the written resolutions that emerged from the proceedings. The leaders' protest was carefully prefaced by an unequivocal declaration of patriotism on the part of a people self-described as "yielding to none in attachment to true principles of the British Constitution and loyalty to Her Most Gracious Majesty."[55] This was followed by a strong protest against the exclusion of Catholics from juries, a statement of solidarity between the Catholics of Canada and the United Kingdom, and a direct appeal to Queen Victoria, all of which Power was to submit directly to Her Majesty.[56] The entire undertaking was vintage Power. He maintained the delicate balance between the interests of the church and the demands of the state, relying on the deference that would be shown him due to his office and his reputation for moderation. He protested the violation of Catholic rights yet couched his criticisms in terms that indicated that he and those he represented were merely upholding principles of British justice. For Power, this was also another opportunity to profess Catholic loyalty to the Crown while defending the Catholic and Protestant liberties enjoyed under its reign. The Toronto meeting set a valuable precedent. Power muted the radical edge of the repeal movement by harnessing its energies to serve a moderate end, and two weeks later, the Catholics of Hamilton under the guiding hand of William Peter MacDonald passed a similar set of resolutions.[57]

Power's reputation as a voice of wisdom and moderation in ecclesiastical and ethnic politics extended far beyond the Diocese of Toronto. As the repeal movement took hold in that diocese, Power was called back to the Diocese of Halifax to help solve problems between the Irish and Scottish communities in the apostolic vicariate of Nova Scotia. The tensions in the Maritime church between Irish and Scottish immigrants had deep roots. In 1827, William Fraser, a Scot, had been appointed successor to Edmund Burke, the first vicar apostolic of Nova Scotia.[58] Preferring to live among his kinsmen, Fraser took up residence in Arichat, on Cape Breton Island, instead of in Halifax, where his predecessor had presided over the predominantly Irish Catholic community. He then sent Father John Loughnan to Halifax as his vicar-general. The Halifax Irish felt snubbed by their bishop and offended by the behaviour of his designate.[59] Fraser's absence prompted a resurrection of lay activism among the Irish, who asserted control over property in St Mary's parish and the congregation's assets. It seemed to them that all of Burke's achievements were unravelling under his successor. This volatile combination of personalities, ethnic politics, and lay assertiveness caused disorder and division in the Nova Scotia church. Adding fuel to the fire, in February 1842, the Roman curia, without warning Fraser, appointed William Walsh, a Dublin priest and a native of Waterford, as coadjutor to Fraser with permanent residence among the Irish in Halifax.[60] Fraser deemed this unnecessary and hurtful, and he refused to recall Loughnan, thus creating a crisis of authority within Halifax's Catholic community.[61] In 1843, Power referred to his home church as being in danger of "scandalous schism."[62]

Given his keen personal interest in the matter, Power did not hesitate to accept the invitation of the bishops of Lower Canada to intercede in the Fraser-Walsh affair. The ongoing disorder in the vicariate of Nova Scotia – and particularly Walsh and Fraser airing their dirty laundry in public – was an embarrassment to other Catholic leaders. It was also a distraction to clerics on both sides of the Atlantic, as it diverted their attention from Ignace Bourget's efforts to create an ecclesiastical province in British North America.[63] Power was the church's last hope: he was a Halifax native; he was of Irish heritage; he was a moderate; and he was trusted by Bishops Bourget, Signay, and Turgeon. He was loyal to his friend Walsh, who felt unwanted by his bishop and was being tormented by the local vicar-general.[64] Power did not mince words in writing to Cardinal Prefect Fransoni of the Propaganda Fide; he described Loughnan as a poorly trained and overly ambitious priest and advised Rome to uphold the authority of the coadjutor. Such comments were typical of Power, who exercised similar authority over the priests of his own diocese. He further characterized Loughnan as embittered because Rome had not named him coadjutor. Making a final, more devastating observation, he wrote that Fraser was the victim of his own weaknesses and was therefore incapable of running the vicariate. Citing evidence gleaned from his correspondence with Walsh, which he copied to Fransoni, and relying on reports from his associates in St Mary's parish, Power maintained that until Walsh's arrival in 1842, the Halifax Catholic Church had been neglected. Inspired by his battles with frontier Catholicism in Upper Canada, Power was intent on bringing strength and order to Catholicism where it was weak and in disarray. Halifax and its Irish community was yet another challenge for him.[65]

Power's efforts were not ignored. His letters of support for Walsh were translated into Italian by none other than the ambitious Irish cleric Paul Cullen, who then sent them through the proper channels.[66] Daniel Murray, the archbishop of Dublin, also wrote glowingly of Walsh, as did Michael Tobin of the Legislative Council of Nova Scotia and other Halifax lay leaders. It appeared that the Irish establishment would push for a resolution of this issue just as it had pushed for the appointment of Walsh behind Fraser's back. John Hughes, the bishop of New York, added his voice, telling Power that he would urge a resolution favourable to Walsh when he made his *ad limina* visit to Rome.[67] Power's role as key Canadian prelate in the affair was confirmed when Pierre-Flavien Turgeon, the coadjutor of Quebec, sent a sheaf of documents to Toronto, none of which were favourable to Walsh, implying that Power could resolve the matter. And Bishop Joseph Signay signalled his support in a letter to Cardinal Fransoni. The Irish-French Canadian alliance pushed an agenda calling for the division of Nova Scotia into two dioceses: one under Fraser for the Scots; another under Walsh for the Irish.[68] It was successful. On 21 September 1844, the Vatican divided the vicariate of Nova Scotia in two, creating the Diocese of Arichat (the seat of the diocese was later moved to Antigonish) for Fraser and the Diocese of Halifax for Walsh.[69] The whole affair elevated Power's stature among his colleagues as a defender of Irish Catholic interests and an emerging player in the Irish Catholic web stretching from Dublin to Rome and across the Atlantic to the United States, Canada, and Britain's Atlantic possessions.

The Walsh-Fraser affair was the first of several intercessions Power made on behalf of Irish Catholics in the years leading up to Black '47. In 1847, Canada's bishops petitioned Rome for a new diocese to be created out of the territories shared by the Dioceses of Montreal and Kingston, which straddled the Ottawa River and extended to the northwest as far as Lake Temiskaming. In April of that year, while in Rome, Power lobbied the Propaganda Fide directly, arguing that the prospective bishop of the new diocese should be English-speaking, due to the tremendous influx of Irish Catholic settlers into the upper Ottawa Valley.[70] Although the Diocese of Bytown was created two months later, in June 1847, Power's expectations were only partially realized. Oblate missionary J.E. Bruno Guigues was appointed Bytown's first bishop in July, but, as he admitted himself, speaking English was a struggle for him.[71]

Although Power was perhaps unaware of it when he set out, his trip to Europe would strengthen his affinity for the Irish and his determination to be their advocate. In January 1847, he was scheduled to make his *ad limina* visit to Rome, an undertaking required of all bishops every five years. If a bishop could not present his report to the pope directly, then he had to file a quinquennial report on the spiritual and statistical profiles of his diocese. Power had attempted an *ad limina* visit as early as the autumn of 1845, but he had been forced to cancel it when he fell ill during a pastoral visit to the Lake Huron-Lake St Clair frontier of his diocese and did not fully recover for several months.[72] The 1847 trip would last for several months and would include an audience with the new pope, Pius IX; the renewal of contacts made in 1841 in Rome, Paris, and London; the attempt to recruit members of religious orders in France and Ireland; and the acquisition of funding for his missions. For one who had been in fragile health in 1845 and 1846, the prospect of a milder winter and warmer spring on the Continent would have been splendid.

But travel from Toronto to Europe was difficult and potentially dangerous, so Power made all the necessary personal arrangements before leaving Toronto for Buffalo, on 13 January.[73] It would be his longest sojourn away from his diocese. Realizing that he might never see the Diocese of Toronto again, he prepared his last will and testament and appointed William Peter MacDonald, J.J. Hay, Edward Gordon, and Pierre Point as co-administrators in his absence. He was still concerned about the "spirit of independence and insubordination" in the diocese, sensing that it could increase while he was abroad, and his anxiety was heightened by the fact that he doubted the ability of any of his priests to succeed him should he perish at sea or in Europe.[74] Nevertheless, he indicated that if a successor was needed, then he should be of either Irish or Canadian birth and fluent in French.[75]

Leaving instructions for his colleagues to follow if he died abroad, Power departed for Buffalo, en route to New York City, where he was to catch a steamer for England.[76] But, due to a mechanical problem with the vessel he was travelling on, he was forced to disembark at Boston and board the steamer *Hibernia*, which was scheduled to stop in Halifax on 3 February before crossing the Atlantic. His stay in his hometown was unexpected and brief – just a refuelling and provisioning stop – and he had barely enough time to visit his mother and sisters on Hollis Street and perhaps see Walsh, who was now firmly in control of the church. Despite the brevity of the visit, local reporters covered the story; one commented that their native son appeared to be "in excellent health and spirits."[77]

This trip would be one of the most important events of Power's career. Travelling alone this time, he modelled his recruitment drive on the one he had conducted with Bourget in 1841. About two weeks after departing Halifax, Power was in London advancing his various causes at the Colonial Office, including that of Jesuit Dominique du Ranquet, who had suffered what Power perceived as unjust treatment on Walpole Island. By early April, Power was in Rome revisiting potential benefactors, making the acquaintance of bureaucrats appointed since his last visit, posing administrative questions to local officials, investigating questions of canonical import, and presenting reports to the Propaganda Fide and the new pope. He was eager to learn how often the Diocese of Rome held synods and what issues they deliberated at such gatherings. His long-range plan was to create parallel structures in Upper Canada. His first days in Rome were all the more interesting because it was Holy Week and the Easter Triduum, which climaxed on Easter Sunday, 4 April. Power was able to celebrate Mass in Rome on the holiest of Christian feasts.

His visit also coincided with a period of heightened church activity, enthusiasm, and energy in Rome, much of it generated by Pope Pius IX,

Giovanni Mastai Ferretti. Elected in July 1846 at the rather youthful age of fifty-four, Pio Nono, as he was affectionately known to the masses, was ready to turn a new page in the history of the Papal States, to leave behind the *zelanti* ethos of his predecessor, Gregory XVI, and move in a more progressive and modern direction. In choosing the name Pius, he implied that he had political leanings and a desire to reconcile the church with the age in the spirit of Pius VII, whom he had succeeded as bishop of Imola and now bishop of Rome. Pio Nono had granted general amnesty to political prisoners and exiles from the Papal States, initiated the building of railways and the installation of gas lighting in Rome, decreased state censorship, and created a bicameral legislature for the Papal States. Young Italians, smitten with this charismatic pontiff, speculated that he was the one who could unite the disparate duchies, principalities, and republics on the Italian peninsula to form a greater "Italia." Even Protestant Americans in Rome, who had gathered to celebrate George Washington's birthday in 1847, toasted the new pontiff as the "Prince Reformer."[78]

There is no doubt that Power's sojourn in Rome was marked by the spirit of renewal and energy generated by the new pope. He would have been struck by how many of his fellow prelates were queuing up in the Vatican for their turn to report to a larger-than-life figure. To William Walsh, he confided that he felt fortunate to have been granted an audience, given the fact that so many other bishops had been forced to wait for weeks to visit Pius IX, some of them during the stifling, mosquito-ridden Roman summer.[79] When his turn came, Power chatted with the pope at some length, reporting not only on the Diocese of Toronto but also on the activities of his colleagues Signay and Bourget.[80] While the pope's answers to some of his questions struck Power as disappointing (he learned, for example, that Roman diocesan synods had not been held for several generations), Power did leave a lasting impression on Pius IX. Many years later, the pope spoke fondly of Power to Bishop Jean-François Jamot of Peterborough, who was making his *ad limina* visit to Rome.[81] Before leaving Rome, Power – still an avid gardener – collected some watermelon seeds to plant in the garden behind his episcopal residence in Toronto.[82]

By 8 May, Power was in Paris trying to convince members of local religious orders to come to Toronto and attempting to solicit funds from potential benefactors. He spent much of his time in the French capital writing to German bishops asking them to support the German-speaking Catholics of Waterloo and Wellington Counties and renewing his rela-

tionship with his principal source of funds, the Society for the Propagation of the Faith.[83] Next, he travelled to England and Ireland, where he
again endeavoured to find replacements for deceased clergy and members
of religious orders to teach school, provide social services, and perform
mission work. To this end, on 1 June, he went to the Dublin suburb
of Rathfarnam, where he scored his first major success since recruiting
the Jesuits five years earlier. At the mother house of the Institute of the
Blessed Virgin Mary, he and Mother Teresa Ball cemented a deal in
which the superior general would send a group of her Loretto Sisters to
the Diocese of Toronto to establish schools. The Lorettos would be the
first women's religious order recruited for western Upper Canada.[84]

Although Ireland provided Power with his greatest success of his 1847
trip, it was also the site of some disturbing revelations. Before Power left
Rome, Pius IX had given him a copy of an encyclical letter concerning
the Irish famine that encouraged the world to pray for those in distress
and to give them charitable aid. The pope promised a special indulgence
for all public prayers for the victims and, as Power explained to his own
flock, such "prayers may be offered with greater alacrity and advantage"
due to the extreme distress in Ireland.[85] From London, Power wrote his
own pastoral letter, in which he made similar requests for prayers and
alms while acknowledging that Canadians were already contributing
to Irish relief with "the greatest generosity." It was a moderate plea for
Canadian action that did not lay blame on any party, including the British government. The timing of this letter is as interesting as its contents.
Power had agreed to promulgate the encyclical letter from Pius IX in
June, the month he expected to get home.[86] Yet, on 13 May, some three
weeks after he had left Rome, Power penned his own pastoral letter and
sent it on to Toronto, knowing that it would precede him by at least a
month. By issuing his letter from London, Power may have been trying
to signal to British authorities that Ireland's hungry must be saved. But
even if the significance of the letter's London origin was lost on the
bureaucrats at the Colonial Office, it would not be lost on the Protestant
or Roman Catholic inhabitants of Power's diocese.

It is also interesting to note that Power issued the letter at least two
weeks *before* he travelled to Ireland. Reports of the tragedy appeared
regularly in the London papers,[87] and Power would have read the alarm-
ing details in the *Mirror* before leaving Toronto. Accounts of the horrifying drama by Donlevy's writers seethed with indignation: "troops are
obliged to escort provisions as they pass through the streets, and the
unfortunate creatures, whose bones are described as protruding through

their skins, are only kept down by the fear of the bayonet."[88] Power would have been informed about the misery in Connaught, Munster, and parts of Leinster in the winter of 1846–47 as stores of food dwindled and imports of maize and grain ceased. He would have known that the starving were forced to eat the few seed potatoes they had, thus ensuring that there would be nothing left to plant in the spring.

Power's arrival in London coincided with one of the famine's worst phases. He got to Ireland in June, and there he would witness a tragedy whose script had been written after the fall of Napoleon, thirty-two years earlier. In 1815, when Britain's continental war with France concluded, the overheated war economy cooled. British army and navy personnel were demobilized, and the consumption of foodstuffs, clothing, and equipment was drastically reduced; trade with the Baltic nations and other providers of raw materials resumed. Between 1815 and 1845, food prices dropped, making it more difficult for Irish farmers to make ends meet, and mechanization and industrialization squeezed the traditional Irish textile trades. Falling incomes, combined with unemployment and underemployment, forced many Irish families to leave their homes and seek a better life elsewhere.[89] They were small farmers, wage labourers, and artisans – the kind of people with whom Power had been so familiar as a missionary priest in Sherbrooke, Drummondville, Petite-Nation, and Ste-Martine.[90] Moreover, they hailed from Ulster and regions near Cork, areas with excellent navigational connections to British North American ports. These people saw that there were problems with the Irish economy that would jeopardize the future of their children, so they sold what they had and sailed for North America.[91]

Another factor contributing to the Irish crisis was land use. For centuries, the Irish countryside had been carved up by landlords; this allowed the British control over Irish real estate and gave the Protestants and Anglicans ascendancy over the Roman Catholic majority. Some landlords remained on their estates in Ireland, rooting themselves in the local culture, but many others lived in England and left the day-to-day management of their holdings to local agents. They sublet land to farmers, both Protestant and Catholic, who in turn sublet pieces to cottiers and subsistence farmers. Since the penal laws prohibited most Catholics from owning land, the economic, cultural, and religious disparities between those who owned land and those who rented it were profound.[92] Tenants – including large-scale farmers, subsistence farmers, and cottiers – were primarily Catholic, whereas the landowners were generally Protestant or Anglican. It was a volatile situation.

A population explosion between 1815 and 1845 increased the burden on the already weakened economy and antiquated landholding system and made family life even more difficult. Between 1821 and 1841, the population of Ireland increased from 6.8 million to 8.2 million.[93] Farmers with small holdings who wanted to furnish their male heirs with land subdivided their tenancies, thereby reducing the acreage they used to sustain the remaining members of their large families.[94] One solution to this shrinking plot problem was to grow more potatoes, because the protein- and carbohydrate-rich tuber offered maximum yield per land used. Potatoes for consumption and for seed could be stored in root cellars for months after the growing season. Thus, as Irish tenants carved their land into ever smaller parcels, their dependence on the potato became more acute. At the same time, landlords were trying to maximize their profits by converting their horticultural lands into pasture for livestock. This conversion, however, required large tracts of land, so the landlords endeavoured to amalgamate the smaller farms. Only the existence of tenants' contracts prevented them from moving ahead quickly with this scheme.[95]

Then, in 1845, the potato crop failed, and the tenant farmers could not pay their rents. Their vulnerability gave the landlords the opportunity they needed to advance their lucrative herding projects. In the summer of that year, rains from continental Europe carried spores of *phytophthora infestans*, a fungus that found a hospitable environment in the damp climate and moist soil of Ireland.[96] It attacked the leaves, stalks, and root systems of the potato plants, quickly reducing the fall harvest to a putrid mess. By October, crop losses had been recorded in at least seventeen counties. Many regarded it as just another crop failure, part of the agricultural cycle; such failures were in the living memory of Irish farmers. Although optimistic that this was just a temporary setback, tens of thousands of cottiers and rural labourers still faced a long, lean winter.

The British administration at Westminster took measures. Sir Robert Peel's government withdrew the Corn Laws, which had protected British grain growers from low-priced imported wheat, and arranged for the importation of American maize in the fall and winter of 1845–46. Although this Indian corn could be purchased for a penny a pound at hastily erected relief centres, it upset the digestive systems of the Irish, who did not know how to prepare the coarse dried kernels. In mid-1846, with a new crop of potatoes in the ground, a newly appointed administration headed by Lord John Russell discontinued food relief.

The administration anticipated a bumper potato crop and stubbornly believed that free-market forces would resolve the Irish economic crisis. The chief executive of the treasury, Charles Edward Trevelyan, put it bluntly: "The only way to prevent people from habitually becoming dependent on government is to bring [relief] operations to a close."[97]

There was no relief for Ireland. The blight struck with even greater ferocity in the autumn of 1846, and thousands of acres of potatoes rotted in most of the country's thirty-two counties. Worse still, starving farmers had eaten the last of their seed potatoes during the winter of 1846–47. By early 1847, the choices facing the tenant farmers, the unemployed, and the landless labourers were grim. Without food or the money to plant new crops, many would default on their rents and face eviction. The poorest would starve to death where their families had tilled the soil for generations; those who had something to sell – emaciated domestic animals, chattels, family keepsakes – left Ireland for the industrial centres of England and the Scottish lowlands.[98] Those with greater means, or a relative willing to give them remittance money, or a landlord eager to send them away, boarded converted timber ships bound for Britain's North American colonies, the United States, or Australia.[99] For those who remained in the distressed districts of Ireland, there was only misery: "There are 800 persons in the poor houses of Dungarvan. Even the coach house and the stables are filled with paupers. In its hospital there are over 200: six persons died there on Friday night, and the master says the poor creatures are quite exhausted with hunger before they are taken into the house at all – so much so they are not able to bear their food ... last week there were twenty-four persons died ... six of this number died from extreme want and destitution."[100] By late spring, when Michael Power arrived in Ireland, famine had transformed the land and the exodus was well underway.

Power's experiences in famine-ravaged Ireland would leave an indelible impression on him, as his writings and activities would later attest. In Dublin, he would see thousands waiting at quayside to board ships. Outside the capital, he would see that the workhouses in the poor-law unions (areas of administration for poverty relief established under the Poor Relief Act of 1838) were unable to deal with the crush of people desperate for food and shelter. Expelled from their homes for not paying the rent, they searched for food, odd jobs, or a place to lie down and die when the hunger became too much to bear. In 1849, 16,686 farmers were evicted from their tenancies.[101] Immersed in this tragedy, Power witnessed the combined effects of an archaic landholding system, a natural disaster, and the intransigence of free-market disciples.

He left Ireland in early June aboard a steamer bound for Boston, via Halifax. He reached North America in a little over ten days – one-third to one-quarter the time it took the famine migrants to travel the same route aboard the converted sailing craft.[102] On his brief 13 June stop in Halifax, he visited his family; he later apologized to William Walsh for not seeing him, as the steamship's schedule was very tight.[103] When he landed in Toronto, on 21 June, he saw that all was not well. The first wave of Irish famine immigrants had arrived, and Power had less help than he would have expected in handling the crisis. In his absence, William Peter MacDonald had died, as had his good friend Sir Charles Chichester, the commander of the local British garrison and scion of the local Catholic Church. A lover of pomp and ceremony, Chichester had made a name for himself by having the Eighty-first Royal Lincoln-shire Regiment Band accompany him each Sunday as he proceeded to morning Mass at St Paul's.[104] Power could only pay these men his last respects and see that their remains were laid in the crypt of his unfinished cathedral.

The situation in Toronto could only have deepened the melancholy and disappointment that had afflicted him in Europe. For his entire adult life, Power had grounded himself in two things – his fidelity to the church and his unwavering loyalty to the British Empire – and now both were shaken. He confessed to William Walsh that in Rome he had experienced the cumbersome, awkward, and frustrating side of ecclesiastical bureaucracy; in London, he had been so disturbed by the policies emanating from 10 Downing Street (particularly the lack of resolution in the Walpole Island case), that he now thought the colonies could do better with "two or three good honest independent Governors untrammelled" by politicians and "colonial secretaries."[105] And, of course, the events in Ireland and their effects on his diocese were also weighing on his mind.

Power's doubts about the abilities of the Colonial Office were not alleviated on his return to Canada. He read newspaper reports that estimated how many famine immigrants were flooding into the ports of Montreal and Quebec, and it became increasingly clear to him that there were too few resources to meet the urgent needs of these people. The hunger and disease of Ireland had merely been transported to the Province of Canada. Over the summer, as the situation worsened, Power sent out a plea to his flock. He asked them to be patient and to understand that many demands were being made upon their priests: "you are well aware that it has been almost impossible for us under the terrible affliction with which this Province has been visited, to call upon the few priests scattered over this immense diocese to enter upon the duties required on such an occasion [the papal jubilee] at a time that every moment and all their energies both of body and mind were needed for the due administration of the last rights of the Church to the many poor, unfortunate emigrants so inhumanely cast upon our shores."[106]

During the period 1846–47, the increase in the volume of immigrants from the United Kingdom was staggering. By the end of the first quarter of 1847, the figure was six times more than it had been in the same period the previous year.[107] By year's end, 109,580 had left the United Kingdom for British North America, and most of them were famine refugees.[108] Emigration agents estimated that six of every seven emigrants were Irish, which suggests that as many as 97,492 Irish famine refugees headed for the Province of Canada and the Atlantic colonies.[109] Of these, some 80,000 targeted Quebec as their port of call, 17,000 selected New Brunswick, and only 3,500 chose Nova Scotia, Prince Edward Island, and Newfoundland.[110] The total number of migrants setting out for British North America in 1847 was over 250 per cent higher than the total number in 1846, and 350 per cent higher than in 1845.[111] The numbers alone clearly showed that Ireland's woes had been passed on to Canada.

Of the nearly 80,000 Irish who ventured down the St Lawrence River, some 38,000 disembarked at Toronto. It is difficult to characterize these new members of Power's flock because the information on them offered by Colonial Office bureaucrats, local port authorities, and immigration agents is contradictory. The Colonial Office reported that these people had the means to travel and were "a class superior to those of former years, and ... carried with them considerable capital."[112] This was confirmed by the fact that it cost an adult four pounds, ten shillings to five pounds, five shillings (not including provisions) to get to Quebec.[113] For those travelling inland to Power's diocese, the cost was an additional twenty-two shillings per adult to reach Toronto, and twenty-nine shillings to Hamilton; it cost even more to travel overland from the head of Lake Ontario to points west. There were additional charges for children, baggage, and food.[114] On top of these costs, immigrants were required to pay a head tax of four shillings, twopence per adult upon arrival in Canada. Two children between seven and fourteen years of age were considered one adult, while three children between one and seven were calculated as one adult. In light of the crisis of 1847, Lord Elgin, Canada's governor, suggested that raising this tax would reduce the likelihood of Canada being used as a port of entry for such migrants in future and that these Irish might not be what the Colonial Office had reported them to be.[115]

Questions remain about the financial self-sufficiency of the Irish migrants. A.C. Buchanan, the imperial agent general for immigration at Quebec, suggested that money had been given to them by relatives already settled in Canada, although little evidence exists to verify this or indicate its extent.[116] However, port records do show that a few immigrants were sponsored by their landlords; in 1847, 6,000 of the nearly 80,000 immigrants who passed through the port of Quebec were assisted by landlords eager to be rid of them.[117] This statistical evidence undermines the popular image of Irish paupers being packed off in droves to North America by conniving landlords. Nevertheless, even if these Irish began their journey with the means to pay for it, there is qualitative evidence to suggest that they had little to sustain them once they arrived. Lord Elgin, for one, was disturbed by the problems that this situation created. Upon returning from an official visit to western Upper Canada, he remarked that immigration's "disastrous consequences have been felt not only in the large towns where the sick and destitute are collected in great numbers, but even in the remote hamlets to which they have penetrated, carrying with them disease and pauperism."[118] Even if one factors in Elgin's patrician social status and bourgeois attitude towards the labouring classes, his comments still testify to the fact that some migrants who once had means were neither healthy nor wealthy by the end of their journey. There may have been mitigating factors: unscrupulous ship's captains overcharged for medicine and food; there was contagion on the ships and at Grosse Île;[119] immigrants' resources were drained by inland transportation and provisioning costs, which were higher than expected. But the lasting image for Power and others attempting to bring relief to the Irish were those of a people desperate for resources, healing, and comfort. Whether or not they had sufficient means at the outset of their journey no longer mattered. Arriving in Toronto's harbour, they were sick, emaciated, impecunious, and vermin-infested, and they were in urgent need of assistance.

Some days in the summer of 1847, lake boats dumped nearly 1,000 Irish immigrants at Toronto. Throughout that summer and autumn, they departed Quebec and Montreal crammed into lake steamers, piled into open boats, or squeezed into sailing ships bound for Kingston, Toronto, Hamilton, and St Catharine's. In late August, the *British Colonist* reported that 1,000 Irish immigrants had left Kingston; 300 of them had landed at Whitby, and 700 had moved on to Toronto. Confirming

"The Famished," Grosse Île, Canada East, 1847, by John Falter (courtesy of the 3M Company, Canada)

what locals generally believed about the poverty of the newcomers, the reports stated that only thirty of them had paid their own expenses.[120] The province that had once welcomed newcomers as a source of labour turned away from the Irish in panic.[121] At the root of the terror shared by many Canadians was the fact that typhus had broken out wherever the Irish had landed. The effort to quarantine potentially infectious immigrants at Grosse Île had failed. No one in Power's time appreciated the nature of typhus, or rickettsia fever, a highly contagious bacterial infection that incubates in the body for at least ten days before any symptoms present themselves. Victims run high fevers and become delirious – hence the disease's name, which is derived from the Greek *typhus*, meaning cloudy (in this case, cloudy in the mind). After fourteen days of abdominal cramping and severe skin rash, up to 70 per cent of those afflicted die.[122] As antibiotics did not yet exist, physicians treating typhus victims, including Dr. George Mellis Douglas at Grosse Île, relied on warm soups, compresses, and prayers. The tragedy was compounded by the fact that at Grosse Île the healthy were housed cheek-by-jowl with the infected. Dozens died every day in the island's tents and hastily erected sheds. By the end of Black '47, 5,424 immigrants had died and been buried there.[123] Those judged healthy by medical authorities on the island were allowed to proceed to Quebec, where they joined those who had already been cleared after their so-called decontamination – they had showered in water containing mercury and their clothes had been steam cleaned. Many of these people did not display symptoms of typhus until they arrived at Quebec, Montreal, Kingston, or even Toronto.

With so many immigrants arriving daily, Power and his colleagues in each of the Canadian dioceses faced the most serious pandemic since the cholera outbreak of 1832.[124] As fever sheds and temporary lodgings were slapped together at Point St-Charles in Montreal and along the Toronto waterfront at Bathurst and King's Quays, city residents fled to the countryside to avoid being infected by the Irish. The Toronto *Mirror* begged citizens to exercise sanity and charity: "Shun dirt – but do not run away from your fellow creature smitten by the hand of Providence with disease, which is the product of destitution and privation of every shape. Better to die in the performance of duty, than to preserve life by the cowardly desertion of the afflicted ... At the sheds of Montreal, the Priests, Nuns, and Medical Men, had to wade through the human excrement ankle deep. Contrast this with the neat comfortable, and scrupulously clean condition of our emigrant sheds, and then say how it has happened that Toronto has fared so much better than other places."[125] There was an air of condescension in the way Toronto's Irish Catholic clarion described the situation in Montreal, although by summer's end much of the sickness and death that had overwhelmed Lower Canada's towns and marshalled its Catholic bishops, clergy, and religious had swept up the St Lawrence and the lower Great Lakes with a vengeance. Typhus would leave thousands sick and hundreds dead in Canada East, including seven of Montreal's Soeurs Grises (of the twenty-eight who had contracted the disease) and Vicar-General Hyacinthe Hudon, Power's old friend.[126] Ignace Bourget, who with pastoral letters, prayers, and alms collections had marshalled his church behind relief efforts, fell ill with typhus, but he recovered.[127] As the news continued to pour in from the east, Power realized that he was facing the greatest challenge of his career.

The patterns set and precedents observed in Lower Canada were soon playing themselves out in Upper Canada. The daily and weekly papers gave grim tallies of those who had perished in the sheds of Kingston, Toronto, and Hamilton.[128] Local politicians demanded that the legislature boost relief payments, which it did, in order to protect communities upstream from Grosse Île from contagion.[129] Bishops Power and

Phelan did what Bishops Bourget and Signay had done and called for patience, prayers, charitable aid, and alms for Ireland.[130] In Toronto, with over 700 immigrants arriving daily,[131] clergy, medical staff, and the managers of receptions sheds were stretched to the limit. Four shelters were built, at King and Adelaide Streets and at John and Peter Streets, but these filled as fast as they were completed, as did the Toronto fever hospital. Soon, local cemeteries and burial grounds were just as busy. Of the nearly 38,000 immigrants who arrived in Toronto in 1847, 1,100 died. Most of them were interred in St Paul's cemetery with a nameless grave marker, and these anonymous dead could not be recorded in the parish burial register.[132]

The sheer numbers of immigrants and the magnitude of their needs overwhelmed Power's meagre resources. Father John O'Reilly from Dundas and Fathers Thaddeus Kerwin and J.J.Hay of St Paul's were principally responsible for administering the sacraments to the sick and burying the dead in the Catholic cemetery. Father Jean-Baptiste Proulx, who had been replaced on Manitoulin Island by the Jesuits several years before, served the immigrants in the mission stations surrounding Toronto.[133] Power had to be careful not to pull too many priests out of the rural parishes to assist during the crisis, lest the small towns and villages be left unattended. If this happened, then there would be a loss of clerical influence and control in the frontier areas; priests were also needed in outlying areas because Irish immigrants were steadily pushing inland to join relatives and friends who had established themselves in Upper Canada. Moreover, the Talbot district, London, Galt, and Gore's Landing near Cobourg (technically in the Diocese of Kingston) were experiencing their own small-scale crises.[134] In these rural areas, a vicious cycle had developed of landlessness, unemployment, and poverty. Farmers and artisans were reluctant to hire the Irish immigrants for fear of contracting the "ship's fever." As a result, the Irish pilgrimage to the countryside boomeranged to the port cities, compounding the strain on municipal resources. The fragmentary empirical data on how many famine refugees managed to purchase or even lease land suggests that some were able to do so in the London, Huron, and Simcoe districts – where some of the cheapest land could be had – although they were a minority compared to those Irish who had already settled in the same areas prior to the famine.[135]

Faced with the increase in the number of immigrants, the intensification of the typhus pandemic, and the diminishment of his resources, Power began to forge links with other leaders – politicians and non-

Catholic clergy – in order to co-ordinate civic relief efforts more effectively. During his absence earlier in the year, Catholics and Protestants in several Upper Canadian towns had formed Irish relief agencies. By mid-March 1847, the Toronto relief agency for Ireland had raised £1,719, which it sent directly to Ireland. In the spring, when fundraising for Ireland was at its peak, Power donated twenty-five pounds of his own money in absentia, joining other Christian pastors from the townships of King, Whitchurch, Woodstock, and Brock.[136] By summer, the Irish crisis had become a Canadian crisis, and local Catholics were criticizing themselves and public authorities for doing too little to alleviate the problems of the Irish immigrants: "Are the charities of our Holy Religion dried up? Are our bowls of compassion closed against the cries of our people? Look sir at the squalor, and haggard aspect of the poor creatures. Look at their fleshless bodies, and bloodless faces – at their despair, and mental torpor – at their unwashed and unclothed persons, and say whether *we* are doing our duty ... Sir, there is not an Irish family in this City that could not find some old vestments which would serve these people ... The dogs licked the sores of Lazarus at the rich man's gate, and were more merciful than their master. We have less commiseration than the rich man's dogs."[137] The continuing flood of refugees soon prompted a shift from collecting for Irish relief to concentrating local resources on the ports of entry, erecting shelters, and providing food.

On 7 July 1847, 1,000 persons disembarked at Toronto, an event described by Charles Dunlevy as the end result of "a horrible traffic in human blood."[138] The fever hospital on King Street had exceeded its capacity and was stuffed with over 300 patients; at least four died every day. Dr. Grassett, Power's colleague on the school board, contracted typhus while working in the hospital.[139] The dead were hauled away by cart,[140] and soon the rutted streets of Toronto were filled with burial parties eager to deposit corpses before they themselves became occupants of the carts. By the end of July, imperial immigration agent Edward McElderry had estimated that Toronto had already received 18,000 immigrants, most of whom had arrived penniless.[141]

The upsurge in arrivals during August and September prompted Power and his ministerial colleagues in the Protestant and Anglican churches to take extraordinary actions. On Saturday, 18 September, Power and the cream of Toronto's civic leadership – the chief justice John Beverly Robinson, Bishop John Strachan, Mayor W.H. Boulton, Alderman Garnett, J.H. Hagarty, Sheriff Jarvis, and John Elmsley (who had assisted in the sheds)[142] – convened a public meeting to pressure the

The Irish memorial at Grosse Île, erected in 1909 by the Ancient
Order of Hibernians, bears an inscription listing the names of clergy
who were stricken with typhus or died during Black '47. Although he
never visited the quarantine station and did not serve in Quebec at the
time, Bishop Michael Power is included on the list (author's photo)

legislature for additional funds for relief efforts.[143] With Mayor Boulton in the chair, participants debated the key issues of the crisis. The chief justice commented that the infection among the newcomers was not as extensive as they had feared, and that Canada should not turn migrants back, as England had done after the Irish poor-law reforms.[144] The group reached a consensus on the issue of Toronto municipal politicians applying pressure on the assembly, which was to be extended to mid-October to work on relief strategies for the Irish immigrants during the coming winter.[145] To several people at that meeting, including Strachan, one of the most important objectives was securing shelter – perhaps converting existing military barracks into winter hostels. Meeting participants also agreed that immigrants should be employed as soon as possible.[146]

In the middle of the meeting, Power rose to his feet and recast the discussion in light of the immigrant experience. He and Elmsley had detected an element of blame in suggestions that the immigrants had concealed their illness to get away from quarantine centres at Grosse Île, Montreal, or Kingston. With characteristic good timing and eloquence, Power described what he had seen on his recent trip to Ireland. He explained that he had seen migrants leave Dublin in evident good health; by the time they had reached Liverpool, they were showing symptoms of disease; many appeared to shake off the illness, however, and they were permitted passage to America; then, once they were at sea, their symptoms reappeared: "such was the nature of the disease." Power maintained that a similar pattern had repeated itself among those arriving at Grosse Île – their symptoms vanished in quarantine and re-emerged at the inland ports. Then he appealed to a priest who was attending the meeting and with whom Power had tended the sick in the Toronto fever sheds. Power wanted the man to corroborate his own views on the crisis. For Power, "the disease seemed to be of that insidious character, as to baffle all the skill that might be employed in treating for its cure and it did not seem to be affected by change of season." Without criticizing anyone present, Power reinforced his principal point: the Irish were not responsible for the epidemic; they were its victims. The bishop's point was taken, and the tone of the proposed resolutions was amended accordingly.[147]

This may have been Power's finest public moment. Thereafter, the energies of Toronto leaders, as reflected in their resolutions, were directed more towards securing government relief than seeking a scapegoat. They asked the provincial government to pay greater attention to the nature of the disease – as described by Power – and requested that immigrants be permitted to continue their inland journey after they had been subjected to a thorough examination. Power seconded the motion that they demand increased government funding for the sick and the dying over the winter months and that the government decommission military buildings or erect new ones to serve as "an Asylum or work house in which these Immigrants who are able to work may be employed."[148] The motion passed, and John Elmsley agreed to serve on a committee to co-ordinate the erection and management of such an asylum. Unfortunately, the petition for this project was not read into the register of the legislature until the first session of the assembly, in 1848.[149] This delay proved fatal to many immigrants and to some of those assisting them.

Power struggled on. In late August, Fathers Kerwin, O'Reilly, and Hay were ill with fever and confined to the upper rooms of the episcopal residence. In early September, Father Ryan, O'Reilly's replacement, took ill after making several visits to the waterfront hospices. Power was the only one left to say Mass at St Paul's and visit the fever sheds. Proulx was healthy, but he was still needed outside the city. As he had been so often earlier in his career, Power was alone. Rising early in the morning, he would don his frock coat and top hat and trudge through the muck to St Paul's, a fifteen-minute walk east along King Street, where he would say a low Mass and tidy up. Leaving St Paul's, he would pass the shell of his unfinished cathedral and head west to the sheds and the hospital, knowing that his afternoon would be spent offering graveside prayers. The only priest on duty in the sheds, Power would pull his easily identifiable stole from his pocket and arrange it around his neck, over his coat. Observers would see a pastor at work. He held the hands of dying migrants, he offered absolution before death, he gently traced the cross on damp foreheads with an oiled finger. Retracing his steps to St Paul's, he would pray over the dead, preside over burials, and return home. There, he would dine alone, check on his ailing colleagues, pray in the tiny second-floor chapel of St Ambrose, and retire for the night.

Occasionally, his daily routine was disrupted. Two days before the public meeting at which he had spoken so eloquently, Power had answered a knock on his front door. To his shock, five young women stood on the doorstep – the Loretto Sisters promised to him by Mother Teresa Ball in June. He had expected them in the autumn, and now here they were in the midst of the typhus epidemic. One of the women, Sister Teresa Dease, would later comment that Power's "heart was evidently oppressed by the scenes of sorrow he had witnessed in the early part of the day, during his visits to the hospital, where the emigrant fever was raging."[150] Power was greatly agitated. He had sent Kerwin to recuperate in Niagara, and John Carroll had just arrived from Niagara to assist the bishop.[151] Fathers Ryan and Hay were still recovering, and now the women he needed desperately for schools had arrived early, thus putting themselves at risk of contagion.

Teresa Dease understood that Power was worried about their well-being because there was "plague raging in the house." The sisters had endured a difficult seven weeks in transit; they were tired and thus more vulnerable to infection. Sailing from Liverpool to New York, they had proceeded northwest to Toronto via Albany and Rochester by coach, train, and lake steamer.[152] As Power had not been expecting them, there was no one to greet them when they disembarked at Toronto harbour. They took a cab, which had lost a wheel en route to the episcopal residence thanks to the poor quality of Toronto's streets. Settling in at the bishop's residence, the sisters changed from their travelling clothes into their habits and had supper with their host and his priests. As Dease described it, Power's anxiety was obvious during the meal, and Hay's "gravity and almost gloom" was balanced by Ryan's "agreeable manners" and Carroll's sense of humour.[153] The demeanour of Power and Hay seemed to fit the residence's Spartan character. Dease remarked that the dining room and the parlour "looked bare and oppressively lonely." She added that "it was evidently an abode on which the sun of this world's prosperity had never shone."[154] Given Power's personal austerity and the fact that he was pouring what little money he had into the cathedral and relief funds for the poor, Dease's observations are not surprising. It became evident as the meal went on that Power was a nervous wreck. Fearful for the sisters' health, he examined every piece of fruit before offering it to them. Dease noted that the bishop himself ate little, if anything, and he appeared flushed. Asked by his guests about his daily labours and the mounting casualties of the pandemic, he responded bluntly, "Don't speak of them, I anointed so many today and heard their confessions."[155] No doubt, Power wore the day's terrible events like a hair shirt.

What no one at the table that evening seems to have realized was that Power may have already been infected by typhus. Given its incubation period, it is likely that the rickettsia had already found a welcoming environment in his cells. Ironically, as he spoke to his civic colleagues about the unpredictability of the disease, the fatal bacteria were multiplying in his body. Local legend has it that he contracted typhus on a late-night call to the sheds to offer extreme unction to a fever-stricken refugee, but there is no evidence to support this story. Nor is there any proof that he cried to heaven that night, cursing the empire: "My God, what crimes England has to answer for!" Such an outburst was not in keeping with his lifelong beliefs, nor did it ring true after his elegant testimony at the public meeting. It is more likely that the Irish-born sisters who recorded such thoughts many years after the fact, and who were somewhat nationalistic, put their own words into Power's mouth.[156] Power may have contracted typhus in any number of ways: from his daily work in the sheds and the hospital, from his bedside visits to his ailing priests, or from presiding over burials of fever victims. He could have been bitten by the fleas that carried the bacteria in their feces; scratching a bite would have introduced the rickettsia into his system. But however he became infected, the disease would soon remove him from his public duties.

If Hay's explanation is correct, Power began to fail on Tuesday, 22 September. For five days, he appeared to be fighting the contagion successfully. He continued to conduct his affairs from home, giving his colleagues hope that he would recover, just as Ryan, Kerwin, and Hay had done. On 26 September, however, the fever attacked him with a vengeance. Suddenly, he was bedridden, unable to write, unable to go to his little chapel to pray, unable to eat. His faculties remained intact, and he seemed aware that his condition was worsening and that he must send word to his mother that he was gravely ill. Unable to lift a pen, he instructed Hay to inform Bishop William Walsh in Halifax of his condition and to tell Walsh to get word to Mary Roach Power.[157] The remaining four days of his life were marked by increasing pain, violent fever, and complete immobility. The attending physician's efforts to relieve his symptoms proved futile. On Friday, 1 October at 6:30 in the morning, Michael Power breathed his last.

⌐ Seeking Stability ⌐

THE DEATH OF Michael Power created an air of crisis in the Canadian church. His sudden loss not only panicked his closest colleagues in the Diocese of Toronto, but it also caused shock waves among his fellow bishops and missionaries across the province. Anticipating his own death, Power had appointed J.J. Hay, John Carroll, and Pierre Point as joint administrators of the diocese, although the young and sickly Hay, as secretary and archdeacon, took on the lion's share of the responsibility. Within days of Power's death, Hay – whom Vincent Quiblier once described as a man "in a continued state of dying"[1] – made it clear to everyone, including the Propaganda Fide, that due to poor health he could not bear the burden. Adding to Hay's distress was his belief that there was no cleric in the diocese capable of filling Power's shoes or dealing with the problems he had left unresolved. Speaking to the Canadian bishops about the state of the diocese, Hay was blunt: "among the people there is much disunion and there is division among the clergy, some of whose members are always opposing their bishop." He insisted that these disobedient clerics and troublesome laymen could only be brought to heel by the speedy reimposition of strong "episcopal authority."[2] Father Thaddeus Kerwin agreed that Power's successor would have "great difficulties to surmount" in a Protestant colony and trouble coping with the "spectacle of human misery" created by the famine. Similarly, the missionary at Bytown, Father P.A. Telmon, referred to the year 1847 as "disastrous and full of perils," citing such tragedies as Bishops Bourget and Prince contracting typhus and the death of Power.[3]

Hay's expressions of self-doubt and his fear that the progress that had been made in the diocese would be undone jolted Archbishop Joseph Signay into action. He engaged in what was perhaps his first meaningful exercise of authority over his surviving suffragan bishops – Bourget,

Turgeon, Gaulin, and Phelan. Using his coadjutor Pierre-Flavien Turgeon and Ignace Bourget as his principal advisors, Signay launched a search for Power's successor within two weeks. The archbishop agreed with Hay that no Toronto priest was fit for the job; Power himself had informed Signay of this in confidence just prior to his last trip to Europe. However, Signay disagreed with Hay's general assessment of the diocese, pointing out that Power had placed the diocesan administration "on a good foot," had succeeding in recruiting the Loretto Sisters and the Jesuits, and had commenced building the cathedral, a project that was now close to completion. In the opinion of the archbishop, this was an excellent foundation upon which the next bishop could build.[4] Nevertheless, Signay's strategy included recruiting as Power's successor someone who would be a strict disciplinarian of his priests, an Anglophone (due to the growing number of Irish Catholic immigrants to Upper Canada), and a British subject (to have optimum familiarity with the culture, customs, and laws of the province).[5]

Signay wrote letters about the matter to his colleagues and to Archbishop Samuel Eccleston of Baltimore, who provided him with a lengthy list of British, Irish, and American priests.[6] Signay passed this list of candidates on to the Canadian bishops for discussion. Sifting through the responses from Gaulin, Bourget, Phelan, and French Sulpician Armand de Charbonnel (himself a nominee),[7] Signay attempted to compile a short list of three names to send to Rome with due haste. He finally decided that certain prospective candidates were too American, and therefore out of touch with Canadian life and law; others were too Irish or too British, and therefore unsuited to the Canadian frontier. The only Canadian possibilities among the priests whose names had been put forward were Patrick McMahon of Quebec and Power's former political agent Angus Macdonell, whom most thought would refuse the position because he knew too well what awaited Power's successor on the frontier.[8]

But all concerned agreed upon one name. Jesuit John Larkin was born in Durham, England, to Irish parents in 1801. He was three years Power's senior, though his rise in the church had been just as meteoric. Larkin had travelled to the United States and then to Montreal, where he was ordained in 1827, the same year as Power. Having received Holy Orders, Larkin remained in Montreal, where he worked among the Irish immigrants and taught at the Sulpician seminary. In 1831, when Alexander Macdonell sought a coadjutor, local clergy put forward Larkin's name, much to the young priest's displeasure.[9] In 1840, Larkin returned to the United States. He joined the Society of Jesus, which would provide him

with the opportunity to continue studying and teaching. While his ties
to the Jesuits might have been advantageous to a diocese already exceed-
ingly dependent on that order in its western missions, Signay acknowledged that only the Holy See could request that Larkin be released from
the Society of Jesus in order to answer the call to Toronto.[10] But to the
Canadians it seemed worth the risk to make such a request, because
Larkin fit most of the desired criteria: he was a learned man known
for his holiness, he was a British subject, he spoke French, and he had
considerable experience working among Irish immigrants. According to
Signay, he was the only candidate capable of "continuing and perfecting
the works commenced by his predecessor."[11]

On 10 January 1848, Signay sent a supplication of the Canadian
bishops to Pope Pius IX. Included in this plea to resolve the growing leadership vacuum and concomitant crisis in Toronto was a *terna* at whose
head – the *dignissimus* – was John Larkin, SJ, followed by Armand de
Charbonnel and Angus Macdonell, as *dignior* and *dignus*, respectively.[12]
As most of those involved suspected he would, Larkin resisted the offer,
and at one point he even refused to open letters from Pius IX. By October 1849, more than two years after Power's death, it was obvious that
Larkin could not be swayed, and the disappointed bishops moved on
in their search.[13] The situation in the diocese had become more acute
that February, when Hay finally died,[14] leaving the day-to-day administration to John Carroll and the missions in the upper lakes to Pierre
Point. If Carroll's correspondence and that of Hay's before him is any
indication, very little had changed in the operation of the diocese since
Power's demise: couples still sidestepped the church's marriage regulations; priests still threatened to move out of the diocese if they were
not left alone; and Irish Catholic poverty cast a pall over the province's
major cities.[15] Finally, on 15 March 1850, nearly two and a half years
after Power's death, the Vatican appointed Armand de Charbonnel as
Power's successor.

As Charbonnel took up his duties as the second bishop of Toronto,
the memory of Michael Power was fading for his priests and laypeople.
Much of the discipline that he had tried to establish at so many levels had
collapsed due to the extended vacancy of the see, and Charbonnel would
essentially have to reinvent it.[16] Using his French connections, he built
upon the foundations erected by Power, inviting new religious orders to
the diocese: the Congregation of the Sisters of St Joseph, the Brothers
of the Christian Schools, and the Congregation of St Basil. Charbonnel
came to depend upon these orders to provide charitable aid for the Irish

refugees, establish new schools, and, in the case of the Basilians, create the college of which Power had long dreamed. Like Power, Charbonnel drew strength from the ultramontane and devotional revivals, and he utilized their principles in founding Canadian chapters of devotional societies, sodalities, and associations like the St Vincent de Paul Society.[17] Sensing that immigration would make the diocese even more unmanageable given its size (he likely knew that Power had had difficulty making adequate visitations), Charbonnel successfully petitioned Rome to divide the diocese. On 9 February 1856, Pope Pius IX created the Diocese of London, which included the western districts of the settlement frontier and some of the mission territories in the St Clair River and Lake Huron region, and the Diocese of Hamilton, which cut across central Ontario along the Niagara escarpment from the head of Lake Ontario and up the Bruce Peninsula, through Manitoulin, and across the north shores of Lakes Huron and Superior. This allowed Charbonnel to focus his efforts on the new, much smaller Diocese of Toronto, which stretched west to east from Peel County to Ontario County and north to south from Georgian Bay to Lake Ontario. Charbonnel would never have to endure the arduous journeys to the upper country that his predecessor had undertaken.

The decade of the 1850s also saw so much political, social, and technological change that Power's era suddenly seemed like the distant past. During that time, the railway pushed rapidly across the province, linking the centres of Upper and Lower Canada with transportation and communication systems unimagined by Power and his contemporaries. The advance of the railway engendered an industrialization and urbanization that transformed the face of Upper Canada; machine shops, foundries, and ironworks sprouted along railway sidings; cities swelled with immigrants who found work in the new industrial establishments, built homes, and demanded consumer goods and services. Growing quantities of new products were churned out of the province's interior and the upper Great Lakes and channelled through Toronto, Hamilton, Port Hope, Cobourg, Sarnia, and Sandwich. From these ports, Canadian products coursed into the American markets, due in large part to Lord Elgin's successfully negotiated 1854 Reciprocity Treaty with the United States.[18]

With the industrial revolution came the communications revolution. New steam presses revitalized written communications – it became easier to produce daily newspapers with more pages of news. Mail service was also a beneficiary of the new technology, as trains carried mail from one end of the province to the other in a fraction of the time it had taken Michael Power's missives to reach his colleagues in Quebec City and Montreal. Eventually, the development of the telegraph would make communications instantaneous. European news still had to take a ten-to-fourteen-day steamship ride to reach North America, but telegraph services from New York and Boston made the surface travel of news on this side of the Atlantic obsolete.

Attracted by all of these things and the fact that the province was open-ing up new lands in the Huron-Ottawa tract and the Queen's Bush (now Bruce, Grey, and Huron Counties), the immigrants came in waves. The Upper Canadian population was bolstered by Irish, Scottish, English, German, and Dutch farmers. The population increase in both rural and urban areas and the rapid advances in technology and publishing precipi-tated a demand for cheaper, more accessible, and better public schools, as well as publicly funded denominational schools. The demand for the latter at a time of deepening social, political, and religious cleavage between French-speaking and English-speaking citizens, Irish Catho-lics and Irish Protestants, and Catholics and non-Catholics in general, made Charbonnel's defence of separate-school rights far more heated and controversial than Power's had been.[19] As non-Catholic Europe pushed back a more assertive Pius IX who was attempting to expand Catholic power and influence, Protestant Upper Canadians envisioned themselves as actors in the same drama, except that the Pio Nono they pushed against was a French-born count, aristocratic and ultramon-tanist. The Orange Order was taking on numerical strength and politi-cal influence, the new Irish Catholic immigrants to the province were a fearless group, and the 1850s would be scarred by sectarian bitterness, public violence, and rhetorical calumny that made the verbal jousting of the *Catholic*, the *Christian Guardian*, and the *Church* seem harm-less. In sum, the decade's changes – technological, political, social, and religious – relegated Power to a distant past.

Other factors contributed to Power's fade from public memory. By the time of his death, ten of his priests had predeceased him: Alexander Kernan, James Campion, Constantine Lee, James Bennet, Félix Gatien, Timothy McGuire, Louis Boué, Thomas Gibney, Jean-Baptiste Morin, and William Peter MacDonald. Within ten years of his death, several more of his colleagues had gone to their reward: J.J. Hay, Hugh Fitz-patrick, Michael Mills, John Butler, and John McLachlan.[20] In 1856, others were incardinated in the two new subdivisions of the Diocese of Toronto; they effectively became priests of London or Hamilton, leaving

Toronto behind, as well as their connection with its first bishop. Even Power's beloved Jesuits were serving the two new dioceses. Du Ranquet, Point, and Choné continued their missionary work, but they were now separated by time, new superiors, and new bishops from the diocese that had recruited them and from its first bishop. So, by the early 1850s, there were few priests who remembered Power, for good or for ill.

In his home province of Nova Scotia, Power was not entirely forgotten. Bishop Walsh celebrated a memorial Mass for him shortly after his death, and in the late 1850s, there was still a plan to erect a memorial to him at St Mary's Cathedral. For reasons unknown, nothing ever came of the plan.[21] The parish of St Mary's would preside over the development of the property that had once encompassed the graveyard adjacent to St Peter's Chapel, but despite the erection of a new parochial building, there are no records indicating that the remains of Power's father, mother, and brothers were removed to the new Holy Cross Cemetery, opened in 1843.[22] While the church may have forgotten about Power's family members, Michael Power had not. He bequeathed the annual sum of thirty pounds to his mother; he also instructed that upon Mary Roach Power's death, his unmarried sisters – Margaret, Frances, and Elizabeth – be given ten pounds each annually.[23] In August 1850, Mary Power died at the age of sixty-eight, and the episcopal corporation of the Diocese of Toronto began paying the bequest to Power's sisters. It continued to do so until 1883, when Margaret, Power's last surviving sister, died in Montreal. His married sister, Mary Ann Mooney, with whom Elizabeth lived in Boston, was also paid the ten pounds when her husband complained that she had been excluded unfairly from the will.[24]

In the Diocese of Toronto, Power's successor bishops and the dwindling number of priests who had served under him met infrequently to celebrate a memorial mass for the repose of the founding bishop's soul. On 1 October 1868, the twenty-first anniversary of Power's death, Bishop John Joseph Lynch and Bishop John Farrell of Hamilton presided over the Eucharist, and Farrell offered "an eloquent panegyric upon the deceased prelate."[25] To an audience of students who had been marched to St Michael's Cathedral from the Christian Brothers' school, the St Joseph's and Loretto convents, and St Michael's College, the bishop of Hamilton spoke of Power as a man who "died a martyr to his zeal and charity on behalf of the fever-stricken immigrants of '47."[26] Similarly, seven years later, at the opening of the first ecclesiastical council of the Archdiocese of Toronto, Bishop Jean-François Jamot of Peterborough paid tribute to the "saintly Bishop Power," who had ended a most "holy

and useful life by falling a martyr to charity."[27] The latter characteriza-
tion had become the most common way of remembering Power, and it
passed from the oral tradition of the diocese into his earliest biographies.
In his biographical essay on Power, published in 1892 in the volume
commemorating the fiftieth anniversary of the diocese, H.F. McIntosh
wrote: "Bishop Power's eulogy is in the simple, unadorned story of his
useful life and holy death."[28] In 1909, the same theme was picked up by
the Ancient Order of Hibernians when they erected a Celtic cross atop
Telegraph Hill on Grosse Île to honour the victims of Black '47. Among
the names of the deceased clergy inscribed on the base of the cross was
that of Michael Power. He was now formally memorialized alongside
his former priestly Quebec colleagues as a famine martyr.

   In light of all of this – the focus on Power's famine martyrdom, the
fact that so many of his colleagues died within a few years of his own
passing, and the massive changes taking place in Canadian society and
life – it is perhaps not surprising that the whole of Michael Power's life
and work seemed to have been reduced to a few memories of his last days.
From 1890 to 1891, when St Michael's Cathedral was being renovated,
the only English-language plaque commemorating Power was removed
from the sanctuary, where it had marked Power's resting place one level
below. A century later, at a conference organized by Canadian historians
to mark the diocese's sesquicentennial, there were no academic papers
delivered on Power or issues relating to his episcopate; the published
conference proceedings contained only six references to Power in its 352
pages.[29] Nearly a century after he had penned it, McIntosh's assessment
of Power prevailed, despite such statements as this: "his richest gifts
to us are his holy memory and his honoured name ... no words can
[more] fittingly close this chapter than those with which it is begun:
'Greater love than this no man hath, that a man lay down his life for
his friends.'"[30] Clearly, the memory of Power's death had eclipsed the
activity of his life.

   Thus, the question arises: Beyond the example of his "martyrdom,"
what legacy did Michael Power leave his diocese and community? Contemporaries like Signay acknowledged that Power had placed the diocese
on a "good footing," and such sentiments were repeated uncritically by
McIntosh, who remarked that although Power's episcopate was "too
short," it was "at least long enough to lay a firm and sure foundation,
upon which his successors have raised a glorious and enduring structure."[31] Perhaps it was Jamot's memorial sermon, delivered at the beginning of the archdiocesan ecclesiastical council of 1875 (the first such

meeting since Power's synod of 1842), that presented Power's lasting contributions to the church and to the people of western Ontario in broad categories. He reminded his audience, most of whom had not known Power, that their founding bishop was a man "who knew so well how to grasp with the difficulties of the times, so inflexible in principle, but also so prudent, and so conciliatory, when required, who as a priest had already distinguished himself by talent of organization, who knew the secret to place in a short time a parish in a flourishing state. The success of his episcopacy shows also clearly that he had a talent to govern a diocese."[32] While Jamot's intention was to laud a deceased hero, and his words should be judged accordingly, the young bishop offered some vague but important insights into Power's material contributions to the diocese. He suggested that Power had bequeathed to his successors administrative structures and tools with which they could continue to order religious and moral life at the "edge of civilization."

Assessing Power's contributions to the Diocese of Toronto and the Canadian church is not a simple undertaking, even when one looks through a wider lens. The famine martyrdom was perhaps the most dramatic moment of his life, and a moment from which those who followed him – both clerical and lay – drew inspiration, but Power's untimely end had prevented him from accomplishing so many vital things. Hay's lament over a rebellious priesthood and a disunited laity signalled the immaturity and fragility of Power's imposed disciplines, ecclesiastical structures, and local canons. Signay's claim that Power had set the diocese on a "good footing" could only have been made in the short term. Jamot's tributes, offered eighteen years after Power's death, had the benefit of a longer perspective, but they still betrayed precious little detail or analysis. Other observers might simply look to Power's contributions in stone and brick – the cathedral, the episcopal palace, several churches, and a handful of Catholic schools – as an enduring legacy of the first bishop. Yet, as Percy Bysshe Shelley reminds us in "Ozymandias," such monuments give way over time to the "lone and level sands"; their builders are forgotten and the structures themselves eventually rot or are destroyed.

Nearly 150 years after Power's death, we at last have the perspective to identify at least four lasting contributions he made to his local church and, in at least one case, to the Canadian church as a whole. The first and perhaps the most significant example beyond the Diocese of Toronto was securing the status of episcopal corporation for bishops in Upper Canada. The fact that Power petitioned civilian authorities for this legal standing for the Catholic bishops of Kingston and Toronto not only demonstrated his often underestimated political skills but also his ability to observe administrative developments in the church universal and apply them in the Canadian context. With bishops and their priests firmly in control of the temporal affairs of all parishes, Power hoped to halt the rise of lay activism (which he had noted among the Halifax churchwardens and the Lower Canadian *marguilliers*) and thus prevent the destabilization of parishes on the Upper Canadian frontier. Episcopal corporation held out the promise that the bishop would hold supreme spiritual authority in the diocese and control all parish properties, finances, and temporal affairs. He would be the piper who called the tune.

The significance of Power's actions in this regard should not be underestimated. Shortly after episcopal corporation was established in Upper Canada, the bishops of the Atlantic colonies petitioned for their own corporate status, and in the process they carefully proscribed the limits of lay activity and potentially lay activism and control of local parishes. Just as significant was the fact that as the church grew in the Atlantic colonies, Upper Canada, and beyond, the institution of episcopal corporation expanded commensurately. In the case of Toronto alone, the subdivision of the diocese that began in 1856 would eventually result in episcopal corporation for Hamilton, London, Sault-Ste-Marie, St Catharine's, and Thunder Bay. All of these places owe a debt to Michael Power, whose foresight and earnestness won for them episcopal authority and control of properties on the frontier. Outside of Quebec, the principle of episcopal corporation is still normative in the Catholic Church. While laypersons can still lead temporal and pastoral councils in their local parishes, they neither own the property they support financially nor have the final say in matters pertaining to the temporal life of their parishes. Although the language and spirit of co-responsibility for the church as expressed by the pastoral constitution of the church, *Lumen Gentium*, at Vatican II (1962–65) prompted a serious rethinking of the relationship between the lay and clerical states, such ideas have not significantly altered the legal standing of Canadian bishops or the proprietary rights won for them in 1845 by Power.

In an effort to stabilize and further evangelize the frontiers – in the wilderness and in the growing urban centres of his diocese – Power secured the services of religious orders and congregations. While such efforts were not innovative in the North American context given the recruitment efforts of his French Canadian and American colleagues,

Power did set a valuable precedent for the diocese. Building upon his successful recruitment of the Jesuits and the Loretto Sisters, his successor bishops liberally sought assistance from Canadian and European religious orders and congregations in delivering social services, Catholic education, and health care. Charbonnel invited the Congregation of the Sisters of St Joseph, the Congregation of St Basil, and the Brothers of the Christian Schools to the diocese. Long after Charbonnel resigned, in 1860, prelates persisted with his initiatives, and by the diocesan sesquicentennial in 1991, there were over eighty-five orders and congregations of male and female religious working in the archdiocese, including Power's original founding orders.[33] The Lorettos, for example, had extended their network of schools to several Canadian dioceses and into the United States, the fruit of the seeds planted by Power, Teresa Dease, and Mother Teresa Ball.

Power's third contribution was keeping the notion of publicly funded Catholic elementary-school education alive in both the collective Catholic memory and in reality. The documentation is clear that upon his arrival in 1842, he found no Catholic school drawing from the public purse, although this had been provided for in the Day Act, passed the previous year. By the time Power died, however, at least eight separate schools were operating under the terms of the Hincks Act of 1843, and they were left untouched by Ryerson's amendments three years later. Serving as chair of the board of education, Power witnessed the ongoing efforts to establish separate schools in his diocese. Nearly a century and a half later, when Power's separate schools were combined with those of the neighbouring Diocese of Kingston, these educational institutions formed the foundations for Ontario's Catholic education system, which by 2001 had educated nearly 600,000 of the province's children.[34] Power's influence on the collective memory of Catholic schools is undeniable. Despite the testimony of Ryerson, Hodgins, and others, the Catholics who supported the development of rights for separate Catholic schools believed that Power provided a bridge between Macdonell and the 1850s in the assertion of these rights. An unbroken chain of oral and documentary testimony beginning with that of John Elmsley in the 1850s, continuing with Franklin Walker's trilogy on the history of separate schools in the 1960s and 1970s, and culminating, ironically, with the work of historian Michael Power in 2002 indicates that Catholics believed that Toronto's first bishop fully supported the principles of Catholic education. The collective Catholic memory has been convinced of an ongoing episcopally supported fight for publicly funded Catholic education.

Finally, Michael Power did not allow the rigours of the frontier to defeat him. He had inherited the adventuresome spirit of his father and he wedded it to the steadfast spirituality of his mother. Although he pleaded with Rome to allow the cup to pass from him, he took up the challenge of a frontier diocese knowing full well that it might break him physically and mentally. In the winter of 1845–46, it nearly did. After a pastoral visit to Sandwich, he was so ill that he had to cancel the second diocesan synod and a planned trip to Europe. He used two instruments in his effort to reign in the frontier: pastoral visitation and the sweeping application of canon law. Although he hated the very thought of the frontier, he threw himself into his task, traversing the vast expanse of his diocese by sail and steam, on horseback or wielding a paddle; at the frontier missions, he dealt with the diversity of religious practice and the litany of excuses offered by practitioners and their pastors. While he may have been very modest in assessing his personal success in the field, he did manage to establish an episcopal presence on the frontier where no prelate had been before, and he engendered a culture – albeit an unpopular one – in which frontier dwellers were expected to abide by the regulations of the church as closely as their counterparts in the more settled regions. In the short term, the success of the venture was debatable, but Power had established a framework for action: bishops would visit the remote areas of the diocese; they would enforce local and universal church laws; and they would own all church property, be it on King Street in Toronto or in the back fifty of the township of Kincardine. Whether they liked it or not, Power was present to the people entrusted to his pastoral care.

For those who sought to memorialize Power beyond the famine moment, there was plenty to discover. The man who had risked so much trudging to the fever sheds every day had been a risk taker for much of his life. Just shy of his twelfth birthday, he had left everything and everyone he knew and ventured deep into Canada and into an alien culture. At twenty-three, he had been hurriedly ordained and thrust onto a settlement frontier that had stolen the best years of the men who had preceded him. He engaged rebels and seigneurs and then accepted a pastorate in a new diocese that he had neither asked for nor desired. Power's pluck and tenacity seemed to be sustained by little more than the faith that had been passed on to him by his mother, nurtured by Burke and the Sulpicians, and roused by the Ultramontane Revolution. Nothing else could explain his willingness to enter the foreign and challenging environment of the frontier. He was shy, frail, and politically unambitious. Had he been as ambitious as his schoolmates at the Petit Séminaire, he may have aspired to law, served loyally with Baldwin, LaFontaine, or Cartier, and perhaps won a place in Canadian political history. He was certainly bright and bicultural enough; he was also gifted linguistically and had the courage of his convictions. Yet he became a priest, not another Dominick Daly or Thomas D'Arcy McGee.

In his personal relationships, he was a difficult man. When he moved to Upper Canada, he left his best friends Joseph Marcoux and Vincent Quiblier behind in the Montreal district. His eye for detail, his punctuality, and his fastidiousness about church rules made him appear hard-nosed, hypercritical, and peevish when dealing with his priests. On first meeting him, his parishioners at Laprairie thought him cold, although this may be attributable to his social awkwardness and the shyness that comes from a love of privacy. But others – Elmsley, Baldwin, Strachan, and Ryerson – displayed a genuine affection for him. Nor was he without mercy; he extended it even to those who consistently disregarded the high standard of order and discipline he set for them. Here, Fathers Mills, O'Flynn, McDonagh, and Vervais come to mind. While at times Power appeared obsessed with legalism and the notion that the bishop's authority ought never to be compromised, he was called back to the greater sense of forgiveness that lay at the heart of his faith, which may have been summoned out of him by his frequent reading of the *Imitatio Christi*.

Non-Catholics such as Strachan, Ryerson, Sydenham, and Baldwin respected Power's intellect, appreciated his moderation, and acknowledged his loyalty. That loyalty was something that he never really surrendered. Burke had modelled a type of Catholic prelate who regarded British citizenship and loyalty to the Crown as complementary to Catholicism. Such a type was reinforced by Power's Sulpician mentors and by the example of Joseph-Octave Plessis, who had held the young Power in such high esteem. Throughout his priesthood and episcopacy, Power did not waver from the principles of fidelity to the church and loyalty to the empire. At times, the lumbering pace of the colonial bureaucracy, the aloofness of Colonial Office bureaucrats, or the indifference of Whitehall towards Ireland (or its implementation of counterproductive initiatives for Ireland) tested Power's patience and caused him to doubt the abilities of the stewards of the empire. Yet he retained a love of British history and British saints like Thomas à Beckett and Edward the Confessor, and he continued to believe that church and empire could work together for mutual benefit.

Michael Power did not have enough time to bring ecclesiastical order to what he described as the "edge of civilization." He passed away knowing that he had taken the first basic steps towards achieving this end, but the results had not come as quickly as he had hoped. Still, Jesuits occupied the mission stations from the Detroit River to Lake Superior; British North American bishops had a legal status that they had not previously enjoyed; Catholic education in various forms existed, and two religious communities were poised to assume a pivotal role in creating an educational network from Whitby to Windsor; church activities were set within the context of diocesan constitutions; and new parishes were being created in accord with canonical norms. Michael Power would not be alive to witness the changes brought to the settlement and mission frontiers by the sweeping technological, commercial, and political innovations of the coming decades. Faced with the challenges posed by these profound changes, others would be called to put out into the deep.

Toronto Diocesan Regulations, 1842

Convenerunt Sacerdotes eâdem die ab hora decimâ ad primam post meridiem et ab horâ quartâ ad sextam et congregationes privatæ in sequentes dies ad easdem horas indictæ sunt. In prima sessione lectæ fuerunt Constitutiones, quas paraverat Episcopus et propositæ fuerunt examini Sacerdotum, quorum sententia, si quid addendum vel mutandum videretur, ab Episcopo exquisita fuit.

The Priests gathered together on the same day from the tenth hour [of the morning] to the first hour after noon and from the fourth to the sixth hour and private congregations were declared for the following days at the same hours. In the first session were read the Constitutions which the Bishop had prepared and they were set forth for the examination of the Priests, whose opinion, if anything seemed to have to be added or changed, was sought by the Bishop.

Secundâ die Synodi, post orationem mentalem et horarum recitationem in Ecclesiâ, Missa pro defuncto Episcopo Regiopolitano Illustrissimo ac Reverendissimo Alexandro McDonnell et defunctis hujus Diœceseos Sacerdotibus celebrata fuit. Absolutione peractâ, Sessio Secunda habita est juxta ritum in Pontificali descriptum.

On the second day of the Synod, after mental prayer and the recitation of the hours in the Church, Mass was celebrated for the late Bishop of Kingston, the Most Illustrious and Right Reverend Alexander McDonnell, and the departed Priests of this Diocese. The Absolution having been performed, the Second Session was held according to the rite described in the Pontifical.

Sabbato, tertiâ die Synodi, horâ sextâ convenit Clerus ad Ecclesiam et post orationem et horas, Missa celebrata fuit pro Clero et populo in honorem Purissimi Cordis B(eatae) Mariæ Virginis et habita est tertia Synodi Sessio. Nonnullæ Sanctæ Sedis decisiones in Congregationibus privatis Clero vivâ voce communicata fuerunt. In Sessione pomeridianâ, declaravit Promotor nomine Cleri Constitutiones Sacerdotum examini propositas omnibus placere et petiit ut auctoritate Episcopali confirmarentur et promulgarentur, et immediatê in eadem Sessione promulgatæ fuerunt.

On Saturday, the third day of the Synod, at the sixth hour the Clergy gathered at the Church and after prayer and the hours, Mass was celebrated for the Clergy and people in honour of the Most Pure Heart of the Blessed Virgin Mary and there was held the third Session of the Synod. Several decisions of the Holy See were communicated to the Clergy aloud [*viva voce*] in private Congregations. In the afternoon Session the Promoter declared in the name of the Clergy that the Constitutions proposed for the examination of the Priests were pleasing to everyone and he asked that they should be confirmed and promulgated by the authority of the Bishop, and they were promulgated immediately in the same Session.

Dominicâ II et die nona Octobris ad Ecclesiam S(an)cti Pauli convenit cum Clero Reverendissimus Episcopus atque Missam Pontificalem de Spiritu Sancto pro gratiarum actione celebravit. Post Evangelium concionem ad populum habuit Rev(eren)d(u)s M.R. Mills et post sacrum de status Sacerdotalis sublimitate præclari disseruit Rev(eren)d(u)s P. Chapelle. Hymnus Te Deum et Oratio pro gratiarum actione cantati fuêre et renovato â Sacerdotibus voto clericali in manibus Episcopi, singulis datum est osculum Pacis. Postea Reverendissimus Episcopus more solito solemnem benedictionem impertitus est et cantatis verbis Recedamus in pace, responderunt omnes, in nomine Domini et tunc omnes pariter surgentes pacificê recesserunt.

On the second Sunday and ninth day of October at St Paul's Church the Right Reverend Bishop gathered with the Clergy and celebrated a Pontifical Mass of the Holy Ghost in thanksgiving. After the Gospel the Reverend M.R. Mills gave an address to the people and after the service the Reverend P. Chapelle spoke concerning the sublimity of the glorious Priestly state. The hymn "We praise thee, O God" [*Te Deum*] and the Prayer for thanksgiving were sung and, the clerical vow having been renewed by the Priests in the hands of the Bishop, there was given to each the kiss of Peace. Thereafter the Right Reverend Bishop imparted the solemn blessing in the accustomed manner and the words "Let us depart in peace" [*Recedamus in pace*] having been sung, everyone replied, "in the name of the Lord" [*in nomine Domini*] and then all rising together departed peacefully.

Vesperæ horâ quartâ P.M. cantatæ sunt, quibus interfuerunt Reverendissimus Episcopus et omnes Presbyteri, vestibus sacerdotalibus induti et concionem habuit admodum Rev(eren)d(u)s G.P. McDonald V(icarius) G(eneralis) et solemnis S(anctissi)mi Sacramenti Benedictio data est.

Vespers were sung at the fourth hour p.m., at which were present the Right Reverend Bishop and all the Presbyters garbed in priestly vestments, and the Very Reverend W.P. McDonald, V.G., gave an address and solemn Benediction of the Most Holy Sacrament was given.

Constitutiones latæ et promulgatæ ab Illustrissimo ac Reverendissimo D(ono) D(ei) Michaeli Power, Primo Torontino Episcopo.

Constitutions passed and promulgated by the Most Illustrious and Right Reverend by the Gift of God Michael Power, First Bishop of Toronto.

In Synodo Diœcesana Torontina prima, habita in Ecclesia Sti Pauli Apostoli a die VI Octobris, ad diem IX, quæ fuit Dominica II Octobris et XXI post Pentecosten.

In the first Diocesan Synod of Toronto, held in the Church of St Paul the Apostle from the sixth day of October to the ninth day, which was the second Sunday of October and the twenty-first after Pentecost.

I. *Meminerint nostræ Diœceseos Sacerdotes, qui curam habent animarum et pastorali munere sive in Missionibus sive in Civitatibus vel Oppidis funguntur, iis haud licere, sine nostrâ veniâ munera pastoralia aggredi extra limites Missionis vel districtùs sibi commissi, nisi proprius pastor diutius absit vel gravis urgeat necessitas. Attamen omnes Sacerdotes ab Epsicopo approbati propriorum Subditorum confessiones ubique excipere possunt vel paschatis vel alio quocumque tempore, et pro quacumque Diœceseos nostræ parte approbati fuerint, semper et ubique, alios presbyteros vel clericos in sacris constitutos in confessione audire poterunt. Sed erga eosdem facultates extraordinarias nullatenus exerceant, nisi in casibus in quibus erga cæteros fideles exercere possent vel quatenus pænitens ad Sacramentum administrandum seu sacrum ordinem exercendum teneretur, antequam ad Superiorem posset recurrere.*

I. Priests of our Diocese, who have the cure of souls and perform a pastoral function whether in Missions or in Cities or Towns, are to remember that they are not allowed, without our permission to attempt pastoral functions outside the borders of the Mission or district entrusted to them, unless the particular pastor should be absent for a rather long time or a grave necessity should urge. Nevertheless all priests approved by the Bishop can receive the confessions of their own subjects everywhere either in Eastertide or at whatsoever other time, and for whatever part of our Diocese they have been approved they will be able, always and everywhere, to hear in confession other presbyters or clerics established in sacred orders. But they are by no means to exercise extraordinary faculties toward these latter except in cases in which they could exercise them toward the rest of the faithful, or insofar as a penitent might be bound to administer a Sacrament or exercise his sacred order before he could have recourse to his Superior.

II. *Sedes Confessionales cum clathrata transenna conficiendas in omnibus Ecclesiis vel Sacellis publicis hujus diœceseos, in loco patenti et publico, juxtâ Ritualis Romani præscriptum, statuimus. Vetamus quoque ne unquam in Sacristiis vel etiam in ædibus privatis ab Episcopo ad confessiones audiendas designatis nisi per crates interpositas et in loco patenti, quantum per loci rationem licebit, confessiones mulierum vel puellarum excipiantur, exceptis tamen confessionibus pænitentium quæ surdæ sunt vel ad quas ægrotantes et infirmas invisendas Sacerdotes arcessuntur vel etiam quæ passim, in Missionibus procul ab Ecclesiâ ad confitendum accedunt.*

II. We determine that Confessional seats with a latticed grill are to be put together in all the Churches or public Chapels of this diocese, in an open and public place, according to the prescription of the Roman Ritual. We forbid also that confessions of women or girls ever be received in Sacristies or even in a private building designated by the Bishop for hearing confessions except through grills placed between and in an open place, as much as will be allowed by the scheme of the place, with the exception nevertheless of confessions of (female) penitents who are deaf or whom, being sick or infirm, Priests are summoned to visit or even who everywhere approach to confession in Missions far from a Church.

III. *Diligenter caveant Sacerdotes ne in Sacramentorum administratione aliquid â fidelibus exigant, sed ea ministrent ut omnis simoniæ atque avaritiæ suspicio longissimê amoveatur. Si quid vero eleemosynæ aut devotionis studio, sive occasione matrimonia celebrandi vel baptismum ministrandi, peracto jam Sacramento, sponte â fidelibus offeratur, id licitê accipere poterunt. Caveant quoque, [source indecipherable] "ne a pænitentibus quicquam tanquam ministerii sui præmium petant vel accipiant."*

III. Priests are diligently to beware in the administration of the Sacraments not to demand anything from the faithful, but they are to minister them so that every suspicion of simony and of avarice may be very far removed. But if out of zeal for alms or devotion, either on the occasion of celebrating marriages or ministering baptism, anything should be offered spontaneously by the faithful when the Sacrament has already been performed, they will be able to accept it lawfully. Let them beware also [source in margin illegible] "not to seek or accept anything from penitents as a reward of their ministry."

IV. *Fontes Baptismales in unâquâque Ecclesiâ hujus Diœceseos quæ proprium residentemque habet pastorem erigendos statuimus, ut Universali Ecclesiæ* *disciplinæ morem geramus. Iuxtâ Ritualis Romani præscriptum, "antequam infans ex Ecclesiâ asportetur aut susceptores discedant, eorum nomina et alia de administrato Baptismo in Baptismali libro <u>Missionarius</u> accuratê describat." Librum in quo referuntur nomina baptizatorum, parentum, et susceptorum, dies nativitatis et baptismatis necnon Confirmatorum nomina in unâquâque Ecclesiâ teneri præcipimus, eumque Ordinario in sua visitatione exhiberi.*

IV. We determine that Baptismal fonts are to be erected in each Church of this Diocese which has its own resident pastor, so that we may be obedient to the Universal discipline of the Church. According to the prescription of the Roman Ritual, "before an infant is carried out of the Church or the sponsors depart, the *Missionary* is to write down accurately in the Baptismal book their names and other things about the Baptism that has been administered." The book in which the names of those baptized and of their parents and sponsors, the day of birth and baptism, and also the names of those Confirmed are reported we command to be kept in each Church and to be shown to the Ordinary on his visitation.

V. Prohibemus ne in oppidis vel locis in quibus Ecclesia aliqua erecta est quis, nisi de vitâ periclitans, in privatis ædibus baptizetur: et tunc, si prope ab Ecclesiâ residet pastor, omissis consuetis ceremoniis, periclitanti administretur tantum Baptisma privatum. Missionariorum judicio relinquimus (eorum tamen conscientiam onerando) ut decernant quandonam rure degentes ob domicilio- rum magnam distantiam ab Ecclesiâ vel viarum difficultatem, infantulos ad Ecclesiam deferre teneantur ut baptismus iis conferatur. Curandum est etiam (verbis utimur Sapientissimi Pontificis Benedicti XIV) ne extra casum necessita- tis, communis et naturalis aqua vel etiam ea quæ pro lustrationibus benedicitur in baptismi administratione adhibeatur, ac temerê omittatur usus aquæ ad hunc præcisê effectum benedictæ, juxta præscriptum Ritualis Romani. Vix enim sine maximâ incuriâ evenire potest ut in Ecclesiis parochialibus, ubi illæ existunt, Baptismales fontes statutis temporibus et ritibus non benedicantur aut sacrorum oleorum ad hoc sufficiens copia non suppetat. Attamen cum in hâc Diœcesi longum spatium percurrendum sit ubi nullæ sint Ecclesiæ, valde difficille [sic] Missionariis esset aquam Sabbatis Sancto vel Pentecostes bene- dictam secum circumferre, facultatem per præsentes damus Missionariis hujus diœceseos, dum Missiones percurrunt, aquam baptismalem benedicandi eâ breviori formulâ qua utuntur ex Concessione Apostolicâ Missionarii Peruani. Petentibus Archiepiscopo Baltimorensi et Episcopis Fœderatarum Americæ Septentionalis Provinciarum omnibus Americæ Septentrionalis Missionariis hæc facultas Apostolicâ auctoritate nuperrimê concessa fuit.

v. We prohibit that anyone in towns or places in which any Church has been erected be baptized, except in peril of life, in a private house: and then, if the pastor resides near to the Church, only private Baptism, with the omission of the accustomed ceremonies, is to be administered to one in peril. We leave to the judgment of Missionaries (nevertheless imposing this on their conscience) to determine when those dwelling in the country on account of the great distance of their dwellings from the Church or the difficulty of the roads are bound to bring their little infants to Church so that baptism may be conferred on them. Care is to be taken also (we use the words of the Most Wise Pontiff, Benedict XIV) that not outside a case of necessity should common and natural water or even that which is blessed for purifications be used in the administration of baptism, and that the use of water blessed precisely for this purpose not be rashly omitted, according to the prescription of the Roman Ritual. For scarcely without the greatest lack of care can it come about that in parochial Churches, where those exist, Baptismal fonts should not be blessed at appointed times and by appointed rites or that a supply of sacred oils sufficient for this not be at hand. Nevertheless, since in this Diocese one must traverse a long distance where there are no Churches, [and] it would be very difficult for Missionaries to carry around with them water blessed on Holy Saturday or the Saturday of Pentecost, we grant the faculty by these present letters to Missionaries of this diocese, while they are traversing the Missions, of blessing baptismal water by that shorter formula which Peruvian Missionaries use according to the Apostolic Concession. At the petition of the Archbishop of Baltimore and the Bishops of the Federated Provinces [sic] of North America, this faculty has very recently been granted by Apostolic authority to all the Missionaries of North America.

VI. *Infantes acatholicorum, quos ipsi parentes ipsi offerunt, baptizandi sunt quoties probabilis affulget spes Catholicæ eorum . educationis. Curandum autem omnino est ut Patrinus vel Matrina, iique Catholici habeantur. Meminerit autem Sacerdos [Ex Concilio Baltimor–], in mortis periculo, quotiescumque occasio se obtulerit, omnes infantes baptizari non solum posse sed etiam debere.*

VI. The infants of non-Catholics, whom the parents themselves present, are to be baptized as often as there appears a probable hope of a Catholic education for them. Complete care must be taken, however, that a Godfather or Godmother, and they Catholic, be had. The Priest is to remember [From the Council of Baltimore], however, that in danger of death, as often as the occasion presents itself, all infants not only can but also ought to be baptized.

VII. *[Ibid.] Cum non sine necessitate atque utilitate invaluerit in his regionibus consuetudo eandem adhibendi formam in baptismo adultorum ac parvulorum, ex cujus abrogatione plura magnaque incommoda sequerentur, eamdem consuetudinem jam invalescentem toleramus, donec sententiam et judicium Sanctæ Sedis Apostolicæ receperimus.*

VII. [*Ibid.*] Since not without necessity and utility has the custom been in force in these regions of applying the same form in the baptism of adults and of infants, and since from the abrogation of this custom more and great inconveniences would follow, we tolerate the same custom now in force, until we shall have received the sentence and judgment of the Holy Apostolic See.

VIII. [*Ibid.*] *Benedictio mulieris post partum, non promiscuê atque nulla ratione habita puerperæ dispositionis neque extra Ecclesiam vel locum ubi Sacrum fit, in posterum conferenda est.*

VIII. [*Ibid.*] The Blessing of a woman after childbirth is not for the future to be conferred promiscuously and with no account taken of the disposition of the woman who has given birth nor for the future is it to be conferred outside a Church or a place where a Service takes place.

IX. *Cum Ecclesiæ proprius Sacramentorum locus sit, præcipimus ne quid sacerdos sine expressa Ordinarii licentia quenquam in matrimonium conjungat in domibus privatorum nisi in ædibus quod Ordinarius designaverit aut dum actu Missionis exercitiis procul ab Ecclesiâ dat operam. Hortentur contrahere consentes ut ad "hoc Sacramentum quod est in Christo et in Ecclesia" non accedant, nisi Sacramentum Pænitentiæ et etiam Sanctissimam Eucharistiam prius cum pietate receperint. [Ex Concilio Tridentino, Sess. XXIV, C. I] Sacrorum Lateranensis et Tridentini Conciliorum vestigiis inhærentes præcipimus ut nullus Sacerdos matrimonio adsistat nisi tribus denunciationibus inter Missarum Solemnia præmissis, tribus dominicis vel festivis continuis diebus. Quod si ad matrimomium accedentes sint diversarum Missionum, non procedat ad matrimonii solemnizationem nisi post tres proclamationes in utriusque domicilio. Vagorum, notorum, peregrinorum vel etiam ab Insulis Brittannicis in provinciam immigrantium matrimoniis non intersit, nisi prævia testium fide dignorum constiterit de libero eorum statu. Si testes de ipsorum libero statu afferre non valeant, tales conjungi non possunt nisi prius [Ibid. C. VII] "diligentem inquisitionem fecerint Missionarii et re ad Ordinarium delatâ, ab eo licentiam id faciendi obtinuerint." Peractis omnibus quæ ad ritum et administrationem hujus Sacramenti pertinent in librum matrimoniorum diligenter ipsa Sacerdotis manu referantur dies, mensis et annus ac nomina et cognomina tam sposorum quam duorum saltem testium qui aderant. Præterea distinctê exprimat Missionarius an denunciationes aliquas omiserit et cujus auctoritate aut in privatis ædibus celebraverit ex licentia Episcopi. Sub pœna suspensionis prohibemus ne fideles ex alienâ Missione, quæ proprium habuerit pastorem, matrimonio conjungant Sacerdotes sine proprii pastoris consensu si ipsius habendi copia sit, vel veniâ nostrâ. Si quæ autem ob matrimonia celebrata ex licentiâ Ordinarii vel consensu Pastoris loci receperint, ea non retinebunt, sed proprio Pastori immediatê et in totum remittent.*

IX. Since the proper place for the Sacraments is the Churches, we command that no priest without the express licence of the Ordinary join anyone in matrimony in the houses of private persons except in a building which the Ordinary shall have designated or while in the carrying out of his Mission he is devoting his attention to exercises far from the Church. Let them encourage those consenting to contract that they not approach to "this Sacrament which is in Christ and in the Church" unless they have first received with reverence the Sacrament of Penance and also the Most Holy Eucharist [from the Council of Trent, session 24, chapter 1]. Adhering to the guidance of the Sacred Councils of the Lateran and Trent, we command that no priest assist at a marriage except after three announcements have been set out during the solemnities of Mass on three Sundays or consecutive feast days. But if those approaching matrimony should be of diverse Missions, he is not to proceed to the solemnization of marriage except after three proclamations in the domicile of each. Wanderers, unknown persons, strangers or even immigrants from the British Isles into the province are to have no part in marriages unless their free state has been established by the previous testimony of worthy witnesses. If the witnesses should not be able to contribute anything about the persons' free state, such persons cannot be joined together unless first [*ibid.*, chapter 7] "the Missionaries have made diligent enquiry and the matter having been reported to the Ordinary they have obtained licence from him for doing it." When everything has been performed which pertains to the rite and administration of this Sacrament, there are to be diligently reported in the book of marriages in the Priest's own hand the day, month and year and also the names and surnames both of the spouses and of at least two witnesses who were present. Moreover the Missionary is to express clearly whether and by whose authority he omitted any announcements or whether he celebrated in a private house by licence of the Bishop. Under penalty of suspension we prohibit Priests from joining in matrimony the faithful from another Mission, which has its own pastor, without the consent of their own pastor, if there should be opportunity of obtaining it, or our permission. Moreover, if they receive anything on account of the marriages that have been celebrated by licence of the Ordinary or by the consent of the local Pastor, they shall not keep it, but shall remit it immediately and in full to the proper Pastor.

X. *Cum præcepto divino mandatum sit omnibus quibus animarum cura commissa est, [Ex Concilio Tridentino, Sess. XXIII, C. I] "oves suas agnoscere, pro his sacrificium offerre, verbique divini prædicatione, Sacramentorum administratione ac bonorum omnium operum exemplo pascere, pauperum aliarumque miserabilium personarum curam paternam gerere, et in cætera munia pastoralia incumbere: quæ omnia nequâquam ab iis præstari et impleri possunt qui gregi suo non invigilant neque assistunt sed mercenariorum more deserunt," Animarum Pastores omnes monemus, ne absque gravi ratione â Missione seu districtu sibi commisso etiam ad breve tempus discedant, præsertim die dominicâ vel festo de præcepto interveniente. Quod si discedendi extiterit necessitas, meminerint discessuri ita ovibus suis providendum ut, quantum fieri poterit, ex ipsorum absentiâ nullum damnum accipiant. Nec sine licentiâ Episcopi abesse poterint â districtibus vel Missionibus per integram hebdomadam, sicut non sufficit licentia tacita. [Ben. XIV. Inst. Eccl. 17, N. 11] Si tamen ex improviso discedere necessarium fuerit, tunc immediatê ad Ordinarium scribendum erit.*

x. Since by divine precept it has been commanded to all to whom the cure of souls has been entrusted [from the Council of Trent, session 23, chapter 1] "to acknowledge their sheep, to offer sacrifice for them, and to feed them with the preaching of the divine word, the administration of the Sacraments and the example of all good works, to bear a paternal care for the poor and other pitiable persons, and to attend to all other pastoral duties: all which things can by no means be performed and fulfilled by those who do not keep watch over or assist their flock but in the manner of mercenaries desert it," we warn all Shepherds of Souls not to depart without grave reason even for a short time from the Mission or district committed to them, especially on Sunday or an intervening feast of precept. But if the necessity of departing arises, let those who are going to depart remember to provide in such a way for their sheep that, as much as may be, they receive no damage from their absence. Neither without licence of the Bishop shall they be able to be absent from the districts or Missions for a whole week, as indeed tacit licence is not sufficient [Benedict XIV, Eccl. Inst. 17, n. 11]. If nevertheless it is necessary to depart unexpectedly, then the Ordinary will have to be written to immediately.

XI. Vetant Universalis Ecclesiæ Canones ne novum templum temerê vel absque Episcopi auctoritate erigatur. (Cap. 9 de Consec. dict [?] I Conc. Chal.Can. 6) Ideo nemini licere declaramus in hac diœcesi de novâ ædificanda Ecclesiâ aut de vetere amplicficandâ statuere aliquid aut moliri, absque facultate nostrâ in scriptis.

XI. The Canons of the Universal Church forbid that a new temple be erected rashly or without the authority of the Bishop (chapter 9 on Consecration, spoken by the [?] First Council of Chalcedon, canon 6). Therefore we declare that no one may decide or undertake anything about building a new church or enlarging an old one without our faculty in writing.

XII. Statuimus nullam in posterum erigi Ecclesiam in hâc diœcesi nisi fundus, in quo erigenda est, fuerit Nobis tanquam fidei Commissario, in cultum divinum et utilitatem fidelium instrumento scripto adsignatus, salvis tamen Regularium privilegiis.

XII. We determine that no Church be erected for the future in this diocese unless the property, on which it is to be erected, shall have been assigned for divine worship and the advantage of the faithful by written instrument to Us as Trustee of the faith, the privileges of Regular (clergy) being nevertheless preserved.

XIII. Sæpius admoneantur fideles [Ex Concilio Balt. I] stipendia seu subsidia quæcumque quæ solent ab ipsis tribui vel ob loca quæ in Ecclesiis occupant, vel ob servitium quod Ecclesiis seu Missionibus Sacerdotes impendunt vel ut fundus ad Ecclesiam ædificandam extruatur (quæ subsidia plerumque tribuuntur collatitiâ stipe) hominibus laicis quibuscumque Missionarios seu pastores sibi eligendi, vel eos quos Episcopus probaverat, dimittendi, vel muneris sui exercitium impediendi, subsidiis ad vitæ sustentationem subductis seu quavis alia ratione, nullum justribuere quod â Sacris Canonibus agnoscatur

XIII. The faithful are to be warned rather often [from the First Council of Baltimore] that whatsoever stipends or subsidies which are wont to be granted by them on account of the places which they occupy in the Churches or on account of the service which the Priests provide to the Churches or Missions or in order that a property for building a Church may be assembled (which subsidies are for the most part granted by a contributed donation) grant no right which is recognized by the Sacred Canons to any laymen whatsoever of choosing Missionaries or pastors for themselves or of dismissing those whom the Bishop had approved or of hindering the exercise of their function by removing the subsidies for the support of life or by any other means.

XIV. Sacrosancti Concilii Tridentini nixi auctoritate, sub pœnâ suspensionis ipso facto incurrendæ prohibemus ne Clerici in nostrâ diœcesi etiam ad tempus commorantes æditius] aliisve quibuscumque jus se ingerendi in Pastoribus vel Missionariis designandis rejiciendis vel dimittendis sibi usurpantibus vel auctoritatis Episcopalis exercitium pravis molitionibus impedientibus faveant vel consentiant.

XIV. Relying on the authority of the Most Holy Council of Trent, we prohibit Clerics in our diocese, even those staying here temporarily in churches or elsewhere, under penalty of suspension to be incurred ipso facto, from favouring or consenting to any persons whatsoever usurping to themselves the right of intruding themselves in designating, rejecting or dismissing Pastors or Missionaries or impeding by base contrivances the exercise of Episcopal authority.

XV. *Nulli vago, ignoto, vel extraneo Sacerdoti permittatur Missam celebrare aut Sacramenta ministrare, etiamsi litteras ordinis exhibeat donec per Ordinarium declaratum fuerit quid sit agendum. Excipiuntur tamen Presbyteri notissimi et in vicinioribus diœcesibus de sui Ordinarii licentiâ munera sacra exercentes.– Prohibemus sub pœnâ suspensionis ipso facto incurrendæ ne Sacerdotes â Nobis ob scandalum publice datum vel propter malam dimissi vel suspensi seu amoti â munere pastorali vel quibus abstulimus facultates, licet fuerint in aliam diœcesim cooptati, sacram aliquod munus intrâ hanc diœcesim absque nostrâ veniâ aggrediantur. Eamdem pœnam incurrunt Sacerdotes ex alia quacumque diœcesi ab Ordinariis ob scandalum publice datum vel propter malam famam suspensi vel facultatibus privati qui munus sacrum intrâ nostræ diœceseos limites absque licentiâ Nostrâ excere audeant.*

XV. No wandering, unknown, or stranger Priest is to be permitted to celebrate the Mass or minister the Sacraments, even if he should show a letter of ordination until it has been declared through the Ordinary what is to be done. There are excepted nevertheless very well known Presbyters and those exercising sacred functions by licence of their own Ordinary in neighbouring dioceses. We prohibit, under penalty of suspension to be incurred ipso facto, Priests dismissed or suspended or removed from pastoral duty by Us on account of scandal publicly given or from whom We have taken away their faculties, although they have been co-opted into another diocese, from undertaking any sacred function within this diocese without our permission. Priests from whatever other diocese suspended or deprived of their faculties by their Ordinaries on account of publicly given scandal or on account of an evil reputation incur the same penalty who dare to exercise a sacred function within the borders of our diocese without Our licence.

XVI. *Cum mulieribus nullam consuetudinem habeant Clerici in Sacris constituti, nec domi apud se retineant nisi matrem, sororem, aut amitam, neque sibi famulas accipiant vel retineant nisi provectæ ætatis (juxtâ receptam Canonum interpretationem) et famæ illibatæ, de quibus nulla possit haberi suscipio.*

XVI. Clerics established in Sacred orders are to have no familiarity with women, nor are they to keep at home with themselves any except a mother, sister, or aunt, nor are they to take to themselves or keep women servants except those of an advanced age (according to the received interpretation of the Canons) and of spotless reputation, of whom no suspicion could be held.

XVII. *Sacerdotibus omnibus injungimus ut veste talari et superpelliceo in omni sacro munere obeundo utantur, præsertim in propriis Ecclesiis. Veste etiam talari constanter, quatenus fieri possit, gerant, semper in loco residentiæ. Si eam induere in itinere peculiaria rerum adjucta [sic] non sinant, iis tantum*

*vestibus quæ suo congruant ordini utantur, scilicet, quæ sint nigri coloris,
infra genua descendentes, anterius claudentes et quæ omni vario et mundano
ornatu careant. Sint semper hujusmodi ex quo eos esse Ecclesiastici ordinis
homines, facile ab omnibus dignosci possit: ad quod assequendum non parum
juvabit si Collare quod â Benedicto XIV nuncupatur "Sacerdotum insigne",
presbyteris conveniens, ab omnibus, ubique deferatur.*

XVII. We enjoin all priests that they use the cassock and surplice in undertaking every sacred function, especially in their own Churches. The cassock also
they are to wear resolutely, as far as may be possible, always in their place of
residence. If the peculiar circumstances of events in a journey should not allow
them to put it on, they are to use only those garments which are suitable to their
order, namely, which are of black colour, reaching below the knees, closing in
front and which lack every varied and worldly adornment. Let these always
be of the sort from which it can be easily recognized by all that they are men
of the Ecclesiastical order: and to attain this end it will help not a little if the
Collar which, suitable to presbyters, is called by Benedict XIV "the badge of
Priests," is worn by all everywhere.

*XVIII. Omnia officia sacra peragantur juxtâ ordinem Missalis et Breviarii
Romani. Rituale Romanum in nostrâ diœcesi adoptamus: usum tamen Ritualis
Romano Conformis, nuper Baltimori editi, ex auctoritate Summi Pontificis,
et Compendii ejus concedimus. Districtê jubemus ut omnes Sacerdotes semel
saltem in anno diligenter perlegant Rubricas generales quæ initio Missalis
Romani apponuntur et eosdem enixê hortamur ut regulas quæ in Rituale
Romano salubriter præscriptæ sunt, attente et frequenter perlegant et adamus-
sim servare conentur.*

XVIII. All the sacred offices are to be performed according to the order of the
Roman Missal and Breviary. We adopt the Roman Ritual in our diocese; nevertheless we concede the use of the Ritual conformable to the Roman, recently
published in Baltimore by the authority of the Supreme Pontiff, and its Compendium. We strictly command that all Priests, at least once in the year, diligently
read through the general Rubrics which are placed at the beginning of the
Roman Missal and we strongly exhort them that they attentively and frequently
read through the rules which are wholesomely prescribed in the Roman Ritual
and try to keep them accurately.

*XIX. Catechismus ab Archiepiscopo Cassaliensi, Jacobo Butler, exaratus et a
quatuor Archiepiscopis Hiberniæ adoptatus, in hujus diœceseos usum adhibeatur. In Missionibus lingua gallica utentibus Catechismi Quebecensis usum
ad tempus permittimus.*

XIX. The Catechism composed by the Archbishop of Cashel, James Butler, and adopted by the four Archbishops of Ireland, is to be taken into the use of this diocese. In Missions using the French language we permit the use of the Catechism of Quebec for the time being.

XX. *Missionariis injungimus ut, â die prima l Januarii 1843, in suis Ecclesiis duos habeant libros in quibus referantur Baptismata, Confirmationes, Matrimonia et Sepulturæ, quo-rum alter penes Missionarium diligenter adservabitur et alter ad Episcopum Diœcesanum in Archivio adservandus mittetur.*

XX. We enjoin Missionaries that, from the first day of January 1843, they keep in their own Churches two books in which are to be reported Baptisms, Confirmations, Marriages and Burials, of which one will be carefully kept in the possession of the Missionary and the other will be sent to the Diocesan Bishop to be kept in the Archive.

XXI. *Pænitentiæ et Sanctissimæ Eucharistiæ Sacramenta administrare non præsumant Missionarii iis qui ad Societatem Liberorum Muratorum vel ad alias hujusmodi secretas aggregationes, quavis nomenclatura nuncupatas publicê pertinere cognoscuntur, nisi de violatis Ecclesiæ legibus vere pœnitentes atque dolentes positive promittunt sese ab hujusmodi societatibus seu conventiculis omnino recessuros nec unquam professuros etiam privatë se ad illas vel illa ullo modo pertinere.*

XXI. Missionaries are not to presume to administer the Sacraments of Penance and the Most Holy Eucharist to those who are known to belong publicly to the Society of Freemasons or to other secret associations of this kind, by whatever title they are called, unless being truly penitent and sorry for having violated the laws of the Church they promise positively that they will withdraw altogether from societies or conventicles of this kind and not ever profess even privately that they belong to them in any way.

XXII. *Volumus ut Constitutiones in hâc Nostrâ Synodo promulgatæ semel in anno a singulis Sacerdotibus attentê perlegantur et fideliter serventur. Et nunc admodum Reverendi et Dilectissimi Fratres "quicumque hanc regulam secuti fuerint, pax super illos et misericordia et super Israel Dei."*

XXII. We will that the Constitutions promulgated in this Our Synod be attentively read through once a year by priests individually and observed faithfully. And now, Very Reverend and Dearly Beloved Brethren "whosoever shall follow this rule, peace on them and mercy and upon the Israel of God" [Galatians 6.16].

Constitutiones hæ omnes lectæ, probatæ et promulgatæ sunt in Ecclesia S(anc)ti Pauli Apostoli in Urbe Toronto in Synodo diœcesanâ Torontinâ primâ, habita diebus, mense et anno quibus supra.

All these Constitutions were read, approved, and promulgated in the Church of St Paul the Apostle in the City of Toronto in the first diocesan Synod of Toronto, held in the days, month and year as above.

Michael Ep(isco)pus Torontinus
De Mandato Ill(ustrissi)mi ac Rev(erendissi)mi
D(ono) D(ei) Toronti Episcopi
J. J. Hay, Secretarius

Michael Bishop of Toronto
By Command of the Most Illustrious and Right Reverend
by the Gift of God Bishop of Toronto,
J. J. Hay, Secretary.

The Prisoners from Ste–Martine, 1838

Name	Occupation	Age	Married (P=by Power)	Children	Charge	Sentence
Michael Azur Jr						
Paul Barré	shoemaker	45	Yes	6		
Charles Bergevin Sr	farmer	50	Yes	7	treason	deported
Charles Bergevin Jr	farmer	23	Yes P			
François Bergevin	farmer	19				
François Bergevin	farmer	18				
Gédéon Brazeau	merchant	23				released
Henri Brien	doctor	22			treason	exiled
Constant Buisson	bailiff	28	Yes	3	treason	deported
Godfroi Chaloux	farmer	23	Yes P			released
Michel Chartrand	farmer	35				
I.G. Chevrefils	farmer	43	Yes	7	treason	deported
Antoine Curty	farmer					
Ben. Delorme	tanner	32				
Michel Desgrosseilliers	farmer	29	Yes			released
Joseph Dumouchel	farmer	43	Yes	4	treason	deported
Louis Dumouchel	innkeeper	40	Yes	6	treason	deported
Amable Duquet	farmer	30				released
Fr. Desgrosseilliers						
René Fabien						
Pierre Hébert	innkeeper	33	Yes	4		released
Jean Laberge						deported
Augustin Legault						released
Antoine Lefebvre	farmer				treason	
J.M. Lefebvre	farmer		Yes			
Fra. Lefebvre	farmer				treason	
Louis Maheux	farmer	27	Yes P		treason	released
J.B. Mercille	farmer				treason	
Louis G. Neveu	bailiff	37	Yes	4		released

Name	Occupation	Age	Married (P=by Power)	Children	Charge	Sentence
Vital St-Onge Payant	farmer	38			treason	released
James Perrigo	farmer	50	Yes P	4	treason	acquitted
Michel Primeau	farmer				treason	released
Pierre Primeau			Yes			
Paul Rivard						
Louis Thibault					treason	
F.X. Touchette	blacksmith	30	Yes		treason	deported
Michel Tremblay	farmer	52			treason	
Louis Turcot	farmer	33	Yes	6	treason	deported
François Vallée	farmer	30	Yes		treason	pardoned
Louis Vallée						

Sources: Derived from data found in Henriette Laberge-Boulianne, *Mariages de la paroisse de Ste-Martine (Co. Châteauguay), 1823–1972* (Montreal: Éditions Bergeron, 1982); Jean-Paul Bernard, *Les rébellions 1837–38: Les patriotes du Bas Canada dans la mémoire collective et chez les historiens* (Montreal: Boréal Express, 1983), 131–5 and 294; Aegidius Fauteux, *Patriotes de 1837–1838* (Montreal: Éditions des Dix, 1950); and the depositions in APQ, Événements 1837–38

Population of the Diocese of Toronto, 1842–48

General Population (GP), Irish by Birth (IB), Roman Catholics (RC), Separate Schools (SS)

District	GP 1842	IB	RC	SS	GP 1848	IB	RC	SS
Western	24,390	2,017	6,635	0	27,440	2,306	7,340	1
London	30,276	2,978	1,222	0	41,986	5,272	1,745	1
London City					4,668	366	804	0
Talbot	11,455	295	157	0	18,082	558	691	0
Brock	17,286	867	342	0	29,224	3,986	1,216	0
Niagara	36,642	3,079	2,165	0	42,968	1,342	5,017	0
Gore	45,059	5,179	2,986	0	58,228	4,941	4,369	0
Hamilton City					9,889	963	2,760	1
Huron	7,190	1,761	842	0	20,450	2,634	3,497	1
Wellington	14,476	1,195	2,107	0	36,865	5,293	5,317	3
Simcoe					23,050	2,871	3,405	0
Home	83,301	17,985	8,500	0	84,312	6,490	7,949	1
Toronto City					23,503	1,695	5,903	2
Total	270,075	35,356	24,956	0	420,665	38,717	50,013	10
Province UC	487,053	78,255	65,203		725,879	57,604	118,810	

Sources: Censuses of Canada, 1665–1871, vol. 4 of Census of Canada, 1870–1871 (Ottawa: I.B. Taylor, 1876), 134–5, 165–6, table II; Documentary History of Education in Upper Canada, ed. J.G. Hodgins (Toronto: L.K. Cameron, 1900), 12:34–5, table 7

∴ Abbreviations ∾

RELIGIOUS ARCHIVES

AAD	Archives of the Archdiocese of Detroit
AAH	Archives of the Archdiocese of Halifax
AAHC	Archives of All Hallows College
AAHQ	Archives of the Archdiocese of Hull-Quebec
AAK	Archives of the Archdiocese of Kingston
AAM	Archives of the Archdiocese of Montreal
ABCSI	Archives of the Brothers of Christian Schools, Ireland
ADN	Archives of the Diocese of Nicolet
ADNO	Archives of the Diocese of New Orleans
ADSJLQ	Archives of the Diocese of St-Jean, Longueuil, Quebec
ADV	Archives of the Diocese of Valleyfield
AIBVM-H	Archives of the Institute of the Blessed Virgin Mary, Hamilton
AIBVM-R	Archives of the Institute of the Blessed Virgin Mary, Rathfarnam
AIBVM-T	Archives of the Institute of the Blessed Virgin Mary, Toronto
AICR	Archives of the Irish College, Rome
APF	Archives of the Congregation of the Propagation of the Faith
ARCAT	Archives of the Roman Catholic Archdiocese of Toronto
ARSI	Archivum Romanum Societas Iesu (Jesuit Archives, Rome)
ASJUCP	Archives of the Society of Jesus, Upper Canada Province
ASN	Archives of the Seminary of Nicolet
ASSS	Archives of the Seminary of St-Sulpice
AUCC	Archives of the United Church of Canada
PH	Power Holograph Collection
PP	Power Papers
PRC	Power, Roman Correspondence
SFXUA	St. Francis Xavier University Archives, Antigonish, Nova Scotia
SOCG	Scritture referite nelle congregazione generali (at Propaganda Fide, Rome)
SPF	Society for the Propagation of the Faith (Paris and Lyons)

PUBLIC ARCHIVES AND OTHERS

AO	Archives of Ontario
APQ	Archives of the Province of Quebec
BPP	British Parliamentary Papers
CI	Canada Inferior (Lower Canada)
CIHM	Canadian Institute of Historical Microfilms
CS	Canada Superior (Upper Canada)
NA	National Archives (Canada)
ODE	Ontario Department of Education
PANS	Provincial Archives of Nova Scotia
TPL-BR	Toronto Public Library, Baldwin Room

◟ Notes ◞

INTRODUCTION

1 *British Colonist*, 5 October 1847.

2 *Nova Scotian*, 25 October 1847.

3 *British Colonist*, 8 October 1847.

4 Ibid.

5 AUCC, Egerton Ryerson Papers, 86.218, Finding Aid, 26, vol. 2, letter 17, Ryerson to Hodgins, 3 October 1847.

6 *Globe*, 9 October 1847. ARCAT, PP, AF 01.15, "Memorial Motion for Michael Power by the Board, 2 October 1847."

7 *British Colonist*, 8 October 1847.

8 Ibid., 5 October 1847; Montreal *Pilot*, 7 October 1847.

9 *Canadian Freeman*, 1 October 1868.

10 *Mirror*, 8 October 1847; also reprinted in the Halifax Catholic weekly *The Cross*, 4 December 1847.

11 *Cross*, 23 October 1847.

12 NA, Archives of the SPF, Paris, microfilm, Armand de Charbonnel to the SPF, 1850, frame, 12357a; also, ARCAT, PRC, Vincent Quiblier, PSS, to the Sacred Congregation of the Propaganda Fide, Rome, 1 November 1847.

13 *Mélanges religiuex*, 5 October 1847.

14 *Cross*, 23 October 1847.

15 *True Witness and Catholic Chronicle*, 25 January 1856.

16 *Irish Canadian*, 7 January 1863.

17 John Francis Maguire, *The Irish in America* (New York and Montreal: D. and J. Sadlier and Son, 1880). In fact, archived copies of Power's will reveal the poetic license of Maguire's description. Other accounts adhering to this theme of martyr of charity and the Irish can be found in *Catholic Weekly Review*, 25 June and 9 July 1887, and Irish Canadian, 15 March 1876, which contains an impressive memorial sermon by Bishop Jean-François Jamot of Peterborough.

18 H.F. McIntosh, "The Life and Times of the Right Reverend Michael Power, D.D.," in *Jubilee Volume: Archbishop Walsh. Diocese of Toronto*, ed. J.R. Teefy (Toronto: George T. Dixon, 1892), 107–40.

19 Ibid., 140.

20 Ibid., 115–17.

21 Ibid., 109, 139.

22 "The Catholic Church in Toronto," in *The Municipality of Toronto: A History*, ed. Jesse Edgar Middleton (Toronto: Dominion Publishing, 1923), 2:715–38. Pages 723–6 deal directly with Power.

23 Murray W. Nicolson, "Michael Power, First Bishop of Toronto, 1842–47," Canadian Catholic Historical Association, *Historical Studies* 54 (1987): 38. The essay itself extends from pages 27 to 38.

24 Murray W. Nicolson, "The Catholic Church and the Irish in Victorian Toronto" (Ph.D. diss., University of Guelph, 1980). Articles authored by Nicolson and based on the dissertation include: "Irish Tridentine Catholicism in Victorian Toronto: Vessel for Ethno-Religious Persistence," Canadian Catholic Historical Association [CCHA], *Study Sessions* 50, no. 2 (1983): 415–36; "Bishop Charbonnel: The Beggar Bishop and the Origins of Catholic Social Action," CCHA, *Historical Studies* 52 (1985): 51–66; "The Growth of Roman Catholic Institutions in the Archdiocese of Toronto," *Creed and Culture: The Place of English-Speaking Catholics in Canadian Society, 1750–1930*, ed. Terrence Murphy and Gerald Stortz (Montreal and Kingston: McGill-Queen's University Press, 1993), 153–70; "Ecclesiastical Metropolitanism and the Evolution of the Catholic Archdiocese of Toronto," *Histoire sociale/Social History* 17 (May 1982): 129–56.

25 Ibid., 138.

26 "Michael Power," *Dictionary of Canadian Biography*, vol. 7. Robert Fraser, currently of the DCB, permitted this author access to the Michael Power file, which contained Robert Choquette's original draft and corresponding endnotes. My sincerest thanks to Dr Fraser.

CHAPTER ONE

1 Cecil Houston and William J. Smyth, *Irish Emigration and Settlement in Canada: Patterns, Links and Letters* (Toronto: University of Toronto Press, 1999), 16–17.

2 W.S. McNutt, *The Atlantic Provinces: The Emergence of Colonial Society, 1712–1857*, Canadian Centenary Series (Toronto: McClelland and Stewart, 1965), 72.

3 John J. Mannion, *Irish Settlements in Eastern Canada: A Study of Cultural Transfer and Adaptation* (Toronto: University of Toronto Press, 1974), 15–23, 36–9, 44–8, 60–72; John J. Mannion, "Old World Ante-

cedents, New World Adaptations: Inistioge (Co. Kilkenny) Immigrants in Newfoundland," in *The Irish in Atlantic Canada, 1780–1900*, ed. Thomas P. Power (Fredericton, NB: New Ireland Press, 1991), 30–95.

4 Mannion, "Old World Antecedents," 50–2, 89–92.

5 Patrick Corish, "The Irish Catholics at the End of the Penal Era," in *Religion and Identity: The Experience of Irish and Scottish Catholics in Atlantic Canada*, ed. Terrence Murphy and Cyril Byrne (St John's: Jesperson Press, 1987), 1–17.

6 Terrence M. Punch, *Irish Halifax: The Immigrant Generation, 1815–1859* (Halifax: International Education Centre, St Mary's University, 1981).

7 Henry Morris, "The Principal Inhabitants of County Waterford, 1746," in *Waterford History and Society: Interdisciplinary Essays on the History of an Irish County*, ed. Thomas Power and William Nolan (Dublin: Geography Publications, 1992), 309.

8 Cyril Byrne, "Waterford History and Society," in Power and Nolan, *Waterford History*, 354.

9 Ibid., 363.

10 A.A. Johnston, *The History of the Catholic Church in Eastern Nova Scotia*, (Antigonish, NS: St Francis Xavier University, 1960), 1:129, 145.

11 Houston and Smyth, *Irish Emigration*, 17; Mannion, *Irish Settlements*, 19–21. Peter Toner makes an exception for New Brunswick while confirming the Waterford dominance of Nova Scotia and Newfoundland patterns of migration from Ireland. Toner, "The Origins of the Irish in New Brunswick," *Journal of Canadian Studies* 23 (1988): 106–7.

12 ARCAT, PP, Series AA 04, Mary Power to Michael Power, various letters, 1820s.

13 *Nova Scotia Royal Gazette*, 17 October 1809.

14 John Bartlett Brebner, *North Atlantic Triangle*, Carleton Library Series (1945; reprint, Toronto: McClelland and Stewart, 1966), 74–6. Generally, trade with the Indies continued despite the European wars and the commercial incursions of the United States.

15 Punch, *Irish Halifax*, 18–19; and Terrence Punch, "Irish Catholics: Halifax's First Minority Group," *Nova Scotia Historical Quarterly* (1980): 34.

16 Punch, *Irish Halifax*, 8.

17 Ibid., 13; Judith Fingard et al., *Halifax: The First 250 Years* (Halifax: Formac Publishing, 1999), 37. By 1805, the Irish were the largest minority group in Halifax. See also Houston and Smyth, 16–17.

18 Punch, *Irish Halifax*, 20. The figures are for 1827.

19 Ibid., 126.

20 Census of Ireland, Youghal, County Cork, 1766. James Doyle is listed as a Protestant.

21 They were fifty-third on the Hollis Street list.

22 PANS, RG 35, Series A, vol. 1, nos 2, 3, 4, 5, 6, 7, City of Halifax Assessment Rolls, 1819–24.

23 Fingard et al., *Halifax: The First 250 Years*, 38; Thomas H. Raddall, *Halifax: Warden of the North* (London: Dent, 1950), 145.

24 Terence Burns, "Public School Education of Catholics in the City of Halifax, 1819-1900" (master's thesis, St Mary's University, Halifax, 1962), 6. The entrance to the chapel was accessible from Barrington Street. Punch, *Irish Halifax*, 22; and Lenore Merrigan, "The Life and Times of Edmund Burke in Nova Scotia, 1801–20" (master's thesis, St Mary's University, Halifax 1971), 41.

25 PANS, RG 35, Series A, vol. 1, nos 1, 3, 5, 6. Walsh and Crowder had properties valued at £200 and Smilie at £300.

26 Thomas Beamish Akins, *History of Halifax City* (1895; reprint, Belleville, ON: Mika Publishers, 1973), 158.

27 Ibid., 158.

28 *Nova Scotia Royal Gazette*, 2 May 1805, 24 July 1806, 31 July 1806.

29 Ibid., 1 September 1807, 5 January 1808, 21 March 1809, 10 October 1809, 3 April 1810, 17 July 1811.

30 Ibid., 10 October 1809, 17 October 1809, 3 April 1810 (a voyage of thirty-two days).

31 Ibid., 2 May 1805, 10 October 1809.

32 ARCAT, P, AA 02.01, PP, baptismal record of Michael Power, signed by Edmund Burke, 23 October 1804; AAH, Register of Baptisms, Marriages and Deaths, St Peter's Chapel, 1801–08: "Michael," "Lawful son of William Power and Mary 'Roche,' sponsors Patrick Gleason and Joanna Martin, 23 October 1804, Edmund Burke, VG," p. 65.

33 Compiled with the assistance of Nova Scotia Newspaper Obituaries, ARCAT, P, AA 04.01, Mary Power to Michael Power, 27 May 1822; *Acadian Recorder*, 8 June 1822; AAH, Register of Baptisms, Marriages and Deaths, St Peter's Chapel, 1801–08, 30 November 1806, "James," p. 103; Loose Sheets, 31 March 1811, "John Power," p. 21; Register of Baptisms, Marriages and Burials, St Peter's Chapel, 1810–September 1816, 17 February 1815, "Mary Ann Catherine Power," p. 105; Register of Baptisms, Marriages and Burials, St Peter's Chapel, 1816–20, 26 November 1816, "Elizabeth," p. 33.

34 High fertility among the Irish is postulated by Donald Akenson, *Small Differences: Irish Catholics and Protestants, 1815–1922* (Montreal and Kingston: McGill-Queen's University Press, 1988), 26–8; and Donald Akenson, *The Irish Diaspora: A Primer* (Toronto: P.D. Meaney, 1993), 26. This perspective of high fertility is moderated (related more exclusively to the Irish who marry at younger ages) by Robert E. Kennedy Jr., *The Irish: Emigration, Marriage and Fertility* (Berkeley: University of California Press, 1973), 15–16.

35 Akins, *History of Halifax City*, 166, 133.

36 Ibid., 136.
37 No pew-rent books remain from the early history of St Peter's Chapel, although obituaries suggest that the captain was a "respectable inhabitant of this town" (*Halifax Journal*, 23 November 1824; *Weekly Chronicle*, 26 November 1824), which makes it difficult to imagine that the Powers would not have had even a modest pew in the church that was so close to Mary's heart. Leonard H. Smith and Norma H. Smith, *Nova Scotia Immigrants to 1867* (Baltimore: Genealogical Publishing, 1992), 1:458.
38 Herbert Leslie Stewart, *The Irish in Nova Scotia: Annals of the Charitable Irish Society of Halifax (1786–1836)* (Kentville, NS: Kentville Publishing, 1949), 147; D.C. Harvey, "Black Beans, Banners and Banquets: The Charitable Irish Society of Halifax at Two Hundred," *Nova Scotia Historical Review* 6, no. 1 (1986): 16.
39 Stewart, *Irish in Nova Scotia*, 12, 71.
40 Merrigan, "Life and Times," 13; Stewart, *Irish in Nova Scotia*, 87.
41 Stewart, *Irish in Nova Scotia*, 85.
42 PANS, MG 60, vol. 66, Minute Book of the Charitable Irish Society, 1808–1835. Power was proposed by Captain M. Herron at the meeting of 17 February 1816 and was voted in unanimously by the sixteen members attending the meeting on 17 May 1816. Captain Power attended meetings on 18 February 1817, 17 February 1818, 17 November 1818, 17 February 1819, and 17 November 1819. He attended no meetings from 1820 to 1823.
43 Ibid., 22, 90.
44 *Irish Canadian*, 7 July 1863.
45 ARCAT, PP, AA 04.01, Mary Power to Michael Power, 2 May 1822.
46 ARCAT, PP, AA 04.03, Mary Power to Michael Power, 17 March 1823.
47 *Nova Scotia Royal Gazette*, 26 December 1805, 21 March 1809 (a report of Nelson being toasted by CIS).
48 Raddall, *Halifax: Warden of the North*, passim; Akins, *History of Halifax City*, passim.
49 Fingard et al., *Halifax: The First 250 Years*, 30.
50 *Cross*, 28 October 1847.
51 David Wilson, *United Irishmen, United States* (Ithaca: Cornell University Press, 1998).
52 Merrigan, "Life and Times," 53.
53 Johnston, *History of the Catholic Church*, 348.
54 Ibid., 111.
55 George II, Cap. 5, *Statutes at Large of the Province of Nova Scotia*, vol. 1, 1758–1804.
56 Hilda Neatby, *The Quebec Act: Protest and Policy* (Scarborough, ON: Prentice-Hall, 1972), 49–51.
57 Corish, "Irish Catholics," 2.

58 Terrence Murphy, "James Jones and the Establishment of Roman Catholic Church Government in the Maritime Provinces," Canadian Catholic Historical Association [CCHA], *Study Sessions* 48 (1981): 26–42; Luca Codignola, "Roman Catholic Ecclesiastics in English North America, 1610–1656: A Comparative Assessment," CCHA, *Historical Studies* 65 (2001): 107–24; Terrence Punch, "Irish Catholics: Halifax's First Minority Group," *Nova Scotia Historical Quarterly* 10 (1980): 30; Johnston, *History of the Catholic Church*, 111–13.

59 Burns, "Public School Education," 6–7.

60 Johnston, *History of the Catholic Church*, 109. Father Bourg is quoted here.

61 Ibid., 128; Terrence Murphy, "Trusteeism in Atlantic Canada: The Struggle for Leadership among the Irish Catholics of Halifax, St. John's, and Saint John, 1780–1850," in *Creed and Culture: The Place of English-Speaking Catholics in Canadian Society, 1750–1930*, ed. Terrence Murphy and Gerald Stortz (Montreal and Kingston: McGill-Queen's University Press, 1993), 129.

62 Murphy, "Trusteeism," 130.

63 Michael Power, *A History of the Roman Catholic Church in the Niagara Peninsula, 1615–1815* (St Catharine's, ON: Diocese of St Catharine's, 1983), 156–7, 159.

64 Johnston, *History of the Catholic Church*, 180; Merrigan, "Life and Times," 1–8.

65 Power, *History of the Roman Catholic Church*, 170–2. Officer Dame accused Burke of violating his wife. Burke described Dame as a scoundrel who had made similar charges against a fellow officer and his own brother as a means of securing a divorce from his wife.

66 ARCAT, P, AA 02.01, baptismal certificate, certified by Archbishop Thomas O'Donnell, 21 April 1930, and by Father John Carroll, 15 January 1823; performed by Edmund Burke. The sponsors were Patrick Gleeson and Joanna Martin. The mother was listed as Mary "Roche."

67 This influence is suggested in Terrence Punch, "Bishop Michael Power (1804–1847)," in his *Some Sons of Erin in Halifax* (Halifax: Petheric Press, 1980), 48.

68 Merrigan, "Life and Times," 43.

69 AAH, Minutes, St Peter's Chapel, 1801–1858, 002-18, p. 32.

70 Terrence Murphy, "Priests, People and Polity: Trusteeism in the First Catholic Congregation in Halifax, 1785–1801," in Murphy and Byrne, *Religion and Identity*, 77.

71 Merrigan, "Life and Times," 97; AAH, Edmund Burke Papers, index, vol. 1, 24 March 1806. Burke indicates that the maintenance of a Catholic school requires the presence of a religious order, of which there are none in Halifax.

72 Raymond Brodeur, "Catéchismes et changements culturels," SCHEC, *Sessions d'étude* 56 (1989): 7–20. Monseigneur Saint-Vallier, *Cathéchisme du Diocèse de Québec, 1702*, ed. Fernand Porter, OFM (Montreal: Les éditions franciscaines, 1958).

73 Edmund Burke, *Letter of Instruction to the Catholic Missionaries of Nova Scotia and Dependencies* (Halifax: A. Gay, 1804), 6–7, 11.

74 Merrigan, "Life and Times," 53; AAH, Index of Letters, Edmund Burke, vol. 1, no. 110, 16 January 1802; PANS, Nova Scotia House of Assembly, vol. 303, no. 33, 1 March 1802.

75 Merrigan, "Life and Times," 93.

76 Sister Francis Xavier, SC, "Educational Legislation in Nova Scotia and the Catholics," Canadian Catholic Historical Association, Report 24 (1957): 54.

77 Burns, "Public School Education," 7–8; Nova Scotia Legislative Assembly, Third School Act, 1786.

78 Burns, "Public School Education," 9–10, 22.

79 Akins, *History of Halifax City*, 96; Fingard et al., *Halifax: The First 250 Years*, 34.

80 Cited in John Crocket, "The Origin and Establishment of Free Schools in Nova Scotia" (master's thesis, Dalhousie University, Halifax, 1940), 53.

81 *Cross*, 23 October 1847.

82 Bruce Cuthbertson, *Johnny Bluenose at the Polls* (Halifax: Formac Publishing, 1994), 311–16; J. Murray Beck, *Conservative Reformer, 1804–1848*, vol. 1 of Joseph Howe (Toronto: University of Toronto Press, 1982), 12, 16–17.

83 Paul Axelrod, *The Promise of Schooling: Education in Canada, 1800–1914* (Toronto: University of Toronto Press, 1997), 6.

84 James Lambert, "Plessis and Metropolitan Influence," Canadian Catholic Historical Association, *Historical Studies* 55 (1987): 5–25.

85 Johnston, *History of the Catholic Church*, 202.

86 Power, *History of the Roman Catholic Church*, 163–4; Terrence Murphy, "The Emergence of Maritime Catholicism, 1781–1830," *Acadiensis* 15 (1984): 41, 45–7.

87 John Jennings, *Tending the Flock: Bishop Joseph-Octave Plessis and Roman Catholics in Early Nineteenth-Century New Brunswick* (Saint John, NB: Diocese of St John, 1998), 29.

88 Johnston, *History of the Catholic Church*, 265.

89 Murphy, "Emergence of Maritime Catholicism," 45; Codignola, "Roman Catholic Ecclesiastics."

90 Ibid., 35.

91 Johnston, *History of the Catholic Church*, 267–8. Carroll would bury Power's younger brother James in 1822. AAH, Register of Baptisms, Marriages and Deaths, 1821–1826, Register 16, 8 June 1822, "James Power," p. 141.

92 Ibid., 264–5.

93 "Le journal des visites pastorales de Mgr Joseph-Octave Plessis (Évêque de Québec) en Acadie, 1811, 1812, 1815," Société historique acadienne, *Les cahiers* (March, June, September 1980): 186.

94 Punch, "Irish Catholics," 31.

95 "Journal des visites," 189.

96 AAQ, 312 CN, Nouvelle Écosse V: 91, Father Vincent to Joseph-Octave Plessis, 16 October 1815.

97 Olivier Maurault, PSS, *Le Collège de Montréal, 1767–1967* (Montreal: n.p., 1967), 211, 216.

98 *Cross*, 28 October 1847; Punch, "Bishop Michael Power."

99 Merrigan, "Life and Times," 55.

100 Maurault, *Collège de Montréal*, 215, 216. William Cleary and Charles McCullagh appear as Halifax students beginning at the same time as Power in the class of 1816-24. McCullagh left in 1816, probably not finishing the term, while Cleary left in 1818. Baptismal registers at PANS indicate that Burke baptised William Cleary, son of Hugh Cleary and Deborah Roche, in the presence of Michael Power and Mary Power. Hugh may have been the "uncle" of whom Mary Roach (sometimes written "Roche") Power spoke. It is possible that Deborah and Mary were sisters.

101 John S. Moir, *The Church in the British Era* (Toronto: McGraw-Hill Ryerson, 1967), 70.

102 "Journal des visites," 189.

103 Akins, *History of Halifax City*, 187; reports of the census for 1816–17 indicated that there were 11,156 people living in Halifax. In 1791, there had been just 4,897, and by 1802, only 8,532. See Fingard et al., *Halifax: The First 250 Years*, 6.

104 "Journal des visites," 187.

105 Ibid., 188; Cornelius O'Brien, *Memories of Bishop Burke* (Ottawa: Thorburn, 1894), 100.

106 Register of Baptisms, Marriages and Burials, 1816–1820, 21 August 1917, p. 60. AAH, Card 196, Edmund Burke to the Bishop of Quebec, 25 August 1817, Copies of Letters, vol. 2, Archdiocese of Quebec, 22-A. Burke comments that Migneault has returned to Quebec and two priests have arrived to replace him.

107 AAH, Card 196, Edmund Burke to the Bishop of Quebec, 25 August 1817, Copies of Letters, vol. 2, Archdiocese of Quebec, 22-A, 23.

108 Ibid., 23–4; *Nova Scotia Royal Gazette*, 14 August 1816, 18 September 1816. Trips from Quebec to Halifax are recorded as fourteen and eight days, respectively.

109 ARCAT, PP, AA 04.03, Mary Power to Michael Power, 17 March 1823. Although the printed sources suggest they left in 1816, the parish registers indicate that Mignault was administering the sacraments throughout the year, with only a short absence between 30 July and 17 August, hardly

enough time to sail to Montreal and back. Register of Baptisms, Marriages and Burials, 1816–1820, 30 July 1816, p. 23; 17 August 1816, p. 24.

110 *Nova Scotia Royal Gazette*, 22 May 1816.

111 Rainer Baehre, ed., *Outrageous Seas: Shipwreck and Survival in the Waters Off Newfoundland, 1583–1893* (Montreal and Kingston: McGill-Queen's University Press; Ottawa: Carleton University Press, 1999), 2–6; ARCAT, PP, AA 04.05, Mary Power to Michael Power, c.1824.

112 PANS, MG 20, vol. 66, Minute Book, Charitable Irish Society, 1808–35. The ledgers for 1820 through to 1823 indicate that the captain was in arrears. Municipal Tax Assessment Records, Halifax, RG 35 A, vol. 1, no. 4 (1822), no. 5 (1823), no. 6 (1824).

113 *Acadian Recorder*, obituary, 27 November 1824. The date of death was 20 November 1824, and the obituary claims that he left seven children. ARCAT, PP, AA 04.03, Mary Power to Michael Power, 17 March 1823; AA 04.06, Mary Power to Michael Power, 20 February 1824.

114 ARCAT, PP, AA 04.01, Mary Power to Michael Power, 27 May 1822; AA 04.02, 16 July 1822; AA 04.04, 24 September 1823.

115 *Nova Scotia Census*, 1838, County of Halifax, no. 19–91, 52. She is listed as Mrs Power, widow, living with one female over fourteen. ARCAT, AA 04.08, Alliance Life and Fire Insurance Company, 4 January 1842; insured for a value of £300, at a premium cost of twenty-four shillings per year.

116 *Cross*, 9 May and 3 October 1846; Burns, "Public School Education," 12.

117 The family profiles are culled from Jean M. Holder, *Nova Scotia Vital Statistics from Newspapers* (Halifax: Halifax General Committee of the Nova Scotia Historical Society, 1980), 1823–28; *Acadian Recorder*, 25 August 1827; Jean M. Holder and Grace Hubly, *Nova Scotia Vital Statistics ... 1835–1839*; *Acadian Recorder*, 7 May 1842; *Acadian Recorder*, 8 June 1822 [James Power, age fourteen, son of Captain Power, died 6 June 1822]; Terrence Punch, *Religious Marriages in Halifax, 1768–1841, from Original Sources* (Halifax: Genealogical Association of Nova Scotia, 1991), 126, file no. 273; Punch, "Bishop Michael Power," 51.

118 AAM, Bourget Papers, Letterbook, Ignace Bourget to Michael Power, 30 July 1840.

CHAPTER TWO

1 See Susannah Moodie, *Roughing It in the Bush*, New Canadian Library Series (Toronto: McClelland and Stewart, 1984), 22–4; Robert Whyte, *The Ocean Plague* (Boston: Coolidge and Wiley, 1848).

2 Pierre Camu, *Le Saint-Laurent et les Grands Lacs au temps de la voile, 1608–1850* (LaSalle, QC: Éditions Hurtubise HMH, 1996): 80–3. Camu includes an excellent map of navigation on the lower St Lawrence and the gulf.

3 Kathleen Jenkins, *Montreal: Island City of the St Lawrence* (Garden City, NY: Doubleday, 1966), 262; Eric McLean, introduction to *The Living Past of Montreal*, by R.D. Wilson and Eric McLean (Montreal: McGill-Queen's University Press, 1964), n.p.

4 Olivier Maurault, PSS, *Le Collège de Montréal, 1767–1967* (Montreal: n.p., 1867), 23; Jenkins, *Montreal: Island City*, 234.

5 Jenkins, *Montreal: Island City*, 253–4.

6 E.R. Adair, "France and the Beginnings of New France," *Canadian Historical Review* 25 (1944): 246–78.

7 François Dollier de Casson, *History of Montreal* (Toronto: Dent, 1928), 97–103.

8 Jenkins, *Montreal: Island City*, 262.

9 Ibid., 251.

10 Ibid., 251, 266.

11 Ibid., 254.

12 "Pierre-Marie Mignault," *Dictionary of Canadian Biography* (Toronto: University of Toronto Press, 1976), 9:548.

13 Maurault, *Collège de Montréal*, 215.

14 Rolland Litalien et al., *Le Grand Séminaire de Montréal, 1840–1990: 150 années au service de la formation des prêtres* (Montreal: Éditions du Grand Séminaire de Montréal, 1990), 68.

15 CIHM, no. 51396, Prospectus of the Course of Studies Adopted in the Little Seminary of Montreal, 1808–50, p. 7.

16 Maurault, *Collège de Montréal*, 209–23.

17 Ibid., 55.

18 Ibid., 27.

19 Brian Young, *In Its Corporate Capacity: The Seminary of Montreal as a Business Institution*, (Montreal and Kingston: McGill-Queen's University Press, 1986), 11.

20 CIHM, no. 51396, Prospectus of the Course of Studies Adopted in the Little Seminary of Montreal, 1808–50, p. 7.

21 Jenkins, *Montreal: Island City*, 254; ASSS, *Les anciens du Collège de Montréal* (November 1984), 3.

22 Leslie Roberts, *Montreal: From Mission Colony to World City* (Toronto: Macmillan, 1969), 145.

23 Jenkins, *Montreal: Island City*, 258–9.

24 Roberts, *Montreal: From Mission Colony*, 143; Phyllis Lambert, "Removing the Fortifications: Toward a New Urban Form," in *Opening the Gates of Eighteenth-Century Montreal*, ed. Phyllis Lambert and Alan Stewart (Cambridge: MIT Press, 1992), 79–80.

25 Maurault, Collège de Montréal, 90–1.

26 ARCAT, PP, AA 04.01, Mary Power to Michael Power, 27 May 1822.

27 Maurault, *Collège de Montréal*, 92; Young, *In Its Corporate Capacity*, 4–5.

28 CIHM, no. 51396, Prospectus of the Course of Studies Adopted in the Little Seminary of Montreal, 1808–50, pp. 3, 8.

29 Ibid., 3-4; Maurault, *Collège de Montréal*, 52–4, 66.

30 ARCAT, PP, AA 04.04, Mary Power to Michael Power, 24 September 1823.

31 Maurault, *Collège de Montréal*, 54.

32 Young, *In Its Corporate Capacity*, 18, 39.

33 Wayne Hankey, "Berulle's Spiritual Revolution: Church and State in French Canada" (paper presented at the Canadian Catholic Historical Association, Halifax, 30 May 2003).

34 Young, *In Its Corporate Capacity*, 41.

35 ARCAT, PP, AA 07.01, Last Will, 1847. This version of the will was altered just before he left for Europe that year. His family became the principal beneficiaries and local priests became the executors. AA 07.02, Court of Probate, Toronto, 12 January 1847; AO, appendix A, MS 638, reel 63, Reverend Michael Power, 15 October 1847.

36 Maurault, *Collège de Montréal*, 216–17.

37 Hilda Neatby, *The Quebec Act: Protest and Policy* (Scarborough, ON: Prentice Hall, 1972), 49–51; *Religion and Identity: The Experience of Irish and Scottish Catholics in Atlantic Canada*, ed. Terrence Murphy and Cyril Byrne (St John's: Jesperson Press, 1987).

38 ASSS, Montreal, List of Classes. Of Power's 109 colleagues, and of those whose future occupations were recorded, twenty-four became liberal professionals and only six were ordained priests. ASSS, *Les anciens de Collège du Montréal* (November 1984), 3.

39 James Lambert, "Joseph-Octave Plessis," *Dictionary of Canadian Biography* (Toronto: University of Toronto Press, 1987), 6:590.

40 ARCAT, PP, AA 04.06, Mary Power to Michael Power, 20 February 1824.

41 Ibid. The letter intimates that the Sulpicians were impressed by Michael Power's conduct and would attempt to keep him until the conclusion of his studies. The family's financial woes are also evident in a letter Mary wrote to Michael Power on 24 September 1823 (ARCAT, PP, AA 04.04) and in another, undated, letter, likely written in 1824 (PP, AA 04.05).

42 ARCAT, PP, AA 04.01, Mary Power to Michael Power, 27 May 1822.

43 ARCAT, PP, AA 04.03, Mary Power to Michael Power, 17 March 1823.

44 ARCAT, PP, AA 04.07, Mary Power to Michael Power, 20 July 1824.

45 Lucien Lemieux, *Les années difficiles*, vol. 1 of *Histoire du catholicisme québécois: Les XVIII et XIX siècles* (Montreal: Boréal Express, 1989), 110.

46 Pierre Savard, "Le catholicisme canadien-français au XIXe siècle," *Histoire sociale/Social History* 3 (1971): 69.

47 Lemieux, *Années difficiles*, 110.

48 Jean-Pierre Wallot, "Religion and French Canadian Mores in the Early Nineteenth Century," in *Prophets, Priests and Prodigals: Readings in Canadian Religious History Since 1608*, ed. Mark G. McGowan and David B. Marshall (Toronto: McGraw-Hill Ryerson, 1992); Olivier Hubert, "Ritual Performance and Parish Sociability: French Canadian Catholic Families at Mass from the Seventeenth to the Nineteenth Century," in *Households of Faith: Family, Gender, and Community in Canada, 1730–1969*, ed. Nancy Christie (Montreal and Kingston: McGill-Queen's University Press, 2002).

49 Savard, "Catholicisme canadien-français," 70.

50 Lemieux, *Années difficiles*, 105.

51 Ibid., 113; Louis Rousseau and Frank W. Remiggi, *Atlas historiques des pratiques religieuses: Le sud-ouest du Québec au XIXe siècle* (Ottawa: University of Ottawa Press, 1998), 208.

52 Germain Lesage, "Un fil d'Ariane: La pensée pastorale des évêques canadien-français," in *Le laïc dans l'église canadien-français de 1830 á nos jours*, by Pierre Hurtubise et al. (Montréal: Fides, 1972), 15.

53 Noel Baillargeon, *Le Séminaire de Québec, 1800 á 1850* (Ste-Foy: Les presses de l'Université Laval, 1994), 193.

54 Ibid., 202; Honorius Provost, *Le Séminaire de Québec, documents et biographes* (Quebec: Publications des archives du Séminaire de Québec, 1964) 302–3.

55 Lemieux, *Années difficiles*, 111.

56 Ibid., 109.

57 ARCAT, PP, AA 02.02, Sacraments, 17 May 1825, 24 May 1825; AAQ Registre des insinuations ecclésiastiques, Register K, f.n. 12, 24 December 1825, Bernard-Claude Panet raises Michael Power to minor orders in the seminary chapel.

58 *Le Canada ecclésiastique* (Montreal: Librairie Beauchemin, 1918), 138; "Noel-Laurent Amiot," *Dictionary of Canadian Biography* (Toronto: University of Toronto Press, 1976), 7:18–20.

59 AAQ, RG 21, Register 13, p. 1, Bernard-Claude Panet to Laurent Amiot, 16 September 1826.

60 AAQ, RG 21, Register 13, p. 30. Bernard-Claude Panet to Laurent Amiot, 18 October 1826.

61 Ibid.

62 AAQ, RG 21, Register 13, p.45, letter 67, Bernard-Claude Panet to Laurent Amiot, 2 November 1826.

63 AAQ, RG 21, Register 13, p. 93, letter 106, Bernard-Claude Panet to François-Joseph Deguise, vicar-general, *curé* of Varennes, 5 January 1827.

64 Rousseau and Remiggi, *Atlas historiques*, 78–88.

65 AAQ, 210-A, Register 13, pp. 128–9, Bernard-Claude Panet to Laurent Amiot, 14 February 1827.

66 AAQ, 21, Register 13, Bernard-Claude Panet to Jean-Jacques Lartigue, 22 February 1827.

67 This type of behaviour would be evident in the future. The parish history of Laprairie is respectful in its description of him, although it does characterize his physical demeanour as "cold." In 1841, he did not feel worthy of being a bishop and begged the Propaganda Fide to drop any suggestion that he be elevated to the episcopacy. His dealings with priests while he was bishop of Toronto were rather curt, at times, suggesting a social awkwardness. During ten years of adolescence and early adulthood, he had known no social life beyond school and seminary.

68 AAQ, 210-A, Register 13, p. 169, Bernard-Claude Panet to Laurent Amiot, 29 April 1827.

69 AAQ, 21, Register 12, p. 509, letter 480, Bernard-Claude Panet to Msgr de Telmesse, 27 May 1827.

70 ASN, F085/0242, Joseph Signay to Jean Rambault, superior of the seminary, 14 June 1827; Signay to Rambault, 24 June 1827.

71 AAQ, CD, Clergé diocèse, vol. 1, p. 108, Laurent Amiot to Bernard-Claude Panet, 29 June 1827.

72 AAQ, 21, Register K, folio 44, verso (in Latin), Joseph Signay, fifth Sunday after Pentecost, Paroisse Saint-Jean-Baptiste, Nicolet, 8 July 1827.

73 AAQ, 210-A, Register 13, p. 205, Bernard-Claude Panet to Jean-Jacques Lartique, 1 August 1827.

74 AAM, Register of Chancery, Pièces et actes, vol. 1, p. 154.

75 Cyprien Tanguay, Repertoire genérale du clergé canadien (Montreal: Sénécal et Fils, 1893), 15, 197–8.

76 AAQ, 210-A, Register 13, p. 203, Bernard-Claude Panet to Michael Power, 1 August 1827.

77 AAQ, 210-A, Register 13, p. 204, Bernard-Claude Panet to Laurent Amiot, 1 August 1827.

78 "Noel-Laurent Amiot," Dictionary of Canadian Biography (Toronto: University of Toronto Press, 1976), 7:20.

79 AAQ, 210-A, Register 13, p. 204, Bernard-Claude Panet to John Holmes, 1 August 1827.

80 Ibid.

81 AAQ, 210-A, Register 13, p. 205, Bernard-Claude Panet to Jean-Jacques Lartique, 1 August 1827.

82 John Holmes, Nouvel abrégé de géographique moderne, suivi d'un appendice et d'un abrégé de géographie sacrée a l'usage de la jeunesse (Quebec: Neilson and Cowan, 1833).

83 ARCAT, PP, AA 04. Mary Power to Michael Power, 20 February, 1824.

84 AAQ, 312 CN, vol. 1: 80, John Carroll to Joseph-Octave Plessis, 27 August 1824.

85 AAM, 4-267, Jean-Jacques Lartigue to Bernard-Claude Panet, 11 October 1827. Lartigue informed Panet that Fraser's letter had arrived, and that the apostolic vicar was not amused.

CHAPTER THREE

1 Gerald R. Cragg, *The Church and the Age of Reason, 1648–1789* (London: Pelican Books, 1960), 34, 223.

2 Cornelius J. Jaenen, *The Role of the Church in New France* (Toronto: McGraw-Hill Ryerson, 1976), 3–36; Cornelius J. Jaenen, *Friend and Foe: Aspects of French-Amerindian Cultural Contact in the Sixteenth and Seventeenth Centuries* (Toronto: McClelland and Stewart, 1976).

3 Stanley Mealing, ed., *Jesuit Relations and Allied Documents* (Ottawa: Carleton University Press, 1985), 111–14, letter from Carheil to Callières sent from Michilimackinac.

4 Frederick Jackson Turner, "The Significance of the Frontier in American History," in *The Frontier Thesis and the Canadas: The Debate on the Impact of the Canadian Environment,* ed. Michael Cross (Toronto: Copp Clark, 1970), 12–22.

5 George Rawlyk, *Ravished by the Spirit: Religious Revivals, Baptists, and Henry Alline* (Kingston and Montreal: McGill-Queen's University Press, 1984); George Rawlyk, "Baptists and Religious Awakenings in Nova Scotia, 1776–1843," in *Prophets, Priests, and Prodigals: Readings in Canadian Religious History, 1608–Present,* ed. Mark G. McGowan and David B. Marshall (Toronto: McGraw-Hill Ryerson, 1992), 37–59.

6 William Westfall, *Two Worlds: The Protestant Culture of Nineteenth-Century Ontario* (Montreal and Kingston: McGill-Queen's University Press, 1989); William Westfall, "Order and Experience: Patterns of Religious Metaphor in Early Nineteenth-Century Upper Canada," in McGowan and Marshall, *Prophets,* 93–113; Neil Semple, *The Lord's Dominion: The History of Canadian Methodism* (Montreal and Kingston: McGill-Queen's University Press, 1996); S.D. Clark, "The Backwoods Society of Upper Canada," in *The Developing Canadian Community* (Toronto: University of Toronto Press, 1962), 63–80; John Webster Grant, *a profusion of spires: religion in nineteenth-century ontario* (Toronto: University of Toronto Press and Ontario Historical Studies Series, 1988), 52–67.

7 ADN, Paroisse St-Frédéric-de-Drummondville, box 1, 39, John Holmes to Bernard-Claude Panet, 24 August 1827.

8 AAM, Lartigue Papers, Register 4, 267/9, Jean-Jacques Lartigue to Bernard-Claude Panet, 29 September 1827.

9 AAQ, Register K, f64 verso, Bernard-Claude Panet, faculties to Michael Power, 28 May 1828.

10 J.I. Little, "Missionary Priests in Quebec's Eastern Townships: The Years of Hardship and Discontent, 1825–1853," Canadian Catholic Historical Association, *Study Sessions* 45 (1978): 21.

11 Ernestine Charland Rayotte, *Drummondville: 150 ans de vie quotidienne au coeur du Québec* (Drummondville, QC: Éditions des Cantons, 1972), 5–7.

12 Ibid., 12

13 Ibid., 36. For an excellent study of church architecture in eastern Canada, see Vicki Bennett, *Sacred Space and Structural Style* (Ottawa: University of Ottawa Press, 1999).

14 AAQ, Bernard-Claude Panet Papers, Registre de visite pastorale de 1830, 5–6 June, St-Frédéric-de-Drummondville, Cahier des visites, 69 CD, vol.8, p. 59.

15 Maurice O'Bready, *De K'tine à Sherbrooke esquisse historique de Sherbrooke: Des origines à 1954* (Sherbrooke: Université de Sherbrooke, 1973), 31; Fernand Ouellet, *Lower Canada, 1791–1840: Social Change and Nationalism*, trans. Patricia Claxton (Toronto: McClelland and Stewart, 1989), 34.

16 ARCAT, P, AB 09.01, Patrick Phelan to Michael Power, 17 November 1829.

17 O'Bready, *K'tine à Sherbrooke*, 32.

18 AAM, Lartigue Papers, Register 4, 366, Jean-Jacques Lartigue to Michael Power, 31 July 1828; Lartigue Papers, 901-085/ 828-1, Michael Power to Jean-Jacques Lartigue, 21 August 1828; O'Bready, *K'tine à Sherbrooke*, 59.

19 Little, "Missionary Priests," 23.

20 ADN, Paroisse St-Frédéric-de-Drummondville, box 1, 40, Michael Power to Bernard-Claude Panet, 19 January 1828.

21 ARCAT, PP, Accounts, AD 01.02, IOU to C.F.H. Goodhue for twelve pounds, ten shillings, 19 January 1830.

22 AAQ, 320 CN, vol. 6:16, Michael Power to Joseph Signay, 24 January 1843; ADN, Paroisse St-Frédéric-de-Drummondville, box 1, 40, Michael Power to Bernard-Claude Panet, 19 January 1828. Responses of John Holmes and Bernard-Claude Panet, 21 January 1828.

23 *St Patrick's Parish, 1887–1987* (Sherbrooke, QC: The Parish, 1987), 10.

24 AAM, Lartigue Papers, 901-085/831-1, Michael Power to Jean-Jacques Lartigue, 18 July 1831.

25 Ibid.

26 Jean-Pierre Wallot, "Religion and French-Canadian Mores in the Early Nineteenth Century," *Canadian Historical Review* 52 (1971): 51–91; Roberto Perin, "Elaborating a Public Culture: The Catholic Church in Nineteenth-Century Quebec," in *Religion and Public Life in Canada: Historical and Comparative Perspectives*, ed. Marguerite Van Die

(Toronto: University of Toronto Press, 2001), 89–107; Olivier Hubert, "Ritual Performance and Parish Sociability: French Canadian Catholic Families at Mass from the Seventeenth to the Nineteenth Century," in *Households of Faith: Family, Gender, and Community in Canada, 1760–1969*, ed. Nancy Christie (Montreal and Kingston: McGill-Queen's University Press, 2002); Lucien Lemieux, *Les années difficiles*, vol. 1 of *Histoire du catholicisme québécois: Les XVIII et XIX siècles* (Montreal: Boréal Express, 1989), 345–67.

27 Emmet Larkin, "The Devotional Revolution in Ireland, 1850–1875," *American Historical Review* 77 (1972): 625–52; Vincent J. McNally, "Who Is Leading? Archbishop John Thomas Troy and the Priests and People in the Archdiocese of Dublin, 1787–1823," Canadian Catholic Historical Association, *Historical Studies* 61 (1995): 153–70.

28 S.J. Connolly, *Priests and People in Pre-famine Ireland, 1780–1845* (New York: St Martin's Press, 1982); Murray J. Nicolson, "Irish Tridentine Catholicism in Victorian Toronto: Vessel for Ethno-Religious Persistence," Canadian Catholic Historical Association, *Study Sessions* 50, no. 2 (1983): 415–36.

29 ADN, Paroisse St-Frédéric-de-Drummondville, box 1, 40, Michael Power to Bernard-Claude Panet, 19 January 1828.

30 ADN, Paroisse St-Frédéric-de-Drummondville, box 1, 41, Michael Power to Bernard-Claude Panet, 10 August 1828.

31 Serge Gagnon, *Plaisirs d'amour et crainte de Dieu* (Ste-Foy, QC: Les presses de l'Université Laval, 1990).

32 ARCAT, Power Accounts, AD01.01, subscription to the *Gazette* (Montreal) and sundry receipts for canon-law texts; AD01.02, receipt, annual subscription for the *Jesuit* (Boston), 16 February 1830; receipts for the *Jesuit* and the *Catholic* (Kingston), 27 April 1831.

33 B. Pontbriand and J.M. Laliberté, *Mariages de Drummondville: St-Frédéric, 1815–1865* (n.p., 1965), 112.

34 Ibid. The following figures were gleaned from Power's 1827–31 tenure at the mission: French Canadian groom and French Canadian bride, 18 (39.1 per cent); French Canadian partner and other, 2 (4.3 per cent); French Canadian partner and Irish partner, 2 (4.3 per cent); Irish groom and Irish bride, 16 (34 per cent); Irish partner and other, 5 (10.9 per cent); other, 3 (6.5 per cent). All calculations are my own.

35 ADN, Paroisse St-Frédéric-de-Drummondville, box 1, 41, Michael Power to Bernard-Claude Panet, 10 August 1828.

36 AAQ, Cahier des visites, vol. 8, 69 CD, p. 59, 2–4 July 1830, 5–6 June 1830.

37 ADN, Paroisse St-Frédéric-de-Drummondville, box 1, 41, Michael Power to Bernard-Claude Panet, 23 April 1831.

38 Louis Rousseau and Frank W. Remiggi, *Atlas historiques des pratiques religieuses: Le sud-ouest du Québec au XIXe siècle* (Ottawa: University of Ottawa Press, 1998), 66.

39 ADN, Paroisse St-Frédéric-de-Drummondville, box 1, 41, Michael Power
    to Bernard-Claude Panet, 23 April 1831.

40 AAQ, 210-A, Register 14, 668, Bernard-Claude Panet to Michael Power,
    22 September 1831; Bernard-Claude Panet to Hugh Paisley, p. 459, 22
    September 1831.

41 AAQ, 210 A, Register 14, p. 457, Bernard-Claude Panet to Jean-Jacques
    Lartigue, 22 September 1831.

42 Cole Harris, "Of Poverty and Helplessness in Petite-Nation," *Canadian
    Historical Review*, 52 (1971): 23–4.

43 *Au coeur de la Petite-Nation: Le Château Montebello* (Ottawa: Les
    éditions de la Petite-Nation, 1984), 30–6.

44 Claude Baribeau, *La seigneurie de la Petite-Nation, 1801–1854: La rôle
    économique et sociale du seigneur* (Hull: Éditions Asticou, 1983), 21–9;
    Harris, "Of Poverty," 26.

45 Michel Chamberland, *Histoire de Notre-Dame-des-Sept-Douleurs de
    Grenville, PQ* (Montreal: Imprimerie des Sourds-Muets, 1931), 42.

46 One *arpent* is roughly equivalent to five-sixths of an acre, so six *arpents*
    is about five acres. Harris, "Of Poverty," 29.

47 John McCallum, *Unequal Beginnings: Agricultural and Economic Devel-
    opment in Quebec and Ontario until 1820* (Toronto: University of Toronto
    Press, 1980); Fernand Ouellet, *Lower Canada, 1791–1840: Social Change
    and Nationalism* (Toronto: McClelland and Stewart, 1980), 52–6; Gilles
    Paquet and Jean-Pierre Wallot, *Lower Canada at the Turn of the Nine-
    teenth Century: Restructuring and Modernization*, CHA Booklet 45
    (Ottawa: Canadian Historical Association, 1988); Harris, "Of Poverty,"
    30.

48 Hector Legros and Soeur Paul-Emile, SGC, *Le diocèse d'Ottawa, 1847–
    1948* (Ottawa: Le Droit, 1948), 139.

49 Andre Bricualt and Lucien Lavoie, *Le mémorial de Plaisance* (St-André
    Avellin: Les éditions de la Petite-Nation, 1986), 161.

50 Alexis de Barbizieux, OFM, *Histoire de la province ecclésiastique
    d'Ottawa et la colonisation dans la Vallée de l'Ottawa* (Ottawa: Imprim-
    erie d'Ottawa, 1897), 142.

51 Ibid., 143.

52 Ibid., 144.

53 Serge Courville, *Paroisses et municipalités de la région de Montréal au
    XIXe siècle (1825–1861): Répertoire documentaire et cartographique*
    (Quebec: Les presses de l'Université Laval, 1988), 81; NA, MG 24, B
    2, vol. 18, Papineau Family Papers, Notre-Dame-de-Bonsecours, 1821–
    1902, Assembly of Parishioners to Bernard-Claude Panet, 6 September
    1831. At that time, there were 120 families, comprising 450 communi-
    cants, in the parish.

54 AAM, Lartigue Papers, Register 6-108, Jean-Jacques Lartigue to Hugh
    Paisley, 8 October 1831.

55 Legros and Paul-Emile, *Diocèse d'Ottawa*, 139.

56 André Boucher, "La fabrique et les marguilliers," in *Le laïc dans l'église canadien-français de 1830 á nos jours*, by Pierre Hurtubise et al. (Montreal: Fides, 1972), 148–9.

57 Christian Dessureault and Christine Hudon, "Conflits sociaux et élites locales au Bas-Canada: Le clergé, les notables, les paysannerie et le contrôle de la fabrique," *Canadian Historical Review* 80 (1999): 414, 438; Boucher, "Fabrique," 149.

58 Rousseau and Remiggi, *Atlas historiques*, 92.

59 Lemieux, *Années difficiles*, 126.

60 Rousseau and Remiggi, *Atlas historiques*, 92.

61 Hubert, "Ritual Performance," 42.

62 NA, FN 8, G 23, vol. 1, Registre de la Paroisse Notre-Dame de Bonsecours, Montebello, Petite-Nation (1831–49), 23 October 1831, p. 67.

63 Baribeau, *Seigneurie de la Petite-Nation*, 32.

64 Ibid., 39.

65 NA, FN 8, G 23, vol. 1, Registre de la Paroisse Notre-Dame de Bonsecours, Montebello, Petite-Nation (1831–49). From 1831 to 1833, couples came from: Tipperary (2), Donegal (1), Tyrone (1), Carlow (2), Wexford (2), Meath (1), Cork (2), Mayo (4), and Down (1).

66 Baribeau, *Seigneurie de la Petite-Nation*, 32, 39, 59.

67 C. Thomas, *History of the Counties of Argenteuil, Quebec and Prescott, Ontario* (1892; reprint, Belleville, ON: Mika Publishing, 1981), 366–7, 380.

68 Verification of travel is in NA, FN 8, G 23, vol. 1, Registre de la Paroisse Notre-Dame de Bonsecours, Montebello, Petite-Nation (1831–49); see the entries from 23 October 1831 to 7 October 1833.

69 Ibid., March 1832 (109–13), and June 1832 (133–5).

70 Chamberland, *Histoire de Notre-Dame-des-Sept-Douleurs*, 42.

71 Geoffrey Bilson, *A Darkened House: Cholera in Nineteenth-Century Canada* (Toronto: University of Toronto Press, 1980), 5.

72 Ibid., introduction.

73 NA, FN 8, G 23, vol. 1, Registre de la Paroisse Notre-Dame de Bonsecours, Montebello, Petite-Nation (1831–49), 136–7.

74 Ibid., 152–6.

75 Donald MacKay, *Flight from Famine: The Coming of the Irish to Canada* (Toronto: McClelland and Stewart, 1990), 145.

76 NA, FN 8, G 23, vol. 1, Registre de la Paroisse Notre-Dame de Bonsecours, Montebello, Petite-Nation (1831–49), 67–180.

77 AAHQ, Michael Power to Jean-Jacques Lartigue, 23 December 1831.

78 Chamberland, *Histoire de Notre-Dame-des-Sept-Douleurs*, 153.

79 Ibid., 48; AAQ, Directories, October 1831.

80 Bricault and Lavoie, *Mémorial de Plaisance*, 162–3.

81 Cited in Bricault and Lavoie, *Mémorial de Plaisance*, 163; Chamberland, *Histoire de Notre-Dame-des-Sept-Douleurs*, 155.

82 Bricault and Lavoie, *Mémorial de Plaisance*, 163.

83 Chamberland, *Histoire de Notre-Dame-des-Sept-Douleurs*, 154.

84 AAHQ, Paroisse de Bonsecours, Montebello, Michael Power to Jean-Jacques Lartigue, 29 July 1833.

85 AAHQ, Paroisse de Bonsecours, Montebello, Michael Power to Jean-Jacques Lartigue, 10 December 1832.

86 Chamberland, *Histoire de Notre-Dame-des-Sept-Douleurs*, 52.

87 AAHQ, Paroisse de Bonsecours, Montebello, Michael Power to Jean-Jacques Lartigue, 10 December 1832.

88 Chamberland, *Histoire de Notre-Dame-des-Sept-Douleurs*, 151; Barbizieux, *Histoire de la province ecclésiastique*, 144.

89 AAHQ, Paroisse de Bonsecours, Montebello, Michael Power to Bernard-Claude Panet, 27 December 1831; NA, Papineau Family Papers, MG 24 B2, 3737; AAQ, 210-A, Register, vol. 15, p. 1, Bernard-Claude Panet to Michael Power, 19 January 1832.

90 AAHQ, Paroisse de Bonsecours, Montebello, Michael Power to Bernard-Claude Panet, 27 December 1831; Michael Power to Jean-Jacques Lartigue, 27 November 1832; Michael Power to Jean-Jacques Lartigue, 10 December 1832.

91 AAHQ, Paroisse de Bonsecours, Montebello, Michael Power to Jean-Jacques Lartigue, 27 November 1832.

92 AAHQ, Paroisse de Bonsecours, Montebello, Michael Power to Jean-Jacques Lartigue, 10 December 1832.

93 Harris, "Of Poverty," 36–7.

94 Ibid., 38–9.

95 AAM, Lartigue Papers, Register 6, no. 153, Jean-Jacques Lartigue to Michael Power, 24 November 1831; Register 6, nos 162–3, Jean-Jacques Lartigue to Alexander Macdonell, 3 December 1831. Power had similar authority in New York; Register 6, no. 464, Jean-Jacques Lartigue to Bishop de Fussala, coadjutor of Quebec, 5 November 1832.

96 AAM, Lartigue Papers, Register 6, no. 430, Jean-Jacques Lartigue to Alexander Macdonell, 18 October 1832; Register 7, no. 52, Jean-Jacques Lartigue to John Cullen, 31 January 1833.

97 AAK, Macdonell Papers, Letterbook, 1829–34, Alexander Macdonell to Jean-Jacques Lartigue, 13 June 1833.

98 AAM, Lartigue Papers, Register 7, nos 167–8, Jean-Jacques Lartigue to Michael Power, 6 July 1833; Register 7, nos 177–9, Jean-Jacques Lartigue to Michael Power, 12 July 1833; Chamberland, *Histoire de Notre-Dame-des-Sept-Douleurs*, 153.

99 Chamberland, *Histoire de Notre-Dame-des-Sept-Douleurs*, and Barbizieux, *Histoire de la province ecclésiastique* offer a kind version of the events.

100 AAM, Lartigue Papers, Register 7, no. 203, Jean-Jacques Lartigue to Alexander Macdonell, 4 August 1833; Register 7, nos 212–13, Jean-Jacques

Lartigue to Alexander Macdonell, 22 August 1833; AAK, Macdonell Letterbook, 1829–34, Alexander Macdonell to Jean-Jacques Lartigue, 29 August 1833.

101 NA, FN 8, G 23, vol. 1, Registre de Paroisse Notre-Dame-de-Bonsecours, 1830–49, pp. 95–147, 161–80. Power's last entry was 7 October 1833.

102 AAHQ, Paroisse de Bonsecours, Montebello, Michael Power to Jean-Jacques Lartigue, 29 July 1833.

103 AAM, Lartigue Papers, Register 7, no. 199, Jean-Jacques Lartigue to Michael Power, 2 August 1833.

104 Ibid.

105 AAM, Lartigue Papers, Register 7, nos 242–3, Jean-Jacques Lartigue to Joseph Signay, 23 September 1833.

106 AAQ, 210-A, Register 15, p. 494, Joseph Signay to Michael Power, 30 September 1833.

107 ARCAT, AB 04.02, Jean-Jacques Lartigue to Michael Power, 26 September 1833; AB 04.03, Jean-Jacques Lartigue to Michael Power, copy for Denis-Benjamin Papineau, 30 September 1833; Chamberland, *Histoire de Notre-Dame-des-Sept-Douleurs*, 158; Baribeau, *Seigneurie de la Petite-Nation*, 28; NA, Papineau Family Papers, MG 24 B2, vol. 18, Notre-Dame-de-Bonsecours, 1821–1982, Denis-Benjamin Papineau to Jean-Jacques Lartigue, 12 December 1833.

108 Turner, "Significance of the Frontier," 13–15.

109 S.D. Clark, *Church and Sect in Canada* (Toronto: University of Toronto Press, 1948), 107–9, 127–9. This is contrasted to William Westfall's appraisal of the convergence of religious order and experience on the frontier in his "Order and Experience: Patterns of Religious Metaphor in Early Nineteenth-Century Upper Canada," in McGowan and Marshall, *Prophets*, 106–9.

CHAPTER FOUR

1 Elie-J. Auclair, *Histoire de Châteauguay, 1735–1935* (Montreal: Beauchemin, 1935), 83.

2 Louis Rousseau and Frank W. Remiggi, *Atlas historiques des pratiques religieuses: Le sud-ouest du Québec au XIXe siècle* (Ottawa: University of Ottawa Press, 1998), 37.

3 Ibid., 53.

4 Ibid., 37; Diocese of Valleyfield, http://www.missa.org/de_val_smart.php; AAM, Register 7, p. 672, Jean-Jacques Lartigue to Michael Power, 25 February 1835.

5 Henriette Laberge-Boulianne, *Mariages de la paroisse de Ste-Martine (Co. Châteauguay), 1823–1972* (Montreal: Éditions Bergeron, 1982).

6 AAM, Register 7, 224/3, Jean-Jacques Lartigue to Joseph Signay, 23 September 1833 (regarding the need for an English-speaking priest in the

area); Register 7, 329, Jean-Jacques Lartigue to François-Xavier Marcoux, 3 December 1833.

7 AAM, Register 8, p. 265, Jean-Jacques Lartigue to Father Ryder, 19 September 1836; Register 8, p. 377, Jean-Jacques Lartigue to Michael Power, 27 March 1837; Register 8, Jean-Jacques Lartigue to Michael Power, 18 September 1837 (concerning Dolan).

8 AAM, Register 7, p. 289, Jean-Jacques Lartigue to Michael Power, 17 October 1833.

9 Auclair, *Histoire de Châteauguay*, 84.

10 Ibid., 87.

11 ARCAT, PP, Receipts 1833–39, receipts dated 31 December 1833 to 1 January 1838. Subscriptions were paid in full to the conservative papers *L'ami de peuple* and the Montreal *Gazette*, and to the radical *Vindicator*, published by Irish expatriate Dr Edmund Bailey O'Callaghan.

12 ARCAT, PP, AB 01.01, Ignace Bourget to Michael Power, 21 October 1833.

13 ARCAT, PP, AB 04.04, Jean-Jacques Lartigue to Michael Power, 4 January 1834 (concerning mixed marriage); AB 04.05, Jean-Jacques Lartigue to Michael Power, 31 December 1834 (cohabitation); ADV, Ste-Martine Parish, Michael Power to Jean-Jacques Lartigue, 20 December 1834 (banns of marriage); ARCAT, AB 04.05, Jean-Jacques Lartigue to Michael Power, 31 December 1834; AB 04.08, Jean-Jacques Lartigue to Michael Power, 11 February 1835 (here they discuss the particularly thorny case of Thomas Moore and Anne Burne, married 26 January 1835; see Laberge-Boulianne, *Mariages de la paroisse de Ste-Martine*, p.101); AB 04.07, Jean-Jacques Lartigue to Michael Power, 21 February 1835 (affinity); AB 04.12, Jean Jacques Lartigue to Michael Power, 12 December 1836 (second degree of consanguinity).

14 ARCAT, AB 04.09, Jean-Jacques Lartigue to Michael Power, 25 July 1835; AAM, Register 9, p.109, Jean-Jacques Lartigue to Michael Power, 7 September 1838.

15 ADV, Ste-Martine, Michael Power to Joseph Signay, 13 August 1834.

16 ARCAT, PP, AD 01.02, Michael Power to Peter Maher, 7 October 1839.

17 ARCAT, AB 04.10, Jean-Jacques Lartigue to Michael Power, 6 May 1836. The issue in question was the erection of a new cemetery.

18 ARCAT, AB 01.02, Ignace Bourget to Michael Power, 4 November 1834.

19 ADV, Ste-Martine, Michael Power to Ignace Bourget, 8 November 1834.

20 AAM, Register 7, pp. 597–8, Jean-Jacques Lartigue to Michael Power, 13 November 1834, marginal notes.

21 AAM, Register 8, p. 60, Jean-Jacques Lartigue to Michael Power, 7 December 1835.

22 AAM, Register 8, p. 197, Jean-Jacques Lartigue to Remi Gaulin, 15 May 1836; ARCAT, AB 04.11, Jean-Jacques Lartigue to Michael Power, 14 May 1836.

23 Pierre Hurtubise, Mark G. McGowan, and Pierre Savard, *Planted by Flowing Water: The Diocese of Ottawa, 1847–1997* (Ottawa: Novalis, 1998), 52, 69; Alexis de Barbizieux, OFM, *Histoire de la province ecclésiastique d'Ottawa et la colonisation dans la Vallée de l'Ottawa* (Ottawa: Imprimerie d'Ottawa, 1897); Louis J. Flynn, *Built on a Rock: The Story of the Roman Catholic Church in Kingston, 1826–1976* (Kingston: Archdiocese of Kingston, 1976).

24 AAM, Pièces et Actes, vol. 2, p.164, List of Clergy Certified by Hyacinthe Hudon and Michael Power; APF, Rome, SOCG, doc. 119, Petition of Quebec, September 1835; doc. 116, Joseph Signay to Hyacinthe Hudon, priest, and Michael Power, priest, 20 October 1836.

25 Rousseau and Remiggi, *Atlas historiques*, 34. The district of Montreal as it existed in 1835 contained the current dioceses of Montreal, St-Jerome, Amos, Hull-Gatineau, Joliette, St-Jean-Longueuil, St-Hyacinthe, Valleyfield, and part of the Archdiocese of Ottawa and the Diocese of Pembroke.

26 Lucien Lemieux, *L'établissement de la premier province ecclésiastique en Canada, 1783–1844* (Montreal: Fides, 1968), 457–8; John Moir, *The Church in the British Era* (Toronto: McGraw-Hill Ryerson, 1968), 64–79; John Moir, *Church and State in Canada*, Carleton Library Series (Toronto: McClelland and Stewart, 1967), 140–9.

27 A superior treatment of Lartigue's relations with the Sulpicians is found in Gilles Chaussé, "Face à Saint-Sulpice," in *Jean-Jacques Lartigue: Premier évêque de Montréal* (Montreal: Fides, 1980), 89–132.

28 AAQ, 320 CN, vol. 6, Haut-Canada, Michael Power to Pierre-Flavien Turgeon, 7 December 1835.

29 Lemieux, *L'établissement de la premier province ecclésiastique*, 376–9, 457–70.

30 AAM, Register 8, p. 672, Jean-Jacques Lartigue to Michael Power, 25 February 1835; Bourget Register 1, p. 65, Ignace Bourget to Michael Power, 4 May 1838; Lartigue Register 9, p. 210, 1 July 1839, Report of St-Philomène.

31 Lucien Lemieux, *Les années difficiles*, vol. 1 of *Histoire du catholicisme québécois: Les XVIII et XIX siècles* (Montreal: Boréal Express, 1989), 71.

32 Sources on the rebellions in Upper and Lower Canada are numerous. This is not surprising, given that during the period when national history was written in Canada, those historians bitten by the Whig tradition of constitutional history were preoccupied with the rebellions, their constitutional implications, and the evolution of parliamentary institutions in their aftermath. For this period of Power's life, I consulted Gerald M. Craig, *Upper Canada: The Formative Years, 1784–1841* (Toronto: McClel-

land and Stewart, 1967); Fernand Ouellet, *Lower Canada, 1791–1840: Social Change and Nationalism Lower Canada*, trans. Patricia Claxton (Toronto: McClelland and Stewart, 1980); Allan Greer, *The Patriots and the People: The Rebellion of 1837 in Lower Canada* (Toronto: University of Toronto Press, 1993); Jean-Paul Bernard, *Les rébellions 1837–38: Les patriotes du Bas Canada dans la mémoire collective et chez les historiens* (Montreal: Boréal Express, 1983); Fernand Ouellet, "The 1837/8 Rebellions in Lower Canada as a Social Phenomenon," in *Before Confederation*, vol. 1 of *Interpreting Canada's Past*, ed. J.M. Bumsted (Toronto: Oxford University Press, 1986); Jean-Paul Bernard, *The Rebellions of 1837 and 1838 in Lower Canada*, CHA Booklet 55 (Ottawa: Canadian Historical Association, 1995). For a basic chronicle of the military events, see Elinor Kyte Senior, *Redcoats and Patriotes: The Rebellions in Lower Canada* (Ottawa: Canadian War Museum, 1985).

33 Ouellet, "1837/8 Rebellions," 226; Jacques Monet, *The Last Cannon Shot* (Toronto: University of Toronto Press, 1966), chapter 1; Pierre Savard, "Le catholicisme canadien-français au XIXe siècle," *Histoire sociale/Social History* 7 (1971): 70–1; François Beaudin, "L'influence de La Mennais sur Mgr Lartigue, premier évêque de Montréal," *Revue d'histoire de l'Amérique française* 25 (1971): 225–37; Thomas Matheson, "La Mennais et l'education au Bas-Canada," *Revue d'histoire de l'Amérique française* 13 (1960): 476–91.

34 Bernard, *Rebellions of 1837 and 1838*, 2–4.

35 Fernand Ouellet, *Economic and Social History of Quebec, 1760–1850*, Carleton Library Series (Ottawa: Carleton University Press, 1980, 333–4.

36 Ibid., 338–9; John McCallum, *Unequal Beginnings: Agricultural and Economic Development in Quebec and Ontario until 1820* (Toronto: University of Toronto Press, 1980), chapters 2–3.

37 Greer, *Patriots and the People*, 52–86.

38 Note Power's earlier comments on the farmers at Williamstown.

39 Ouellet, "1837/8 Rebellions," 216–17; *Report of the State Trials before a General Court Martial Held at Montreal, 1838–9* (Montreal: Armour and Ramsay, 1839), 1:314.

40 Ouellet, *Economic and Social History*, 284; Greer, *Patriots and the People*, 270–2.

41 Allan Greer, "L'habitant, la paroisse rurale et la politique locale au XVIIIe siècle: Quelques cas dans la Vallée du Richelieu," Société canadienne d'histoire de l'église catholique, *Sessions d'études* 47 (1980): 30–1; Christian Dessureault and Christine Hudon, "Conflits sociaux et élites locales au Bas-Canada: Le clergé, les notables, les paysannerie et le contrôle de la fabrique," *Canadian Historical Review* 80 (1999): 413–39.

42 Mary Finnegan, "Irish-French Relations in Lower Canada," Canadian Catholic Historical Association, *Historical Studies* 52 (1985): 45; Greer, *Patriots and the People*, 66.

43 Greer, *Patriots and the People*, 77.

44 Jack Verney, *O'Callaghan: The Making and Unmaking of a Rebel* (Ottawa: Carleton University Press, 1994), 67–8; Robert C. Daly, "The Irish of Lower Canada and the Rise of French Canadian Nationalism" (paper presented at the annual meeting of the Canadian Historical Association, Guelph, ON, 1984); Maureen Slattery, "Irish Radicalism in Montreal and Dublin, 1833–34: O'Callaghan and O'Connell Compared," Canadian Catholic Historical Association, *Historical Studies* 63 (1997): 31–2.

45 Ouellet, *Economic and Social History*, 425–6.

46 Jean-Jacques Lartigue, "Mandement, 24 October 1837," in *Mandements, lettres pastorales, circulaires et autres documents publie dans le Diocèse de Montréal* (Montreal: J. Chapleau et Fils, 1887), 1:20–1.

47 Lemieux, *Années difficiles*, 384.

48 Senior, *Redcoats and Patriotes*, 94.

49 One can glean a considerable knowledge of Power's library and regular reading by examining his receipts. ARCAT, PP, box 1, group AA, Receipts for Books and Newspapers, 1830–41.

50 Slattery, "Irish Radicalism," 47–51.

51 Verney, *O'Callaghan*, 93–4, 99, 105–8.

52 Chaussé, *Jean-Jacques Lartigue*, 247; ARCAT, PP, Subscriptions and Receipts, *L'ami de peuple*, 28 November 1838.

53 Brian Young, *In Its Corporate Capacity: The Seminary of Montreal as a Business Institution* (Montreal and Kingston: McGill-Queen's University Press, 1986), 47–8.

54 AAM, Bourget Register 1, p. 230, Ignace Bourget to Michael Power, 19 October 1838.

55 Senior, *Redcoats and Patriotes*, 75–92.

56 Ibid., 132.

57 See Craig, *Upper Canada*.

58 "Circulaire: À Sa Tres-Éxcellent Majesté la Reine, December 1837," in *Mandements, lettres pastorales, circulaires et autres documents*, 23–4.

59 ADSJQ, 3/A 190, Note from Priests, Châteauguay, 16 January1838.

60 Jean-Jacques Lartigue, "Mandement: À l'occasion des troubles de 1837, 8 January 1838," in *Mandements, lettres pastorales, circulaires et autres documents*, 24–31.

61 *Report of the State Trials*, 2:162; see also 1:314, 318.

62 Senior explains the leadership structure of the Frères Chasseurs as follows: Grand Eagle (a district commander); Eagle (akin to a colonel over 500 men); Castor (a captain over a company); Raquette (a junior officer; six of them reported to the Castor); nine Frères Chasseurs reported to each Raquette. Senior, *Redcoats and Patriotes*, 155.

63 Montreal *Gazette*, 19 October 1839; APQ, Événements 1837–8, Examination of Louis Thibault, 24 November 1838, no. 2,052.

64 *Report of the State Trials*, Extract from the Copy of a Voluntary Deposition, Montreal Prison, November 1838 [Jean-Baptiste-Henri Brien], 2:548–61; Montreal *Gazette*, 19 October 1839.

65 *Report of the State Trials*, 1:304.

66 APQ, Événements 1837–8, reel M165/4, Depositions of Paul Barré, 24 November 1838, frame 2,275; Louis Gédéon Neveau, 22 November 1838, frame 2,372; Vital St-Onge Payant, frame 2,049; Louis Thibault, 24 November 1838, frame 2,052; Michel Tremblay, 24 November 1838, frame 2,051; Louis Turcot, 27 December 1838, frame 2,042; François Vallée, 27 December 1838, frame 2,391.

67 Ouellet, "1837/8 Rebellions," 37–8, 215; Michael Power, as we will see, would intervene on behalf of those whom he believed were unjustly arrested.

68 Senior, *Redcoats and Patriotes*, 171; Bernard, *Rébellions de 1837–38*, 124–5; APQ, Événements 1837–38, Examination of Vital St-Onge Payant, 24 November 1838, no. 2,049. Payant alleged that only about 100 of the 300 who left Ste-Martine were carrying firearms.

69 Montreal *Gazette*, 19 October 1839. The issue contained Brien's full confession, which earned him exile instead of execution. Report of the State Trials, 1:305, Testimony of Lawrence George Brown, 295–9.

70 Senior, *Redcoats and Patriotes*, 171–2; *Beauharnois ... d'hier à aujourd'hui*, preface by Claude Haineault (Beauharnois: Ville de Beauharnois, 1986), 49–53; Monteal *Gazette*, 6 November 1838, 20 November 1838; APQ, Événements 1837–8, Examination of Michel Tremblay, 24 November 1838, no. 2,051.

71 *Report of the State Trials*, 1:304–15; Montreal *Gazette*, 19 October 1839.

72 APQ, Événements 1837–8, Examination of Joseph Dumouchel, 7 December 1838, no. 2040.

73 *Report of the State Trials*, 2:154–6, 158–64 (helpful are the testimonies of Robert Feeny, Robert Orr Wilson, Catherine Anne Cairns, and David McClennaghan); Montreal *Gazette*, 20 November 1838.

74 *Report of the State Trials*, 1:308, Testimony of John Ross, 12 January 1839; Montreal *Gazette*, 19 October 1839; Bernard, *Rébellions de 1837–38*, 131–5, 294 (list of *patriotes*); Aegidius Fauteux, *Patriotes de 1837–1838* (Montreal: Éditions des Dix, 1950), 139, 235–6.

75 See appendix 2.

76 Montreal *Gazette*, 20 May 1842.

77 *Cross*, 23 October 1847.

78 *Report of the State Trials*, 2:146–7; Montreal *Gazette*, 20 November 1838.

79 Montreal *Gazette*, 8 November 1838, 13 November 1838; *L'ami de peuple*, 21 November 1838.

80 Laberge-Boulianne, *Mariages de la paroisse de Ste-Martine*, 108.

81 NA, MG 24, A 40, vol. 19, Colbourne Papers, Major John Campbell to Captain T. L Goldies, 11 November 1838, frame 5,578.

82 AAM, Register 9, p. 639, Jean-Jacques Lartigue to Michael Power, 26 November 1838; p. 148, Jean-Jacques Lartigue to Michael Power, 2 January 1839.

83 NA, Colbourne Papers, Major John Campbell to Captain T. L Goldies, 11 November 1838, frame 5,578. Campbell asserts, "yesterday two hundred and thirty-seven of the Stormont Militia joined with a few hundred Indians when Rebels immediately left their camp which we took possession of and destroyed Bakers, Perrigods and Vallées houses."

84 See appendix 2. These fifty-one children can be attributed to only ten of the married men.

85 APQ, Événements 1837–8, List of Michael Power, no. 2,236–8. The list is supplemented by lists found in Bernard, Rébellions de 1837–38, 131–5.

86 *Report of the State Trials*, 2:141–86.

87 Bernard, *Rébellions de 1837–38*, 125.

88 APQ, Événements 1837–8, Michael Power to military authorities, 24 January 1839, no. 2,390; Examination of Gédéon Brazeau, no. 2,291; Examination of François Vallée, no. 2,391.

89 APQ, Événements 1837–8, Court Transcript, François Vallée, 2 December 1839, no. 3,132.

90 APQ, Événements 1837–8, Examination of Louis Turcot, 27 December 1838, no. 2,042.

91 F. Murray Greenwood, trans. and ed., *Land of a Thousand Sorrows: The Australia Prison Journal, 1840–1842, of the Exiled Canadian Patriote François-Maurice Depailleur* (Vancouver: University of British Columbia Press, 1980), 96. These transcriptions are not without their problems, as Brian M. Petrie indicates in "Social Misconstructions in the Analysis of the Australian Experiences of the French-Canadian Patriote Convicts, 1839–1848," *Histoire sociale/Social History* 22 (1999): 63–72.

92 APQ, Événements 1837–8, Deposition of Louis Gédéon Neveu, no. 2,372; Examination of Louis Thibault, no. 2,052.

93 *Seigneurie de Beauharnois, cadastre abrégé*, 1854, Williamstown, Village of Ste-Martine, ref. no. 2,995 www.rootsweb.com/~qcchatea/cadastre/vil-mart.htm.

94 *Report of the State Trials*, 1:369–79; Montreal *Gazette*, 19 October 1839; Fauteux, *Patriotes*, 141–3; APQ, Événements 1837–8, Examination of Jean-Baptiste-Henri Brien, no. 2,037.

95 See Greenwood, *Land of a Thousand Sorrows*.

96 Ibid., 65, 113.

97 Fauteux, *Patriotes*, 109 (Bergevin), 150 (Buisson), 235 (Dumouchel), and 386 (Turcot); *Seigneurie de Beauharnois*, 60–1 (Bergevin).

98 NA, Lord Stanley Papers, Roman Catholic Bishopric, 1841–51, appendix 1, Michael Power to Lord Stanley, 27 September 1841, reel A-31.

99 Montreal *Gazette*, 20 May 1842.

100 NA, Bagot Papers, MG 24, A 13, vol. 6, Letterbook, p. 313, Sir Charles Bagot to Lord Stanley (confidential letter), 8 July 1842; Lemieux indicates that Sydenham regarded Power as thoroughly loyal (Lemieux, *L'établissement de la premier province ecclésiastique*, 407).

CHAPTER FIVE

1 AAM, Register 9, p. 230, Jean-Jacques Lartigue to Michael Power, 15 September 1839.

2 Louis Rousseau and Frank W. Remiggi, *Atlas historiques des pratiques religieuses: Le sud-ouest du Québec au XIXe siècle* (Ottawa: University of Ottawa Press, 1998), 217–18.

3 Louis Lavallée, *Laprairie en Nouvelle France, 1647–1760* (Montreal and Kingston: McGill-Queen's University Press, 1992), 113–14.

4 Ibid., 12, 53 (maps).

5 Rousseau and Remiggi, 217–18.

6 Allan Greer, *The Patriots and the People: The Rebellion of 1837 in Lower Canada* (Toronto: University of Toronto Press, 1993), 81–2, 343, 345–6, 355.

7 Ibid., 239; APQ, Événements 1837–8, Wetherel to Civil Secretary, 14 November 1839, no. 3,731.

8 Chanoine J. Chevalier, *Laprairie: Notes historiques à l'occasion de centenaire de l'église* (Laprairie: Paroisse, 1941), 128.

9 AAM, Bourget Papers, Register 2, p. 276, Ignace Bourget to Michael Power, 12 December 1840.

10 AAM, Bourget Papers, Register 2, p. 56, Ignace Bourget to Michael Power, 6 March 1840; Chevalier, *Laprairie*, 22.

11 AAM, Pièces et actes de Msgr Bourget, vol. 4, p.6, 5 May 1842; ARCAT, PP, AD 01.03, Antoine Bourdon to Michael Power, 14 December 1840; AAM Register 2, p. 261, 2 December 1841 (approval for the use of the old sacristy); Chevalier, *Laprairie*, 123–5.

12 Chevalier, *Laprairie*, 123-5.

13 AAQ, 26 CP, Montreal D:112, Joseph Marcoux to Pierre-Flavien Turgeon, 22 May 1841.

14 ADSJLQ, Laprairie Parish, 2A/125, Michael Power to "Monseigneur," 27 March 1841. This particular case brought into question the canonicity of a Catholic taking an active role in the funeral of a Protestant. The letter is presumably written to Bourget, since it indicates that the normal communication route to Montreal was cut off and the letter had to take a more circuitous journey to the chancery via Longueuil. Power saved his

casebooks from his seminary years, including applications of the canon laws of marriage and confession in the Quebec context. ARCAT, Holograph Collection, HO C001.03, Bishop Power's Notes While a Student, pp. 23, 56; a good copy of this notebook is found in ARCAT, PP, AA 03.01.

15 Lucien Lemieux, *L'établissement de la premier province ecclésiastique en Canada, 1783–1844* (Montreal: Fides, 1968).

16 ADSJLQ, Laprairie Parish, 3A/235, Michael Power to Ignace Bourget, 5 August 1840.

17 For a brief biography of MacDonald, consult Art O'Shea, *A Faith Walk, Diocese of Charlottetown. Un sentir de foi* (Strasbourg: Éditions de Signe, 2002), 33–4.

18 John Edward FitzGerald, "Conflict and Culture in Irish-Newfoundland Roman Catholicism" (Ph.D. diss., University of Ottawa, 1997), 426. As late as 1843, Fleming remained intransigent in his opposition to being included in the proposed metropolitan province of Quebec. AAQ 320 CN, vol. 6:22, Michael Power to Pierre-Flavien Turgeon, 6 November 1843.

19 AAQ, 320 cn, vol. 6, Haut-Canada, Michael Power to Pierre-Flavien Turgeon, 12 November 1840.

20 Ibid.

21 *Cross*, 23 October 1847.

22 Among the best discussions of Ultramontanism in Quebec are: Nive Voisine and Jean Hamelin, *Les ultramontanes canadiens-français: Études d'histoire religieuses presentées en hommage au professeur Philippe Sylvain* (Montreal: Boréal Express, 1985); Philippe Sylvain and Nive Voisine, *Réveil et consolidation, 1840–1898*, vol. 2 of *L'histoire du catholicisme québécois* (Montreal: Boréal Express, 1991); Roberto Perin, "Elaborating a Public Culture: The Catholic Church in Nineteenth Century Quebec," in *Religion and Public Life in Canada: Historical and Comparative Perspectives*, ed. Marguerite Van Die (Toronto: University of Toronto Press, 2001), 87–105; *A Concise History of Christianity in Canada*, ed. Terrence Murphy and Roberto Perin (Toronto: Oxford University Press, 1996), of note is Perin's chapter, "French-Speaking Canada From 1840," 190–260; Jacques Monet, "French Canadian Nationalism and the Challenge of Ultramontanism," Canadian Historical Association, *Historical Papers* (1966): 41–55.

23 Joseph de Maistre, *Considerations on France*, trans. Richard LeBrun (Montreal and Kingston: McGill-Queen's University Press, 1974).

24 Marie-Joseph Le Guillou, OP, "The Mennaisian Crisis," in *Progress and Decline in the History of Church Renewal*, ed. Roger Aubert, Concilium Series 27 (New York: Paulist Press, 1967, 109–18; Marvin O'Connell, "Montalembert at Mechlin: A Reprise of 1830," *Journal of Church and State* 26 (1984): 515–36; Félicité de Lamennais, "L'avenir," in *Lamennais and the Dilemma of French Catholicism*, ed. Peter Stearns (New York: Harper and Row, 1967), 168–81; Thomas Bokenkotter, *Church and*

Revolution: Catholics in the Struggle for Democracy and Social Justice (New York: Image, 1998), 39–81.

25 Marvin R. O'Connell, "Ultramontanism and Dupanloup: The Compromise of 1865," *Church History* 53 (1984): 200–17; Frank J. Coppa, "Cardinal Antonelli, the Papal States, and the Counter-Risorgimento," *Journal of Church and State* 16 (1974): 453–71; Gene Burns, *The Frontiers of Catholicism: The Politics of Ideology in a Liberal World* (Berkeley: University of California Press, 1994), 25–8; E.E.Y. Hales, *The Catholic Church in the Modern World* (New York: Image, 1960), 82–99; Gregory XVI, "Mirari Vos," "Singulari Nos," *The Papal Encyclicals*, ed. Claudia Carlen (New York: McGrath Publishing, 1981), 1:235–350.

26 Gilles Chaussé, "Un évêque mannaisien au Canada: Monseigneur Jean-Jacques Lartigue," in *Voisine and Hamelin, Ultramontanes*, 104–20.

27 Monet, "French Canadian Nationalism," 41–7.

28 Ann Taves, *The Household of Faith: Roman Catholic Devotions in Mid-Nineteenth-Century America* (Notre Dame: University of Notre Dame Press, 1986), 21–46, 89–112.

29 Brian P. Clarke, *Piety and Nationalism: Lay Voluntary Associations and the Creation of an Irish-Catholic Community in Toronto, 1850–1895* (Montreal and Kingston: McGill-Queen's University Press, 1993), 62–96, 97–126.

30 Francis Xavier Curran, SJ, *The Return of the Jesuits* (Chicago: Loyola University Press, 1966), 57–97; Paul Desjardins, SJ, *Le Collège Sainte-Marie de Montréal: La fondation, le fondateur* (Montreal: Collège Sainte-Marie, 1940), 17–29; Mary Alban Bouchard, CSJ, "Pioneers Forever: The Sisters of St Joseph of Toronto and their Ventures in Social Welfare and Health Care," in *"Catholics at the Gathering Place": Historical Essays on the Archdiocese of Toronto, 1841–1991*, ed. Mark G. McGowan and Brian P. Clarke (Toronto: Canadian Catholic Historical Association; Dundurn Press, 1993), 105–18; Donat Levasseur, OMI, *Les Oblats de Marie Immaculée dans l'ouest et le nord du Canada, 1845–1967* (Edmonton: University of Alberta Press; Western Canadian Publishers, 1995), 21–36; Robert Choquette, *The Oblate Assault on Canada's Northwest* (Ottawa: University of Ottawa Press, 1995), 6–11; Leon Pouliot, SJ, *Monseigneur Bourget et sons temps* (Montreal: Bellarmin, 1972), 3:75–97.

31 Gilles Chaussé, *Jean-Jacques Lartigue: Premier évêque de Montréal* (Montreal: Fides, 1980), chapter 6.

32 Louis Rousseau, "Les missions populaires de 1840–1842: Acteurs principaux et consequences," Société canadienne d'histoire de l'église catholique, *Sessions d'études* 53 (1986): 9; Pouliot, *Monseigneur Bourget*, chapter 3; Roberto Perin, "Nationalism and the Church in French Canada, 1840–1880," *Bulletin of Canadian Studies* 1, no. 1 (1973): 30.

33 Mason Wade, *The French Canadians, 1760–1967* (Toronto: Macmillan, 1968), 1:360; Clarke, *Piety and Nationalism*, 1.

34 Murray Nicolson, "Michael Power: First Catholic Bishop of Toronto," Canadian Catholic Historical Association, *Historical Studies* 54 (1987): 28; ARCAT, PP, Ignace Bourget to Michael Power, 25 April 1841.

35 Rousseau and Remeggi, *Atlas historiques*, 70; *L'aurore des Canadas*, 6 October 1840.

36. *Prémices des mélanges religieux*, 14 December 1840, 26 December 1840, 8 January 1841, 20 January 1841.

37 Rousseau and Remeggi, *Atlas historiques*, 11–12.

38 *Prémices des mélanges religieux*, 21 December 1840.

39 Rousseau, "Missions populaires," 10–13.

40 William Westfall, *Two Worlds: The Protestant Culture of Nineteenth-Century Ontario* (Montreal and Kingston: McGill-Queen's University Press, 1989), 57; George Rawlyk, "New Lights, Baptists and Religious Awakenings in Nova Scotia, 1776–1843," in *Prophets, Priests, and Prodigals: Readings in Canadian Religious History, 1608–Present*, ed. Mark G. McGowan and David B. Marshall (Toronto: McGraw, Hill Ryerson, 1992), 53–6.

41 *Prémices des mélanges religieux*, 29 January 1841.

42 Rousseau, "Missions populaires," 20; *Prémices des mélanges religieux*, 15 October 1841, 12 November 1841.

43 AAM, Bourget Papers, 255.104, 840-1, Michael Power to Ignace Bourget, 14 December 1840; ARCAT, PP, Ignace Bourget to Michael Power, 25 April 1841.

44 Pouliot, *Monseigneur Bourget*, 2:54.

45 AAM, Bourget Papers, Register 1, p. 347, Ignace Bourget to Remi Gaulin, 25 April 1841.

46 Pouliot, *Monseigneur Bourget*, 2:52–3; Lemieux, *L'établissement*, 460.

47 AAQ, 26 CP, Montreal 8:51, Ignace Bourget to Pierre-Flavien Turgeon, 25 April 1841; Pouliot, Monseigneur Bourget, 2:54; Vincent McNally, *The Lord's Distant Vineyard: A History of the Oblates and the Catholic Community in British Columbia* (Edmonton: University of Alberta Press; Western Canadian Publishers, 2000), 6–9.

48 AAM, Register 1, pp. 335–6, Ignace Bourget to Remi Gaulin, 13 April 1841; *Prémices des mélanges religieux*, 30 April 1841.

49 AAM, Bourget Papers, Register 1, p.347, Ignace Bourget to Remi Gaulin, 25 April 1841.

50 APF, SOCG, doc. 176, Testimony of Bishop Joseph Signay of Quebec and Pierre-Flavien Turgeon, Bishop of Sidyme, 29 April 1841, pp. 778–9; ARCAT, LB .004, Remi Gaulin to Pope Gregory XVI, 2 June 1841; AAM, Bourget Papers, Register 1, Ignace Bourget to Pierre-Flavien Turgeon, 25 April 1841.

51 APF, SOCG, doc. 175, Ignace Bourget and Remi Gaulin to Propaganda Fide.

52 AAQ, 26 CP, Montreal D:112, Joseph Marcoux to Pierre-Flavien Turgeon, 22 May 1841.

53 Pouliot, *Monseigneur Bourget*, 2:57–8.

54 Ibid., 2:55–9.

55 Ibid., 2:59.

56 Rousseau, "Missions populaires," 15.

57 See Choquette, *Oblate Assault*; Raymond Huel, *Preaching the Gospel to the Indians and the Métis* (Edmonton: University of Alberta Press, 1996); Levasseur, *Oblats de Marie Immaculée*; Martha McCarthy, *From the Great River to the Ends of the Earth: Oblate Missions to the Dene, 1847–1921* (Edmonton: University of Alberta Press, 1995); McNally, *Lord's Distant Vineyard*.

58 Herbert Thurston, SJ, and Donald Attwater, eds., *Butler's Lives of the Saints*, (New York: P.J. Kennedy and Sons, 1956), 2:668–9. In *The Count of Monte Cristo* (1844), Alexandre Dumas offers some of the most vivid and contemporary imagery of Roman feasts as they were practised during the pontificate of Gregory XVI. *The Count of Monte Cristo*, trans. Robin Buss (London: Penguin, 1996), 284.

59 Stendhal, *A Roman Journal*, trans. and ed. Haakon Chevalier (New York: Collier, 1961), 23–4.

60 A similar voyage to Italy is outlined by Eugénie de la Rochère in *Rome: Souvenirs religieux, historiques, artistiques* (Tours: A. Mame, 1854), 4.

61 Pouliot, *Monseigneur Bourget*, 2:66.

62 Stendhal, *Roman Journal*, 104.

63 *Journals of Francis Parkman*, ed. Mason Wade (New York: Houston and Brothers Publishing, 1947), 1:176 (the log of his Roman trip is found on pages 175–201); Dumas, *Count of Monte Cristo*, 342–56.

64 Christopher Hibbert, *Rome: The Biography of the City* (New York: W.W. Norton and Company, 1985), 243.

65 Ibid., 244–6.

66 Rochère, *Rome: Souvenirs*, 84a.

67 Pouliot, *Monseigneur Bourget*, 2:69; see also Gregory XVI, "Mirari Vos," "Singulari Nos."

68 ARCAT, PP, AB 08.01, Pierre-Flavien Turgeon to Michael Power, 29 April 1841.

69 APF–SOCG, vol. 960, doc. 161, Relazione della cose del Canada, voto Msgr Corboli, 21 November 1841, p. 747; APF-SOCG, 1841, doc. 193, Ignace Bourget to Ignazio Giovanni Cadolini, 20 July 1841.

70 APF-SOCG, vol. 920, doc. 161, Voti di Msgr Corboli, relazione della cose del Canada, 21 November 1841, p. 748.

71 Pouliot, *Monseigneur Bourget*, 2:69.

72 APF-SOCG, vol. 960, doc. 197, Michael Power to Ignazio Giovanni Cadolini, 28 July 1841.

73 Ibid.

74 ARCAT, PP, F 01.10, undated.

75 APF-SOCG, vol. 920, doc. 161, Voti di Msgr Corboli, relazione della cose del Canada, 21 November 1841, p. 752.

76 APF, Series 2, Acta 204, folio 536, pp. 540–3, Cardinal Castruccio Castracane to Ignazio Giovanni Cadolini, Propaganda Fide, 15 November 1841. It was recommended that Kingston be divided and Power named bishop of Upper Canada.

77 McNally, *Lord's Distant Vineyard*, 9. François Blanchet was appointed vicar apostolic of Oregon on 1 December 1843, and in 1845 he was consecrated in Montreal by Bourget, Gaulin, and Patrick Phelan.

78 APF-SOCG, vol. 965, folio 249–252, doc. 289, p. 262, Lord Glenelg to the Earl of Gosford, 26 May 1836 (copy).

79 Lemieux, *L'établissement*, 462, 464, 466. APF, Series 2, Acta 204, folio 536, p. 543, Cardinal Castruccio Castracane to Ignazio Giovanni Cadolini, Propaganda Fide, 15 November 1841.

80 ARCAT, LB 01.010, Ignace Bourget to Ignazio Giovanni Cadolini, 18 August 1841 (copy).

81 APF-SOCG, doc. 195, Ignace Bourget to Lord John Russell, 15 June 1841 (copy).

82 Lemieux, *L'établissement*, 463.

83 Pouliot, *Monseigneur Bourget*, 2:72; *Prémices des mélanges religieux*, 24 September 1841. He left Liverpool on 4 September and arrived in Montreal on 23 September.

84 NA, Lord Stanley Papers, Summary of Roman Catholic Archbishop for North American Colonies, excerpt from Ignace Bourget to Lord Stanley, 4 September 1841.

85 Pouliot, *Monseigneur Bourget*, 2:72, n.43.

86 Peter Ackroyd, *Dickens* (London: Vintage, 1994), 45, 227.

87 Peter Ackroyd, *London: The Biography* (London: Chatto and Windus, 2000), 137–8.

88 NA, Stanley Papers, Summary of Roman Catholic Archbishop for North American Colonies, appendix 1, Michael Power to Lord Stanley, 27 September 1841.

89 Ibid.

90 Ibid.

91 NA, Stanley Papers, Summary of Roman Catholic Archbishop for North American Colonies, appendix 9, letter 217, Lord Stanley to Sir Charles Bagot, 3 August 1842.

92 The precedent for new Catholic bishops in the Canadas had already been set with the appointment of Lartigue to Montreal in 1830. NA, Stanley Papers, Summary of Roman Catholic Archbishop for North American Colonies, appendix 2, A.B. to Lord Stanley, 3 October 1841; appendix 5, Lord Stanley to Sir Charles Bagot, 20 May 1842.

93 NA, Stanley Papers, Summary of Roman Catholic Archbishop for North American Colonies, appendix 1, Michael Power to Lord Stanley, 27 September 1841.

94 Ibid.

95 NA, Stanley Papers, Summary of Roman Catholic Archbishop for North American Colonies, appendix 2, A.B. to Lord Stanley, 3 October 1841.

96 Edward Norman, *The English Catholic Church in the Nineteenth Century* (New York: Oxford University Press, 1984), 124.

97 NA, Stanley Papers, Summary of Roman Catholic Archbishop for North American Colonies, appendix 3, Nicholas Wiseman to Lord Stanley, 14 January 1842.

98 NA Stanley Papers, Summary of Roman Catholic Archbishop for North American Colonies, appendix 4, Extract from Opinion of Law Officers, 11 April 1842.

99 APF-SOCG, vol. 299, William Walsh to Cardinal Giacomo Fransoni, Prefect of the Propaganda Fide, 29 June 1844.

100 APF-SOCG, vol. 965, item 281, Decree, Luigi Amat di San Filippo e Sasi, Prefect, 13 May 1844, 1; ARCAT, LB 01.127/128, Bishop Joseph Signay to Michael Power, 3 December 1844 (copy); LB 01.129, Bull Read at Solemn Mass, 29 December 1844.

101 NA, Stanley Papers, Summary of Roman Catholic Archbishop for North American Colonies, appendix 8, Sir Charles Bagot to Lord Stanley, 8 July 1842; appendix 10, Sir Charles Metcalfe to Lord Stanley, 20 February 1845.

102 NA, Stanley Papers, Summary of Roman Catholic Archbishop for North American Colonies, appendix 2, William Hope to Michael Power, 27 September 1841.

103 AAM, Bourget Papers, 420.085, doc. 841-4, Michael Power to Ignace Bourget, 2 October 1841; 420.085, 841-1, Notes Mr Power; AAM, Register 1, p. 421, Ignace Bourget to Pierre-Flavien Turgeon, 25 November 1841.

104 Pouliot, *Monseigneur Bourget*, 2:80–3.

105 NA, Stanley Papers, Summary of Roman Catholic Archbishop for North American Colonies, appendix 2, Michael Power to Lord Stanley, 13 October 1841; ARCAT, LB 01.023, C.W. Hope to Michael Power, 19 October 1841 (copy). Hope told Power that he did not know when decisions would be made regarding Bourget's applications.

106 ARCAT, LB 01.013, Papal Bull of Gregory XVI, 17 December 1841; LB 01.014, Gregory XVI, Appointment to Ecclesia Occidentalis Provinciae Canadae Superioris, 17 December 1841.

107 ARCAT, LB 01.018, Michael Power to The Most Holy Father, 9 January 1842.

108 AAM, Kingston Correspondence, 255-102, 842-4, Remi Gaulin to Ignace Bourget, 20 March 1842.

109 AAM, Register 1, pp. 512–13, Ignace Bourget to Remi Gaulin, 8 April 1842.

110 ADSJLQ, Laprairie Parish, 2A/126, Michael Power to Ignace Bourget, 10 April 1842; a copy of this letter is held in ARCAT, LB 01.012.

111 ARCAT, LB 02.001, Michael Power to Remi Gaulin, 19 April 1842; *Prémices des mélanges religieux*, 15 April 1842.

112 AAM, Register 1, Ignace Bourget to Michael Power, 15 April 1842; Kingston Correspondence, Remi Gaulin to Ignace Bourget, 255-102, 842-5, 11 April 1842.

113 James A. Schmeiser, "The Development of Canadian Ecclesiastical Provinces, Councils, Rituals, and Catechisms from the Time of Bishop François Montmorency Laval (1658) to the Plenary Council of Quebec," *Studia Canonica* 5, no.1 (1971): 135–65.

114 Thomas à Kempis, *The Imitation of Christ*, trans. and ed. Joseph N. Tylenda, SJ (New York: Vintage, 1998).

115 AAQ, 320 CN, vol. 6:7, Haute Canada, Michael Power to Pierre-Flavien Turgeon, 19 April 1842.

116 *Prémices des mélanges religieux*, 10 May 1842, 13 May 1842.

117 Ibid., 13 May 1842.

118 Ibid.

119 Ibid.

120 Ibid., 10 May 1842; AAQ 320 CN, vol. 6, Haut Canada, Michael Power to Joseph Signay, 10 June 1842; AAQ 320 CN, vol. 6:99, Michael Power to Pierre-Flavien Turgeon, undated (likely June 1842).

CHAPTER SIX

1 AAM, Toronto Correspondence, 255.104, doc. 846, Michael Power to Joseph Marcoux, 21 September 1846.

2 Catherine Parr Traill, *The Backwoods of Canada* (1836; reprint, Toronto: Prospero Books, 2000), 44–6.

3 Edwin C. Guillet, *Pioneer Travel in Upper Canada* (1933; reprint, Toronto: University of Toronto Press, 1972), 109–10; Eric Ross, *Full of Hope and Promise: The Canadas in 1841* (Montreal and Kingston: McGill-Queen's University Press, 1991), 48–9.

4 Guillet, *Pioneer Travel*, 109–10, 186–9.

5 Ross, *Full of Hope*, 51.

6 J.M.S. Careless, *The Union of the Canadas: The Growth of Canadian Institutions, 1841–1857*, Canadian Centenary Series (Toronto: McClelland and Stewart, 1967), 28.

7 ARCAT, Report to Bishop Milde of Vienna, LB 02.229, Michael Power to Archbishop Milde, 16 January 1845; Archives of the Pontifical Mission Works, Montreal, Michael Power to the President of the Society for the Propagation of the Faith, 10 May 1842 (copy).

8 Anna Brownell Jameson, *Winter Studies and Summer Rambles in Canada*, New Canadian Library (1838; reprint, Toronto: McClelland and Stewart, 1990), 15.

9 *British Colonist*, 13 July 1842.

10 Ibid., 29 June 1842.

11 Ibid.; Ross, *Full of Hope*, 70. The lucrative development of the wheat economy in Toronto's immediate hinterland facilitated the city's commercial success as a market centre. Evidence of the importance of wheat is noted in Douglas McCalla, *Planting the Province: The Economic History of Upper Canada, 1784–1870*, Ontario Historical Studies Series (Toronto: University of Toronto Press, 1993), 71–4; David Gagan, *Hopeful Travellers: Families, Land and Social Change in Mid-Victorian Peel County, Canada West*, Ontario Historical Studies Series (Toronto: University of Toronto Press, 1981), 14–16.

12 Gerald Craig, *Upper Canada: The Formative Years, 1784–1841*, Canadian Centenary Series (1963; reprint, Toronto: McClelland and Stewart, 1979), 127.

13 *Catholic*, 13 April 1843; *Mirror*, 28 July 1843.

14 *Mirror*, 2 August 1844.

15 McCalla, *Planting the Province*, 118–21.

16 Ibid., 134–7.

17 Vivid descriptions of the province's roadways are offered in Jameson, *Winter Studies*, 239–40; Sharon Bagnato and John Strange, eds., *Footpaths to Freeways: The Story of Ontario Roads* (Toronto: Ministry of Transportation and Communication, 1984), 4–5.

18 Craig, *Upper Canada*, 143; Jameson, *Winter Studies*, 270; Bagnato and Strange, *Footpaths to Freeways*, 27–8.

19 Guillet, *Pioneer Travel*, 92–102, 107–10; Jameson, *Winter Studies*, 234.

20 *Mirror*, 4 February 1842, 4 June 1842.

21 Guillet, *Pioneer Travel*, 158; Bagnato and Strange, *Footpaths to Freeways*, 31.

22 Guillet, *Pioneer Travel*, 148.

23 "Journal of Father Claude Allouez's Voyage into Outaouac Country, from the Relation for 1666–67," in *The Jesuit Relations and Allied Documents: A Selection*, ed. Stanley Mealing, (1963; reprint, Ottawa: Carleton University Press, 1985), 95; Susannah Moodie, *Roughing It in the Bush*, New Canadian Library (Toronto: McClelland and Stewart, 1962), 68, 151–5.

24 Donald B. Smith, "The Dispossession of the Mississauga Indians: A Missing Chapter in the Early History of Upper Canada," in *Historical Essays on Upper Canada*, ed. J.K. Johnston and Bruce G. Wilson (Ottawa: Carleton University Press, 1989), 25–7; Donald Smith, *Sacred Feathers: The Reverend Peter Jones (Kahkewaquonaby) and the Mississauga Indians* (Toronto: University of Toronto Press, 1987), 17–33.

25 Peter S. Schmalz, *The Ojibwa of Southern Ontario* (Toronto: University of Toronto Press, 1991).

26 Curtis Fahey, *In His Name: The Anglican Experience in Upper Canada, 1791–1854* (Ottawa: Carleton University Press, 1991), 39–41; John Webster Grant, *A Profusion of Spires: Religion in Nineteenth Century Ontario*, Ontario Historical Studies Series (Toronto: University of Toronto Press, 1988), 109–10.

27 Good background on the French Canadian is found in Brother Alfred, "The Honourable James Baby," in *Catholic Pioneers in Upper Canada* (Toronto: Macmillan, 1947), 35–54; *Outline History of Assumption Parish* (n.p., 1967).

28 Jean R. Burnet, *Ethnic Groups in Upper Canada*, OHS Research Publication 1 (Toronto: Ontario Historical Society, 1972), 8, 26–7, 104–6.

29 Derek Nile Tucker, "Successful Pioneers: Irish Catholic Settlers in the Township of Hibbert, Ontario, 1845–1887" (master's thesis, McMaster University, Hamilton, 2001); Cecil J. Houston and William J. Smyth, "Community Development and Institutional Support: Life on the Agricultural Frontier of Adjala and Mono Townships," in *"Catholics at the Gathering Place": Historical Essays on the Archdiocese of Toronto, 1841–1991*, ed. Mark G. McGowan and Brian P. Clarke (Toronto: Canadian Catholic Historical Association; Dundurn Press, 1993), 5–22; Cecil J. Houston and William J. Smyth, *Irish Emigration and Canadian Settlement: Patterns, Links and Letters* (Toronto: University of Toronto Press, 1990), 178.

30 ARCAT, PP, AB 11.09, Marriage Register of the Mission of St Thomas, 1846, and List of Baptisms, 1846. The issue of the prominence of pre-famine immigrants in Ontario is discussed with great force in Donald H. Akenson, *The Irish in Ontario: A Study in Rural History* (Montreal and Kingston: McGill-Queen's University Press, 1984).

31 John McCallum, *Unequal Beginnings: Agricultural and Economic Development in Quebec and Ontario until 1820* (Toronto: University of Toronto Press, 1980), 9–24. In June 1840, wheat commanded four shillings and sixpence per bushel, while barley garnered only two shillings and oats fetched one shilling and fivepence. In October 1845, the following prices were posted: wheat, 3s6d to 4s10d; barley, 2s2d to 2s4d; oats, 1s5d to1s9d. In 1846, the prices were: wheat, 3s6d to 4s9d; barley, 2s to 2s6d; oats, 1s2d to 1s3d. The source for these figures is *Mirror*, 12 June 1840, 3 October 1845, 9 October 1846.

32 ARCAT, LB 02.042, J.J. Hay to T. Douglas Harrington (Bagot), 19 December 1842.

33 ARCAT, LB 02.193, Michael Power to Father F. Guth, Buffalo, 19 September 1844.

34 ARCAT, LB 02.250, Michael Power to Very Reverend A. Czvitkovitcz, CSSR, 18 August 1845; LB 02.229, Michael Power to Archbishop Milde, 16 January 1845.

35 Reiner Baehre, "Pauper Immigration to Upper Canada in the 1830's," *Histoire sociale/Social History* 14 (1981): 339–67; Michael Katz, *The People of Hamilton, Canada West: Family and Class in a Mid-Nineteenth-Century City* (Cambridge: Harvard University Press, 1975), 94–175; Andrew Carl Holman, "Corktown, 1832–1847: The Founding of Hamilton's Pre-famine Catholic Irish Settlement" (master's thesis, McMaster University, Hamilton, 1989), chapter 4.

36 *Mirror*, 8 May 1840, 1 November 1839.

37 Ibid., 22 October 1841. John Elmsley, Reverend W.P. McDonagh, and Dr. King were involved in a "formidable array of libel cases."

38 ARCAT, LB 02.004, Michael Power to Msgr de Jessé, Society for the Propagation of the Faith, 10 May 1842; LB 02.028, Michael Power to Msgr de Jessé, 16 November 1842; *Mirror*, 19 June 1842. The population statistics from the *Mirror* were gleaned from the census of 1842: Church of England, 120,000; Presbyterians, 114,000; Methodists, 100,000; Catholics, 78,000; Baptists, 20,000; miscellaneous (Quakers, Lutherans, Congregationalists, Mennonites, Dutch), 19,000; Jews, 1,000; other, 24,000 (the *Mirror*, however, did not report accurate numbers for the Catholics – see appendix 3); AAK, Letterbook 1833–68, Census of the Catholic Population in Upper Canada, 1834, pp.17–18. At that time, the portion of Upper Canada that would become Power's diocese contained twelve of the thirty-six parishes and 24,248 of the province's 52,248 Catholics. In less than a decade, immigration and natural population growth had increased the Catholic population to majority status in Power's diocese. See also NA, Rapports sur les état des missions, Society for the Propagation of the Faith (SPF), Toronto, F1999, pp. 12345–419, 1842–74 (microfilm); Michael Power to Msgr Choiselat-Galliea, 15 February 1843, p. 12350; Report of Michael Power for 1843 (1844) to SPF, p. 12348.

39 ARCAT, LB 02.042, James Hay to Douglas Harrington, 19 December 1842; NA, APF, Report from Michael Power to Society for the Propagation of the Faith, p. 12349.

40 ARCAT, PP, Directory of the Diocese of Toronto, December 1843.

41 ARCAT, LB 02.004, Michael Power to Msgr de Jessé, 10 May 1842.

42 Murray W. Nicolson, "William O'Grady and the Catholic Church in Toronto Prior to the Irish Famine," McGowan and Clarke, "*Catholics at the Gathering Place*," 23–40.

43 ARCAT, Macdonell Papers, BB 06.03, W.P. McDonagh to Remi Gaulin, 18 August 1840. McDonagh reports that O'Grady died in Whitby and says that he would prefer that the former priest be buried there, not in Toronto, as had been O'Grady's wish.

44 AAK, Gaulin Papers, B I I C 18, W.P. McDonagh to Patrick Dollard, Secretary to Bishop Gaulin, 23 November 1841; Brother Alfred, "John Elmsley," in *Catholic Pioneers in Upper Canada* (Toronto: Macmillan, 1947); Murray Nicolson, "John Elmsley and the Rise of Irish Catholic

Social Action in Victorian Toronto," *Canadian Catholic Historical Association, Historical Studies* 51 (1984): 47–66.

45 AAK, Gaulin Papers, B I I C 15, William Peter MacDonald to Patrick Dollard, 8 January 1841.

46 AAK, Gaulin Papers, B I I C 19, Father Alexander McDonell to Patrick Dollard, 12 June 1841; W.P. McDonagh to Patrick Dollard, 5 July 1841.

47 AAK, Gaulin Papers, B I I C, 15, William Peter MacDonald to Patrick Dollard, 2 February 1840; B I I C 15, William Peter MacDonald to Patrick Dollard, 21 June 1841.

48 AAK, Gaulin Papers, B I I C 15, William Peter MacDonald to Patrick Dollard, 21 June 1841.

49 AAK, Gaulin Papers, B I I C 15, William Peter MacDonald to Patrick Dollard, 1 October 1841. For more on MacDonald, see Stewart Gill, "The Sword in the Bishop's Hand: Father William Peter MacDonald, a Scottish Defender of the Catholic Faith in Upper Canada," *Canadian Catholic Historical Association, Study Sessions* 50, no. 2 (1983): 437–52.

50 AAM, Toronto Correspondence, 225.104, doc. 842–7, Michael Power to Joseph Marcoux, 16 July 1842.

51 ARCAT, PP, AD 01.03, Bill to Michael Power from the North American Hotel, 9 July 1842; LB 02.226, Michael Power to Msgr Ferret, Vice-President, Society for the Propagation of the Faith, 7 January 1845.

52 Reverend Edward Kelly, *The Story of St Paul's Parish, 1822–1922* (Toronto, 1922), 46.

53 *Catholic*, 6 July 1842.

54 Ibid., 8 June 1842.

55 ARCAT, AA 05.06, Pastoral Letters; *Catholic*, 8 June 1842.

56 *Catholic*, 8 June 1842.

57 Ibid.

58 Ibid.

59 Ibid., 6 July 1842.

60 AAM, Toronto Correspondence, 225.104, doc. 842-2, Michael Power to Ignace Bourget, 16 July 1842; *Catholic*, 27 July 1842.

61 ARCAT, PP, Accounts, AD 01.03, Bills of Sale, John Mulholland and Company, Importers, 29 August 1842; AD 01.04-06, Assessment Rolls no. 61 (1845), no. 72 (1845), and no. 726 (1846) indicate that Power owned his residence in St David's ward, presumably on Jarvis Street.

62 ARCAT, LB 01.035, 01.036, 01.039; LB 02.080, 02.052; *Catholic*, 14 September 1842.

63 ARCAT, LB 02.028, Michael Power to Msgr de Jessé, Society for the Propagation of the Faith, 16 November 1842; AAM, Toronto Correspondence, 255.104, doc. 843-4, Michael Power to "Cher Monsieur" (Joseph Marcoux), 5 July 1843.

64 AAM, Toronto Correspondence, 255.104, 842-2, Michael Power to Ignace Bourget, 16 July 1842.

65 ARCAT, LB 02.120, Michael Power to M.A. Tesse, Society for the Propagation of the Faith 12 December 1843.

66 ARCAT, LB 02.018, Circular Letter to the Clergy of the Diocese, 10 September 1842.

67 *Catholic*, 14 September 1842.

68 Francis Xavier Curran, SJ, *The Return of the Jesuits* (Chicago: Loyola University Press, 1966), 82–9.

69 See Thomas à Kempis, *The Imitation of Christ*, trans. and ed. Joseph N. Tylenda, SJ (New York: Vintage, 1998), book 3, "The Disciple and Christ."

70 Curran, *Return of the Jesuits*, 93.

71 AAM, Toronto Correspondence, Michael Power to Ignace Bourget, 255.104, doc. 842-4, 4 November 1842.

72 ARCAT, PP, AG 01.01, Circulaire du clergé du Diocèse de Montréal, 16 February 1843; AAM, Toronto Correspondence, 255.104, file 846-6, Michael Power to J.O. Paré, 31 October 1846. There are many examples of Power keeping his eye on developments in the Lower Canadian church and seeking the advice of former colleagues.

73 ARCAT, AB 02. Power exchanged many letters and receipts with bookseller Thomas Casserly of New York.

74 ARCAT, PP, AD 01.03, Bill to R. Cuthbert, Bookbinder, 17 September 1842.

75 AAM, Toronto Correspondence, Michael Power to Ignace Bourget, 255.104, doc. 842-4, 4 November 1842.

76 AAM, Bourget Papers, Register 1, p. 628, Ignace Bourget to Michael Power, 9 November 1842.

77 Peter Ward, *Courtship, Love and Marriage in Nineteenth-Century Canada* (Montreal: McGill-Queen's University Press, 1990), 15–31; Mark G. McGowan, *The Waning of the Green: Catholics, the Irish, and Identity in Toronto, 1887–1922* (Montreal and Kingston: McGill-Queen's University Press, 1998), 104–7; John S. Moir, "The Canadian Protestant Reaction to the *Ne Temere* Decrees," Canadian Catholic Historical Association, *Study Sessions* 48 (1981): 78–80.

78 ARCAT, LB 01.049-056, Constitutions of the Diocese of Toronto; note constitutions I–IX, XIX–XX. A translation of the original Latin document is provided in appendix 1. The author expresses his great appreciation to Dr Richard Toporoski, St Michael's College, University of Toronto, for preparing this translation.

79 Ibid., constitution I.

80 Ibid., constitution XVIII.

81 Murray Nicolson, "Michael Power: First Catholic Bishop of Toronto," Canadian Catholic Historical Association, *Historical Studies* 54 (1987): 31.

82   ARCAT, LB 01.049-056, Constitutions of the Diocese of Toronto, constitution XVI.

83   AAQ, 320 CN, vol. 6:24, Michael Power to Pierre-Flavien Turgeon, 2 September 1844.

84   ARCAT, LB 01.098, Michael Power to Pierre Point, SJ, 29 December 1843.

85   ARCAT, LB 02.020, Michael Power to Angus Macdonell, 14 October 1842; AAM, Toronto Correspondence, 255.104, doc. 843-12, Antoine Vervais to Michael Power, 23 October 1843.

86   AAM, Toronto Correspondence, 255.104, doc. 843-8, Michael Power to Ignace Bourget, 19 June 1843.

87   The confidence Power had in these men is noted in ARCAT, LB 02.207, Michael Power to Patrick Phelan (regarding Quinlan), 4 December 1844; LB 01.104-5, Michael Power to Alexandre Czvitkovitcz, CSSR, 28 February 1844; LB 01.104-5, Alexandre Czvitkovitcz to Michael Power, 20 February 1844 (regarding Sanderl [copy]); LB 01.101, Bishop Antoine Blanc to Michael Power, Exeat of Father Boué to Upper Canada, 22 July 1840 (copy); ADNO, Blanc Papers, Michael Power to Antoine Blanc, 9 January 1844; Michael Power to Antoine Blanc, 15 December 1845; ARCAT, LB 02.225, Michael Power to John Carroll, 3 January 1845; *Mirror*, 7 July 1842; *Catholic*, 12 July 1843 (regarding Edward Gordon). For information on William Peter MacDonald, see Gill, "Sword in the Bishop's Hand"; *Catholic*, 16 February 1842; *Mirror*, 9 April 1847 (obituary); ARCAT, Priest's Files, William P. MacDonald, clippings.

88   ARCAT, LB 01.056, Michael Power to Giovanni Corboli, 14 November 1842.

89   ARCAT, PP, AB 10.05, Jan Roothan to Michael Power, 5 April 1843.

90   ARSI, CI, 1,001 (1842–63), vol. 3, fasc. IX, Michael Power to Jan Roothan, 12 November 1842.

91   ARCAT, PP, ab 14.08, John Ainance, J.B. Tagewinine, P. Chegechi, J.R. Anowatin, request for government funds to be sent to Power for a priest at Georgian Bay, undated (c. 1842–43).

92   ARSI, CI, 1,001, vol. 3, fasc. IX, Michael Power to Jan Roothan, 12 November 1842.

93   ARCAT, LB 02.028, Michael Power to Msgr de Jessé, Society for the Propagation of the Faith, 16 November 1842; NA, SPF, Paris, F 199, Diocese of Toronto, Reports on the State of the Missions, 1842–74, docs 12,345–6.

94   ARCAT, PP, AB 10.05, Jan Roothan to Michael Power, 5 April 1843.

95   ARSI, CI, 1,001, vol. 1, fasc. II, Pierre Chazelle to Jan Roothan, 28 July 1843; Pierre Chazelle to Jan Roothan, 20 May 1843.

96   ARSI, CI, 1,001, vol. 1, fasc. II, Pierre Chazelle to Jan Roothan, 20 January 1843.

97 Ibid.; ARSI, CI, 1,001, vol. 1, fasc. II, Pierre Chazelle to Jan Roothan, 30 January 1843.

98 ARSI, CI, 1,001, vol. 1, fasc. II, Pierre Chazelle to Jan Roothan, 20 May 1843; Pierre Chazelle to Jan Roothan, 8 August 1843; ARCAT, PP, AB 10.10, Jan Roothan to Michael Power, 12 October 1843; "Pierre Chazelle," in *Dictionary of Jesuit Biography: Ministry to English Canada, 1842–1987* (Toronto: Canadian Institute of Jesuit Studies, 1991), 56; AAM, Register 3, pp. 138–9, Ignace Bourget to Pierre-Flavien Turgeon, 22 July 1843.

99 ARCAT, LB 02.008, Michael Power to Ignace Bourget, 16 July 1842.

100 AAM, Toronto Correspondence, 255.104, doc. 842-5, Michael Power to Ignace Bourget, 17 November 1842.

101 ARSI, CI, 1,001, vol. 1, fasc. II, Pierre Chazelle to Jan Roothan, 20 May 1843 (regarding du Ranquet).

102 AAM, Toronto Correspondence, 255.104, doc. 843-2, Michael Power to François-Xavier Marcoux, 11 February 1843.

103 AAM, Register 3, pp. 491–3, Ignace Bourget to Michael Power, 8 February 1845.

104 AAK, Gaulin Papers, B I I C 27, Michael Power to Angus Macdonell, 3 June 1843; ARCAT, LB 02.089, Michael Power to Angus Macdonell, 18 April 1843.

105 ARSI, CI, 1,001, vol. 3, fasc., IX, Pierre Chazelle to Jan Roothan, 20 June 1844.

106 AAD, Paul Papers, Pierre Paul to Michael Power, 24 April 1845 (regarding Sault Ste Marie); ARCAT, LB 02.244, Michael Power to Ignace Bourget, 29 May 1845 (regarding Manitoulin, Proulx, and the Superior country); Elizabeth Arthur, ed., *The Thunder Bay District, 1821–1892* (Toronto: Champlain Society, 1973), xxix, 13–16.

107 ARCAT, LB 02.286, Michael Power to Pierre Point, 22 November 1846; LB 02.293, Michael Power to Pierre Point, 1 January 1847.

108 ASJUCP, CH 06, 4, Michael Power, Appointment and Faculties to Bernard Fritsch, SJ, 1847.

109 ARCAT, LB 02.150, Michael Power to Dominique du Ranquet and Jean-Pierre Choné, 26 April 1844.

110 ARCAT, PP, AD 01.03, Antoine Vervais to Angus Macdonell, 23 October 1842; AD 01.03, Angus Macdonell to Michael Power, 23 October 1842. The actual amounts per priest are indicated in AAK, B I I C 11, Gaulin Papers, Francis Hincks to Remi Gaulin, 14 March 1843.

111 AAK, B I I C 11, Gaulin Papers, Francis Hincks to Remi Gaulin, 14 November 1842 (this letter indicates that the total amount available was about £500 semi-annually; for more information on Hincks, see William Ormsby, "Sir Francis Hincks," in *The Pre-Confederation Premiers: Ontario Government Leaders, 1841–1867*, ed. J.M.S. Careless [Toronto:

University of Toronto Press, 1980], 155); ARCAT, LB 02.064, Michael Power to Angus Macdonell, 1 February 1843.

112   ARCAT, LB 02.068, Michael Power to Patrick Dollard, 8 February 1843; LB 02.066, Michael Power to John H. Dunn, 8 February 1843; 02.067, Michael Power to H.H. Killaly, 8 February 1843; 02.072, Michael Power to Remi Gaulin, 15 February 1843.

113   ARCAT, PP, AB 10.04, Robert Baldwin and Louis-Hyppolyte LaFontaine to Francis Hincks, 12 March 1843 (copy).

114   AAK, Phelan Papers, C 1 3 C 16, Michael Power to Patrick Phelan, 3 March 1844.

115   ARCAT, LB 02.258, Michael Power to Patrick Phelan, 25 November 1845; LB 02.259, Michael Power to Patrick Phelan, 7 January 1846.

116   "Canons of the Council of Chalcedon, 451," in *A New Eusebius: Documents Illustrating the History of the Church to AD 337*, ed. W.C.H. Frend and J. Stevenson (London: SPCK, 1966), 324–31.

117   Gerald J. Stortz, "The Clergy of the Archdiocese of Toronto, 1841–1901," in McGowan and Clarke, *"Catholics at the Gathering Place,"* 73–88.

118   ARCAT, LB 02.232, Michael Power to Vincent Quiblier, 29 January 1845.

119   ARCAT, PP, AA 05.06, Pastoral Letters, 8 May 1842.

120   Kempis, *Imitation of Christ*, book 1, p. 12.

121   ARCAT, LB 02.232, Michael Power to Vincent Quiblier, 29 January 1845.

122   Terrence Murphy, "The Emergence of Maritime Catholicism," *Acadiensis* 13 (1984): 29–49; John Edward FitzGerald, "Conflict and Culture in Irish-Newfoundland Catholicism, 1829–1850" (Ph.D. diss., University of Ottawa, 1997); AAK, Macdonell Papers, A 1 2 C 4, William P. MacDonald to Patrick Dollard, 22 March 1837; AAM, Bourget Letterbook, Ignace Bourget to Michael Power, 9 December 1842; ARCAT, Macdonell Papers, BB 07.02, William P. MacDonald to Remi Gaulin, 28 October 1841 (scandal of Father Lee); BB 05.02, Constantine Lee to Remi Gaulin, 30 March 1841 (problems with Father O'Flynn).

123   ARCAT, LB 02.278, Michael Power to William P. McDonagh, 1 October 1846; LB 02.238, Michael Power to Patrick O'Dwyer, 11 March 1845; LB 02.136, Michael Power to P. Connolly, 29 February 1844; LB 02.129, Michael Power to Patrick O'Dwyer, 13 February 1844.

124   ARCAT, LB 02.154, Michael Power to Samuel Brown, 29 April 1844 (the activities of Father Fergus).

125   ARCAT, LB 02.294, Michael Power to William Nightengale, 11 January 1847 (drunkeness); LB 02.197, Michael Power to William P. MacDonald, 23 October 1844 (P. Connolly of Dundas as a drunk); LB 02.237, Michael Power to W.P. McDonagh, 4 March 1845 (women); LB 02.251, Michael Power to Father Michael Mills, 25 August 1845 (verbal abuse of parishioners).

126 ARCAT, LB 02.240, Michael Power to James O'Flynn (violent temper), 2 April 1845; LB 02.262, Michael Power to James O'Flynn, 15 February 1846.

127 ARCAT, LB 02.015, Michael Power to W.P. McDonagh, 6 September 1842; LB 02.009, Michael Power to James O'Flynn, 15 July 1842.

128 ARCAT, LB 02.130, Michael Power to James O'Flynn, 14 February 1844.

129 ARCAT, LB 02.188, Michael Power to James O'Flynn, undated (c. August 1844).

130 ARCAT, LB 02.199, Michael Power to Angus Macdonell, 29 October 1844 (regarding Father Michael MacDonell of Maidstone); LB 02.161, Michael Power to Michael MacDonell, 28 May 1844; AAD, Lefebvre Letterbook, vol. 1, 1843–49, Bishop Pierre Paul to Michael Power, 6 March 1844 (confirming MacDonell's neglect of his parish duties). Father Vervais was accused of neglecting dying parishioners, ARCAT, LB 02.038, Michael Power to Antoine Vervais, 10 December 1842.

131 ARCAT, LB 02.130, Michael Power to James O'Flynn, 14 February 1844.

132 ARCAT, LB 02.081, Michael Power to Angus Macdonell, 20 March 1843 (regarding Fathers J.B. Morin and Michael MacDonell); LB 02.033, Michael Power to J.B. Morin, 22 November 1842 (in this letter, Power indicates that although Morin was absent from the synod, he was still subject to the constitutions it produced).

133 ARCAT, LB 02.104, Michael Power to Patrick O'Dwyer, 30 September 1843; LB 02.184, Michael Power to Father McIntosh, 6 August 1844.

134 ARCAT, LB 02.064, Michael Power to Michael MacDonell, 1 February 1843; LB 02.063, Michael Power to J.B. Morin, 1 February 1843; LB 02.104, Michael Power to Patrick O'Dwyer, 30 September 1843.

135 J.M. Bumsted, "Scottish Catholicism in Canada," in *Creed and Culture: The Place of English-Speaking Catholics in Canadian Society, 1750–1930*, ed. Terrence Murphy and Gerald Stortz (Montreal and Kingston: McGill-Queen's University Press, 1993), 82–3, 89–90. The problems that existed between priestly cultures in English-speaking and French-speaking Canada did not subside; see Robert Choquette, "Problèmes et mœurs et disciplines ecclésiastique: Les catholiques des prairies canadiennes, 1900 à 1930," *Histoire sociale/Social History* 8 (1975):102–19.

136 William Westfall, *Two Worlds: The Protestant Culture of Nineteenth-Century Ontario* (Montreal and Kingston: McGill-Queen's University Press, 1989), 19–49.

137 ARCAT, LB 02.104, Michael Power to Patrick O'Dwyer, 30 September 1843.

138 ARCAT, LB 02.156, Michael Power to William P. MacDonald, 4 May 1844.

139 ARCAT, LB 02.139, Michael Power to William P. MacDonald, 6 March 1844.

140 Example include: ARCAT, LB 02.017, Michael Power to Constantine Lee, 9 September 1842; LB 02.283, Michael Power to W.P. McDonagh, 2 November 1846; LB 02.154, Michael Power to Samuel Brown, 29 April 1844 (regarding Father Stephen Fergus); LB 02.167, Michael Power to Father Stephen Fergus, 1 June 1844; LB 02.101, Michael Power to Antoine Vervais, 13 September 1843.

141 ARCAT, LB 02.170, Michael Power to Stephen Fergus, 12 June 1844.

142 ARCAT, LB 02.105, Michael Power to Antoine Vervais, 14 October 1843.

143 See appendix 1, Toronto Diocesan Regulations, 1842. Michael Robert Mills (1798-1851) was ordained in 1823 and left the diocese after Power's death to become a Cistercian monk in the United States. See *They Honoured Their Vestments of Holiness*, ed. Robert Scollard (Toronto: Archdiocese of Toronto, 1990), 68; ARCAT, LB 02.075, Michael Power to Michael Mills, 21 February 1843; LB 02.077, Michael Power to Michael Mills, 26 February 1843.

144 The litany of accusations made against Mills are found in ARCAT, LB 02.222, Michael Power to Michael Mills, 19 December 1844 (church collections); LB 02.185, Michael Power to Michael Mills, 8 August 1844 (clerical dress); LB 02.101, Michael Power to Michael Mills, 12 July 1843 (improper use of cemetery); LB 02.069, Michael Power to Michael Mills, 9 February 1843 (women and drink); LB 02.019, Michael Power to Michael Mills, 12 September 1842 (women and residence); LB 02.108, Michael Power to Michael Mills, 30 September 1843 (dress regulations, interference, poor state of parish, filthy altar).

145 ARCAT, LB 02.101, Michael Power to Michael Mills, 12 July 1843.

146 ARCAT, LB 02.062, Michael Power to Michael Mills, 31 January 1843; LB 02.056, Michael Power to John Hawkins, 23 January 1843; LB 02.022, Michael Power to William Murphy, 25 October 1842.

147 ARCAT, AA 10.08, Michael Power to Michael Mills, 22 July 1846 (copy).

148 AAQ, 320 CN 6:26, Upper Canada, Michael Power to Pierre-Flavien Turgeon, 15 December 1845.

149 ARCAT, PP, AA 11.08, Michael Mills to Michael Power, 26 November 1846.

150 ARCAT, LB 02.290, Michael Power to Michael Mills, 19 December 1846.

151 ARCAT, PP, Circular Letters, Circular Letter X, 31 December 1846.

CHAPTER SEVEN

1 AAM, Toronto Correspondence, 255.104, file 843-4, Michael Power to Joseph Marcoux, 5–6 July 1843.

2 Ibid.; *Biblia Sacra iuxta Vulgatam Clementinam*, ed. Alberto Colunga and Laurentio Turrado (Madrid: Biblioteca de Autores Cristianos, 1977), rev. 16:10–11, p. 1190.

3 Lactantius, "The Divine Institutes," book VII, chapter XIV, in *Ante-Nicene Fathers*, ed. Alexander Roberts and James Donaldson (Peabody, MA: Hendrickson Publishers, 1995), 211.

4 Gilles Chaussé, *Jean-Jacques Lartigue: Premier évêque de Montréal* (Montreal: Fides, 1980), 140–2; Thomas Matheson, "La Mennais et l'education au Bas-Canada," *Revue d'histoire de l'Amérique française* 13 (1960): 476–91; Philippe Sylvain, "Un disciple canadien de Lamennais: Louis-Antoine Dessaules," *Cahiers des Dix* 37 (1972): 61–83; François Beaudin, "L'influence de La Mennais sur Mgr Lartigue, premier évêque de Montréal," *Revue d'histoire de l'Amérique française* 25 (1971): 225–37; ARCAT, AA 03.04, Copy of Aphorisms of an "Old Author," 1682.

5 Eugen Weber, *apocalypses: prophecies, cults and millennial beliefs through the ages* (Toronto: Random House, 1999), 127.

6 AAK, A I 2 C 3, Msgr Le Saulnier to Alexander Macdonell, 27 February 1827.

7 Anna Brownell Jameson, *Winter Studies and Summer Rambles in Canada*, New Canadian Library (1838; reprint, Toronto: McClelland and Stewart, 1990), 235–6, 239, 255.

8 *Mirror*, 30 April 1841, 24 December 1841; *Catholic* 14 December 1842.

9 *Mirror*, 16 May 1845.

10 Father James O'Flynn, open letter, *Mirror*, 25 August 1843.

11 ARCAT, LB 02.061, Michael Power to W.P. McDonagh, 28 January 1843; LB 02.053, Michael Power to W.P. McDonagh, 13 January 1843.

12 ARCAT, LB 02.122, Michael Power to Patrick O'Dwyer, 5 January 1844.

13 *Mirror*, 20 September 1844.

14 *Mirror*, 22 March 1843; ARCAT, LB 02.140, Michael Power to W.P. McDonagh, 18 March 1844.

15 A sense of this is evident in ARCAT, LB 02.122, Michael Power to Patrick O'Dwyer, 5 January 1844.

16 AAD, Lefebvre Letterbook, vol. 1, 1843–49, Pierre Paul to Michael Power, 6 March 1844.

17 AAM, Toronto Correspondence, 255.104, file 845-3, Michael Power to Ignace Bourget.

18 *Catholic*, 11 January 1843; ARCAT, LB 02.156, Michael Power to William P. MacDonald, 4 May 1844 (regarding remarks made in the issue of 17 April). The CIHM microfilm version of the *Catholic* was actually filmed from a bound volume inscribed, in Power's own hand, as being from the collection of the "Bishop of Toronto."

19 The final issue was published on 17 April 1844. The *Catholic* was succeeded by the *Liberal*, edited by Catholic layman John Robertson of

Hamilton. Good examples of the type of fare offered by the *Catholic* appear in the issue of 10 April 1844. Bishop William Fraser encouraged Nova Scotians to become subscribers until the paper became more overtly an organ of political reform. ARCAT, Macdonell Papers, AE 20.11, William Fraser to William P. MacDonald, 23 September 1842; AE 20.13, William Fraser to William P. MacDonald, 23 December 1842.

20 A reprinted version appears as *The General Catechism, Revised, Corrected and Enlarged and Prescribed to Be Taught throughout the Dioceses of Kingston and Toronto* (Kingston, ON: P. McTavey, 1844), authorized on the Feast of St Edward the Confessor, 13 October 1842, in Toronto, by Michael Power and Remi Gaulin; reauthorized by Patrick Phelan, 7 August 1844.

21 ARCAT, PP, AB 10.11, Comte de Forbin-Janson to Michael Power, 8 December 1843.

22 ARCAT, LB 02.079, J.J. Hay to Antoine Vervais, 13 March 1843.

23 ARCAT, LB 02.116, Michael Power to Cardinal Fransoni, 30 November 1843.

24 ARCAT, LB 01.144, Michael Power to Father Menet, SJ, 17 December 1845.

25 ARCAT, PP AB 11.01, Johannes Brunelli, Secretary of the Propaganda Fide, to Michael Power, 11 February 1844; LB 01.140, Copy of Plenary Indulgence, 11 February 1786, Pius VI, Feast of the Assumption, 19 September 1845.

26 ARCAT, LB 01.112, Perpetual Faculties Given to Michael Power by Pope Gregory XVI, 11 February 1844; LB 02.116, Michael Power to Cardinal Fransoni, 30 November 1843; AAK, C I 4 ER I, Report of Patrick Phelan to Rome Regarding Feast Days, 10 January 1847 (listed in *General Catechism*, p.3).

27 AAM, Register of Letters, p. 498, Ignace Bourget to Joseph Signay, 17 February 1845; ARCAT, PP, AA 03.06, *Calendarium Romanum ad usum Quebecensis*, 1825. This schedule was revised in Power's own handwriting as the *Calendarium ad usum Diocesis Torontinae*, 1843, specifying the dates of Septuagesima, Ash Wednesday, Easter, Ascension, Pentecost, Corpus Christi, and Advent for the years 1843–47. To the calendar of non-obligatory feast days, Power added minor monthly feasts, including St Peter Damien (23 February), St Gabriel Archangel (18 March), Pope Urban and Martyrs (28 May), St Aloysius Gonzaga (21 June), St Martha (30 July), St Alphonsus Ligouri (9 August), St Raphael Archangel (24 October), St Stanlislaus Kotska (16 November), and St Elizabeth of Hungary (26 November).

28 *Catholic*, 21 February 1844; ARCAT, AA 06.04, Pastoral Letter IV, 2 February 1844. Similar relaxations, in this case by Power's colleague William Walsh, were noted when the potato crop failed in Nova Scotia. *Cross*, 14 February 1846.

29 ARCAT, LB 01.126, Michael Power to Edward Gordon, 13 December 1844; LB 01.141, Michael Power to Pierre Point, 17 December 1845.

30 ARCAT, LB 02.112, Michael Power to J.B. Morin, 20 September 1843; AF 01.14, *Formula Benedicendi Aquam Baptismatam.*

31 ARCAT, LB 02.158, Michael Power to P.T. Sanderl, CSSR, 8 May 1844; LB 02.142, Michael Power to Patrick O'Dwyer, 22 March 1844.

32 ARCAT, LB 02.091, Michael Power to Patrick O'Dwyer, 17 May 1843.

33 Ibid.

34 Decrees of the Council of Trent, session 29, canon 1.

35 ARCAT, PP, LB 02.005, Michael Power to Bishop Kenrick of Philadelphia, July 1842. Power indicated that he was willing to go further than his colleagues in Quebec had in applying the *Tametsi* decrees of the Council of Trent.

36 *Butler's Catechism* (1947 ed.), lesson 29; *Le catéchisme des provinces ecclésiastiques de Québec, Montréal, et Ottawa* (Montreal, 1888), 58–61; Arthur Devine, *The Law of Christian Marriage* (New York: Benzinger, 1908), 3–4; Peter Ward, *Courtship, Love and Marriage in Nineteenth-Century Canada* (Montreal: McGill-Queen's University Press, 1990), 15–31.

37 ARCAT, LB 02.070, Michael Power to W.P. McDonagh, 11 February 1843; LB 02.014, Michael Power to James O'Flynn, 2 September 1842.

38 AAD, Pierre Paul to Michael Power, 6 March 1844.

39 ARCAT, PP, AA 10.03, Michael Power to Father Boul, 29 April 1844; LB 02.50, Michael Power to Patrick O'Dwyer, 5 January 1843; LB 02.18, Michael Power to Patrick O'Dwyer, 22 July 1844.

40 ARCAT, LB 02.246, Michael Power to Michael Mills, 3 July 1845 (high fees); LB 02.190, Michael Power to Patrick O'Dwyer, 22 August 1844; LB 02.061, Michael Power to W.P. McDonagh, 28 January 1843 (concubinage); LB 02.083, Michael Power to Patrick O'Dwyer, 23 March 1843.

41 ARCAT, LB 02.049, Michael Power to W.P. McDonagh, 31 January 1843; LB 02.044, Michael Power to William Whelan, 23 December 1842.

42 Mark G. McGowan, *The Waning of the Green: Catholics, the Irish, and Identity in Toronto, 1887–1922* (Montreal and Kingston: McGill-Queen's University Press, 1998), 104–7.

43 ARCAT, AA 10.01, Michael Power to Patrick O'Dwyer, 17 November 1842; LB 02.026, Michael Power to Michael Mills, 9 November 1842; LB 02.155, Michael Power to Father Boue, 29 April 1844.

44 ARCAT, LB 02.039, Michael Power to Angus Macdonell, 10 December 1842. Power states to Macdonell: "I disapprove of all marriages between Catholics and non-Catholics."

45 ARCAT, LB 02.02, Michael Power to Michael Mills, 9 November 1842.

46 ARCAT, LB 02.251, Michael Power to Michael Mills, 25 August 1845.

47 ARCAT, LB 02.005, Michael Power to Bishop Kenrick of Philadelphia, n.d. (c. 1842); LB 02.034, Michael Power to Angus Macdonell, 22 November 1842.

48 ARCAT, LB 02.027, Michael Power to Patrick O'Dwyer, 16 November 1842.

49 ARCAT, LB 02.030, Michael Power to Patrick O'Dwyer, 18 November 1842.

50 McGowan, *Waning of the Green*, 104–5; John S. Moir, *The Church in the British Era, from the British Conquest to Confederation* (Toronto and New York: McGraw-Hill Ryerson, 1972), 89; John S. Moir, *Church and State in Canada West* (Toronto: University of Toronto Press, 1959), 140–8; Raymond Lahey, "Catholicism and Colonial Policy in Newfoundland, 1779-1845," in *Creed and Culture: The Place of English-Speaking Catholics in Canadian Society, 1750–1930*, ed. Terrence Murphy and Gerald Stortz (Montreal and Kingston: McGill-Queen's University Press, 1993), 59–64; William Renwick Riddell, "The Law of Marriage in Upper Canada," *Canadian Historical Review* 2 (1921): 226–48.

51 ARCAT, LB 02.051, Michael Power to William Whelan, 10 January 1843; LB 02.230, Michael Power to William Whelan, 22 January 1845. Power informed Whelan that he was in violation of article 12 of the statutes of the Diocese of New York. This indicated not only Power's knowledge of the canons but also his careful reading of the regulations of other dioceses, which may well have had an influence on the drafting of the regulations at the Toronto synod.

52 ARCAT, LB 02.203, Michael Power to W.P McDonagh, 25 November 1844.

53 ARCAT, LB 02.190, Michael Power to Patrick O'Dwyer, 22 August 1844; LB 02.037, Michael Power to Angus Macdonell, 30 November 1842; Catholic, 24 January 1844.

54 Patrick Carey, *People, Priests, and Prelates: Ecclesiastical Democracy and the Tensions of Trusteeism* (Notre Dame: University of Notre Dame Press, 1987); Terrence Murphy, "Trusteeism in Atlantic Canada: The Struggle for Leadership among the Irish Catholics of Halifax, St John's, and Saint John, 1780–1850," in Murphy and Stortz, *Creed and Culture*, 126–51.

55 ARCAT, Macdonell Papers, BB 07.01, W.P. MacDonald to Remi Gaulin, 9 March 1841.

56 Allan Greer, *The Patriots and the People: The Rebellion of 1837 in Lower Canada* (Toronto: University of Toronto Press, 1993).

57 ARCAT, PP, AB 14.02, Meeting of the Catholic Inhabitants of the Guelph Mission, 3 December 1844; AB 11.05, Catholic Residents of Adelaide to Bishop Power, 27 May 1844.

58 ARCAT, LB 02.021, Michael Power to Antoine Vervais, 25 October 1842; LB 01.122, Episcopal Ordinance to the Fabrique of St-Jean-Baptiste Parish,

Amherstburg, n.d. (c. 1843); LB 02.038, Michael Power to Antoine Vervais, 10 December 1842.

59 ARCAT, LB 02.087, Michael Power to Charles Coquohn and Lawrence Doyle, 1 April 1843.

60 ARCAT, LB 02.158, Michael Power to P.T. Sanderl, CSSR, 8 May 1844; LB 02.131, J.J. Hay to Otto Klotz, 14 February 1844.

61 Such measures are evidenced in ARCAT, PP, AB 14.02, Meeting of the Catholic Inhabitants of Guelph, 3 December 1844 and 5 January 1845.

62 ARCAT, PP, AA 10.01, Michael Power to Patrick O'Dwyer, 17 November 1842; LB 02.177, Michael Power to Pierre Point, SJ, 29 June 1844.

63 ARCAT, LB 02.164, Michael Power to Michael Mills, 30 May 1844.

64 ARCAT, LB 02.169, Michael Power to Michael Mills, 10 June 1844.

65 ARCAT, LB 02.164, Michael Power to Michael Mills, 30 May 1844.

66 ARCAT, LB 02.264, Michael Power to Michael Mills, 22 February 1846.

67 ARCAT, LB 01.124, Episcopal Ordinance from Michael Power to the Parish of St Margaret, Adjala, 16 September 1844.

68 ARCAT, PP, AB 03.01, Amable Charest to Michael Power, n.d. (c. 1843).

69 ARCAT, LB 01.138, Mandement to the Mission of Sandwich, 19 September 1845; LB 02.141, Michael Power to Father J.B. Morin, 19 March 1844.

70 *Journals of the Legislative Assembly of the Province of Canada*, session 1844–45, 29 November 1844–29 March 1845, Petition, 16 December 1844, p. 52.

71 ARCAT, LB 02.048, Michael Power to Angus Macdonell, 30 December 1842.

72 ARCAT, PP, AB 10.01, John B. Gildea to Michael Power, 21 September 1842. This letter included a copy of the Maryland statutes outlining the manner of holding and transmitting title to church property; note chapter 308.

73 AAM, Toronto Correspondence, 255.104, file 843-10, Michael Power to Ignace Bourget, 21 October 1843; 255.104, file 843-11, Michael Power to Ignace Bourget, 6 November 1843.

74 AAM, Toronto Correspondence, 255.104, file 845-7, Angus Macdonell to Michael Power, 12 February 1845; Elizabeth Nash, ed., *Debates of the Legislative Assembly of United Canada* (Montreal: Presses de l'École des Hautes Études Commerciales, 1970), 300, 365–6, 1101, 1106.

75 *Journals of the Legislative Assembly of the Province of Canada*, session 1844–45, 29 March 1845, p. 440; ARCAT, PP, AA 12.01, 8 Victoria cap. LXXXII.

76 ARCAT, PP, LB 02.248, Michael Power to Cardinal Fransoni, 5 August 1845.

77 AAM, Toronto Correspondence, 255.104, file 845-7, Michael Power to Angus Macdonell, 12 February 1845.

78 ARCAT, PP, AA 10.07, Michael Power to Reverend William MacIntosh, 7 April 1846.

79 ARCAT, LB 02.272, Michael Power to Charles Baby, 23 August 1846.

80 ARCAT, LB 02.256, Michael Power to Simon Sanderl, CSSR, 12 November 1845.

81 ARCAT, PP, AB 14.12, Articles of Agreement, John Butler, Township of Durham, District of Brock, and Michael Power, 19 February 1846; AB 14.13, Articles of Agreement, John Bingham and Michael Power, 19 February 1846, Township of Durham, District of Brock.

82 Murphy, "Trusteeism in Atlantic Canada," 134, 139–40.

83 See appendix 3.

84 "Seaforth Log Church," *Canadian Freeman*, 24 March 1863.

85 ARCAT, LB 02.261, Michael Power to the President of the Society for the Propagation of the Faith (SPF), 20 January 1846; NA, SPF Papers, letter 58, p. 12352.

86 ARCAT, PP, AB 14.05, Building Committee at Guelph, 1845; *Mirror*, 11 September 1846; "Church of St Thomas," *Mirror*, 31 July 1846.

87 ARCAT, AA 06.09, Pastoral Address IX, 29 December 1846, "Inviting the Catholics of the Diocese of Toronto to Contribute Towards the Building of the Cathedral Church of St Michael's in That City."

88 J.R. Teefy, ed., *Jubilee Volume of the Archdiocese of Toronto, 1842–1892* (Toronto: George T. Dixon, 1892), 127; Brian Cook, *The Voice of the Archangel Michael: "Who Is Like God?" A Short History and Guide to St Michael's Cathedral, Toronto* (Toronto: St Michael's Cathedral, 1989), 8.

89 *Mirror*, 11 April 1845.

90 Ibid., 18 April 1845.

91 *Christian Guardian*, quoted in *Mirror*, 18 April 1845.

92 This was calculated by multiplying a 5-foot depth by a 190-foot length and a 100-foot width.

93 ARCAT, LB 01.133, Dedication of the Cornerstone of St Michael's Cathedral, 8 May 1845.

94 *Mirror*, 9 May 1845.

95 Ibid.

96 Teefy, *Jubilee Volume*, 279.

97 ARCAT, LB 02.260, Michael Power to M. Ferret, SPF, 20 January 1846; AAM, Toronto Correspondence, 255.104, file 846-1, Michael Power to Joseph Marcoux, 7 February 1846.

98 NA, SPF Papers, Copies from the Archives of the SPF, Paris, Diocese of Toronto, 1 February 1847, p. 12354.

99 ARCAT, AA 06.10, Circular Letter, 31 December 1846.

100 NA, SPF Papers, Paris, p. 12355a, 1846.

101 NA, SPF Papers, Paris, Diocese of Toronto, 17 August [1850].

102 Cook, *Voice of the Archangel Michael*, 10.

103 Teefy, *Jubilee Volume*, 128.

104 AIBVM-T, *Annals, 1847–1870*, by Mother Teresa Dease, transcribed by Maggie Lyons, 25 August 1875, p. 11.

105 ARCAT, LB 01.163, Chapel Dedication, 7 December 1846.

106 NA, SPF Papers, Paris, J.J. Hay to the SPF, 1848.

107 NA, SPF Papers, Paris, Michael Power's Report, 1 February 1847.

108 ARCAT, AA 06.10, Pastoral Letter, 31 December 1846.

109 ARCAT, LB 02.296, Michael Power to John Carroll, 15 January 1847; LB 02.297, J.J. Hay to Patrick O'Dwyer, 5 June 1847.

110 ARCAT, LB 01.120, Michael Power on the Ordination of Charles Kileen, 6 June 1844.

111 ARCAT, LB 01.152, Record of the Ordination of John O'Reilly, 5 July 1846.

112 ARCAT, LB 02.124, Michael Power to Father A. Neyron, 11 January 1844.

113 ARCAT, PP, Testimonial Letters for Charles Kileen, 3 July 1844.

114 ARCAT, LB 02.054, Michael Power to Father W. Dolan, 14 January 1843; LB 02.109, Michael Power to Father Hugh Fitzpatrick, 22 October 1843.

115 ARCAT, LB 01.097, Faculties Granted to Hugh Fitzpatrick, 29 October 1843.

116 ARCAT, LB 01.119, Michael Power on Agreement with Bishop Henni, 6 June 1844. Power indicated that Bishop Henni of Milwaukee was supervising the northwestern regions of the Diocese of Toronto. Similar responsibilities were undertaken by missionary and future bishop Frederic Baraga. See "Frederic Baraga," *Dictionary of Canadian Biography* (Toronto: University of Toronto Press, 1976), 9:30–2.

117 ARSI, CI, (1842–63), vol. 1, fasc. II, Pierre Chazelle to Jan Roothan, 20 May 1843.

118 ARSI, CI, vol. 1, fasc. II, Pierre Chazelle to Jan Roothan, 11 September 1843. Anglican missionary John Carey alludes to the limited successes; see ASJUCP, C-406, no. 1, Testimony of John Carey, 20 May 1844. Although biased, the Jesuits were aware of Protestant difficulties on the island; see "Le Père Pierre Point, missionaire de la Compagnie de Jésus dans le Haut-Canada, à son supérieur en France," 10 May 1844, in *Lettres des nouvelles missions du Canada, 1843–1852*, ed. Lorenzo Cadieux, SJ (Montreal: Bellarmin, 1973), 165.

119 ARSI, CI, vol. 3, fasc. IX, Pierre Chazelle to Jan Roothan, 20 June 1844; ARCAT, LB 02.211, note from Michael Power appended to a letter to Father H. Hudon (LB 02.209, 7 December 1844); LB 02.212, Samuel Jarvis to John Keating, 8 May 1844 (copy; the date on the copy is wrong – the correct date is 10 March).

120 ASJUCP, C-401, no. 1, Samuel Jarvis to John Keating, 10 March 1844.

121 ASJUCP, C-401, no. 1, "To Our Great Father the Governor General at Montreal" [Metcalfe], 25 July 1844; John Webster Grant, *Moon of Wintertime: Missionaries and the Indians of Canada in Encounter since 1534* (Toronto: University of Toronto Press, 1984), 80.

122 ASJUCP, C-401, no. 1, "To Our Great Father the Governor General at Montreal" [Metcalfe], 25 July 1844.

123 ASJUCP, C-401, no. 1, John Keating to J.M. Higginson, Civil Secretary, Indian Department, 1 September 1844; NA, RG 10, vol. 456, reel C–13328, item 256, Agents, Western Superintendency, Civil Secretary Higginson to John Keating, 13 September 1844.

124 "Le Frère Joseph Jennesseaux de la Compagnie de Jésus à un frère coad-juteur de la même compagnie," 9 August 1844, in *Cadieux, Lettres des nouvelles missions*, 176–87; see also "Le Père Pierre Point, missionaire de la Compagnie de Jésus dans le Haut-Canada, à son supérieur en France," 10 May 1844, in Cadieux, *Lettres des nouvelles missions*, 165.

125 "Le R.P. Chazelle, supérieur des missions de la Compagnie de Jésus au Canada, à son supérieur en France," 10 August 1844, in Cadieux, *Lettres des nouvelles missions*, 188–96.

126 ARCAT, LB 02.209, Michael Power to Father H. Hudon, 7 December 1844.

127 ARCAT, LB 02.269, Michael Power to Dominick Daly, 15 June 1846.

128 ARCAT, LB 02.209, Michael Power to Father H. Hudon, 7 December 1844.

129 ARCAT, LB 02.269, Michael Power to Dominick Daly, 15 June 1846. Evidence from du Ranquet was derived from a letter he sent to Indian Department Secretary Vardon, ARCAT, LB 2.280, 29 September 1846 (copy).

130 ARCAT, LB 02.291, Petition from Michael Power to the Right Honourable Earl of Cathcart, 17 December 1846.

131 ARCAT, LB 02.269, Michael Power to Dominick Daly, 15 June 1846; LB 02.291, Petition from Michael Power to the Right Honourable Earl of Cathcart, 17 December 1846.

132 Quoted in ARCAT, LB 02.298, Michael Power to Earl Grey, 19 February 1847.

133 Ibid.

134 ASJUCP, C-401, no. 3, Her Majesty the Queen vs Dominique du Ranquet, Conviction, Province of Canada, Western District, J.B. Clench, 30 March 1847; C-401, no. 3, Proceedings of the Enquiry, 29–30 March, 1847.

135 NA, RG 10, vol. 439, Superintendency Records, Western (Sarnia) Superin-tendency, Correspondence of J.B. Clench, 1842–54, Oshaogimaw Nautel to J.B. Clench, 5 May 1848.

136 ARCAT, Macdonell Papers, Louis Labasque et al. to Bishop Jean-Jacques Lartigue, 27 June 1833; Lorenzo Cadieux, "Aperçu historique," in *Les*

robes noires a l'Île du Manitou, 1853–1870, ed. Lorenzo Cadieux, SJ, and Robert Toupin, SJ, Documents historiques 75 (Sudbury, ON: Société historique du Nouvel-Ontario, 1982), 8.

137 Ruth Bleasdale, "Manitowaning: An Experiment in Indian Settlement," Ontario History 66 (1974): 148; Cadieux, "Aperçu historique," 11.

138 "Wikwemikong, Unceded First Nation," *Akwesasne to Wunnumin Lake: Profiles of Aboriginal Communities in Ontario* (Toronto: Ontario Native Affairs Secretariat; Ministry of Citizenship, 1992), 258–9.

139 "Jean-Baptiste Proulx," *Dictionary of Canadian Biography* (Toronto: University of Toronto Press, 1976), 11:714–15; Bleasdale, "Manitowaning," 152–4.

140 Robert Toupin, SJ, "La vie interne de la mission," in Cadieux and Toupin, *Robes noires*, 35–6; Cadieux, "Aperçu historique," 14–16.

141 ARCAT, LB 02.010, Michael Power to Jean-Baptiste Proulx, 15 August 1842; LB 02.031, Michael Power to Jean-Baptiste Proulx, 22 November 1842; LB 02.032, Michael Power to George Gordon, 22 November 1842.

142 ARCAT, LB 02.092, Jean-Baptiste Proulx to Samuel P. Jarvis, Chief Superintendent of Indian Affairs, 15 May 1843 (copy).

143 ARCAT, LB 02.242, Michael Power to Ignace Bourget, 21 May 1845.

144 ARCAT, LB 02.244, Michael Power to Ignace Bourget, 29 May 1845; "Le Père Choné, missionaire de la Compagnie de Jésus au Canada, à son supérieur en France," 3 September 1844, in Cadieux, *Lettres des nouvelles missions*, 209–13.

145 ARSI, CI, I-XV, doc. 4, Jean-Pierre Choné to Jan Roothan, 12 January 1846. This "relation" contains rich descriptions of Native religious practice and the Ojibwa deities and stories; see also I-XV, doc. 9, Jean-Pierre Choné to Jan Roothan, 14 April 1847. Statistics for the Manitoulin missions are offered by Choné in ARSI, Missio CI, I-XV, doc. 1, Jean-Pierre Choné to Jan Roothan, 2 February 1845.

146 "Jean Véroneau," *Dictionary of Jesuit Biography* (Toronto: Canadian Institute of Jesuit Studies, 1991), 337–8; ARSI, Missio CI, I-XV, doc. 9, Jean-Pierre Choné to Jan Roothan, 14 April 1847.

147 Toupin, "Vie interne," 46; Cadieux, "Aperçu historique," 21.

148 ARSI, CI, I-XV, doc. 6, Jean-Pierre Choné to Jan Roothan, 26 June 1846; I-XV, doc. 7, Jean-Pierre Choné to Jan Roothan, 16 December 1846.

149 ARSI, CI, I-IX, doc. 11, Pierre Point to Jan Roothan, 22 September 1847. The statistics for the northern missionary expansion are found in ARSI, Missio CI, I-IX, doc. 8, Pierre Point to Jan Roothan, 29 October 1846.

150 AAM, Toronto Correspondence, 255.104, file 845-4, Michael Power to Ignace Bourget, 28 May 1845; a copy of this letter is also held in ARCAT, LB 02.244, 29 May 1845.

151 ARCAT, LB 01.145, Case of the Faculties of William Nightengale, 20 September 1845.

152 ARCAT, LB 02.302, Michael Power to Stephen Fergus, 9 May 1844.

153 ARCAT, LB 02.300, Michael Power to Prince Archbishop Milde of Vienna, 8 May 1847; LB 02.007, Michael Power to Bishop Kinsella of Ossory, Ireland, 8 July 1842; LB 02.302, Michael Power to Archbishop Reisach of Munich, 8 May 1847; AAHC, Michael Power to Rev. B. Woodlock, President of All Hallows College, 17 July 1847.

154 ARCAT, LB 02.295, Michael Power to Joseph Signay, 13 January 1847.

155 NA, SPF Papers, Paris, Armand de Charbonnel to the SPF, 17 August 1850, p. 12367.

156 ARCAT, LB 01.139, Michael Power's Proclamation at Belle Rivière, 19 September 1845; AAM, Toronto Correspondence, 255.104, file 846-1, Michael Power to Joseph Marcoux, 7 February 1846; ARCAT, AA 06.10, Pastoral Letter X, 31 December 1846.

CHAPTER EIGHT

1 Diane Ravitch, *The Great School Wars: New York City, 1804–1973* (New York: Basic Books, 1974); Ed Rea, *Bishop Alexander Macdonell and the Politics of Upper Canada* (Toronto: Ontario Historical Society, 1974); John Edward Fitzgerald, "Conflict and Culture in Irish-Newfoundland Catholicism, 1829–1850" (Ph.D diss., University of Ottawa, 1997); Léon Pouliot, SJ, *Monseigneur Bourget et son temps*, 3 vols. (Montreal: Bellarmin, 1955–72).

2 Thomas à Kempis, *The Imitation of Christ*, trans. and ed. Joseph N. Tylenda, SJ (New York: Vintage, 1998), 49, 50–1, 11.

3 AAM, Toronto Correspondence, 255.104, file 846-1, Michael Power to Joseph Marcoux, 7 February 1846.

4 ARCAT, PP, LB 01.135, Pope Gregory XVI, Conferral of Doctor of Sacred Theology on Michael Power, 16 March 1845; ARCAT, PRC, no. 2701, Indult of Pope Gregory XVI to Michael Power, 16 March 1845. Power was officially recognized as the Catholic bishop of the western portion of the province shortly after his arrival, in 1842. ARCAT, PP, Rawson W. Rawson, Chief Secretary of the Governor General, to Michael Power, 15 September 1842.

5 C.B. Sissons, *Egerton Ryerson: His Life and Letters* (Toronto: Clarke-Irwin, 1937–1947), 2:149.

6 ARCAT, LB 02.229, Michael Power to Archbishop Milde, 16 January 1845; Census of Canada, 1848 (see appendix 3). Power reported to Milde that in 1842, the population of Toronto was 20,000, and of this figure 4,500 were Catholics; six years later, the figures were 5,900 Catholics out of a population of 23,503.

7 See appendix 3.

8 *Census of Canada, 1870–71* (Ottawa: Queen's Printer, 1876). This includes Censuses of Canada, 1665–1871; Census of Canada, 1842, Upper Canada, table II, table I.

9 Glenn Lockwood, "Eastern Upper Canadian Perceptions of Irish Immigrants, 1824–1868" (Ph.D diss., University of Ottawa, 1988).

10 John S. Moir, "Toronto's Protestants and Their Perceptions of Their Catholic Neighbours," in *"Catholics at the Gathering Place": Historical Essays on the Archdiocese of Toronto, 1841–1991*, ed. Mark G. McGowan and Brian P. Clarke (Toronto: Canadian Catholic Historical Association; Dundurn Press, 1993), 314–15.

11 *Mirror*, 5 February 1841.

12 Brother Alfred, *Catholic Pioneers in Upper Canada* (Toronto: Macmillan, 1947), 1–74.

13 Moir, "Toronto's Protestants," 315; see also ARCAT, Macdonell Papers, AD 01.01, "A Friend" to Alexander Macdonell, 23 March 1833; Hereward Senior, "The Orange, the Green and the Snow in Between," in *The Untold Story: The Irish in Canada*, ed. Robert O'Driscoll and Lorna Reynolds (Toronto: Celtic Arts of Canada, 1988), 2:565–70; John S. Moir, *Church and State in Canada West: Three Studies in the Relation of Denominationalism and Nationalism, 1841–1867* (Toronto: University of Toronto Press, 1959), 146–9, 161–5.

14 *Mirror*, 6 March 1846.

15 *Catholic*, 2 March 1842.

16 Bruce Elliott, *The City Beyond: A History of Nepean, Birthplace of Canada's Capital, 1792–1990* (Nepean, ON: Corporation of the City of Nepean, 1991), 32–5.

17 Murray Nicolson, "Irish Tridentine Catholicism in Victorian Toronto: Vessel for Ethno-Religious Persistence," Canadian Catholic Historical Association, *Study Sessions* 50, vol. 2 (1983): 418.

18 Mark G. McGowan, "Ecumenism," in *Planted by Flowing Waters: The Diocese of Ottawa, 1847–1997*, ed. Pierre Hurtubise, Mark G. McGowan, and Pierre Savard (Ottawa: Novalis, 1998), 219–25.

19 NA, SPF Papers, Paris, Michael Power to Msgr Ferret, 7 January 1845, p. 12351.

20 *Bathurst Courier*, 11 August 1837; Elliott, *City Beyond*, 68, 32.

21 Murray Nicolson, "John Elmsley and the Rise of Irish Catholic Social Action in Victorian Toronto," Canadian Catholic Historical Association, *Historical Studies* 51 (1984): 49.

22 Stewart Gill, "The Sword in the Bishop's Hand: Father William Peter MacDonald, a Scottish Defender of the Catholic Faith in Upper Canada," Canadian Catholic Historical Association, *Study Sessions* 50, vol. 2 (1983): 448–9. MacDonald's newspaper was published from 1830–31, and from 1841–44.

23 A few examples: *Catholic*, 22 December 1841, 5 January 1842, 14 September 1842, 9 November 1842, 31 May 1843. The *Church* was founded in 1837 by John Strachan, and it was intended to be the paper of the Upper Canadian majority. See Curtis Fahey, *In His Name: The Anglican Experience in Upper Canada, 1791–1854* (Ottawa: Carleton University Press,

1991), 49, 51, 139–40, 166–8, 170, 179; Robert Black, "Established in the Faith: The Church of England in Upper Canada, 1780–1867," in *By Grace Co-workers: Building the Anglican Diocese of Toronto, 1780–1989*, ed. Allan Hayes (Toronto: Anglican Book Centre, 1989), 28.

24 *Catholic*, 31 May 1843. A.N. Bethune was the editor of the *Church* until 1842. He was replaced by John Kent in February of that year, and Kent was unseated in July 1843 by the returning Bethune. Fahey, *In His Name*, 245–6.

25 AAK, B I 1CI5, W.P. MacDonald to Patrick Dollard, 26 October 1841.

26 Fahey, *In His Name*, 244–6.

27 Moir, "Toronto's Protestants," 315–16; Neil Gregor Smith, "Religious Tensions in Pre-Confederation Politics," *Canadian Journal of Theology* 9 (1963): 248–62; Franklin Walker, "Protestant Reaction in Upper Canada to the 'Popish Threat,'" Canadian Catholic Historical Association, *Report* 21 (1954): 91–107.

28 John S. Moir, *Church and State in Canada, 1627–1867*, Carleton Library Series (Toronto: McClelland and Stewart, 1967), 145–9.

29 Moir, *Church and State in Canada West*, contains an excellent study of the secularization of King's College and the battle over separate schools.

30 J.M.S. Careless, "Mid-Victorian Liberalism in Central Canadian Newspapers, 1850–1867," *Canadian Historical Review* 31 (1950): 221–36.

31 *Mirror*, 18 July 1845, 17 January 1846.

32 Ibid., 20 September 1844.

33 Ibid., 16 May 1845, 2 June 1843.

34 Ibid., 15 November 1844.

35 Hereward Senior, *Orangeism: The Canadian Phase* (Toronto: McGraw-Hill Ryerson, 1972), 2–6.

36 ARCAT, Macdonell Papers, BB 05.01, Constantine Lee to Remi Gaulin, 15 March 1841.

37 Cecil Houston and William Smyth, *The Sash Canada Wore: A Historical Geography of the Orange Order in Canada* (Toronto: University of Toronto Press, 1980), 16–23.

38 Ibid., 112–41.

39 *Catholic*, 2 August 1843, 6 September 1843, 27 September 1843. Similar sentiments can be found in *Mirror*, 26 June 1846.

40 *Mirror*, 26 June 1846.

41 AO, MU 1375, Hodgins Papers, Egerton Ryerson to William H. Draper, 14 May 1846; J.G. Hodgins, "The Opening of the Normal School for Upper Canada, 1847," chapter 10, in *Documentary History of Education in Upper Canada*, ed. J.G. Hodgins (Toronto: L.K. Cameron, 1900), 7:99–100.

42 Moir, *Church and State in Canada West*, 138.

43 *Catholic*, 16 August 1843.

44 NA, SPF Papers, Paris, J.J. Hay to the SPF, 15 February 1848.

45 Pastoral Letter I, reprinted in *Catholic*, 8 June 1842.

46 ARCAT, AA 06.02, Pastoral Letter, Jubilee of 1842, 29 June 1842.

47 Ibid.; Pastoral Letter VI, 2 February 1846.

48 ARCAT, AA 05.06, Pastoral Letters, 2 February 1843, 2 February 1844, 29 December 1844, 2 February 1846.

49 ARCAT, LB 02.132, Michael Power to W.P. MacDonald, 22 February 1844. Power expresses his distress upon hearing of a family who had "lately adjured to the Errors of Protestantism."

50 ARCAT, LB 02.227, Michael Power to Charles Daly, 14 January 1845; PP, AB 11.06, Charles Daly to Michael Power, 20 January 1845. Daly refers the matter to the architect for the proposed asylum.

51 J.M.S. Careless, *The Union of the Canadas: The Growth of Canadian Institutions, 1841–1857*, Canadian Centenary Series (Toronto: McClelland and Stewart, 1967); Jacques Monet, SJ, *The Last Canon Shot: A Study of French-Canadian Nationalism, 1837–1850* (Toronto: University of Toronto Press, 1969), 11–41. Monet's excellent study examines how French-Canadians responded successfully to the challenges of the union and defeated the notion, fed by Durham, that the union would complete an Anglo ascendancy.

52 David Mills, *The Idea of Loyalty in Upper Canada, 1784–1850* (Montreal and Kingston: McGill-Queen's University Press, 1988).

53 *Mirror*, 7 January 1842. Much the same was happening in Nova Scotia; see *Cross*, 31 July 1847.

54 *Mirror*, 5 July 1839, 12 July 1839, 1 November 1839, 7 January 1842, 16 September 1842, 17 June 1842, 17 March 1843. On 13 January 1843, the *Mirror* reprinted a statement of loyalty to the governor general issued by Bishop Remi Gaulin of Kingston; see also *Catholic*, 12 January 1842. MacDonald's paper noted that Catholics were loyal, yet reform-minded. According to the *Catholic*, even Father Étienne Chartier, the rebel priest of 1837, was reported to have abjured his participation in the Lower Canadian rebellion.

55 ARCAT, LB 02.047, Michael Power to W.P. MacDonald, December 1842; *Catholic*, 27 March 1844, 3 April 1844, 10 April 1844. Power was a subscriber to the paper; the CIHM microfiche of the *Catholic* is of a bound version with his autograph on the cover page.

56 *Catholic*, 1 June 1842.

57 ARCAT, AA 10.06, Michael Power to Angus Macdonell, 11 December 1844. Baldwin was a subscriber to the *Catholic*; see Metropolitan Toronto Reference Library, Baldwin Room (TPL-BR), Baldwin Papers, L5, Family Correspondence, A80, no. 42, Eliza Baldwin to Robert Baldwin, 9 November 1843; no. 46, Eliza Baldwin to Robert Baldwin, Good Friday, 1845 (Eliza mentions that she and Maria were at the convent together).

58 ARCAT, PP, AB 11.07, Soeur St-André to Michael Power, 25 July 1845.

59 "Dominick Daly," *Dictionary of Canadian Biography* (Toronto: University of Toronto Press, 1986), 9:189–93.

60 ARCAT, LB 02.133, Michael Power to Dominick Daly, 22 February 1844.

61 AAM, Toronto Correspondence, 255.104, file 842-4, Michael Power to Ignace Bourget, 4 November 1842; 255.104, file 843-7, Michael Power to Ignace Bourget, 5 June 1843.

62 ARCAT, AB 10.09, Remi Gaulin to Michael Power, 27 June 1843; AB 08.02, Pierre-Flavien Turgeon to Michael Power, 14 July 1843; AAQ, 320 CN, vol. 6:19, Michael Power to Pierre-Flavien Turgeon, 1 July 1843.

63 AAM, Register of Letters, Ignace Bourget to Michael Power, 10 July 1843, pp. 122–5.

64 AAM, Register of Letters, Ignace Bourget to Pierre-Flavien Turgeon, 30 June 1843, p. 119. Gaulin eventually took up residence in Montreal. "Remi Gaulin," *Dictionary of Canadian Biography* (Toronto: University of Toronto Press, 1976), 8:318.

65 AAQ, 320 CN 6:26, Michael Power to Pierre-Flavien Turgeon, 15 December 1845.

66 *True Witness and Catholic Chronicle*, 28 March 1856.

67 Franklin Walker, *Catholic Education and Politics in Upper Canada* (Toronto: J.M. Dent and Sons, 1955), 37–75; Franklin Walker, *Historical Sketch of Separate Schools of Ontario and Minority Report, 1950* (Toronto: English Catholic Education Association of Ontario, 1950), 15–27; Robert T. Dixon, "The Ontario Separate School System and Section 93 of the British North America Act," (Ph.D diss., Ontario Institute for Studies in Education, University of Toronto, 1976); James F. White, "Separate School Law and the Separate Schools of the Archdiocese," in *Jubilee Volume of the Archdiocese of Toronto, 1842–1892*, ed. J.R. Teefy (Toronto: George T. Dixon, 1892), 252–3. Sir Richard Scott, architect of the separate school legislation of 1863, makes no mention of Power in his "Establishment and Growth of the Separate School System in Ontario," in *Canada: An Encyclopaedia of the Country*, ed. J. Castell Hopkins (Toronto: Linscott Publishing, 1898), 3:180–7. The most recent affirmation of this Catholic position is Michael Power, *A Promise Fulfilled: Highlights in the Political History of Catholic Separate Schools in Ontario* (Toronto: Ontario Catholic School Trustees' Association, 2003), 17–22.

68 Hodgins, "Opening of the Normal School," 100.

69 J. George Hodgins, *The Legislation and History of Separate Schools in Upper Canada* (Toronto: William Briggs, 1897), 28–32; C.B. Sissons, *Church and State in Canadian Education* (Toronto: Ryerson Press, 1959), 21–3; John S. Moir, "The Origins of the Separate School Question in Ontario," *Canadian Journal of Theology* 5 (1959): 107–8; Murray W. Nicolson, "Irish Catholic Education in Victorian Toronto: An Ethnic Res-

ponse to Urban Conformity," *Histoire sociale/Social History* 17 (1984): 292; John Webster Grant, *A Profusion of Spires: Religion in Nineteenth Century Ontario* (Toronto: University of Toronto Press, 1988), 146–7.

70 Alison Prentice, *The School Promoters: Education and Social Class in Mid-Nineteenth-Century Upper Canada* (Toronto: McClelland and Stewart, 1977), 128–9. For more on Ryerson and the religious character of common schools, see Albert F. Fiorino, "The Moral Education of Egerton Ryerson's Idea of Education," in *Egerton Ryerson and His Times*, ed. Neil McDonald and Alf Chaiton (Toronto: Macmillan of Canada, 1978), 59–80.

71 Nicolson, "John Elmsley"; Prentice, *School Promoters*; Sissons, *Egerton Ryerson*.

72 Robert Gidney and W.P.J. Millar, *Inventing Secondary Education: The Rise of the High School in the Nineteenth Century* (Montreal and Kingston: McGill-Queen's University Press, 1990), 4–7.

73 "An Act ... Further to Provision for the Establishment of Common Schools throughout the Province, 18 September 1841," in Hodgins, *Documentary History*, 1:142.

74 *Catholic*, 21 June 1843. The priests were J.J. Hay, W.P. MacDonald, and C.P. O'Dwyer.

75 ARCAT, PP, LB 02.110, Michael Power to Dominick Daly, 7 November 1843.

76 "The Separate Schools Question in 1855," table 7, "Protestant and Roman Catholic Separate Schools in Upper Canada, 1841–1854," in Hodgins, *Documentary History*, 12:34–5.

77 An Act for the Establishment and Maintenance of Common Schools in Upper Canada, 7 Victoria, chapter 29, sections 54–6, 1843.

78 *Mirror*, 1 December 1843.

79 An Act for the Establishment and Maintenance of Common Schools in Upper Canada, 7 Victoria, chapter 29, sections 50–1, 1843; ARCAT, LB 02.176, Michael Power to Simon Sanderl, 17 January 1844.

80 ARCAT, LB 02.219, Michael Power to Angus Macdonell, 18 December 1844; AAHQ, 320 CN, vol. 6:22, Michael Power to Pierre-Flavien Turgeon, 6 November 1843.

81 "Separate Schools Question," table 7, in Hodgins, *Documentary History*, 12:34–5.

82 ARCAT, LB 02.247, Michael Power to Michael Mills, 8 July 1845.

83 ARCAT, LB 01.139, Mandement to the Inhabitants of St Jude Parish, Belle Rivière, 19 September 1845; LB 02.158, Michael Power to Simon Sanderl, 28 June 1844.

84 ARCAT, LB 02.158, Michael Power to Simon Sanderl, 28 June 1844.

85 NA, SPF Papers, Paris, letter 151, Michael Power to the President of the SPF, 8 May 1847, p. 12353. Power informed his French benefactors that

the laws of his province were favourable to Catholics while acknowledging that the overwhelming majority of Upper Canadians were Protestant or Anglican.

86 AO, RG 2-12, Ontario Department of Education, Incoming Correspondence, container 5, John Dwyer to Dominick Daly, 12 January 1846. Dwyer was petitioning for money owed to the separate school for the 1842–3 academic year.

87 AO, RG 2-12, Ontario Department of Education, Incoming Correspondence, container 5, John Hopkins to Egerton Ryerson, 10 September 1846.

88 AO, RG 2-12, Ontario Department of Education, Incoming Correspondence, container 5, William H. Robinson to Egerton Ryerson, 3 October 1846; R.H. Thornton to Egerton Ryerson, 25 December 1846; RG 2-8-0-3, Ontario Department of Education, Outgoing Correspondence, container 5, Egerton Ryerson to R.H. Thornton, 28 December 1846.

89 AO, RG 2-12, Ontario Department of Education, Incoming Correspondence, container 5, Roderick MacDonald to Egerton Ryerson, 26 January 1846; Ludwig Kribs to Egerton Ryerson, 11 February 1846; RG 2-8-0-3, Ontario Department of Education, Outgoing Correspondence, container 5, Egerton Ryerson to Ludwig Kribs, 24 January 1846.

90 An Act for the Establishment and Maintenance of Common Schools in Upper Canada, 7 Victoria, chapter 29, sections 8–23, 1843; AO, RG 2-8-0-3, Ontario Department of Education, Outgoing Correspondence, container 5, Egerton Ryerson to R.H. Thornton, 28 December 1846.

91 Hodgins, "The Opening of the Normal School," 7:99–100; "Separate Schools Question," table 7, in Hodgins, *Documentary History*, 12:34–5.

92 *Mirror*, 8 August 1845.

93 "Separate Schools Question," table 7, in Hodgins, *Documentary History*, 12:34–5; John Ross Robertson, Robertson's Landmarks of Toronto (Belleville, ON: Mika, 1974), 4:124–5.

94 Ibid., 124.

95 *Mirror*, 8 August 1845.

96 AO, RG 2-12, Ontario Department of Education, Trustee P.J. O'Neill, Chair D.R. Bradley, and C. Donlevy to Egerton Ryerson, 18 August 1846.

97 AO, RG 2-12, Ontario Department of Education, Incoming Correspondence, container 5, Denis Heffernan to Egerton Ryerson, 21 December 1846; RG 2-8-0-3, Ontario Department of Education, Outgoing Correspondence, container 5, Egerton Ryerson to Denis Heffernan, 24 December 1846; Egerton Ryerson to George A. Barber, 19 August 1846.

98 *Mirror*, 9 April 1847. The school in District 7 was soon joined by a second Catholic school, in Toronto District 8.

99 ARCAT, LB 02.269, Michael Power to Dominick Daly, 15 June 1846; LB 01.138, Mandement of Michael Power, 19 September 1845; LB 01.139, Episcopal Mandate of Michael Power, 19 September 1845; *Mirror*, 1 August 1845.

100 ARCAT, LB 02.040, Michael Power to John A. Dunn, 14 December 1842; LB 02.133, Michael Power to Dominick Daly, 22 February 1844; LB 02.215, Michael Power to Governor General Metcalfe, 11 December 1844.

101 Roy C. Dalton, *The Jesuits' Estates Question, 1760–1888: A Study of the Background for the Agitation of 1889* (Toronto: University of Toronto Press, 1968), 48, 78–9; J.R. Miller, *Equal Rights: The Jesuits' Estates Controversy* (Montreal and Kingston: McGill-Queen's University Press, 1979), chapter 1; William V. Bangert, SJ, *A History of the Jesuits* (St Louis, MO: Institute of Jesuit Sources, 1986), 408.

102 Monet, *Last Canon Shot*, 244–5.

103 Dalton, *Jesuits' Estates Question*, 96.

104 ARCAT, PP, AA 10.06, Michael Power to Angus Macdonell, 11 December 1844 (copy); LB 02.219, Michael Power to Angus Macdonell, 18 December 1844; LB 02.233, Petition from the Bishops of Canada to Governor General Metcalfe, January 1845; LB 02.231, Michael Power to Ignace Bourget, 27 January 1845.

105 ARCAT, LB 02.110, Michael Power to Dominick Daly, 7 November 1843.

106 Dalton, *Jesuits' Estates Question*, 112–13; AAK, Phelan Papers, C I 3 C16, Michael Power to Angus Macdonell, 18 November 1846.

107 Gidney and Millar, *Inventing Secondary Education*, 32.

108 Ibid., 12–17, 34–6.

109 *British Colonist*, 15 October 1847. For a solid overview of the early years of the Ladies of Loretto in Toronto, see Marion Norman, "Making a Path by Walking: Loretto Pioneers Facing the Challenges of Catholic Education on the North American Frontier," Canadian Catholic Historical Association, *Historical Studies* 65 (1999): 92–106.

110 Letter from Michael Power to Teresa Ball, dated 25 June 1847, quoted in *Life and Letters of Rev. Mother Teresa Dease, Foundress and Superior General of the Institute of the Blessed Virgin Mary in America* (Toronto: McClelland Goodchild Stewart, 1916), 37–9.

111 Even by the time of Confederation, in 1867, the notion of a free school was not universally accepted. In that year, only 86.8 per cent of common schools in Ontario were entirely free. "The Chief Superintendent's Annual Report for 1847," in *Papers and Documents Illustrative of the Educational System in Ontario, 1842–1861*, ed. J.G. Hodgins (Toronto: L.K. Cameron, 1912), 5:52–3.

112 ARCAT, LB 02.302, Michael Power to Archbishop Reisach of Bavaria, 8 May 1847.

113 AIBVM-R, P2/1/B2/1, Michael Power to "Mrs" Teresa Ball, 25 June 1847.

114 "Separate Schools Question," table 7, in Hodgins, *Documentary History*, 12:34–5.

115 Ibid.

116 AO, Hodgins Papers, MU 1375, Egerton Ryerson to William Draper, 3 March 1846.

117 Common School Act, 9 Victoria, chapter 20, 1846; AO, RG 2-3-5, Ontario Department of Education, container 1, General Board of Education, Minutes, Drafts, 21 July 1846; Hodgins Papers, MU 1375, Egerton Ryerson to William Draper, 3 March 1846, 4 May 1846, 14 May 1846; RG 2, Ontario Department of Education, Inventory 2, Administrative Histories, A-L, General Board of Education for Canada West; RG 2-12, Ontario Department of Education, General Correspondence 1846, container 5, Appointments to the General Board of Education, 1 July 1846; Sissons, *Church and State*, 21.

118 AO, RG 2-3-5, Ontario Department of Education, container 1, General Board of Education, Minutes of Meeting (rough draft), 21 July 1846.

119 AO, RG 2-3-1-1, Ontario Department of Education, container 1, General Board of Education, Minute Book, 9 October 1846 (readers); RG 2-12, Ontario Department of Education, General Correspondence, container 5, Dominick Daly to Egerton Ryerson, 11 June 1846. The governor general turned over the old legislature building of Upper Canada for the creation of a normal school; RG 2-8-0-3, Ontario Department of Education, Outgoing Correspondence, Circular, 4 August 1846; *Globe*, 9 October 1847; "Proceedings of the Board of Education for Upper Canada, 1847," in Hodgins, *Documentary History*, 8:89–95.

120 Hodgins, *Documentary History*, 7:100; Sissons, *Egerton Ryerson*, 2:49.

121 Hodgins, *Documentary History*, 7:26–7; Amendment to the Common School Act, 1847, 11 Victoria, chapter 19.

122 Hodgins, *Documentary History*, 7:27.

123 Ibid., 7:27–8.

124 Ibid., "Draft of the City and Town Common School Bill of 1847," 7:189.

125 AO, RG 2-12, Ontario Department of Education, General Incoming Correspondence, container 5, John Strachan to Egerton Ryerson, 17 March 1846; Hodgins Papers, Egerton Ryerson to William Draper, 29 March 1847. Ryerson's purpose is reiterated in "Chief Superintendent's Annual Report," in Hodgins, *Papers and Documents*, 5:52–3; AO, Strachan Papers, MS 35, reel 12, Letterbook 6, John Strachan to Solicitor General Livius Sherwood, 27 April 1846; Strachan Papers, MS 35, reel 12, Letterbook 6, John Strachan to Egerton Ryerson, 26 May 1846. In the former letter, to Sherwood, Strachan criticizes attempts by Ryerson and Draper

to amalgamate all non-Catholics into one category for Protestant schools as an "infidel principle" that members of the Church of England could never accept.

126 White, "Separate Schools," 252.

127 An Act for Amending the Common School Act of Upper Canada, 11 Victoria, chapter 19, 1847 (first reading, 18 June 1847; second reading, 25 June 1847, amendment to section V, clause 3); AO, RG 2-3-1-1, Ontario Department of Education, container 1, General Board of Education, Minute Book. Power was absent from the chair as of 5 February 1847. He returned on 29 June 1847. There is no record that the amendments were ever discussed at that meeting.

128 "Chief Superintendent's Annual Report," in Hodgins, *Papers and Documents*, 5:38.

129 "Separate Schools Question," table 7, in Hodgins, *Documentary History*, 12:34–5.

130 *Globe*, 5 November 1856, 11 February 1858.

131 Walker, *Catholic Education*, 76–139; *The Roman Catholic Bishop of Toronto and the Chief Superintendent of Schools on the Subject of Separate Common Schools in Upper Canada* (Quebec: John Lovell, 1852).

CHAPTER NINE

1 *Mirror*, 1 January 1847.

2 Marianna O'Gallagher and Rose Dompierre, *Eyewitness, Grosse Île* (Ste-Foy, QC: Carraig Books, 1995), map.

3 André Charbonneau and André Sévigny, *1847, Grosse Île: A Record of Daily Events* (Ottawa: Canadian Heritage; Parks Canada, 1997), 16; Robert Whyte, *The Ocean Plague* (Boston: Coolidge and Wiley, 1848), 84.

4 Charbonneau and Sévigny, *Grosse Île*, 1.

5 Gilbert Tucker, "Famine Immigration to Canada, 1847," *American Historical Review* 36 (1931): 540.

6 *Mirror*, 12 November 1847, citing *Orleanian*.

7 Mark G. McGowan, *A Peoples' History: Creating Historical Memory, The Irish Famine Migration to Canada* (forthcoming).

8 Cecil J. Houston and William J. Smyth, *Irish Emigration and Canadian Settlement: Patterns, Links and Letters* (Toronto: University of Toronto Press, 1990), 14.

9 Donald H. Akenson, *The Irish in Ontario: A Study in Rural History* (Montreal and Kingston: McGill-Queen's University Press, 1984), 4–5. Examples of rural settlement patterns can be found in Glenn Lockwood, "Success and the Doubtful Image of the Irish Immigrants in Upper Canada: The Case of Montague Township, 1820–1900," in *The Untold Story: The*

Irish in Canada, ed. Robert O'Driscoll and Lorna Reynolds (Toronto: Celtic Arts of Canada, 1988), 319–41.

10 Houston and Smyth, *Irish Emigration*, 71.

11 Wendy Cameron, "Selecting Peter Robinson's Irish Emigrants," *Histoire sociale/Social History* 9 (1976): 29–46.

12 Carol Bennett, *Valley Irish* (Renfrew, ON: Juniper Books, 1983); Carol Bennett McCuaig, *People of St Patrick's: Mount St Patrick Parish, 1843–1993* (Renfrew, ON: Juniper Books, 1993); Carol Bennett McCuaig, *The Kerry Chain, The Limerick Link* (Renfrew, ON: Juniper Books, 2003); Louis J. Flynn, *Built on a Rock: The Story of the Roman Catholic Church in Kingston, 1826–1976* (Kingston: Roman Catholic Archdiocese of Kingston, 1976); Bill La Branche, *The Peter Robinson Settlement of 1825: The Story of Irish Immigration to the City and County of Peterborough*, official homecoming souvenir booklet (Peterborough, 1975).

13 Paul Hutchison and Michael Power, *Goaded to Madness: The Battle of Slabtown* (Ste Catharine's, ON: Slabtown Press, 1999); Dean William Harris, *The Catholic Church in the Niagara Peninsula, 1626–1895* (Toronto: William Briggs, 1895), 226–51; Derek Nile Tucker, "Successful Pioneers: Irish Catholic Settlers in the Township of Hibbert, Ontario, 1845–1887" (master's thesis, McMaster University, Hamilton, 2001), 35; Cecil J. Houston and William J. Smyth, "Community Development and Institutional Support: Life on the Agricultural Frontier of Adjala and Mono Townships," in *"Catholics at the Gathering Place": Historical Essays on the Archdiocese of Toronto, 1841–1991*, ed. Mark G. McGowan and Brian P. Clarke (Toronto: Canadian Catholic Historical Association; Dundurn Press, 1993), 5–22; AO, Census of Canada, 1851–52, Township of Biddulph, County of Huron.

14 See appendix 3. The general census indicates that there were 17,985 Irish in the home district of western Upper Canada. A rough calculation of the Catholic population minus the French Canadians would put the Irish Catholics at about 7,673 (42.6 per cent), or just slightly higher than the 1:2 ratio of Catholics to Protestant Irish suggested by Houston and Smyth in *Irish Emigration*.

15 Akenson, *Irish in Ontario*, 3–47; BPP, Migration Statistics, 1840s.

16 NA, MG 24 A 1 3, Bagot Papers, vol. 7, doc. 164, Charles Bagot to Lord Stanley, 28 July 1842.

17 *Mirror*, 16 October 1840.

18 Helen I. Cowan, *British Emigration to British North America* (Toronto: University of Toronto Press, 1961), 105, 123–5.

19 *Mirror*, 16 October 1840.

20 The motif of exile has been fully explored in Kerby Miller's award-winning *Emigrants and Exiles: Ireland and the Irish Exodus to North America* (New York: Oxford University Press, 1985).

21 *Mirror*, 16 October 1840.

22 Ibid., 5 April 1844.

23 Ibid.

24 *Pilot* (Boston), 5 October 1844, 28 March 1845.

25 Ibid., 28 March 1845; *Mirror*, 22 March 1844, 28 March 1845 (Galt festivities), 26 March 1847 (Hamilton festivities).

26 *Mirror*, 28 March 1845.

27 Ibid., 17 April 1846.

28 Ibid., 26 March 1847.

29 Ibid., 8 March 1844.

30 Ibid., 12 February 1841.

31 Maxine Kerr and Thomas Booth, *The St Patrick's Benevolent Society of Toronto: A History* (Toronto: St Patrick's Benevolent Society, 1995), 15–20.

32 Ibid., 20, 25, 30.

33 Ibid., 35.

34 *Catholic*, 14 June 1843.

35 *Mirror*, 15 December 1843, 9 February 1844; *Pilot*, 28 March 1845. The growth of the associations was also noted outside of the diocese, in Halifax, Saint John, and Quebec City. *Pilot*, 27 April 1844, 23 March 1844.

36 *Mirror*, 15 December 1843; *Catholic*, 10 January 1844; *Pilot*, 20 January 1844, 19 April 1845. The *Pilot* reported that similar collections were made across the Irish diaspora. The Montreal repeal association was drawing as many as 800 people to its meetings, although at one such event only forty-two pounds was raised. By December 1845, however, Montrealers had remitted an additional fifty pounds.

37 *Catholic*, 23 November 1843.

38 Ibid.

39 AAHQ, 320 CN vol. 6:21, Michael Power to Pierre-Flavien Turgeon, 27 July 1843.

40 *Catholic*, 5 April 1843. Violence was also reported in Kingston and Montreal. See *Mirror*, 10 March 1842; *Pilot*, 28 December 1844.

41 AAHQ, 320 CN vol. 6:24, Michael Power to Pierre-Flavien Turgeon, 2 September 1844.

42 *Mirror*, 26 May 1843; Hutchison and Power, *Goaded to Madness*, 11–12.

43 See Hutchison and Power, *Goaded to Madness*; *Catholic*, 5 April 1842. For an overview of labour issues, see Ruth Bleasdale, "Irish Labourers on the Cornwall, Welland, and Williamsburg Canals in the 1840s" (master's thesis, University of Western Ontario, London, 1975).

44 *Mirror*, 15 July 1842.

45 Gregory S. Kealey, *Toronto Workers Respond to Industrial Capitalism, 1867–1892* (Toronto: University of Toronto Press, 1980), 98–123; Michael Cross, "The Shiners' War: Social Violence in the Ottawa Valley in the 1830s," *Canadian Historical Review* 54 (1973): 1–26.

46 *Mirror*, 30 April 1846.

47 Ibid., 1 December 1843.

48 *Catholic*, 14 February 1844.

49 Ibid.; *Mirror*, 30 April 1846.

50 Hutchison and Power, *Goaded to Madness*, 10; Cecil Houston and William Smyth, *The Sash Canada Wore: A Historical Geography of the Orange Order in Canada* (Toronto: University of Toronto Press, 1980), 33, 43, 57. The last major riot in the area erupted on 12 July 1849, and it was known thereafter by locals as the Battle of Slabtown; see Hutchison and Power, *Goaded to Madness*, 24.

51 Hutchison and Power, *Goaded to Madness*, 19.

52 *Pilot*, 9 March 1844; *Catholic*, 14 February 1844.

53 *Mirror*, 22 March 1844.

54 *Cross*, 25 April 1846.

55 *Catholic*, 24 April 1844; ARCAT, LB 02.151, Record of Public Meeting, 15 April 1844.

56 ARCAT, PP, AB 11.04, Petition, 22 April 1844.

57 *Mirror*, 3 May 1844.

58 Terrence Murphy, *Creed and Culture: The Place of English-Speaking Catholics in Canada* (Montreal and Kingston: McGill-Queen's University Press, 1993), 131.

59 J. Brian Hanington, *Every Popish Person: The Story of Roman Catholicism in Nova Scotia and the Church of Halifax, 1604–1984* (Halifax: Archdiocese of Halifax, 1984), 89–95.

60 André Chapeau, OSB, Louis-Philippe Normand, OMI, and Lucienne Plante, CND, *Canadian R.C. Bishops, 1658–1979* (Ottawa: St Paul University, Research Centre in the Religious History of Canada, 1980), 24.

61 Murphy, *Creed and Culture*, 133–4; APF, series 3, SOCG, vol. 965 (1844), folio 619–20, William Fraser to Giacomo Filippo Fransoni, Cardinal Prefect of the Propaganda Fide, 24 May 1842.

62 ARCAT, LB 02.093, Michael Power to Cardinal Fransoni, 23 May 1843; APF, series 3, SOCG, vol. 965 (1844), folio 646–49, Michael Power to Cardinal Fransoni, 22 May 1843.

63 APF, series 3, SOCG, vol. 960 (1841), folio 794–5, Hyacinthe Hudon to Propaganda Fide, 27 April 1841. Hudon offers evidence that the Lower Canadians were concerned about Nova Scotia well in advance of Walsh's appearance on the scene. AAH, Michael Power to William Walsh, 17 January 1844 (copied from the Cullen Files, Irish College of Rome).

64 SFXUA, Johnston Collection, MG 75/1, ScF2, Michael Power to William Walsh, 4 November 1842 (copied from the Cullen Files, Irish College of Rome); APF, series 3, SOCG, vol. 965 (1844), folio 647–8, Michael Power to Cardinal Fransoni, 22 May 1843; series 3, SOCG, vol. 965 (1844), folio 647–8, William Walsh to Michael Power, 27 April 1843 (copy).

65 ARCAT, LB 02.093, Michael Power to Cardinal Fransoni, 22 May 1843; APF, series 3, SOCG, vol. 966 (1844), folio 10–11, Daniel Murray to Joseph Warmington, OFM, 20 June 1844; series 3, SOCG, vol. 965 (1844), folio 784–5, Antonio de Luca to Cardinal Charles J.E. Acton, Propaganda Fide, 14 July 1844; series 3, SOCG, vol. 965 (1844), folio 786–811, Michael Tobin to William Walsh, 19 March 1844.

66 AAH, Michael Power to William Walsh, 23 May 1843 (copy).

67 ARCAT, PP, AB 10.08, John Hughes to Michael Power, 29 May 1843.

68 APF, series 3, SOCG, vol. 965 (1844), folio 600–1, Joseph Signay to Cardinal Fransoni, 11 November 1843; series 3, SOCG, vol. 965 (1844), folio 590–9, four letters from Colin MacKinnon to Cardinal Fransoni, 25 April, 1 July, 21 August, and 21 October 1844; ARCAT, AB 08.03, Pierre-Flavien Turgeon to Michael Power, 11 September 1843; AAM, 255.10, file 844–4, Vincent Quiblier to Michael Power, 6 March 1844; AAH, Michael Power to William Walsh, 17 January 1844 (copy).

69 Hanington, Every Popish Person, 94–5; Murphy, Creed and Culture, 133–4.

70 ARCAT, PP, AA 10.10, Michael Power to the Propaganda Fide, 12 April 1847 (copy).

71 Robert Choquette, "A Historical Overview," in Planted by Flowing Waters: The Diocese of Ottawa, 1847–1997, ed. Pierre Hurtubise, Mark G. McGowan, and Pierre Savard (Ottawa: Novalis, 1998), 13.

72 AAM, Toronto Correspondence, 255.104, file 846-1, Michael Power to Joseph Marcoux, 7 February 1846.

73 AAH, Walsh Papers, vol. 2, Michael Power to William Walsh, 10 August 1847.

74 AAHQ, 320 CN vol. 6, Michael Power to Joseph Signay, 13 January 1847.

75 ARCAT, PP, AA 10.09, Michael Power to "Monseigneur," 13 January 1847; AAHQ, 320 CN vol. 6, Michael Power to Joseph Signay, 13 January 1847

76 Cross, 6 February 1847.

77 Ibid.

78 Frank Coppa, "Cardinal Antonelli, the Papal States and the Counter Resorgimento," Journal of Church and State 16 (1974): 453–71; Howard Marraro, "The Religious Problem of the Italian Resorgimento as Seen by Americans," Church History 25 (1956): 41–62; Bill McSweeny, "Catholic Piety in the Nineteenth Century," Social Compass 34, nos 2–3 (1987): 203–10.

79 AAH, Walsh Papers, vol. 2, Michael Power to William Walsh, 10 August 1847.

80 AAHQ, 320 CN, vol. 6, Michael Power to Joseph Signay, 26 June 1847.

81 Eulogy by Bishop Jamot of Peterborough, Irish Canadian, 15 March 1876.

82 AIBVM-T, Transcribed Annals of Mother Teresa Dease.

83 ARCAT, LB 02.300, Michael Power to Archbishop Milde, 8 May 1847; LB 02.301, Michael Power to M. Le Barron, Leopoldine Association, Vienna, 8 May 1847; LB 02.302, Michael Power to Archbishop of Munich, 8 May 1847.

84 AIBVM-H, Mother Teresa Ball, "Annals of Loretto, 1814–1860," typed copy.

85 ARCAT, PP, Pastoral Letter, 13 May 1847.

86 Ibid.

87 *Times, London Illustrated News, Nation*, 24 April 1847. All of these London papers are cited in Peter Gray, *The Irish Famine* (New York: Harry N. Abrams, 1995).

88 *Mirror*, 8 May 1846, 16 May 1846; *Cross*, 9 May 1846.

89 Miller, *Emigrants and Exiles*, 204.

90 Houston and Smyth, *Irish Emigration*, 82.

91 S.H. Cousins, "The Regional Pattern of Migration During the Great Irish Famine, 1846–1851," *Transactions and Papers of the Institute of British Geographers* 28 (1960): 16.

92 Patrick Corish, *The Irish Catholic Experience: A Historical Survey* (Wilmington, DE: Michael Glazier, 1985), 123–38; S.J. Connolly, *Priests and People in Pre-famine Ireland* (New York: St Martin's Press, 1982), 10–11.

93 *Irish Historical Documents Since 1800*, ed. Alan O'Day and John Stevenson (Dublin: Gill and Macmillan, 1992), 73.

94 Gray, *Irish Famine*, 26.

95 Miller, *Emigrants and Exiles*, 193–279; R.F. Foster, *Modern Ireland, 1600–1972* (Harmondsworth, UK: Penguin, 1988), 318–45; J.C. Beckett, *Modern Ireland, 1603–1923* (London: Faber, 1966), 284–350; Christine Kinealy, *This Great Calamity: The Irish Famine, 1845–42* (Dublin: Gill and Macmillan, 1994), 6–11.

96 Gray, *Irish Famine*, 35.

97 Cited in Donald MacKay, *Flight from Famine: The Coming of the Irish to Canada* (Toronto: McClelland and Stewart, 1990), 230.

98 *Mirror*, 26 February 1847.

99 Val Noone, *Melbourne and the Irish Famine* (Melbourne: Irish Famine Commemoration Committee, 1998); NA, Colonial Office Papers, 384/80, John Flaherty to Lord John Russell, 20 July 1847; Colonial Office Papers, 384/80, Earl Grey to John Flaherty, 12 August 1847. Westminster offered farmers facing eviction no relief or exemption from paying rent.

100 *Mirror*, 5 March 1847.

101 O'Day and Stevenson, *Irish Historical Documents*.

102 NA, Colonial Office Papers, 384/80, Guide for Emigrants to British North America, March 1847, p. 197. Emigrants were advised to carry with them provisions for a minimum of forty-six days, although they were also

told that trans-Atlantic passage by sailing craft could take up to seventy days.

103 AAH, Walsh Papers, vol. 2, Michael Power to William Walsh, 10 August 1847.

104 Brother Alfred, *Catholic Pioneers in Upper Canada* (Toronto: Macmillan, 1947), 237.

105 AAH, Walsh Papers, vol. 2, Michael Power to William Walsh, 10 August 1847.

106 ARCAT, PP, AA 06.12, Pastoral Letter IX, 10 August 1847.

107 NA, Colonial Office Papers, 384/80, *Seventh General Report of the Colonial Land and Emigration Commissioners, 1847* (London: William Clowes and Sons, 1847), 6. Figures indicate a rise in the number of immigrants from United Kingdom ports to British North American ports – from 235 in the first quarter of 1846 to 1,395 in the first quarter of 1847.

108 NA, Colonial Office Papers, 384/80, *Eighth General Report of the Colonial Land and Emigration Commissioners, 1848* (London: William Clowes and Sons, 1848), 33.

109 Ibid., 17. This is my own calculation.

110 Ibid. Nova Scotia, 2,000; Prince Edward Island, 536; Newfoundland, 993.

111 NA, Colonial Office Papers, 384/80, *Seventh General Report*, 5. The total for 1846 was 43,439; for 1845, it was a mere 31,771. See *Mirror, 20 August 1847*.

112 NA, Colonial Office Papers, 384/80, *Ninth General Report of the Colonial Land and Emigration Commission, 1849* (London: William Clowes and Sons, 1849), 1.

113 NA, Colonial Office Papers, 384/80, Guide for Emigrants to British North America, March 1847, p. 1.

114 Ibid.

115 *Elgin-Grey Papers, 1846–1852*, ed. Sir Arthur Doughty, vol. 1 (Ottawa: Public Archives of Canada; J.O. Patenaude; King's Printer, 1937). See Earl of Elgin to Lord Grey, 27 May 1847; Elgin to Grey, 13 August 1847; Grey to Elgin 1 March 1849.

116 NA, Colonial Office Papers, 384/80, *Ninth General Report*, 1. Some additional but still not definitive evidence has been presented in Robert Grace, "Irish Immigration and Settlement in a Catholic City: Quebec, 1842–61," *Canadian Historical Review* 84 (2003): 237–8, 240.

117 G.J. Parr, "The Welcome and the Wake: Attitudes in Canada West toward the Irish Famine Migration," *Ontario History* 66 (1974): 101.

118 Doughty, *Elgin-Grey Papers*, vol. 1, appendix VI, Copy of Dispatch from Governor-General Elgin to Earl Grey, 29 October 1847; also Elgin to Grey, 13 August 1847.

119 The estimated death rates at sea and in quarantine were: 0.43 per cent at sea, 1845; 0.55 per cent in quarantine, 1845; 0.62 per cent at sea, 1846;

0.82 per cent in quarantine, 1846; 5.9 per cent at sea to Canada only, 1847; 5.7 per cent at sea to all of British North America, 1847. *Journals of the Legislative Assembly, Province of Canada* 7 (1848): appendix W, 22 March 1848. See also NA, Colonial Office Papers, 384/82, *Eighth General Report*, 13; Colonial Office Papers, 384/80, Papers Relating to Emigrations to the British Provinces in North America, enclosure 1, Mortality in Canadian Immigration, p. 2.

120 *British Colonist*, 20 August 1847.

121 *Mirror*, 20 August 1847.

122 O'Gallagher and Dompierre, *Eyewitness*, 52.

123 Daily reports of the dead were published in the press. *Mirror*, 20 August 1847; *British Colonist*, 7 September 1847, 20 August 1847; *Chronicle* (Quebec), 2 August 1847, 3 August 1847, 7 August 1847 (2,148 sick at Grosse Île), 4 August 1847, 21 August 1847, 4 September 1847, 9 September 1847, 11 September 1847. The government could not erect new buildings to supplement the existing lazarettos and tents quickly enough; see *Journals of the Legislative Assembly, Province of Canada* 7 (1848): appendix W, 22 March 1848. Statistics generated from the registers of Grosse Île indicate that 3,597 of the dead were Roman Catholic (86.6 per cent) and 557 were Protestant (13.4 per cent). These calculations were derived from burial registers reprinted in O'Gallagher and Dompierre, *Eyewitness*.

124 AAM, Bourget Papers, 295.101, file 847-16, Pierre-FlavienTurgeon to Ignace Bourget, 28 May 1847.

125 *Mirror*, 5 August 1847. Word of the suffering in Montreal was spread via the weeklies of British North America: *Mirror*, 13 August 1847; *Cross*, 31 July 1847, 13 November 1847.

126 AAM, Soeurs Grises de Montréal, 1841–48, 525.103, file 847-3, "Notes sur les ... sheds depuis 25 septembre 1847, jusqu'au 16 avril 1848"; Soeurs Grises de Montréal, 1841–48, 525.103, file 847-6, Sister McMullen to Ignace Bourget, 7 August 1847; Soeurs Grises de Montréal, 1841–48, 525.103, file 847-9, Sister McMullen to Ignace Bourget, October 1847. On Hudon, see *British Colonist*, 20 August 1847, 3 September 1847 (regarding Point St-Charles); Doughty, *Elgin-Grey Correspondence*, Elgin to Grey, 13 August 1847.

127 "Lettre pastoral ... en faveur de la malheureuse Irlande, Ignace Bourget, 27 juin 1847," in *Mandements, lettres pastorales, circulaires et autres documents publie dans le Diocèse de Montréal* (Montreal: J. Chapleau et Fils, 1887), 1:370–89; "Lettre pastorale, Ignace Bourget, 13 août 1847, au sujet de l'épidémie de 1847," in *Mandements, lettres pastorales, circulaires et autres documents*, 1:399–407; AAM, Bourget Papers, 901.055, 847-8, Ignace Bourget to Monsignor Charles Prince, 28 January 1847.

128 *British Colonist*, 20 August 1847; *Mirror*, 14 September 1847.

129 *Journals of the Legislative Assembly, Province of Canada* 6 (1847): 132–3, Petition of A. Laroque, 13 July 1847; 12, Speech of Mr Colville, 8 June 1847.

130 AAK, C I 3 C14, Phelan Papers, Patrick Phelan to Daniel Murray, 22 March 1847 (donation).

131 *British Colonist*, 27 August 1847.

132 ARCAT, St Paul's Roman Catholic Parish Box, St Paul's Sacramental Register, 1833–50; Official Burial Register, 1849–57; Gilbert Tucker, "Famine Immigration to Canada, 1847," *American Historical Review* 36 (1931): 540.

133 *British Colonist*, 24 August 1847.

134 Ibid., 3 September 1847.

135 Kitanya Petgrave, "Small Differences?: Looking at Early Irish Catholics and Protestants through the Lens of Hibbert Township," 2001; Derek Nile Tucker, "Successful Pioneers"; Houston and Smyth, "Community Development"; *British Colonist*, 2 July 1847. The latter source lists land purchase prices per acre: "Huron District, 12'6 to 20'0/ac; Western District, 8'9 to 20'0/ac; London/Brock/Talbot 20'0 to 30'0/ac; Gore 11'3 to 20'0/ac; Wellington 11'3 to 20'0/ac; and Home/Simcoe, 8'9 to 17'6/ac."

136 *Mirror*, 20 April 1847. More on fundraising for Ireland is found in *Mirror*, 12 February 1847, 5 March 1847.

137 Ibid., 2 July 1847.

138 Ibid., 9 July 1847.

139 Ibid.

140 Evangeline MacDonald, *Joyful Mother of Children, Mother Frances Mary Teresa Ball* (Dublin: M.H. Gill and Son, 1961), 215.

141 *British Colonist*, 3 August 1847. On 13 August, it was reported that of the 550 arrivals in Toronto that day, 500 were without any means.

142 *Canadian Freeman*, 14 May 1863.

143 *British Colonist*, 21 September 1847. The situation was critical, according to issues published on 13 August and 14 September 1847; this was corroborated by *Mirror*, 13 August 1847. The government was in touch with local authorities to assess the situation; NA, Papers of the Provincial Secretary, Dominick Daly to Edward McElderry, 13 July 1847.

144 NA, Papers of the Provincial Secretary, Dominick Daly to Edward McElderry, 13 July 1847.

145 *British Colonist*, 17 September 1847.

146 AO, MS 35 R 11, Strachan Papers, Letterbook 5, John Strachan to Daniel Murray, 1 December 1847, p. 26; *British Colonist*, 17 September 1847.

147 *Mirror*, 24 September 1847.

148 Ibid.

149 *Journals of the Legislative Assembly, Province of Canada* 7 (1848): 19.

150 AIBVM-T, *Annals, 1847–1870*, by Mother Teresa Dease, transcribed by Maggie Lyons, 25 August 1875.

151 Ibid., 14.
152 AIBVM-R, B2/2, Mother Ignatia Hutchison to Mother Teresa Ball, 2 September 1847; Mother Ignatia Hutchison to Mother Teresa Ball, 9 September 1847; AIBVM-T, *Annals, 1847–1870*, by Mother Teresa Dease, transcribed by Maggie Lyons, 25 August 1875, 8–9.
153 Ibid., 14.
154 Ibid., 11.
155 Ibid., 17.
156 *Life and Letters of Rev. Mother Teresa Dease, Foundress and Superior General of the Institute of the Blessed Virgin Mary in America* (Toronto: McClelland Goodchild Stewart, 1916), 40; AIBVM-T, Earliest Annals Box, "Mary Evangelista O'Sullivan's Black Scribbler," 1929. Margaret Costello drew the comment from O'Sullivan's scribbler. Costello herself was born in Ireland in 1852, in the wake of the famine, and she would have been subject to the popular nationalist interpretations of the famine fuelled by the writings of John Mitchell as well as the Young Ireland Movement and its organ, the *Nation*. Received into the Institute of the Blessed Virgin Mary (IBVM) in 1876 and professed in 1878, Costello was a career teacher. In 1916, she published the *Life and Letters* volume under the anonymous heading "a member of the community." O'Sullivan, from whose writings Costello clearly adapted the story, was born in Ireland in 1846, during the famine, and she was educated there until her family immigrated to New York and then to Canada. She was a teacher and a contemporary of Costello's. She would have been in Toronto in 1916 when Costello was secretary-general of the order. See Sister Mary Aloysius Kerr, IBVM, *Dictionary of Biography of the Institute of the Blessed Virgin Mary in North America* (Toronto: Mission Press, 1984), 27, 152–3. They would have been subject to the nationalist interpretation of Irish history, including the collective historical memories of the famine so evident in popular and Irish historical literatures. See McGowan, *People's History*; James Donnelly Jr, *The Great Irish Potato Famine* (Phoenix Mill, UK: Sutton Publishing, 2001); R.F. Foster, *The Irish Story: Telling Tales and Making It up in Ireland* (London: Allan Lane; Penguin, 2001).
157 AAH, Walsh Papers, vol. 3, J.J. Hay to William Walsh, 2 October 1847.

CONCLUSION

1 ARCAT, PP, PRC, 2904, Vincent Quiblier to Pro-secretary of the Sacred Congregation of the Propaganda Fide, 1 November 1847 (copy).
2 AAQ, 320 CN vol. 6:50, J.J. Hay to Joseph Signay, 3 October 1847.
3 ARCAT, PP, PRC, 3003, Thaddeus Kerwin to Propaganda Fide, 22 February 1848; AAK, C 1 3 C28, P.A. Telmon to Patrick Phelan, 30 December 1847.

4 AAM, Toronto Correspondence, 255.104, file 847–13, Joseph Signay to Ignace Bourget, 14 October 1847.

5 Ibid.

6 AAM, Toronto Correspondence, 255.104, file 847–15, Samuel Eccleston to Joseph Signay, 31 October 1847 (copy).

7 AAM, Toronto Correspondence, 255.104, file 847-5, Pierre-Flavien Turgeon to Ignace Bourget, 4 October 1847.

8 AAM, Toronto Correspondence, 255.104, file 847-19, Joseph Signay to Ignace Bourget, 9 December 1847; Toronto Correspondence, 255.104, file 847–17, Patrick Phelan to Joseph Signay, 20 November 1847 (copy).

9 "John Larkin," *Dictionary of Jesuit Biography* (Toronto: Canadian Institute of Jesuit Studies, 1991), 181–2.

10 ARCAT, PP, PRC, 2905, Joseph Signay to Propaganda Fide, 10 January 1848 (copy).

11 Ibid.

12 AAM, Toronto Correspondence, 255.104, file 848-1, "Supplique" of the Bishops of Canada to Pius IX, 10 January 1848.

13 ARCAT, PP, PRC, 3102, Canadian Bishops to Pope Pius IX, October 1849.

14 *They Honoured Their Vestments of Holiness*, ed. Robert Scollard (Toronto: Archdiocese of Toronto, 1990), 60.

15 ARCAT, PP, AB 05.02, Patrick Phelan to J.J. Hay, 29 January 1849; AB 05.03, Scrope Beardmore to J.J. Hay, 29 January 1849; LB 02.305, J.J. Hay to Father Edward Smith, 9 August 1848 (drunkenness); LB 02.306, J.J. Hay to Father William McIntosh, 22 August 1848 (scandal in Hamilton); LB 02.308, J.J. Hay to Patrick O'Dwyer, 12 January 1849 (priest protests being transferred to the "backwoods"); AE 01.03, John Elmsley to John Carroll, 27 October 1849 (orphanage).

16 Murray Nicolson, "Irish Tridentine Catholicism in Victorian Toronto: Vessel for Ethno-Religious Persistence," Canadian Catholic Historical Association, *Study Sessions* 50, vol. 2 (1983): 415–36; Murray Nicolson, "Bishop Charbonnel: The Beggar Bishop and the Origins of Catholic Social Action," Canadian Catholic Historical Association, *Historical Studies* 52 (1985): 51–66; Murray Nicolson, "The Growth of Roman Catholic Institutions in the Archdiocese of Toronto," in *Creed and Culture: The Place of English-Speaking Catholics in Canadian Society, 1750–1930*, ed. Terrence Murphy and Gerald Stortz (Montreal and Kingston: McGill-Queen's University Press, 1993), 153–70; Murray Nicolson, "Ecclesiastical Metropolitanism and the Evolution of the Catholic Archdiocese of Toronto," *Histoire sociale/Social History* 17 (1982): 129–56.

17 Brian P. Clarke, "'To Bribe the Porters of Heaven': Poverty and Salvation in the St Vincent de Paul Society in Victorian Toronto," Canadian Society of Church History, *Papers 1983*, pp. 97–115; Brian P. Clarke, "Poverty

and Piety: The Saint Vincent de Paul Society's Mission to Irish Catholics in Toronto, 1850–1890," in *Canadian Protestant and Catholic Missions, 1820s to 1960s: Historical Essays in Honour of John Webster Grant*, ed. John S. Moir and C.T. McIntire (New York: Peter Lang, 1988), 75–102; Paula Maurutto, *Governing Charities: Church and State in Toronto's Catholic Archdiocese, 1850–1950* (Montreal and Kingston: McGill-Queen's University Press, 2003), 20–3.

18 J.M.S. Careless, *The Union of the Canadas: The Growth of Canadian Institutions, 1841–1857*, Canadian Centenary Series (Toronto: McClelland and Stewart, 1967); John McCallum, *Unequal Beginnings: Agricultural and Economic Development in Quebec and Ontario until 1870* (Toronto: University of Toronto Press, 1980); D.C. Masters, *The Reciprocity Treaty of 1854* (Toronto: McClelland and Stewart, 1963).

19 Franklin Walker, *Catholic Education and Politics in Upper Canada* (Toronto: English Catholic Education Association of Ontario, 1955).

20 Scollard, *They Honoured Their Vestments*, 39–40.

21 *Mirror*, 3 December 1858.

22 A search for records of reinterrment at AAH and PANS proved futile, and two visits to Holy Cross Cemetery yielded no evidence that Michael Power's family even had a marked grave.

23 AO, RG 22-155, Court of Probate, appendix A1, MS 638, reel 63, Reverend Michael Power, 15 October 1847.

24 ARCAT, PP, AA 09.01, Articles of Agreement Between J.J. Hay and Misses Margaret, Eliza, and Frances Power, 14 December 1850 (copy); AA 09.06, W.M. Mooney to Bishop Charbonnel, 24 September 1857; AA 09.24, William Compton to John Joseph Lynch, 7 August 1883 (report of the death of Margaret Power). Information on the death of Mary Roach Power is found in *Nova Scotian*, 26 August 1850; AAH, Cemeteries, Holy Cross, reel 12050-52; *Acadian Recorder*, 24 August 1850; PANS, microfilm 19358, Wills, vol. 6, 1847–1958, Mary Power, 11 May 1850, pp. 94–5.

25 *Canadian Freeman*, 1 October 1868.

26 Ibid.; *Canadian Freeman*, 8 October 1868.

27 *Irish Canadian*, 15 March 1876.

28 H.F. McIntosh, "Life and Times of Bishop Power," in *Jubilee Volume of the Archdiocese of Toronto, 1842–1892*, ed. J.R. Teefy (Toronto: George T. Dixon, 1892), 138–9.

29 *"Catholics at the Gathering Place": Historical Essays on the Archdiocese of Toronto, 1841–1991*, ed. Mark G. McGowan and Brian P. Clarke (Toronto: Canadian Catholic Historical Association; Dundurn Press, 1993).

30 McIntosh, "Life and Times," 139.

31 Ibid.

32 *Irish Canadian*, 15 March 1876.

33 *Walking the Less Travelled Road: A History of Religious Communities within the Archdiocese of Toronto, 1841–1991*, ed. William O'Brien et al. (Toronto: Archdiocese of Toronto, 1993).

34 Institute for Catholic Education, Documents, *Ontario Catholic Education: Enduring Truths, Changing Realities, Re-igniting the Spirit* (Toronto: Institute for Catholic Education, 2002), 11 (excerpt from Carl Matthews, SJ, "Profiles in Courage").

~: Index :~